CW01301606

COLIN CAMPBELL is a Senior Lecturer in the Faculty of Law, Monash University. Colin holds Masters degrees in law from the Universities of Melbourne and Cambridge, and a PhD in law from the University of Cambridge. Formerly a solicitor and a judge's associate, Colin's main research interests lie in the areas of Administrative Law and Anti-discrimination Law. Colin has published articles in leading journals, including the *Cambridge Law Journal*, the *Law Quarterly Review* and the *University of Toronto Law Journal*. He is the co-editor, along with Matthew Groves, of *Australian Charters of Rights a Decade On* (2017).

PATRICK EMERTON is an Associate Professor in the Faculty of Law, Monash University. He researches in constitutional law and theory, just war theory, human rights theory, and anti-terrorism law. His recent work includes contributions to *The Oxford Handbook of the Australian Constitution* (2018) and *The Oxford Handbook of Ethics of War* (2018). In 2010 the *Federal Law Review* awarded him the inaugural Leslie Zines Prize for Excellence in Legal Research.

EMERGENCY POWERS IN AUSTRALIA

SECOND EDITION

Democratic countries, such as Australia, face the dilemma of preserving public and national security without sacrificing fundamental freedoms. In the context where the rule of law is an underlying assumption of the constitutional framework, *Emergency Powers in Australia* provides a succinct analysis of the sorts of emergency which have been experienced in Australia and an evaluation of the legal weapons available to the authorities to cope with these emergencies. It analyses the scope of the defence power to determine the constitutionality of federal legislation to deal with wartime crises and the 'war' on terrorism, the extent of the executive power and its relationship to the prerogative, the deployment of the defence forces in aid of the civil power, the statutory frameworks regulating the responses to civil unrest, and natural disasters. The role of the courts when faced with challenges to the invocation of emergency powers is explained and analysed.

HOONG PHUN (H. P.) LEE held the Sir John Latham Chair of Law at Monash University from 1995-2014, where he had also served as the Deputy Dean and Acting Dean. He is the co-author of *The Australian Judiciary* (2nd ed, 2013) and author of *Constitutional Conflicts in Contemporary Malaysia* (2nd ed, 2017). Professor Lee's other publications include: *Judiciaries in Comparative Perspective* (2011) (editor) and *Asia-Pacific Judiciaries: Independence, Impartiality and Integrity* (2017) (co-editor). He was awarded the Australian Press Council Medal in 2011. In 2015, he was appointed Emeritus Professor of Law at Monash University.

MICHAEL W. R. ADAMS obtained his Bachelor of Laws degree from Monash University and his Bachelor of Media degree from Adelaide University. Michael most recently acted as a counsel and fellow in the International Justice Program at Human Rights Watch. Previously, Michael was the Associate to the Honourable Justice Pamela Tate of the Court of Appeal of Victoria and a researcher at the Victorian Law Reform Commission. As the Charles B. Bretzfelder Constitutional Law Scholar, he obtained his LLM from Columbia University, where he is currently doing doctoral research.

EMERGENCY POWERS IN AUSTRALIA

SECOND EDITION

HOONG PHUN (H. P.) LEE
Emeritus Professor of Law at Monash University

MICHAEL W. R. ADAMS
Candidate, Doctor of the Science of Law, Columbia Law School

COLIN CAMPBELL
Senior Lecturer, Monash University

PATRICK EMERTON
Associate Professor, Monash University

CAMBRIDGE UNIVERSITY PRESS

CAMBRIDGE
UNIVERSITY PRESS

University Printing House, Cambridge CB2 8BS, United Kingdom

One Liberty Plaza, 20th Floor, New York, NY 10006, USA

477 Williamstown Road, Port Melbourne, VIC 3207, Australia

314–321, 3rd Floor, Plot 3, Splendor Forum, Jasola District Centre, New Delhi – 110025, India

79 Anson Road, #06–04/06, Singapore 079906

Cambridge University Press is part of the University of Cambridge.

It furthers the University's mission by disseminating knowledge in the pursuit of education, learning, and research at the highest international levels of excellence.

www.cambridge.org
Information on this title: www.cambridge.org/9781107166530
DOI: 10.1017/9781316711125

© Hoong Phun (H. P.) Lee, Michael Adams, Colin Campbell and Patrick Emerton 2019

This publication is in copyright. Subject to statutory exception and to the provisions of relevant collective licensing agreements, no reproduction of any part may take place without the written permission of Cambridge University Press.

First edition published as *Emergency Powers*, The Law Book Company Limited, 1984
Second edition 2019

Printed and bound in Great Britain by Clays Ltd, Elcograf S.p.A.

A catalogue record for this publication is available from the British Library.

Library of Congress Cataloging-in-Publication Data
Names: Lee, H. P., 1947–, author.
Title: Emergency powers in Australia / Hoong Phun (H. P.) Lee, Emeritus Professor of Law at Monash University, Michael W. R. Adams, Candidate, Doctor of the Science of Law, Columbia Law School, Colin Campbell, Senior Lecturer, Monash University, Patrick Emerton, Associate Professor, Monash University.
Description: Second edition. | New York : Cambridge University Press, 2018. | Includes bibliographical references and index.
Identifiers: LCCN 2018021307 | ISBN 9781107166530 (hardback : alk. paper)
Subjects: LCSH: War and emergency powers–Australia.
Classification: LCC KU2232 .E44 2018 | DDC 342.94/062–dc23
LC record available at https://lccn.loc.gov/2018021307

ISBN 978-1-107-16653-0 Hardback

Cambridge University Press has no responsibility for the persistence or accuracy of URLs for external or third-party internet websites referred to in this publication and does not guarantee that any content on such websites is, or will remain, accurate or appropriate.

CONTENTS

Preface vii
Notes on Authors x
Table of Cases xii
Table of Statutes xviii

1 Introduction   1
2 The Defence Power   17
3 The Executive, the Prerogative and Emergencies   54
4 Maintenance of Public Order   82
5 Public Safety and the War on Terror   136
6 Civil Emergencies and Special Powers Legislation   170
7 Military Aid to the Civil Power   218
8 The Judiciary and Emergency Powers   232
9 Conclusion   261

Index   264

PREFACE

> *A study of emergency powers might seem at first to be an arcane area of constitutional law ... On the contrary, a study of emergency powers quickly leads us to the bedrock of constitutionalism and conceptual foundations of constitutional theory. It forces us to consider the relationship between law, politics, history and the modern state and to ask whether and in what circumstances liberal constitutionalism is the best way forward.*
> – Victor V. Ramraj and Arun K. Thiruvengadam (eds) *Emergency Powers in Asia: Exploring the Limits of Legality* (CUP 2010) 17

Today, the problem of emergency powers is more relevant than ever before. In many countries, where constitutionalism is either very weak or virtually non-existent, states of emergency are a common occurrence; indeed, even in some countries with relatively strong rule of law traditions, the use of emergency powers has become increasingly normalised.

Prior to the 11 September 2001 attacks in the United States (commonly referred to as '9/11'), the subject of emergency powers was viewed as an esoteric area of study. Ever since 9/11, interest in the topic in liberal democracies has intensified. Today, there is a mushrooming of scholarship on the 'war on terror' and its impact on the state of constitutionalism. In recent times, a number of scholarly books and many articles have been published.[1]

Emergencies can arise in many contexts, ranging from political crises, industrial disputes impacting severely on essential services and commodities, natural disasters, nuclear incidents, terrorism and full-scale war. Apart from the two world wars, Australia has, fortunately, not been

---

[1] David Dyzenhaus, *The Constitution of Law: Legality in a Time of Emergency* (CUP 2006); Oren Gross and Fionnuala Ni Aolain, *Law in Times of Crisis: Emergency Powers in Theory and Practice* (CUP 2006); Austin Sarat (ed), *Sovereignty, Emergency, Legality* (CUP 2010); Victor V Ramraj (ed), *Emergencies and the Limits of Legality* (CUP 2008); Victor V Ramraj and Arun K Thiruvengadam (eds), *Emergency Powers in Asia: Exploring the Limits of Legality* (CUP 2010).

confronted by the sorts of crises that have, in other countries, posed a threat to constitutional rule. However, in contemporary times, Australia cannot be fully insulated against threats to public safety, particularly in an era darkened by the brutal and cruel attacks of militant terrorists and suicide bombers.

The first edition of this work was published by H. P. Lee in 1984, at a time when the global 'war on terrorism' was not in existence. No doubt there had been sporadic terrorist movements and cults, but they were not of the same magnitude as the contemporary threats posed by militant 'Islamic State' terrorists. Without an end in sight for the 'war on terror', a dilemma is posed for democratic countries. Abnormal powers that are invoked may, over a prolonged period, seep into public consciousness as normal powers. Hence, it is said that 'Perhaps there is no more foundational question than what a constitutional democracy can do to defend itself when confronted with an emergency that has the potential to undermine the democracy itself'.[2] The true test of the viability of a constitutional and legal system of a democratic country is its ability to respond to emergencies without permanently sacrificing fundamental freedoms.

The Australian Constitution does not contain an entrenched framework of emergency powers, and yet, despite the intrusion of two World Wars, the Australian Constitution remains the instrument underpinning the governance of the Australian nation. This book seeks to canvass the panoply of constitutional and legal powers available to the authorities in Australia to deal with emergency situations, and the reconciliation of these powers with the rule of law which, according to Sir Owen Dixon, forms an underlying assumption of the Constitution.

This second edition is the work of a team of four authors who are individually responsible substantially for the writing of their allocated chapters. H. P. Lee is mainly responsible for Chapters 2 and 7; Michael Adams for Chapters 4 and 6; Colin Campbell for Chapter 8; and Patrick Emerton for Chapter 3. We are also jointly responsible for Chapters 1, 5 and 9, and the overall shape and design of the book.

This book is not a mere updating of the first edition. A number of chapters have been completely reworked and a new chapter in relation to public safety and the war on terror (Chapter 5) has been added. This new chapter incorporates selected materials from Chapter 3 ('The judiciary as

---

[2] The Editors, 'Introduction' (2004) 2 *I.CON* 207 (Symposium: Emergency Powers and Constitutionalism).

a branch of government') in H. P. Lee and Enid Campbell, *The Australian Judiciary* (2nd ed, Cambridge University Press, 2013) and chapter 20 (Patrick Emerton and H. P. Lee, 'Judges and non-judicial functions in Australia') in H. P. Lee (ed), *Judiciaries in Comparative Perspective* (Cambridge University Press, 2011).

This book would not have seen the light of day without the encouragement and unstinting support of Finola O'Sullivan of Cambridge University Press. We are truly indebted to her and the staff of Cambridge University Press for their wonderful help in editing and publishing the second edition of this book. We are grateful to Matthew O'Neill for his research assistance in relation to Chapters 3 and 8 and Michael Smyth for his research assistance with regard to Chapter 8. We express our gratitude and appreciation to our respective partners (Rose, Jaclyn, Tamara and Natasha) and families for their understanding of the time devoted by us in bringing this book to fruition.

NOTES ON AUTHORS

H. P. LEE held the Sir John Latham Chair of Law at Monash University from 1995 to 2014, where he had also served as the Deputy Dean and Acting Dean. He is the co-author of *The Australian Judiciary* (2nd ed, Cambridge University Press, 2013) and author of *Constitutional Conflicts in Contemporary Malaysia* (2nd ed, 2017). Professor Lee is the editor of *Judiciaries in Comparative Perspective* (Cambridge University Press, 2011), and the co-editor of *Asia-Pacific Judiciaries: Independence, Impartiality and Integrity* (Cambridge University Press, 2017), *Australian Administrative Law: Fundamentals, Principles and Doctrines* (Cambridge University Press, 2007), and *Australian Constitutional Landmarks* (Cambridge University Press, 2003). He was awarded the Australian Press Council Medal in 2011. In 2015, he was appointed Emeritus Professor of Law at Monash University.

MICHAEL W. R. ADAMS obtained his Bachelor of Laws degree from Monash University, his Bachelor of Media degree from Adelaide University and his LLM from Columbia University, where he is currently doing doctoral research. He has acted as a counsel and public interest and government fellow in Human Rights Watch's International Justice Program, was an associate to the Honourable Justice Pamela Tate of the Victorian Court of Appeal, and was the research and executive assistant to the chair of the Victorian Law Reform Commission, the Honourable Philip Cummins AM. He was a sessional lecturer at Monash University in 2015. Michael has published in leading journals, including the *Journal of International and Comparative Law*, *Asia Pacific Law Review* and *Monash University Law Review*.

COLIN CAMPBELL is a senior lecturer in the Faculty of Law, Monash University. Colin holds Masters degrees in law from the Universities of Melbourne and Cambridge, and a PhD in law from the University of Cambridge. Formerly a solicitor and a judge's associate, Colin's main research interests lie in the areas of Administrative Law and Anti-discrimination Law. Colin has published articles in leading journals, including the *Cambridge Law Journal*, the *Law Quarterly Review* and the *University of Toronto Law Journal*. He is the co-editor, along with Matthew Groves, of *Australian Charters of Rights a Decade On* (2017).

PATRICK EMERTON is Associate Professor in the Faculty of Law, Monash University. He researches in constitutional law and theory, just war theory, human rights theory and anti-terrorism law. His recent work includes contributions to *The Oxford Handbook of the Australian Constitution* and *The Oxford Handbook of Ethics of War*. In 2010 the *Federal Law Review* awarded him the inaugural Leslie Zines Prize for Excellence in Legal Research.

CASES

A v. Hayden (1984) 156 CLR 532 76, 77, 232
A v. Secretary of State for the Home Department [2005] 2 AC 68 142, 249, 263
Adelaide Company of Jehovah's Witnesses Inc v. Commonwealth (1943) 67 CLR 116 50–51
Al-Kateb v. Godwin (2004) 219 CLR 562 64, 155, 203
Andrews v. Howell (1941) 65 CLR 255 30, 38, 50
Associated Provincial Picture Houses Ltd v. Wednesbury Corporation [1948] 1 KB 223 239
Attorney-General for the Commonwealth v. Colonial Sugar Refining Co. Ltd. [1914] AC 237 84
Attorney-General of the Commonwealth of Australia v. The Queen (1957) 95 CLR 529 148
Attorney-General (NSW) v. Quin (1990) 170 CLR 1 248
Attorney-General (NSW) v. Trethowan (1931) 44 CLR 395 180
Attorney-General (NT) v. Emmerson (2014) 253 CLR 393 88, 159
Attorney-General (SA) v. Corporation of the City of Adelaide (2013) 249 CLR 1 102
Attorney-General (Vic) v. Commonwealth (1935) 52 CLR 533 40
Attorney-General (Vic); Ex rel Dale v. Commonwealth (1945) 71 CLR 237 76
Austin v. Commonwealth (2003) 215 CLR 185 204
Australian Communist Party v. Commonwealth (1951) 83 CLR 1 18, 54, 66, 67, 128
Australian Woollen Mills v. Commonwealth (1944) 69 CLR 476 38
Aye v. Minister for Immigration and Citizenship (2010) 187 FCR 449 234, 236

Bank of NSW v. Commonwealth (1948) 76 CLR 1 61
Barton v. Commonwealth (1974) 131 CLR 477 56, 57
Beatty v. Gillbanks (1882) 9 QBD 308 89
Black v. Corkery (1988) 33 A Crim R 134 90
Bropho v. Western Australia (1990) 171 CLR 1 90
Brown v. Tasmania [2017] HCA 43 86, 111, 112, 114, 116
Burkard v. Oakley (1918) 25 CLR 422 37
Burmah Oil Co Ltd v. Lord Advocate [1965] AC 75 79
Burns v. Ransley (1949) 79 CLR 101 129, 130–131

TABLE OF CASES

Cadia Holdings Pty Ltd v. New South Wales (2010) 242 CLR 195 57, 59, 60
Cantwell v. Connecticut 310 US 296 (1940)
Chevron USA Inc v. Natural Resources Defence Council Inc 467 US 837 (1984) 248
Chu Kheng Lim v. Minister for Immigration, Local Government and Ethnic Affairs (1992) 176 CLR 1 76, 88, 154
Clarke v. Commissioner of Taxation (2009) 240 CLR 272 204
Clough v. Leahy (1904) 2 CLR 139 76
Clunies-Ross v. The Commonwealth (1984) 155 CLR 193 80
Coal Miners' Industrial Union of Workers (WA) v. Amalgamated Collieries of Western Australia Ltd (1960) 104 CLR 437 254
Cobb and Co Ltd v. Kropp [1967] 1 AC 141 182
Coco v. The Queen (1994) 179 CLR 427 90
Coleman v. Power (2004) 220 CLR 1 82, 87, 92, 131
Commissioner of Police v. Rintoul [2003] NSWSC 662 96
Commissioner of Taxation v. Futuris Corporation Ltd (2008) 237 CLR 146 258
Commonwealth v. Australian Commonwealth Shipping Board (1926) 39 CLR 1 40
The Commonwealth v. Cigamatic Pty Ltd (in liq) (1962) 108 CLR 372 61
Commonwealth v. Tasmania (1983) 158 CLR 1 58, 80
Condon v. Pompano (2013) 252 CLR 38 88, 118, 161
Cooper v. The Queen (1961) 105 CLR 177 131
Corporation of the City of Enfield v. Development Assessment Commission (2000) 199 CLR 135 248
Council of Civil Service Unions v. Minister for the Civil Service [1985] AC 374 233, 238, 247
CPCF v. Minister for Immigration and Border Protection (2015) 255 CLR 514 78, 78, 253
Cunliffe v. Commonwealth (1994) 182 CLR 272 131

Davis v. Commonwealth (1988) 166 CLR 79 45, 57
De Mestre v. Chisholm (1944) 69 CLR 51 38
Deputy Commissioner of Taxation (Cth) v. Richard Walter Pty Ltd (1995) 183 CLR 168 254

Fardon v. Attorney-General (2004) 223 CLR 575 162
Farey v. Burvett (1916) 21 CLR 433 17, 19, 20, 21–22, 49, 50
Federal Commissioner of Taxation v. Official Liquidator of EO Farley Ltd (1940) 63 CLR 278 60
Ferguson v. Commonwealth (1943) 66 CLR 432 38
Ferrando v. Pearce (1918) 25 CLR 241 37
Fraser v. County Court of Victoria [2017] VSC 83 93

Gonzwa v. Commonwealth (1944) 68 CLR 469 38
Gratwick v. Johnson (1945) 70 CLR 1 51
Grollo v. Palmer (1995) 184 CLR 348 149, 150, 169

TABLE OF CASES

Groves v. Commonwealth (1982) 150 CLR 113 79
Gypsy Jokers Motorcycle Club Inc. v. Commissioner of Police (2008) 234 CLR 532 88, 161

Habib v. Commonwealth of Australia (2010) 183 FCR 62 242
Holland v. Jones (1917) 23 CLR 149 30
Hubbard v. Pitt [1976] QB 142 89
Huddart Parker and Co Pty Ltd v. Moorehead (1908) 8 CLR 330 148

Illawarra District County Council v. Wickham (1959) 101 CLR 467 40
In re Debs 158 US 564 (1895) 45, 84
International Finance Trust Company Limited v. New South Wales Crime Commission (2009) 240 CLR 319
IRC v. Rossminster Ltd [1980] AC 592 145

Johanson v. Dixon (1979) 143 CLR 376 121
Johnston Fear & Kingham & the Offset Printing Co. Pty Ltd v. Commonwealth (1943) 67 CLR 314 51, 79, 80
JT International SA v. Commonwealth (2012) 250 CLR 1 80

Kable v. Director of Public Prosecutions (NSW) (1996) 189 CLR 51 88, 140, 158–159
Kamm v. State of New South Wales (No 4) [2017] NSWCA 189 167
Kerrison v. Melbourne City Council (2014) 228 FCR 87 103
K-Generation Pty Ltd v. Liquor Licensing Court (2009) 237 CLR 501 161
Kirk v. Industrial Court of New South Wales (2010) 239 CLR 531 88, 161, 162, 257
Kruger v. Commonwealth (1997) 190 CLR 1 203

Lange v. Australian Broadcasting Corporation (1997) 189 CLR 520 68, 86
Levy v. Victoria (1997) 189 CLR 579 87, 112
Little v. Commonwealth (1947) 75 CLR 94 143–144, 145
Liversidge v. Anderson [1942] AC 206 144–145, 169
Lloyd v. Wallach (1915) 20 CLR 299 37, 142–143

Madzimbamuto v. Lardner-Burke [1969] 1 AC 645 78, 79
Marbury v. Madison (1803) 1 Cranch 137 (5 US 87) 248
Marchiori v. Environment Agency [2002] Eur LR 225 236, 239
Marcus Clark & Co Ltd v. Commonwealth (1952) 87 CLR 177 33–36
Marks v. The Commonwealth (1964) 111 CLR 549 79
McCloy v. New South Wales (2015) 257 CLR 178 69, 86
McCulloch v. Maryland 4 Wheat. 316 (1819) 22
Melbourne Corporation v. Barry (1922) 31 CLR 174 85
Melbourne Corporation v. Commonwealth (1947) 74 CLR 31 171
Miller v. TCN Channel Nine Pty Ltd (1986) 161 CLR 556 87, 126

TABLE OF CASES   xv

Minister for Immigration and Citizenship v. Li (2013) 249 CLR 332 239, 240
Minister for Immigration and Citizenship v. SZMDS (2010) 240 CLR 611 238
Minister for Immigration and Multicultural Affairs v. Al Khafaji (2004) 219 CLR 664 155
Minister for Immigration and Multicultural Affairs v. Rajamanikkam (2002) 210 CLR 222 240
Minister of Arts, Heritage and the Environment v. Peko Wallsend (1987) 15 FCR 274 233
Minister of State for the Army v. Dalziel (1944) 68 CLR 261 79
Momcilovic v. The Queen (2011) 245 CLR 1 86, 88
Monis v. The Queen (2013) 249 CLR 92 69, 87
Muldoon v. Melbourne City Council (2013) 217 FCR 450 103
Mulholland v. Australian Electoral Commission (2004) 220 CLR 181 85
Murphy v. Electoral Commissioner (2016) 90 ALJR 1027 61

New South Wales v. Commonwealth (1915) 20 CLR 54 148
New South Wales v. Commonwealth [2006] HCA 42 45
North Australian Aboriginal Justice Agency Ltd v. Northern Territory (2015) 256 CLR 569 88, 165
North Australian Aboriginal Legal Aid Service Inc v. Bradley (2004) 218 CLR 146 165

O'Flaherty v. City of Sydney Council (2013) 210 FCR 484 103
O'Flaherty v. City of Sydney Council (2014) 221 FCR 382 103

Pankhurst v. Kiernan (1917) 24 CLR 120 37
Pape v. Federal Commissioner of Taxation (2009) 238 CLR 1 72, 73, 76, 127, 138, 171, 175, 245
Pirrie v. McFarlane (1925) 36 CLR 170
Plaintiff M68/2015 v. Minister for Immigration and Border Protection (2016) 257 CLR 42 56, 58, 71, 76–77
Plaintiff S157/2002 v. Commonwealth (2003) 211 CLR 476 256, 257
Polyukhovich v. The Commonwealth (1991) 172 CLR 501 17
Potter v. Minahan (1908) 7 CLR 277 90

R v. Bow Street Metropolitan Stipendiary Magistrate; Ex parte Pinochet Ugarte (No 1) [2000] 1 AC 61 242
R v. Commonwealth Court of Conciliation and Arbitration; Ex parte State of Victoria (1942) 66 CLR 488 49, 50
R v. Commonwealth Court of Conciliation and Arbitration; Ex parte Victoria (sub nom Victoria v. Foster) (1944) 68 CLR 485 50
R v. Commonwealth Rent Controller; Ex parte National Mututal Life Assurance Association of Australasia Ltd (1947) 75 CLR 361 255
R v. Davey [1899] 2 QB 301 252

R v. Graham and Burns (1888) 16 Cox CC 420 90
R v. Foster (1949) 79 CLR 43 38
R v. Hegarty; Ex parte City of Salisbury (1981) 147 CLR 617 149
R v. Hickman; ex parte Fox (1945) 70 CLR 598 254
R v. Hughes (2000) 202 CLR 535 76
R v. McCormack [1981] VR 104 90
R v. Murray; Ex parte Proctor (1949) 77 CLR 387 259
R v. Neale (1839) 173 ER 899 90
R v. Kirby; Ex parte Boilermakers' Society of Australia (1956) 94 CLR 254 148, 175
R (on the application of Miller and another) v. Secretary of State for Exiting the European Union [2017] UKSC 5 56
R v. Sharkey (1949) 79 CLR 121 84, 127, 129, 130–131, 171, 227
R v. Toohey; Ex parte Northern Land Council (1981) 151 CLR 170 61
R v. Trade Practices Tribunal, Ex parte Tasmanian Breweries Pty Ltd (1970) 123 CLR 361 149
R v. University of Sydney (1943) 67 CLR 95 50
R v. Vincent (1839) 173 ER 754 90
Re Ditfort; Ex parte Deputy Commissioner of Taxation (NSW) (1988) 19 FCR 347 247
Re Residential Tenancies Tribunal (NSW); Ex parte Defence Housing Authority (1997) 190 CLR 410 76
Reid v. Sindberry (1944) 68 CLR 504 38
Richardson v. Forestry Commission (1988) 164 CLR 261 19
RJR-MacDonald Inc. v. Canada [1994] 1 SCR 311 112
Ruddock v. Vadarlis (2001) 110 FCR 491 58, 77–78, 247

Shaw Savill and Albion Co Ltd v. The Commonwealth (1940) 66 CLR 344 79
Sickerdick v. Ashton (1918) 25 CLR 506 37
Somerset v. Stewart (1772) 98 ER 499 90
South Australia v. Commonwealth (First Uniform Tax Case) (1942) 65 CLR 373 38
South Australia v. Totani (2010) 242 CLR 1 88, 118, 164
Spratt v. Hermes (1965) 114 CLR 226 215
Stenhouse v. Coleman (1944) 69 CLR 457 23–24, 38
Sue v. Hill (1999) 199 CLR 462 55

Tajjour v. New South Wales (2014) 254 CLR 508 85, 121
Thomas v. Mowbray [2007] HCA 33; (2007) 233 CLR 307 15, 18, 19, 40–44, 48, 53, 67, 138–139, 145–146, 151–152, 168–169, 262
Thompson v. Randwick Municipal Council (1950) 81 CLR 87 241
Totani v. The State of South Australia [2009] SASC 301 163

Union Steamship Co of Australia Pty Ltd v. King (1988) 166 CLR 1 175

TABLE OF CASES   xvii

Victoria v. Commonwealth and Hayden (1975) 134 CLR 338 127, 171
Victorian Chamber of Manufactures v. Commonwealth (1943) 67 CLR 335 38, 50

Wainohu v. New South Wales (2011) 243 CLR 181 85, 88, 118
Walker Corporation Pty Ltd v. Sydney Harbour Foreshore Authority (2008) 233 CLR 259 80
Waterside Workers' Federation v. J W Alexander (1918) 25 CLR 434 148
Wenn v. Attorney-General (Victoria) (1948) 77 CLR 84 41
White v. Redfern (1879) 5 QBD 15 252
Wilcox Mofflin Ltd. v. New South Wales (1952) 85 CLR 488 126
Williams v. Commonwealth (No.1) [2012] HCA 23; (2012) 248 CLR 156 57, 69–71
Williams v. Commonwealth (No.2) [2014] HCA 23; (2014) 252 CLR 416 69, 246
Wilson v. Minister for Aboriginal and Torres Strait Islander Affairs (1995) 184 CLR 348 150
Wotton v. Queensland (2012) 246 CLR 1 87, 102
Wotton v. State of Queensland (No. 5) [2016] FCA 1457 126, 191

STATUTES

Imperial

Commonwealth of Australia Constitution Act 1900 64, 225
  s 5:
  s 9:

Australia

Commonwealth

Aboriginal Land Rights (Northern Territory) Act 1976 216
Administrative Decisions (Judicial Review) Act 1977 212
Anti-Terrorism Act 2005 [No.2] 132–133
  sch 7:
Appropriation (Nation Building and Jobs) Act (No. 1) 2009 217
Appropriation (Nation Building and Jobs) Act (No. 2) 2009 217
Australian Radiation Protection and Nuclear Safety Act 1998 201
  s 63:
Australia Act 1986 59, 60, 64–65
  s 2(1):
  s 15:
Australian Security Intelligence Organisation Act 1979 156–158
  s 8:
  s 34AB:
  s 34D:
  s 34E:
  s 34F:
  s 34G:
  s 34K:
  s 34L:
  s 34S:
  s 34ZS:
Australian Security Intelligence Organisation Legislation Amendment (Terrorism) Act 2003 157

TABLE OF STATUTES

Biosecurity Act 2015 209–214
  ch 1 pt 3 div 2.
  ch 2 pt 2 div 2.
  ch 2 pt 2 div 5.
  ch 2 pt 3 div 3 subdiv B.
  ch 8.
  ch 8 pt 1.
  s 3:
  s 8:
  s 12:
  s 32(2):
  s 34(1):
  s 34(2):
  s 42(1):
  s 42(2):
  s 71:
  s 72:
  s 74(1):
  s 74(2):
  s 74(3):
  s 74(4):
  s 84:
  s 113(1):
  s 113(3):
  s 113(4):
  s 172:
  s 475(1):
  s 477:
  s 477(1):
  s 477(6):
  s 478:
  s 478(1):
  s 478(6):
  s 540:
  s 544:
Charter of the United Nations Act 1945 67
  s 15:
  s 18:
Classification (Publications, Films and Computer Games) Act 1995 216
  pt 10:
Commonwealth Inscribed Stock Amendment Act 2009 217

TABLE OF STATUTES

Communist Party Dissolution Act 1950 26, 28–29, 35–36, 47, 128
   s 4:
   s 5:
   s 5(1):
   s 5(2):
   s 6:
   s 9:
   s 10:
Constitution
   s 2:
   s 7:
   s 12:
   s 15:
   s 21:
   s 24:
   s 51:
   s 51(i):
   s 51(vi):
   s 51(ix):
   s 51(xxix):
   s 51(xxxi):
   s 51(xxxii):
   s 51(xxxvii):
   s 51(xxxix):
   s 52:
   s 52(ii):
   s 53:
   s 54:
   s 55:
   s 56:
   s 61:
   s 64:
   s 68:
   s 69:
   s 70:
   s 81:
   s 83:
   s 92:
   s 96:
   s 107:
   s 109:
   s 114:

TABLE OF STATUTES

s 116:
s 119:
s 122:
Crimes Act 1914 127, 129, 131–133, 135, 153
   pt IAA, div 4B, subdiv C
   s 3(1):
   s 3W:
   s 3ZQS:
   s 3ZQT:
   s 24A(1):
   s 24B(2):
   s 24D:
Crimes (Internationally Protected Persons) Act 1976 229
Criminal Code 1995 127, 132–135, 141
   div 105:
   div 105A:
   s 80.2:
   s 80.2(5):
   s 80.2C(3):
   s 80.3:
   s 80.3(2):
   s 100.1:
   s 101.1:
   s 101.4:
   s 101.6:
   s 102.1:
   s 102.5(2):
   s 102.8:
   s 105.2:
   s 105.4:
   s 105.4(7):
   s 105.8:
   s 105.12:
   s 105.14:
   s 105.14A:
   s 105.15:
   s 105.16:
   s 105.18:
   s 105.34:
   s 105.35:
   s 105.36:
   s 105.37:

Criminal Code 1995 (cont.)
 s 105.40:
 s 105.41:
 s 105A.7(1):
 s 471.12:
Criminal Code Amendment (High Risk Terrorist Offenders) Act 2016   140
Defence Act 1903   139, 219, 226–227, 229–231
 pt IIIA:
 s 51A:
 s 51B:
 s 51B(1)(a):
 s 51B (2):
 s 51T:
 s 51WB:
Defence Preparations Act 1951   34
Household Stimulus Package Act (No. 2)   217
Income Tax Rates Amendment (Temporary Flood and Cyclone Reconstruction Levy) Act 2011   215
Liquid Fuel Emergency Act 1984   180
 pt III:
Migration Act 1958   154, 256
National Health Security Act 2007   201, 204
 s 31(1):
 s 73(1):
 s 73(2):
 s 73(4):
National Security Act 1939–1940   38, 51, 143
National Security Act 1939–1943   38
National Security Legislation Amendment Act 2010   135
Northern Territory National Emergency Response Act 2007
 pt 10 div 2:
 s 18:
Northern Territory (Self-Government) Act 1978   216
Nuclear Non-Proliferation (Safeguards) Act 1987   201
 s 63:
Parliamentary Precincts Act 1988   93, 96
 s 4(2):
 s 4(3):
 s 5(1):
 s 5(2):
 s 6:
 s 11:

TABLE OF STATUTES xxiii

Public Order (Protection of Persons and Property) Act 1971 90, 91, 93–94, 228–229
   s 4:
   s 6:
   s 6(1):
   s 6(2):
   s 6(1A):
   s 6 (3):
   s 6(1):
   s 8:
   s 15(1):
Surveillance Devices Act 2004 153
   s 12:
   s 14:
Tax Bonus for Working Australians Act (No. 2) 2009 217
Tax Bonus for Working Australians (Consequential Amendments) Act (No. 2) 2009 217
Tax Laws Amendment (Temporary Flood and Cyclone Reconstruction Levy) Act 2011 215
Telecommunications (Interception and Access) Act 1979 156
   s 44:
   s 49:
Trade Practices Act 1974 133–134
Racial Discrimination Act 1975 193
   s 9(1):
Sex Discrimination Act 1984 172
Unlawful Associations Act 1916 37
   s 4:
War Precautions Act 1914 21, 142
War Precautions Act 1914–1915 37
   s 4:

Australian Capital Territory

Crimes Act 1900 104
   pt 9:
Crimes (Sentencing) Act 2005 117
   pt 3.4:
Emergencies Act 2004 122, 180, 181, 194
   s 150(3):
   s 150A:
   s 150B:
   s 150C:

Emergencies Act 2004 (cont.)
  s 151:
  s 156:
Environment Protection Act 1997 199, 200
  pt 11 div 11.3:
  pt 12:
  s 105(b):
  s 106:
  s 107:
  s.108:
  s 109:
Fuel Control Act 1979 180
  s 11:
Health Act 1993 116
Health (Patient Privacy) Amendment Act 2015 116
Human Rights Act 2004 86, 172
  s 30:
Public Health Act 1997 205–208
  s 4:
  s 119(1):
  s 119(3):
Radiation Protection Act 2006 202
  pt 3 div 3.7:
  s 47(2):
Terrorism (Extraordinary Temporary Powers) Act 2006 137, 140
Utilities Act 2000 180
  pt 9:

Northern Territory

Criminal Code
  s 63:
  s 63(4):
Emergency Management Act 2013 122, 180, 181, 184–190, 201
  s 4:
  s 19:
  s 21:
Essential Goods and Services Act 1981 180
  s 5:
Local Government Act 2008 100
  s 33:
Police Administration Act 1978 216
  pt VII div 4:
  pt VII div 4AA:

TABLE OF STATUTES XXV

Radiation Protection Act 2004 202
   s 62:
Serious Crime Control Act 2009 117
Summary Offences Act 104, 121
   s 47A:
   s 55A:
   s 56(1):
Terrorism (Emergency Powers) Act 137, 140
Trespass Act 1987 92
   s 5:
   s 6:

New South Wales

APEC Meeting (Police Powers) Act 2007 214
Biosecurity Act 2015 209–214
Community Protection Act 1994 159
Constitution Act 1902 59
   pt 4:
   s 35B:
Crimes Act 1900 90, 91, 105, 107, 113, 115, 121, 141
   s 35A:
   s 93B:
   s 93C:
   s 93W:
   s 93X:
   s 93Y:
   s 201(1):
   s 545C:
   sch 3 s 3:
Crimes (Criminal Organisations Control) Act 2012 117, 120
Crimes (High Risk Offenders) Act 2006 167
Crimes (Serious Crime Prevention Orders) Act 2016 120
   s 3:
   s 5(1):
Criminal Assets Recovery Act 1990 120, 161
   s 6(2):
   s 10:
Emergency Powers Act 1949 180
Energy and Utilities Administration Act 1987 180
   pt 6:
Environmental Trust Act 1998 199
   s 16:

xxvi   TABLE OF STATUTES

Essential Services Act 1988 180
  s 10:
Inclosed Lands, Crimes and Law Enforcement Legislation Amendment (Interference)
    Act 2016 113, 115
Inclosed Lands Protection Act 1901 113, 115
  s 4:
  s 4B:
Law Enforcement (Powers and Responsibilities) Act 2002 115, 122–126
  pt 6A:
  pt 14:
  s 45A:
  s 45B:
  s 87A(1):
  s 87B:
  s 87C:
  s 87D(1):
  s 87F(1):
  s 87G(2):
  s 87G(4):
  s 87I:
  s 87J:
  s 87J(2):
  s 87K(1):
  s 87K(3):
  s 87L:
  s 87M(1):
  s 87MA:
  s 87MB:
  s 87N:
  s 87O:
  s 200:
  s 200(3):
  s 200(4):
Local Government Act 1993
  s 8(1):
  s 632(1):
Public Health Act 2010 205–208
  s 3(1):
  s 8:
  s 8(1):
  s 8(2):
  s 198(1):

TABLE OF STATUTES   xxvii

Radiation Control Act 1990 202
   s 19:
   s 19(1):
Road Obstructions (Special Provisions) Act 1979 214
State Emergency and Rescue Management Act 1989 122, 180, 181, 193, 194, 201, 207
   pt 2 div 1 subdiv 2:
   pt 2 div 1 subdiv 3:
   s 4(1):
   s 4(2):
   s 7:
   s 18:
   s 20A:
   s 33:
   s 60L:
Summary Offences Act 1988 91–92, 95, 108
   pt 4:
   s 4:
   s 4A:
   s 6:
   s 11A:
   s 23:
   s 23(1):
   s 24:
   s 25:
Terrorism (High Risk Offenders) Act 2017 140–141, 167
   pt 2:
   pt 3:
   div 1.3:
   s 7:
   s 8:
   s 9:
   s 10:
   s 26(6):
   s 40(1):
Terrorism (Police Powers) Act 2002 137, 140

Queensland

Biosecurity Act 2014 209, 258
Commonwealth Games Act 1982 214
Constitution Act 1867 59
   pt 3:
   s 11A:

Constitution of Queensland 2001 59
   ch 3 pt 2:
   s 7:
   s 12:
   s 15:
   s 21:
   s 29(1):
   s 33:
   s 110:
Criminal Code Act 1899 91, 92, 120, 127
   sch 1 pt 9A:
   sch 1 s 61:
   sch 1 s 71:
   sch 1 s 199:
   sch 1 s 230:
   sch 1 s 340(2AA):
Dangerous Prisoners (Sexual Offenders) Act 2003 162
Disaster Management Act 2003 122, 180–181, 190–191, 195–196
   pt 2:
   pt 2 div 1 subdiv 2:
   pt 3:
   s 13(1):
   s 13(2):
   s 64:
   s 66:
   s 67A:
   s 69:
   s 72:
   s 72A:
   s 73(1):
   s 75:
   s 77(1):
Electricity Act 1994 180
   ch 5 pt 2:
Environmental Protection Act 1994 199–200
   ch 9 pt 4:
   s 466B(iii):
   s 467:
G20 (Safety and Security) Act 2013 110–111
   pt 2 div 1:
   pt 4:
   s 17:

TABLE OF STATUTES xxix

    s 18:
    s 19:
    s 50(2):
Peaceful Assembly Act 1992 95–96, 108, 111
    pt 9D div 3
    s 5(1):
    s 5(2):
    s 6(1):
    s 9:
    s 12:
    s 13(1):
Police Powers and Responsibilities Act 2000 104–105, 107–108, 124
    pt 5:
    s 29:
    s 29(1):
    s 31(1):
    s 45:
    s 46(1):
    s 47(1):
    s 48(1):
Penalties and Sentences Act 1992 117–119
    pt 9D div 3:
Public Health Act 2005 205–208
    ch 8:
    ch 8 pt 7:
    s 7:
    s 319(3):
    s 322(b):
Public Safety Preservation Act 1986 122, 124–125, 137, 190–191, 193–194, 201
    pt 2A:
    pt 3:
    s 5:
    s 8(1):
    s 8(2):
    s 8(3):
Radiation Safety Act 1999 202
    s 148:
Serious and Organised Crime Legislation Amendment Act 2016 118
    s 492:
State Transport Act 1938 180
    s 2:

xxx TABLE OF STATUTES

Summary Offences Act 2005 90–92
   s 6:
   s 6(2):
   s 10A(1):
   s 11:
Vicious Lawless Association Disestablishment Act 2013 118

South Australia

Constitution Act 1934 59
   pt 3:
Criminal Law Consolidation Act 1935 90–91
   sch 11 s 1:
Emergency Powers Act 1974 180
Emergency Management Act 2004 122, 180–181, 195–197, 201, 206
   pt 1A:
   pt 2:
   pt 3:
   s 3:
   s 4(2):
   s 14:
   s 21:
   s 22:
   s 23:
   s 24:
   s 25(1):
   s 25(2):
Environment Protection Act 1997 199–200
   pt 10 div 2:
   s 93(3):
   s 99(3):
   s 103J(5):
Essential Services Act 1981 180
   s 3:
Liquor Licensing Act 1997 161
   s 28A:
Mental Health Act 2009 208
Motor Fuel Rationing (Temporary Provisions) Act 1977 214
Motor Fuel (Temporary Restriction) Act 1980 214
Public Assemblies Act 1972 96–97
   s 3:
   s 4(6):
   s 5(1):

TABLE OF STATUTES   xxxi

   s 5(2):
   s 6:
   s 6(2):
Radiation Protection and Control Act 1982 202
   s 42:
Serious and Organised Crime (Control) Act 2008 117, 163–164
South Australian Public Health Act 2011 205–207
   pt 2:
   pt 10:
   pt 11:
   s 75:
   s 77(1)(b):
   s 87(1):
   s 87(2):
   s 88:
   s 88(2):
   s 90(3):
Statutes Amendment (Public Health Incidents and Emergencies) Act 2009 205
Summary Offences Act 1953 91–93, 104, 121, 124
   s 6:
   s 6A:
   s 7:
   s 13:
   s 17A:
   s 17AB:
   s 18:
   s 18A:
   s 18A(2):
   s 18A(3):
   s 58:
   s 72B:
   s 72B(3):
Terrorism (Police Powers) Act 2005 137

Tasmania

Constitution Act 1934 59
   pt II:
Criminal Code Act 1924 90–91, 127
   s 6:
   s 34:
   s 73:
   s 73(1)(b):

Criminal Code Act 1924 (cont.)
   s 75:
   s 80:
Electricity Supply Industry Act 1995 180
   pt 6:
Emergency Management Act 2006 122, 180–181, 197–198, 201
   pt 3:
   sch 1 s 1:
   sch 1 s 1(1):
   sch 1 s 1(4):
   s 3:
   s 4:
   s 7:
   s 10:
   s 10(1):
   s 40(2):
   s 40(4):
   s 40(5):
   s 40(6):
   s 40(2):
   s 42:
   s 44:
Environmental Management and Pollution Control Act 1994 199
   s 74E:
   s 74F:
Mineral Resources Development Act 1995 113
Police Offences Act 1935 91–92, 98–99, 104–105, 120
   pt 2 div 1A:
   pt 2 div IIIAA:
   s 3:
   s 6:
   s 7:
   s 12:
   s 13:
   s 15B:
   s 34B:
   s 49AA:
   s 49AB(1):
   s 49AB(2):
   s 49AB(4):
   s 49AB(5):
   s 49AB(8):

Police Powers (Public Safety) Act 2005 137
Public Health Act 1997 205
  pt 2 div 2:
  s 14(1):
  s 16:
  s 16(2):
  s 15(1)(a):
Radiation Protection Act 2005 202
  s 64:
Reproductive Health (Access to Terminations) Act 2013 116
Traffic Act 1925 99
  s 3:
Workplaces (Protection from Protesters) Act 2014 111–114
  s 3:
  s 4(2):
  s 5(1):
  s 6:
  s 6(1):
  s 6(2):
  s 6(3):
  s 6(4):
  s 6(5):
  s 7:
  s 7(1):
  s 7(2):
  s 7(3):
  s 8(1):
  s 11(1):
  s 11(6):
  s 13:
  s 14:
  s 18(1):
  s 18(2):
  s 18(5):
  s 18(6):
  s 18(7):
  s 18(8):

Victoria

Administrative Law Act 1978
  s 8:
Beer Prices Regulation (Temporary Provisions) Act 1983 214

Constitution Act 1975 59
 pt I:
 s 6(1):
Charter of Human Rights and Responsibilities 2006 86, 172
 s 7(2):
 s 15(3):
 s 32:
 s 38(1):
Control of Weapons Act 1990 124
 s 3:
 s 10:
 s 10(7):
Crimes Act 1958 90–91
 div 2C:
 s 195G:
 s 195I:
 s 320:
Crimes Legislation Amendment (Public Order) Act 2017 91, 100
 s 8:
Criminal Organisations Control Act 2012 120
 pt 5A:
Electricity Industry Act 2000 180
 pt 6:
Emergency Management Act 1986 180, 184–186, 195, 201
 s 4:
 s 23(1A):
 s 23(1)
 s 23(7):
 s 24(1):
 s 24(2):
 s 24(3):
 s 36A:
Emergency Management Act 2013 122, 180–181, 184–190, 194, 201
 pt 2:
 pt 4:
 s 3:
 s 12:
 s 32:
 s 37(1):
 s 39(1):
 s 40(b):
 s 45:

TABLE OF STATUTES xxxv

    s 45(2)(b):
    s 53:
    s 55A(2):
Environment Protection Act 1970 199–200
    s 30A:
Essential Services Act 1958 180, 183–184, 186
    s 3:
    s 3(1):
    s 4:
    s 4(1):
    s 5(1):
    s 11:
    s 12:
    s 13:
    s 14:
    s 15:
Fire Services Commissioner Act 2010 186, 188
    s 3:
Fuel Prices Regulation Act 1981 214
Fuel Emergency Act 1977 184
    s 3:
Local Government Act 1989 99
    s 3E(1):
    s 111(1):
Plant Biosecurity Act 2010
Public Health and Wellbeing Amendment (Safe Access Zones) Act 2015 209
Public Health and Wellbeing Act 2008 116, 205–208, 236, 249
    pt 9A:
    pt 10 div 3:
    s 9:
    s 10:
    s 167(2)(a):
    s 185B:
    s 185D:
    s 198(1):
    s 198(7):
    s 198(8):
    s 200(1):
Public Safety Preservation Act 1928 180
Public Safety Preservation Act 1958 180, 183–184, 189
    s 3(1):
    s 3(2):

Public Safety Preservation Act 1958 (cont.)
    s 4(a):
    s 4(b):
    s 5:
    s 9:
Radiation Act 2005 202
    pt 8:
    s 96(1):
Sentencing Act 1991 91
    s 10AA(8):
Summary Offences Act 1966 91–93, 104–105, 107–108
    pt 1 div 1A:
    s 4(e):
    s 5:
    s 6(1):
    s 6(3):
    s 6(4):
    s 6(5):
    s 9:
    s 17:
    s 17(2):
    s 51:
    s 52(1A):
Summary Offences Amendment (Move-on Laws) Act 2015 108
Summary Offences and Sentencing Amendment Act 2014 108
State Disasters Act 1983 185
    s 4:
Terrorism (Community Protection) Act 2003 137, 140
    pt 3A:
Unlawful Assemblies and Processions Act 1958 90, 94
    s 5:
Vagrancy Act 1966 121
    s 6(1):
Vital State Industries (Works and Services) Act 1992 180
    s 4:
    s 5:
    s 6:
    s 7:
    s 8:

Western Australia

Biosecurity and Agriculture Management Act 2007 209
    pt 2 div 7:

Commonwealth Heads of Government Meeting (Special Powers) Act 2011 214
Constitution Act 1889 59
  pt IIIA:
  s 50(1):
Corruption and Crime Commission Act 2003 161
  s 76(2):
Criminal Code Act Compilation Act 1913 90–92, 127
  s 63:
  s 65:
  s 67:
  s 70A:
  s 74A:
  s 75A:
  s 172:
Criminal Investigation Act 2006 104–105, 107, 124–125
  s 27:
  s 27(3):
  s 68:
  s 68(1):
Criminal Organisations Control Act 2012 117
Emergency Management Act 2005 122, 180–181, 194–195, 201
  pt 2 div 1:
  pt 2 div 2:
  s 3:
  s 9(b):
  s 18:
  s 50:
  s 56
  s 56(2):
  s 70:
Environmental Protection Act 1986 199
  pt 5 div 4:
Essential Foodstuffs and Commodities Act 1979 214
Fuel, Energy and Power Resources Act 1972 180
  pt III:
Police Act 1892 83
  s 34:
Public Health Act 2016 205–208, 258
  pt 12:
  s 3:
  s 167(2):
  s 168(b):
  s 183:

Public Health Act 2016 (cont.)
    s 184:
    s 185:
Public Order in Streets Act 1984 97–98
    s 4(1):
    s 4(3):
    s 4(4):
    s 5(3):
    s 5(4):
    s 6:
    s 7(1):
    s 7(2):
    s 9:
    s 9(1):
    s 9(2):
    s 9(3):
    s 9(4):
    s 10:
Radiation Safety Act 1975 202
    s 55:
Terrorism (Extraordinary Powers) Act 2005 137

South Africa

Constitution of the Republic of South Africa (1996) 63
    s 37:
    s 37(2)(b):

United Kingdom

Act of Settlement 1701 56
Australia Act 1986 59, 60, 64–65
    s 2(1):
    s 15:
Bill of Rights 1688/89 56
Civil Contingencies Act 2004 177–181, 191
    pt 1:
    pt 2:
    s 5:
    s 19:
    s 20:
    s 21:
    s 22:

s 22(1):
s 22(2):
s 22(3):
s 24(3):
s 27:
Defence of the Realm Act 1914 177
Emergency Powers Act 1920 176–177, 180, 183
   s 1:
   s 2(1):
   s 2(3):
   s 2(4):
Emergency Powers (Defence) Act 1939 144
Habeas Corpus Suspension Act 1817 82
Public Health Act 1875 252
Serious Crimes Act 2007 119

United States

U.S. Constitution
   Art. IV, s 4:
   17th Amendment

1

Introduction

The invocation of emergency powers by the state in response to a perceived crisis is the subject of considerable controversy in liberal democracies because these powers appear on their face to pose a direct challenge to the liberal ideal of constitutional government.

Victor V. Ramraj and Arun K. Thiruvengadam (eds) *Emergency Powers in Asia: Exploring the Limits of Legality* (Cambridge University Press, 2010) 1.

1.1 Emergency Powers: Some General Themes

Many countries will occasionally be confronted with crises of such magnitude that they will pose a threat to the stability, and even possibly the existence, of the state if not contained. These crises or emergencies can arise from any of a multitude of causes: political, financial, large-scale natural disasters[1] and armed insurrection. Today many countries, including Australia, are engaged in an ongoing 'war on terror'. It has been asserted:

> The terrorist attacks of September 11, 2001 and the ensuing 'war on terror' have focused much attention on issues that have previously lurked in a dark corner at the edge of the legal universe. Politicians and academics alike are now preoccupied with a wide range of questions about the possible responses of democratic regimes to violent challenges. The resort to emergency powers at both the national and international level has been so extensive and penetrating that the exercise of these powers and the

---

[1] 'The Indian Ocean earthquake and tsunami of 26 December 2004 was one of the most catastrophic events of its kind': C Raj Kumar and DK Srivastava (eds) *Tsunami and Disaster Management: Law and Governance* (Sweet & Maxwell Asia 2006) vii (Foreword). They added: 'The sheer magnitude of the impact, affecting a number of countries in south and South-east Asia, killing nearly 300,000 and displacing thousands of people, was beyond anyone's wildest expectation': ibid.

complex questions that arise in that connection now play a critical role in discussions about the rule of law, legitimacy, and legality.[2]

The horrendous 9/11 attacks on the World Trade Center towers in New York, the bomb blasts in Bali nightclubs in Indonesia, the bombing of a train in Madrid in 2004 and other terrorist attacks in recent times in a number of cities[3] around the world have compelled liberal democracies to devise new forms of legislation to provide the authorities ample emergency powers to counter the activities of these terrorists, and to ensure the safety of the people. This hurried burst of legislative activity in countries around the world has posed the vexing question of how to strike the proper balance between public safety and the rule of law. Exegesis on this difficult question by eminent scholars has resulted in an increased output of works, with the result that emergency powers may no longer be regarded as an esoteric subject.[4] Professor Robert Martin wrote:

---

[2] Oren Gross and Fionuala Ni Aolain, *Law in Times of Crisis: Emergency Powers in Theory and Practice* (CUP 2006) 1. Herbert V Morais wrote:

> Even before September 11, 2001, international terrorist attacks have been carried out for many years, albeit on a smaller scale, in several parts of the world. He provided the following examples of some major terrorist attacks: Attack on the U.S.S. Cole in Aden, Yemen, in October 2000, which killed 17 American sailors and wounded more than twice that number. Bombings of the United States embassies in Nairobi, Kenya and Dar-es-Salam, Tanzania, in August 1998, which killed more than 200 people and injured several thousand. Attack on the Khobar Towers air base in Saudi Arabia in June 1996, which resulted in the deaths of 19 Americans, the hospitalization of 64 others, and the treatment of about 200. Tokyo subway nerve gas attack in March 1995, which resulted in the hospitalization of more than 600 subway passengers and 12 deaths. Pan Am 103 explosion and crash in Lockerbie, Scotland in December 1988, which killed 270 passengers, mostly Americans.

See Herbert V Morais, 'The War against Money Laundering, Terrorism, and the Financing of Terrorism' (2002) Lawasia J 1, 14–15.

[3] The recent attacks include attacks in Paris (7 January 2015 – on the newspaper *Charlie Hebdo*; 13 November 2015 – Bataclan and Stade de France); Brussels (22 March 2016 – airport and metro station); Istanbul (28 June 2016 – Atatürk Airport; 1 January 2017 – nightclub); Nice (14 July 2016 – attack using a truck); London (22 March 2017 – using a car on Westminster Bridge; 3 June 2017 – London Bridge); Stockholm (7 April 2017 – attack using a truck); Manchester (22 May 2017 – Ariana Grande concert); Barcelona (16–18 August 2017).

[4] See as examples Gross and Ni Aolain (n 2); David Dyzenhaus, *The Constitution of Law: Legality in a Time of Emergency* (CUP 2006); Austin Sarat (ed), *Sovereignty, Emergency, Legality* (CUP 2010); Victor V Ramraj, Michael Hor and Kent Roach (eds), *Global Anti-Terrorism Law and Policy* (CUP 2005); Victor V Ramraj (ed), *Emergencies and the Limits*

> The very notion of emergency powers is contradictory. The defining principle of constitutional government is the Rule of Law. This principle requires that the state always act in accordance with the law... The notion of emergency powers contradicts the Rule of Law because it posits that, in times of national crisis, the state may act outside constitutional norms. The idea is that whenever the existence of the state is imperilled, it may take extraordinary steps in order to save itself.[5]

In vibrant democracies, where the rule of law prevails, the invocation of exceptional powers poses a significant conundrum of how to balance the preservation of public safety with the maintenance of the rule of law. This conundrum is particularly accentuated when national security is claimed by governments to be at stake. It is generally accepted that in a time of crisis the panoply of legal powers available to the authorities trusted with protecting the state will be amplified commensurate with the intensity of the emergency. The remarkable trait of a liberal democracy is that while the powers to cope with the emergency provide the potential for authoritarian rule, such powers are terminated with the restoration of normalcy.

1.1.1 Definition of 'Emergency'

The word 'emergency' is elastic. Lord Dunedin, delivering the judgment of the Privy Council in *Bhagat Singh & Ors* v. *The King Emperor*,[6] said: 'A state of emergency is something that does not permit of any exact definition: it connotes a state of matters calling for drastic action...' Lord MacDermott, delivering the advice of the Privy Council in *Stephen Kalong Ningkan* v. *Government of Malaysia*,[7] observed that the natural meaning of the word itself is capable of covering a very wide range of situations and occurrences, including such diverse events as wars, famines, earthquakes, floods and the collapse of civil government. Professor Robert Martin said:

> While there is no universally accepted definition of emergency, it is generally understood that an emergency is, and must be, temporary. This is because an emergency involves conditions which are aberrant, atypical,

---

of Legality (CUP 2008); Victor V Ramraj and Arun K Thiruvengadam (eds), *Emergency Powers in Asia: Exploring the Limits of Legality* (CUP 2010).
[5] Robert Martin, 'Notes on Emergency Powers in Canada' (2005) 54 UNBLJ 161, 162.
[6] AIR 1931 PC 111.
[7] (1968) 2 MLJ 238, 242; [1970] AC 379, 390.

and extreme powers intended to deal with unusual situations must, by definition, be unusual and temporary.[8]

This general understanding must now yield to the reality that in today's on-going 'war on terror' many societies are placed on an unending 'emergency' footing, in which exceptional powers are given long leases of life.

In those countries that have an entrenched framework of emergency powers, the invocation of emergency powers depends on the claimed existence of a state of emergency. The controversial issue for the courts in these countries is the role of the courts in exercising judicial review over this claim. Hence, it is of importance to have criteria for identifying the existence of a genuine emergency. The danger of allowing the executive arm of government an unconstrained power to proclaim a state of emergency was put aptly by Heydon J in *Pape v. Commissioner of Taxation*:[9]

> Modern linguistic usage suggests that the present age is one of 'emergencies', 'crises', 'dangers' and 'intense difficulties', of 'scourges' and other problems. They relate to things as diverse as terrorism, water shortages, drug abuse, child abuse, poverty, pandemics, obesity, and global warming, as well as global financial affairs. In relation to them, the public is endlessly told, 'wars' must be waged, 'campaigns' conducted, 'strategies' devised and 'battles' fought. Often these problems are said to arise suddenly and unexpectedly. Sections of the public constantly demand urgent action to meet particular problems. The public is continually told that it is facing 'decisive' junctures, 'crucial' turning points and 'critical' decisions. Even if only a very narrow power to deal with an emergency on the scale of the global financial crisis were recognised, it would not take long before constitutional lawyers and politicians between them managed to convert that power into something capable of almost daily use. The great maxim of governments seeking to widen their constitutional powers would be: 'Never allow a crisis to go to waste.'[10]

Heydon J added:

> [I]t is far from clear what, for constitutional purposes, the meanings of the words 'crises' and 'emergencies' would be. It would be regrettable if the field were one in which the courts deferred to, and declined to substitute their judgment for, the opinion of the Executive or the legislature. That

---

[8] Martin (n 5) 161.
[9] [2009] HCA 23; (2009) 238 CLR 1.
[10] Ibid [551].

would be to give an 'unexaminable' power to the Executive, and history has shown, as Dixon J said, that it is often the Executive which engages in the unconstitutional supersession of democratic institutions. On the other hand, if the courts do not defer to the Executive or the legislature, it would be difficult for the courts to assess what is within and what is beyond power.[11]

In a 1991 report, the New Zealand Law Reform Commission[12] identified a number of distinguishing characteristics of emergencies in which extraordinary powers are made available to the authorities to respond to them:

> Scale: The emergency will pose a serious danger to the safety or welfare of the...public or a serious threat to the security of the [country] as a whole, it will have a widespread impact or potential impact, and it will require substantial resources to counter the danger effectively.
>
> Urgency: Generally the emergency threat will be an immediate one, although an event which is imminent or likely to occur may justify the taking of emergency measures. A common perception, clearly accurate in the case of an emergency such as a serious earthquake, is that emergencies occur suddenly and are unexpected. But an emergency situation, such as a drought, may develop gradually over a period of time.
>
> Temporary character: Generally the emergency will be temporary, although a drought or a lengthy war both illustrate that this is not invariably the case.
>
> Inadequacy of normal measures: The emergency will be a situation that cannot be dealt with without recourse to extraordinary measures.[13]

In a number of the constitutions promulgated after the end of the Second World War, the word 'emergency' has taken on a special meaning as a result of the entrenchment of a framework of emergency powers within these constitutions.[14] The main concern of the framers of these post-World War II constitutions was to ensure an appropriate balance between the protection of fundamental liberties and the preservation of national safety. The high-powered Reid Commission which crafted the Malayan (later, Malaysian) Constitution said:

---

[11] Ibid [552].
[12] NZLC R22 (*Final Report on Emergencies*).
[13] Ibid 8 para [1.20].
[14] Article 150, Malaysian Constitution. The Malaysian Constitution, for example, provides that the Malaysian King is empowered to issue a proclamation of emergency if the King 'is satisfied that a grave emergency exists whereby the security, or the economic life, or public order in the Federation or any part thereof is threatened'.

Neither the existence of fundamental rights nor the division of power between the Federation and the States ought to be permitted to imperil the safety of the State or the preservation of a democratic way of life. The Federation must have adequate power in the last resort to protect these essential national interests. But in our opinion, infringement of fundamental rights or of State rights is only justified to such extent as may be necessary to meet a particular danger which threatens the nation. We therefore recommend that the Constitution should authorize the use of emergency powers by the Federation but that the occasions on which, and so far as possible the extent to which, such powers can be used should be limited and defined'.[15]

It is the standpoint of this book that, as the Australian Constitution does not embody an explicit framework of emergency powers, it is unnecessary as of now to attempt a formulation of an all-embracing definition of the term 'emergency'. Exceptional powers, whenever needed, are provided in ordinary legislation. A pragmatic approach is to identify the nature of an emergency: by doing so, it would enable a proper evaluation of the response by the authorities to cope with the emergency. Thus, the panoply of emergency powers which should be made available to the relevant authorities should vary with the type of emergency involved. The New Zealand Law Commission rejected the approach of 'a single general statute dealing with a wide range of emergencies' and confirmed its support for a 'sectoral approach to emergency legislation', in the sense of support for 'a series of separate statutes, each concerned with a particular emergency situation'.[16]

Emergencies can be broadly classified into 'wartime', emergencies pertaining to 'serious civil disturbances',[17] and 'civil' emergencies. A wartime emergency poses the gravest threat to the life of a nation. Emergencies pertaining to serious civil disturbances relate largely to 'widespread public disorder, or actions threatening the security of the State such as treason, sabotage or terrorism'.[18] Civil emergencies vary in

---

[15] *Report of the Federation of Malaya Constitutional Commission* (1957) 74 para [172].

[16] *Final Report on Emergencies* (NZLC R22) 9 para [1.22]. Originally, the Public Safety Conservation Act 1932 (NZ) was available as a general statute but it never defined 'those threats to public safety or public order that were sufficiently serious to justify the declaration of emergency'. Concerned that the broad regulation-making power vested too much discretion in the executive, the Act was repealed in 1987: see *Final Report on Emergencies* (NZLC R22) 184 para [7.3].

[17] Adopting the description of this category of emergency by the New Zealand Law Commission: NZLC R22, 60 para [3.16].

[18] Ibid 60 para [3.16].

magnitude and severity. They can be short-lived or of a lengthy duration. Conditions giving rise to civil emergencies can range from natural and industrial disasters, strikes in essential services, to economic emergencies.

In Australia, the executive arm of government cannot resort to a 'constitutionalised' framework of emergency powers. In other words, the Australian Constitution does not contain a set of provisions providing for a power to declare a state of emergency, the circumstances justifying the invocation of emergency powers, express safeguards circumscribing the use of such powers or the scope of judicial review. Similarly, emergency powers are not set out expressly in the constitutions of the States. However, a broad spectrum of emergency powers is contained in ordinary statutes at both Commonwealth and State levels.

One of the reasons why it has not yet been necessary to define 'emergency' is because that question has traditionally fallen to the States to answer. Because State Parliaments exercise plenary legislative powers, and are not bound to adhere to their own constitutions, they are generally free to define 'emergency' as they see fit, and confer emergency powers in conformity with that definition, without any significant boundaries. To the extent that there are constitutional limits on State emergency powers, they are imposed by the limited freedoms guaranteed by the Australian Constitution and, at the margins, the requirement that Parliaments not permanently abdicate their legislative powers. This means, essentially, that a State Parliament may redistribute legislative and executive power as it deems necessary in response to a state of emergency that it is free to define.

However, the increasingly national character of Australian emergency laws, in the face of existential dangers posed by epidemics, terrorism and massive environmental disasters, may yet require a constitutionally satisfactory definition of 'emergency' to be implied from the Australian Constitution. Moreover, any legislative or executive powers that derive from that definition being satisfied would have to contend with the fact that the Commonwealth is a government of limited powers, with certain obligations to preserve the federal and representative character of the Australian constitutional system of government.

If emergency does become 'nationalised', the risk, here as in elsewhere, is that an approach to emergency which simply sweeps the ordinary constitutional framework aside risks doing extensive damage to the underlying constitutional structure that empowers the government to deal with emergency on the people's behalf in the first place.

1.2 Dangers of Over-Reaction

When a country without a well-thought out framework of emergency powers is suddenly confronted by a crisis, there is a danger that the authorities, in responding, may adopt disproportionate measures, causing excessive encroachments upon fundamental liberties. When there is an outbreak of war between countries, governments are compelled to counter the perceived threat to national survival by placing the country in a state of emergency.

A controversial episode which provides a neat illustration of the difficulties in balancing national security and civil liberties was when members of an extremist separatist group known as Le Front de Liberation du Quebec (or 'FLQ') kidnapped the Quebec Labour Minister, Pierre Laporte, and the British Trade Commissioner, James Cross. At the request of Quebec provincial authorities, the Prime Minister invoked a piece of legislation called the War Measures Act[19] to deal with the crisis. This legislation was enacted in 1914 as a response to wartime conditions. Though used extensively in both World Wars, this was the first occasion for its use in peacetime. Initially, there was some political opposition to the invocation of the Act, but that opposition faded out after it was discovered that the Quebec Labour Minister had been murdered by the FLQ.[20]

The War Measures Act provided:

> The Governor in Council may do and authorize such acts and things, and make from time to time such orders and regulations, as he may by reason of the existence of real or apprehended war, invasion, or insurrection deem necessary or advisable for the security, defence, peace, order or welfare of Canada...

To exercise these powers, all that was required was a proclamation of the Governor in Council declaring that war, invasion or insurrection, real or apprehended, existed. Significantly, section 2 of the Act stated:

> The issue of a proclamation ... shall be conclusive evidence that war, invasion, or insurrection, real or apprehended, exists and has existed for any period of time therein stated, and of its continuance, until by the issue of a further proclamation it is declared that the war, invasion or insurrection no longer exists.

---

[19] RSC 1970, c. W-2.
[20] John J McGonagle, Jr, 'Emergency Detention Acts: Peacetime Suspension of Civil Rights – With a Postscript on the Recent Canadian Crisis' (1970) 20 Cath U L Rev 203, 233–36.

1.2 DANGERS OF OVER-REACTION

Pursuant to the Act, the Governor in Council made regulations which declared the FLQ an unlawful association, and rendered membership in or support of it a criminal offence, punishable by imprisonment for up to five years. The regulations also provided for heavy penalties for knowingly assisting persons in the FLQ or providing accommodation for the organisation. The regulations conferred on the authorities special powers of search and detention of persons arrested for alleged violation of the regulations. In November 1970, the Canadian Parliament enacted the Public Order (Temporary Measures) Act 1970 to come into effect upon the termination of the proclamation of the War Measures Act.

Cheffins and Tucker, in commenting on the crisis, said:

> Viewed in hindsight, it is hard to say that there existed the 'war, invasion, or insurrection, real or apprehended' required for the proclamation of the War Measures Act. There seems to be little doubt, however, that the government was justified in taking the position that it needed some special temporary powers, but the fact remains that these could probably have been obtained by the quick passage by Parliament of a special powers act designed specifically to deal with the FLQ crisis.[21]

Craig Forcese and Aaron Freeman have remarked:

> What Canada learned from the October Crisis is that during political emergencies, the executive branch is typically strengthened at the expense of the legislative and judicial branches. Urgency tends to trump sober second thought, and the rule of law may be suspended for a perceived greater good.[22]

A stark illustration of an overreaction which resulted in staining the democratic credentials of the United States was provided by the Korematsu affair.[23] The launching of a surprise attack on Pearl Harbor on 7 December 1941 (described by President Franklin Roosevelt as 'a date which will live in infamy'[24]) led to a response by the US authorities which today has been acknowledged to be gravely erroneous.

---

[21] Ronald Cheffins and Ronald Tucker, *The Constitutional Process in Canada* (2nd ed., McGraw-Hill Ryerson Ltd 1976) 133. See also Herbert Marx, 'The Apprehended Insurrection of October 1970 and the Judicial Function' (1972) 7 UBC L Rev 55.
[22] Craig Forcese and Aaron Freeman, *The Laws of Government: The Legal Foundation of Canadian Democracy* (Irwin Law 2005) 577.
[23] *Korematsu v. United States* 323 US 214 (1944). See also HP Lee, 'Of Lions and Squeaking Mice in Anxious Times' (2016) 42(1) Monash LR 1, 8–10.
[24] President Franklin D Roosevelt, 'A Date Which Will Live in Infamy' (Speech delivered at a joint session of Congress, Washington DC, United States, 8 December 1941).

On 19 February 1942, President Franklin Roosevelt signed Executive Order 9066. Pursuant to this executive order, over 110,000 Japanese-Americans were rounded up and sent to a number of internment camps. Those interned included 'immigrants, citizens, men, women, children and infants'.[25]

The constitutionality of Executive Order 9066 was challenged by Fred Korematsu, who was born and raised in California. The constitutionality of the executive order was upheld by a 6–3 decision of the Supreme Court. Black J, delivering the opinion of the Court, acknowledged that the compulsory exclusion of large groups of citizens from their homes, would be inconsistent with American basic governmental institutions, 'except under circumstances of direst emergency and peril'. He added: 'But when under conditions of modern warfare our shores are threatened by hostile forces, the power to protect must be commensurate with the threatened danger'.[26]

Jackson J, one of three dissenting justices, pointed out that Korematsu had been born in the United States and, under the *Constitution*, he was a citizen of the United States. He added:

> No claim is made that he is not loyal to this country. There is no suggestion that apart from the matter involved here he is not law-abiding and well disposed. Korematsu, however, has been convicted of an act not commonly a crime. It consists merely of being present in the state whereof he is a citizen, near the place where he was born, and where all his life he has lived.[27]

Jackson J warned that 'the principle of racial discrimination in criminal procedure and of transplanting American citizens' would '[lie] about like a loaded weapon ready for the hand of any authority that can bring forward a plausible claim of an urgent need. Every repetition imbeds that principle more deeply in our law and thinking and expands it to new purposes'.[28]

A report published in 1983 by a commission set up by Congress stated that the decisions that followed the executive order were shaped by 'race

---

[25] Neil Gotanda, 'The Story of Korematsu: The Japanese–American Cases' in Michael C Dorf (ed), *Constitutional Law Stories* (Foundation Press 2004) 249.
[26] 323 US 214, 219–20 (1944).
[27] Ibid 242–43.
[28] Ibid 246.

prejudice, war hysteria and a failure of political leadership'.[29] Indeed, the rationale for the order, that it was necessary to prevent Japanese-Americans in the region from planning attacks on naval assets, was later revealed to have been fabricated.[30] *Korematsu* was highlighted to serve as a caution to Australia that 'in times of distress the shield of military necessity and national security must not be used to protect governmental actions from close scrutiny and accountability'.[31]

1.3 Emergency Powers: International Norms

It has been said that the law is made for the state and not the state for the law. If the circumstances are such that a choice must be made between the two, it is the law which must be sacrificed to the state, with the maxim *salus populi suprema lex esto* ('Let the welfare of the people be the supreme law') often cited.[32] The need for normal constitutional principles to yield temporarily to the invocation of special or emergency powers to deal with a crisis is expressly recognised not only by most constitutional frameworks, but also by various international instruments and the general international law.

International law is predicated on the sovereignty of nation-states; and an attribute of sovereign statehood in international law is a government's capacity to exercise effective control over its territory and its people by, inter alia, guaranteeing public order.[33] When a government's capacity to guarantee public order, and thus its effective control over territory and people, is threatened by an emergency, international law is faced with the same problem that emergency poses to law generally. The argument goes

---

[29] Commission on Wartime Relocation and Internment of Civilians, 'Personal Justice denied: Recommendations' (June 1983) quoted in Greg Robinson, *By Order of the President: FDR and the Internment of Japanese Americans* (HUP 2001) 251 n 55. The executive order was finally revoked by President Gerald Ford in 1976. In 1988, President Ronald Reagan signed into law legislation which provided 'for an official apology and a tax-free payment of $20 000 to each person who had been evacuated'. The conviction of Korematsu was ultimately evacuated by the Federal District Court.

[30] See: Susan Kiyomi Serrano and Dale Minami, '*Korematsu v. United States*: A Constant Caution in a Time of Crisis' (2003) 10 Asian Am L J 37, 38.

[31] Justice Michael Kirby, 'Liberty, Terrorism and the Courts' (2005) 9 UWS L Rev 11, 27.

[32] Joseph Barthelemy, *Problems de Politique et Finances de Guerre* (Alcan 1915) cited in Clinton Rossiter, *Constitutional Dictatorship* (Harcourt 1963) (Rep) 12.

[33] James Crawford, *The Creation of States in International Law* (2nd edn, OUP 2006) 55–61, 91–92; Mario Silva, *State Legitimacy and Failure in International Law* (Brill Nijhoff 2014) 13–17.

that it cannot be the case that a nation-state is bound to fully comply with various legal restraints where its very sovereignty, the quality that supposedly makes it a subject of international law, is threatened.[34] This is particularly apposite in the age of humanitarian military intervention; there is some suggestion that states of emergency which speak to a loss of control can, in some cases, justify intervention by other nation-states through the United Nations Security Council or, more controversially, unilaterally.[35]

It would appear that the drafters of international conventions have appreciated this tension. The record suggests that they have incorporated limited exceptions and derogations into the international instruments that obligate nation-states to adhere to human rights law with the objective of restoring the nation-state to a state of affairs in which it can fully comply with those obligations.[36]

For example, Article 15 of the European Convention on Human Rights expressly permits a member State to take measures derogating from the obligations under the convention 'in times of war or other public emergency threatening the life of the nation'. However, the Convention permits no derogation, even in times of emergency, from guarantees of the right to life (save through lawful acts of war), guarantees against torture or inhuman or degrading treatment or punishment, the guarantee that no one shall be held in slavery or servitude and the guarantee against retrospective legislation in the criminal law.

Article 4(1) of the International Covenant on Civil and Political Rights, 1966 states:

> In time of public emergency which threatens the life of the nation and the existence of which is officially proclaimed, the State Parties to the present Covenant may take measures derogating from their obligations under the present Covenant to the extent strictly required by the exigencies of the

---

[34] Gross and Ni Aolain (n 2) 110–11.

[35] See Gerry Simpson and Nicholas Wheeler, 'Preemption and Exception: International Law and the Revolutionary Power' in Thomas J Biersteker, Peter J Spiro, Chandra Lekha Sriram, Veronica I Raffo (eds) *International Law and International Relations: Bridging Theory and Practice* (Routledge 2007) 112; Silva (n 33) 13–17, 151–52.

[36] As Diane A Desierto has argued, 'the text, context, and *travaux préparatoires* of the international human rights treaties manifest that States agreed to the inclusion of derogation clauses or limitation clauses in these treaties, on the condition that derogation or non-compliance in situations of emergency would only be temporary, clearly exigent, transparent, and designed to expedite the restoration of the State's ability to fully comply with its treaty obligations'. See Diane A Desierto, *Necessity and National Emergency Clauses: Sovereignty in Modern Treaty Interpretation* (Martinus Nijhoff 2012) 261.

situation, provided that such measures are not inconsistent with their other obligations under international law and do not involve discrimination solely on the ground of race, colour, sex, language, religion or social origin.[37]

While recognition is accorded to the need for emergency powers, the recognition is qualified to the extent that there are limits which a State cannot exceed. As Dominic McGoldrick has observed, the UN Human Rights Committee has understood Article 4(1) to require nation-states to exercise emergency powers that derogate from their human rights commitments in a way that is not only necessary in the exigencies of the situation but proportionate to that particular situation.[38]

Some of these limits go to the nation-state's constitutional structure. When considering the compatibility of a nation-state's emergency powers with civil and political rights, the Committee has taken an interest in, inter alia, the degree of Parliamentary control and other procedural constraints over the invocation and use of emergency powers, as well as the availability of judicial review.[39] This reflects that international law has an interest in the constitutional dimensions of emergency powers; it amounts to a recognition that the control of emergency through the preservation of a separation of powers is an important institutional ingredient in the protection of human rights.

1.4 The Frequency of Emergencies

The 'depressingly large number of emergencies'[40] encountered in the Asian region is conspicuous and bears a correlation to the high degree of instability in many countries in the region and other developing societies. In a number of emergent nations, emergency rule has tended

---

[37] The limitations and derogations provisions of the International Covenant on Civil and Political Rights were examined by a group of 31 experts in international law convened by the International Commission of Jurists and various international bodies and they produced 'The Siracusa Principles' (UN Document E/CN.4/1984/4: see 'The Siracusa Principles' (1986) 36 *The Review* (Int Comm of Jurists) 47.

[38] Dominic McGoldrick, 'The Interface between Public Emergency Powers and International Law' (2004) 2 Int J Const L 380, 408.

[39] Ibid 406–07.

[40] Ramraj and Thiruvengadam (n 4) 1, 3. In an early study, it was pointed out that from 1946 to 1960, states of emergency were proclaimed on no less than 29 separate occasions in British dependent territories alone: see Denys C Holland, 'Emergency Legislation in the Commonwealth' (1960) 13 CLP 148.

to become a norm rather than an exception.[41] It has been remarked: 'Regrettably, in more and more countries states of emergencies are being proclaimed and maintained for very long periods accompanied by restrictions on basic human rights which appear to go beyond what is strictly required for protecting the "life of the nation" as opposed to the life of the government in power'.[42] There are many factors which have contributed to this sad state of affairs. Many emergent nations are faced with problems arising from a diversity of religion, race or language. Furthermore, many of the fledgling legal systems of these countries are placed under great strain by unscrupulous politicians in trying to manipulate the system to entrench themselves and cronies in power. Nwabueze explained:

> The process of transforming a primitive, traditional society into a modern one has also imposed its own strain. The society is in a state of flux, and change, especially rapid change such as these countries are undergoing, creates tension. The forces of change, urbanisation, industrialisation, vast increases in literacy and education all have to be reconciled within the society, and they inevitably operate to undermine the traditional basis of authority and established values. On the other hand, the new political organisation, the modern state, is as yet not sufficiently rooted or legitimised to provide the alternative base of authority needed to contain the pressure of these forces, and the struggle between the various groups for the right to administer the state has weakened it still further. All these factors react upon one another to make the society of the new nations into a kind of cauldron, which continually gives off vapours of conflict and instability. Now and again the uneasy equilibrium breaks down, giving way to violence.[43]

Fortunately, Australia is a very stable democratic polity, and hence, the number of emergency situations it has experienced over its life span is small. The gravest emergencies were the two World Wars. However, Australia today, like many other democratic countries around the world, has created legislative frameworks to empower the authorities to prevent terrorists from carrying out their nefarious activities and to place curbs on people suspected of involvement with terrorist groups. It is important that emergency powers legislation must be crafted so as to accord with certain internationally acknowledged minimum standards. These

---

[41] Benjamin Obi Nwabueze, *Constitutionalism in the Emergent States* (C. Hurst & Co 1973).
[42] 'Editorial Note' (1976) *The Review* (International Commission of Jurists) 8.
[43] Nwabueze (n 41) 173.

minimum standards are essential to ensure, in the words of Lord MacDermott, that 'the protection cannot be allowed to choke or warp the essence of what is protected'.[44]

1.5 Scope of the Book

This book evaluates the state of the law in Australia pertaining to the capacity of government to handle a crisis which threatens public safety and tranquillity. It considers the scope of the constitutional and statutory powers available to the authorities to deal with wartime emergencies, global terrorism, civil disorders, and natural disasters against the backdrop of a commitment to the rule of law, which is viewed as underlying the Australian constitutional system. In the face of an emergency, the executive and legislative arms of government inevitably bear the responsibility of securing public safety and national survival, and the scope of the executive power in relation to emergencies is discussed.

The defence power in the Australian Constitution and the established jurisprudence pertaining to it, particularly in the light of *Thomas v. Mowbray*,[45] will be analysed. It explores the legislative framework regulating such deployment in light of the enactment of the *Defence Legislation Amendments (Aid to Civilian Authorities) Act 2000* (Cth), particularly, Part III AAA – 'Utilisation of Defence Force to Protect Commonwealth Interests, and State and self-governing Territories, against domestic violence'.

For a democratic polity, it is essential to ensure that there is a proper accommodation of the right to protest within a framework of public order. The offences of unlawful assembly, rout and riot and offences relating to the protection of state security are considered. Also considered are the increasingly uniform and national frameworks that have been adopted at the State and Commonwealth level to deal with civil emergencies, such as environmental disasters and global epidemics.

The judicial arm plays a vital role by ensuring that the invocation of exceptional powers does not lead to unacceptable encroachments upon the fundamental liberties of the people. In that connection, the role of the courts as constitutional guardians involves a judicious balancing of competing interests. The techniques employed by the courts in reviewing

---

[44] Rt. Hon. Lord MacDermott, 'Law and Order in Times of Emergency' (1972) *Jur Rev* 1.
[45] (2007) 233 CLR 307.

the exercise of emergency powers is discussed, with special emphasis on doctrines, such as 'justiciability' and 'deference'.

Any criticisms made, and solutions suggested, are in the spirit of principled pragmatism that must accompany any realistic consideration of emergency powers. In *Conway* v. *Rimmer*,[46] Lord Pearce remarked: 'The flame of individual liberty and justice must burn more palely when it is ringed by the more dramatic light of bombed buildings'.[47] However, the resort to emergency powers in a liberal democracy does not permit the *extinguishment* of the flame.

[46] [1968] AC 910.
[47] Ibid 982.

2

The Defence Power

A war imperilling our very existence, involving not the internal development of progress, but the array of the whole community in mortal combat with the common enemy, is a fact of such transcendent and dominating character as to take precedence of every other fact of life. It is the ultima ratio *of the nation. The defence power : . . passing into action becomes the pivot of the Constitution, because it is the bulwark of the State. Its limits then are bounded only by the requirements of self-preservation.*

Justice Isaacs, *Farey* v. *Burvett* (1916) 21 CLR 433, 453.

2.1 Introduction

'The Constitution', declared Isaacs J in *Farey* v. *Burvett*,[1] '...is not so impotent a document as to fail at the very moment when the whole existence of the nation it is designed to serve is imperilled'.[2] The experience in Australia so far is that the federal nature of the Constitution has not posed and does not pose a hindrance to action by the Commonwealth to cope with emergencies threatening the survival of the nation. In times of war, it is axiomatic that the survival of the nation must override interstate rivalries or obsession with States' rights. It is also acknowledged that the struggle for national survival may have an adverse impact on fundamental freedoms. Brennan J in *Polyukhovich* v. *The Commonwealth*[3] said:

> In times of war, laws abridging the freedoms which the law assures to the Australian people are supported in order to ensure the survival of those freedoms in times of peace. In times of peace, an abridging of those freedoms ... cannot be supported unless the Court can perceive that the abridging of the freedom in question is proportionate to the defence

---

[1] (1916) 21 CLR 433.
[2] Ibid 451.
[3] (1991) 172 CLR 501.

interest to be served. What is necessary and appropriate for the defence of the Commonwealth in times of war is different from what is necessary and appropriate in times of peace.[4]

The national effort to ensure survival is bolstered by an express provision in the Commonwealth constitution. Latham CJ in *Australian Communist Party v. Commonwealth*[5] (hereinafter referred to as the *Communist Party Case*) similarly observed: '[T]he Constitution of the Commonwealth has not been so imperfectly framed that, in what the Government and Parliament consider a time of crisis when the national existence is at stake, they can act promptly and effectively, by means of executive action and legislation, only by breaking the law'.[6] Section 51(vi) provides:

> The Parliament shall, subject to this Constitution, have power to make laws for the peace, order, and good government of the Commonwealth with respect to ... The naval and military defence of the Commonwealth and of the several States, and the control of the forces to execute and maintain the laws of the Commonwealth.

The jurisprudence on the reach and operation of the defence power was developed over two phases: pre-*Thomas* phase and post-*Thomas* phase.[7] In the pre-*Thomas* phase, the 'classical' exegesis of the power emerged from decisions of the High Court in the context of the two World Wars. The context was a factual scenario in which the enemies of Australia were state polities which were clearly identified, a state of war was openly declared and terminated and large armies were deployed on both side of the conflagration. In the post-*Thomas* phase, the defence power has been and is still being deployed in a so-called 'war on terror'. This so-called 'war on terror' involves a 'shadowy' enemy which has no state boundaries, and it has no analogy with the two World Wars in which Australia was a participant. The defence power in the post-*Thomas* phase is utilised to justify the enactment of Commonwealth legislation investing the executive authorities with broad powers, such as the power of preventative detention and the imposition of control orders.

---

[4] Ibid 592–93.
[5] (1951) 83 CLR 1.
[6] Ibid 164.
[7] The *Thomas* reference is to the High Court decision in *Thomas v. Mowbray* [2007] HCA 33; (2007) 233 CLR 307. See Kate Chetty, 'A History of the Defence Power: Its Uniqueness, Elasticity and Use in Limiting Rights' (2016) 16 Macq L J 17.

2.2 Pre-*Thomas* v. *Mowbray* Phase of the Defence Power

Unlike many of the other powers in s 51, the defence power is remarkable in that its scope is not static. Its variable nature can be likened to the mercury column of a thermometer. As the conditions of a war emergency become more intense, the scope of the defence power increases; as the war emergency cools down, the scope of the defence power similarly contracts. It has been described as a power which 'expands or contracts'[8] or 'waxes and wanes'.[9] These descriptions of the defence power are quite surprising in view of the fact that the power on a literal reading of its terms would tend to suggest a rather restricted scope. As Derham[10] has pointed out, ordinary assumptions about statutory interpretation would require some value to be given to the words 'naval and military' in s 51(vi). 'In their natural meaning', Derham said, 'those words would have a limiting effect upon the ambit of the power'.[11] This is not so, according to the High Court in *Farey* v. *Burvett*, wherein Griffith CJ said:

> [T]he words "naval" and "military" are not words of limitation, but rather of extension, showing that the subject matter includes all kinds of warlike operations.... In my opinion the word "defence" of itself includes all acts of such a kind as may be done in the United Kingdom, either under the authority of Parliament or under the Royal Prerogative, for the purpose of the defence of the realm, except so far as they are prohibited by other provisions of the Constitution ... It is obvious, however, that the question whether a particular legislative act is within it may fall to be determined upon very different considerations in time of war and time of peace ...[12]

The constitutional source of the Commonwealth Parliament's power to legislate for the defence of the nation is not confined to s 51(vi). The magnitude of the power should be seen in the operation of the power with other supporting sections of the Constitution: s 51(xxxii), empowering the Commonwealth Parliament to legislate with respect to the control of railways for the transportation for naval and military purposes; s 51(xxxix), the incidental power; s 52(ii), the exclusive power of the Commonwealth Parliament to make laws with respect to matters relating to any department of the public service the control of which is by the

---

[8] *Richardson* v. *Forestry Commission* (1988) 164 CLR 261, 326 (Dawson J).
[9] *Thomas* v. *Mowbray* [2007] HCA 33, [236] (Kirby J).
[10] David Derham, 'The Defence Power' in Rae Else-Mitchell (ed), *Essays on the Australian Constitution* (2nd edn, Law Book 1961) 157.
[11] Ibid 159.
[12] (1916) 21 CLR 433, 410.

Constitution transferred to the executive government of the Commonwealth; s 68 vesting the command in chief of the naval and military forces of the Commonwealth in the Governor-General as the Queen's representative; s 69, transferring the departments of naval and military defence from the States to the Commonwealth; s 70, transferring all powers and functions from the State executive governments to the executive government of the Commonwealth in relation to those matters within the exclusive power of the Commonwealth; s 114, which prohibits the States from raising or maintaining any naval or military force; s 119, imposing an obligation upon the Commonwealth to protect the States from invasion and domestic violence.

The defence power in its full expansion has enabled the Commonwealth to impose 'extensive and detailed controls on the community of a kind that, in time of peace, would ordinarily be thought to fall under some other heads of legislative power and to have nothing significant to do with the defence power of the Commonwealth'.[13] Higgins J in *Farey v. Burvett* remarked:

> But, from the nature of defence, the necessity for supreme national effort to preserve national existence, the power to legislate as to defence, although it shows itself on the same level as the other powers, has a deeper tap-root, far greater height of growth, wider branches, and overshadows all the other powers.[14]

Griffith CJ, in the same case, asserted that the power to make laws with respect to defence was 'a paramount power' and that if there was a conflict between the defence power and 'any reserved State rights', 'the latter must give way'.[15] On the other hand, Dixon J in the *Communist Party Case*[16] has cautioned that the federal nature of the Constitution 'is not lost during a perilous war'.[17] The key features of the defence power in the pre-*Thomas* phase were worked out in a number of significant cases.[18]

---

[13] Derham (n 10) 158.
[14] (1916) 21 CLR 433, 457–58.
[15] Ibid 441.
[16] (1951) 83 CLR 1.
[17] Ibid 203.
[18] It is outside the purview of this chapter to explore in minutiae the full ramifications of the defence power. There is ample literature on the subject: Derham (n 10) 157; William Wynes, *Legislative, Executive and Judicial Powers in Australia* (5th edn, Law Book Co 1976); Colin Howard, *Australian Federal Constitutional Law* (Law Book Co 1972) 422–41; Patrick Lane, *The Australian Federal System* (Law Book Co 1979) 121–52;

2.2.1 Farey v. Burvett

Farey sold bread in a proclaimed area at a price greater than the maximum price prescribed by an Order authorised by the Regulations. Farey was charged under the War Precautions (Prices Adjustment) Regulations 1916, made under the War Precautions Act 1914 as amended by Act No 3 of 1916. He appealed to the High Court against his conviction, claiming that, insofar as the Act authorised the making of Regulations dealing with the price of bread, the Act was not within the defence power.

It was argued that the word 'defence' in s 51(vi) must bear a single and uniform meaning at all times, in the sense that an act which was not authorised to be done in time of peace could not be authorised in time of war. It was undisputed that an attempt by the Commonwealth Parliament to fix the price of food in time of peace was an encroachment on the reserved powers of the States. Equally, it was argued that there was a trespass on the powers of the States in time of war.

The appeal was dismissed by a majority of the High Court (Griffith CJ, Barton, Isaacs, Higgins and Powers JJ; Gavan Duffy and Rich JJ dissenting). The majority judges rejected a restrictive approach in defining the scope of the defence power. In their dissent, Gavan Duffy J and Rich J were only prepared to extend the meaning of the words 'naval and military defence of the Commonwealth and the several States' to the raising, training and equipment of the naval and military forces, to the maintenance, control and use of such forces, to supply of arms, ammunitions and other things necessary for naval and military operations, to all matters strictly ancillary to these purposes, 'and to nothing more'. They added that if the power to fix the price of bread was really necessary it could be exercised by the States or delegated by the States to the Commonwealth. They said: 'It is a gross and pernicious error to suppose that in the conduct of the present war the interests of the States and the Commonwealth are diverse, they are identical, and the people of Australia will no doubt be as willing to protect and forward those interests through their State Legislatures as through the Commonwealth Parliament'.[19]

Christopher Gilbert, 'There Will be Wars and Rumours of Wars: A Comparison of the Treatment of Defence and Emergency Powers in the Federal Constitutions of Australia and Canada' (1980) 18 Osgoode Hall LJ 307.

[19] (1916) 21 CLR 433, 468.

Gavan Duffy J and Rich J adopted too myopic a viewpoint of the operation of the defence power, and this narrow view was rightly rejected by the majority judges, who favoured a broader approach. While one can accept that during the exigencies of war the interests of the States will not conflict with the interests of the Commonwealth, it is not to the point. The more important aim is to ensure a successful prosecution of the war strategy, and such an aim should not be undermined by a disagreement of the States over the desirability or sufficiency of measures to be adopted to achieve that aim.

Griffith CJ viewed the defence power as one in which the extent of its application is dependent on the prevailing circumstances. Given the variable scope of operation of the defence power, one test must always be applied, namely: 'Can the measure in question conduce to the efficiency of the forces of the Empire, or is the connection of cause and effect between the measure and the desired efficiency so remote that the one cannot reasonably be regarded as affecting the other?'[20] He noted that sumptuary laws had always been common war measures and that the legislative act that the case sought to impugn was in substance such a law. He proceeded to cite the regulation of the supply and pricing of food in a beleaguered city as an example of a proper and even necessary war measure. Barton likewise said: 'If the thing be capable, during war, of aiding our arms by land or sea, here or elsewhere, we are to say so, but we say no more'.[21]

Another fundamental aspect of the decision in *Farey* v. *Burvett* pertained to the role of the court regarding the desirability or necessity of making the law. Griffith CJ and Barton J invoked the following passage from the judgment of Marshall CJ in *McCulloch* v. *Maryland*:[22] 'Where the law is not prohibited, and is really calculated to effect any of the objects entrusted to the Government, to undertake here to inquire into the degree of its necessity, would be to pass the line which circumscribes the judicial department, and to tread on legislative ground'.[23] Isaacs J displayed an extremely deferential approach to the determination of the validity of federal legislation in a wartime situation. He said:

> If the measure questioned may conceivably in such circumstances even incidentally aid the effectuation of the power of defence, the Court must

---

[20] Ibid 441.
[21] Ibid 449.
[22] 4 Wheat. 316 (1819).
[23] Ibid 423.

hold its hand and leave the rest to the judgment and wisdom and discretion of the Parliament and the Executive it controls for they alone have the information, the knowledge and the experience and also, by the Constitution, the authority to judge of the situation and lead the nation to the desired end.[24]

By 'such circumstances', Isaacs J was referring to 'a mighty and unexampled struggle'.[25] This view of Isaacs J 'went considerably further than the other members of the majority' and 'have not been adopted by the Court in subsequent cases' and that the majority required the provision to have a connection to a legitimate defence purpose. However, once this connection was established, it was not for the Court to judge 'the efficiency or the reasonableness of the measure'.[26] The distinction between the sufficiency or necessity of a legislative measure and its constitutional validity can be a fine one. A danger in leaving the Parliament with an almost uncontrolled discretion, is that it could lead to an abdication by the court of its function of determining constitutional validity of a proposed legislative measure.

2.2.2 Stenhouse v. Coleman

In *Stenhouse* v. *Coleman*,[27] Dixon J illuminated some of the essential features of the defence power. First, he underlined the purposive nature of the defence power. He added:

> ...unlike most other powers conferred by s 51 of the Constitution, it involves the notion of purpose or object. In most of the paragraphs of s 51 the subject of the power is described either by reference to a class of legal, commercial, economic or social transaction or activity..., or by specifying some class of public service ..., or undertaking or operation ..., or by naming a recognized category of legislation. In such cases it is usual, when the validity of legislation is in question, to consider whether the legislation operates upon or affects the subject matter, or in the last case answers the description, and to disregard purpose or object. But 'a law with respect to the defence of the Commonwealth' is an expression which seems rather to treat defence or war as the purpose to which the legislation must be addressed.[28]

---

[24] (1916) 21 CLR 433, 455–56.
[25] Ibid.
[26] Derham (n 10) 160–61.
[27] (1944) 69 CLR 457.
[28] Ibid.

With regard to the purpose, Dixon J explained that it must be collected from 'the instrument in question, the facts to which it applies and the circumstances which called it forth'. He added:

> It is evident that among these circumstances the character of the war, its notorious incidents, and its far-reaching consequences must take first place. In some cases they must form controlling considerations, because from them will appear the cause and the justification for the challenged measure. They are considerations arising from matters about which, in case of doubt, courts can inform themselves by looking at materials that are the subject of judicial notice.[29]

This description of the nature of the defence power was later adopted with approval by Fullagar J and reiterated by Dixon, presiding as Chief Justice, in the *Communist Party Case*.[30] In that same case, Kitto J stressed that the word 'purpose' had nothing to do with 'the motives or the policy lying behind the legislation'. 'It refers', he added, 'to an end or object which legislation may serve; and the consequence which follows from the recognition of defence as a "purpose" in this sense of the word is that the relevance to defence which stamps a measure with the character of a law with respect to defence is to be found in a capacity to assist that purpose'.[31]

In *Stenhouse v. Coleman*, the second important aspect of the defence power touched upon by Dixon J focused on the task of relating an impugned law to the power. Whether a measure was incidental or conducive to the prosecution of a war that was being fought depended 'much less upon the abstract formulation of the general test or criterion to be applied than upon a correct ascertainment of the true nature and operation of the provisions impugned and of their bearing upon the prosecution of the war'.[32] Dixon J elaborated:

> If the actual and possible factors could be openly and exhaustively examined and laid bare before it, a court would probably find little difficulty in deciding whether a given measure was, or was not, incidental or conducive to the prosecution of the war. But in many cases this cannot be done. Apart from other reasons, information and considerations which may have guided the authors of a statutory instrument under attack may be of such a nature that they cannot be publicly canvassed without prejudicing the conduct of the war or imperilling the national interest.

---

[29] Ibid 471.
[30] (1951) 83 CLR 1, 253.
[31] Ibid 273.
[32] (1944) 69 CLR 457, 469.

> In any case, there are limitations upon the material which a court can receive or take into account for the purpose of considering the validity of a general law. If the form of the power makes the existence of some special or particular state of fact a condition of its exercise, then, no doubt, the existence of that state of fact may be proved or disproved by evidence like any other matter of fact. But ordinarily the court does not go beyond matters of which it may take judicial notice. This means that for its facts the court must depend upon matters of general public knowledge. It may be that in this respect the field open to the court is wider than has been commonly supposed...[33]

Dixon J observed that 'common experience' showed that much of the difficulty and uncertainty that attends the discussion of the validity of a purported exercise of a purposive legislative power arose from the 'inferential, not to say speculative, character of the grounds connecting the provision with the prosecution of the war'.[34] He noted that those who would support the validity of a measure would often place reliance upon the 'presumption in favour of validity', remarking that since the question was one of law and not of fact, a presumption would seldom provide a solution; 'at best it supplies a step in legal reasoning'. However, in relation to the prosecution of the war, the presumption would be reinforced by the respect accorded by the court to 'the opinion or judgment of the other organs of government with whom the responsibility for carrying on the war rests'.[35] Dixon J added:

> When, for example, it appears that a challenged regulation is a means adopted to secure some end relating to the prosecution of the war, the court does not substitute for that of the Executive its own opinion of the appropriateness or sufficiency of the means to promote the desired end. But great as must be the weight given to these considerations, it is finally the court which must form and act upon a judgment upon the question whether the legislation, be it direct or be it subordinate, is a true exercise of the legislative power with respect to defence.[36]

There surely would be occasions when the fine distinction drawn by Dixon J would be difficult to operate. When the court engages in the task of determining whether a measure is 'designed' to attain a desired end, it may at times be perceived to be examining whether the measure is 'sufficient' to attain the desired end. Such perception would lend weight

---

[33] Ibid.
[34] Ibid.
[35] Ibid 470.
[36] Ibid.

to the criticism that the court was intruding upon the executive sphere. In a wartime context, the task of the court taking 'judicial notice' based upon general public knowledge is not problematic. In a context not involving military matters, how is the court to go about the task of establishing the linkage between the defence power and the legislative measure adopted by the Parliament? If, for example, the impugned law seeks to dissolve an organisation on the basis that the executive government is of the view that such an organisation poses a threat to the security of the country, how is the court to adjudge the validity of such a law? Could the court be bound by the expression of a 'conclusive' opinion of the Commonwealth Parliament that a certain state of affairs existed necessitating the invocation of draconian measures? This perplexing question was encountered in the *Communist Party Case*.

2.2.3 Communist Party Case

The *Communist Party Case*, described by Professor George Winterton as 'one of the greatest triumphs' scored by Australian constitutionalism and a 'celebrated victory for the rule of law',[37] involved a challenge to the validity of the Communist Party Dissolution Act 1950, primarily on the ground that its chief provisions did not relate to matters falling within any legislative power expressly or impliedly given by the Constitution to the Commonwealth Parliament.

The Communist Party Dissolution Act 1950 received the Royal Assent on 20 October 1950 and was prefaced by a preamble consisting of nine paragraphs. The first three paragraphs merely set out the terms of ss 51(vi), 61 and 51(xxxix) of the Constitution. The other paragraphs were set out by Latham CJ as follows:-

> 4. And whereas the Australian Communist Party, in accordance with the basic theory of communism, as expounded by Marx and Lenin, engages in activities or operations designed to assist or accelerate the coming of a

---

[37] George Winterton, 'The Communist Party Case' in HP Lee & George Winterton (eds), *Australian Constitutional Landmarks* (CUP 2003) 108. Professor Winterton published an earlier version of this article as 'The Significance of the Communist Party Case' (1992) 18 MULR 630. The legislative history of the Act is set out in Frank Beasley, 'Australia's Communist Party Dissolution Act' (1951) 29 Can Bar Rev 490. See also Ross Anderson, '*Australian Communist Party v. The Commonwealth*' (1951) 1 UQLJ 34; Geoffrey Sawer, 'Defence Power of the Commonwealth in Time of Peace' (1953) 6 Res Jud 214; Wolfgang Friedmann, 'Some Reflections on the Anti-Communist Act' (1950) 1 UWA Law Rev 516; Edward McWhinney, 'Judicial Positivism in Australia' (1953) 2 Am J Comp L 36.

revolutionary situation, in which the Australian Communist Party, acting as a revolutionary minority, would be able to seize power and establish a dictatorship of the proletariat:

5. And whereas the Australian Communist Party also engages in activities or operations designed to bring about the overthrow or dislocation of the established system of government of Australia and the attainment of economic industrial or political ends by force, violence, intimidation or fraudulent practices:

6. And whereas the Australian Communist Party is an integral part of the world communist revolutionary movement, which, in the King's dominions and elsewhere, engages in espionage and sabotage and in activities or operations of a treasonable or subversive nature and also engages in activities or operations similar to those, or having an object similar to the object of those, referred to in the last two preceding paragraphs of this preamble:

7. And whereas certain industries are vital to the security and defence of Australia (including the coal-mining industry, the iron and steel industry, the engineering industry, the building industry, the transport industry and the power industry):

8. And whereas activities or operations of, or encouraged by, the Australian Communist Party, and activities or operations of, or encouraged by, members or officers of that party and other persons who are communists, are designed to cause, by means of strikes or stoppages of work, and have, by those means, caused, dislocation, disruption or retardation of production or work in those vital industries:

9. And whereas it is necessary, for the security and defence of Australia and for the execution and maintenance of the Constitution and of the laws of the Commonwealth, that the Australian Communist Party, and bodies of persons affiliated with that Party, should be dissolved and their property forfeited to the Commonwealth, and that members and officers of that Party or of any of those bodies and other persons who are communists should be disqualified from employment by the Commonwealth and from holding office in an industrial organization a substantial number of whose members are engaged in a vital industry.

Latham CJ described paragraphs 4–8 as consisting of allegations of fact and paragraph 9 as expressing the opinion of the Commonwealth Parliament that it was necessary for reasons of defence and the maintenance of the Constitution to enact the provisions of the Act.

Section 4 declared that the Australian Communist Party was an unlawful association and was by force of the Act itself dissolved. Any other association could be declared to be unlawful if it fell within one of the descriptions contained in s 5(1). These descriptions spelt out some degree of association with the Communist Party or with communism. The Governor-General was authorised under s 5(2) to declare an association unlawful if he was satisfied that the association fitted one of the statutory descriptions and that the continued existence of that body of persons would be prejudicial to the security and defence of the Commonwealth or to the execution or maintenance of the Constitution or of the laws of the Commonwealth. Section 5 also contained provisions enabling an association to challenge before a court the declaration that it had associated with the Communist Party or with communism in the manner set out in s 5(1). However, it would not be able to challenge the declaration of the Governor-General that the continued existence of the association would be prejudicial to defence or to the maintenance and execution of the Constitution, etc.

Section 6 provided that the effect of the declaration was to dissolve the body.

Section 9 contained provisions in relation to individual persons. It empowered the Governor-General to make a declaration if he was satisfied that a person was a member or officer of the Australian Communist Party, or was a communist and was engaged in or likely to engage in activities prejudicial to the security and defence of the Commonwealth or to the execution or maintenance of the Constitution or of the laws of the Commonwealth. Section 9 contained provisions corresponding to those contained in s 5 with respect to an application to a court to set aside a declaration. As in the case of s 5, s 9 did not provide for any application to a court in respect of the declaration that the person was engaged in or likely to engage in the prejudicial activities specified in the section. A declared person would be subject to some civil disqualifications.

Section 10 provided that a declared person would be incapable of holding office under or of being employed by the Commonwealth or an authority of the Commonwealth or of holding office as a member of an incorporated authority of the Commonwealth. He or she would also be rendered incapable of holding office in an industrial organisation (whether registered under Commonwealth or State law or not) to which s 10 applied.

The Australian Communist Party, various federal trade unions and certain of their office-bearers commenced actions before Dixon J with the object of obtaining a declaration that the provisions of the Communist Party Dissolution Act 1950 were *ultra vires* and void and injunctions restraining the Commonwealth from acting to their prejudice. They attacked the validity of the Act primarily on the ground the chief provisions of the Act did not relate to matters falling within any legislative power expressly or impliedly given by the Constitution to the Commonwealth Parliament. Instead, the provisions trenched upon matters contained within the residue of legislative power belonging to the States. The Commonwealth sought to justify the validity of the Act on the defence power in s 51(vi), and the power of making laws in respect of the maintenance of the Constitution or the execution of the laws, whether that power be derived from a combination of s 51(xxxix) and s 61, or 'whether it be a power which comes or arises from the very existence of the Commonwealth itself as a body politic'.

Dixon J stated a case for the Full Court and referred two questions to it:

1. (a) Does the decision of the question of the validity or invalidity of the provisions of the *Communist Party Dissolution Act* 1950 depend upon a judicial determination or ascertainment of the facts of any of them stated in the fourth, fifth, seventh, eighth and ninth recitals of the preamble of that Act and denied by the plaintiffs, and (b) are the plaintiffs entitled to adduce evidence in support of their denial of the facts so stated in order to establish that the Act is outside the legislative power of the Commonwealth?
2. If no to either part of question 1 are the provisions of the *Communist Party Dissolution Act* 1950 invalid in whole or in some part affecting the plaintiffs?

Latham CJ, Dixon, McTiernan, Williams, Fullagar and Kitto JJ said that the recitals would not assist the Court in determining the validity of the Act. Neither was it permissible for evidence to be adduced to challenge the truth of the assertions as embodied in the recitals. Instead, the Court would rely on facts of which it could take 'judicial notice'. In relation to the second question, the Court, with the exception of Latham CJ who dissented, held the Act to be invalid.

The Court was concerned with 'constitutional facts' and not 'ordinary facts'.[38] The latter, which requires proof by evidence tendered, refers to 'particular facts peculiar to the immediate parties, facts to which the law (antecedently fixed by legislative facts) is applied'. On the other hand, constitutional facts are 'described as "background facts", furnishing "information which the Court should have in order to judge properly of the validity of this or that statute or of this or that application by the executive government of State or Commonwealth of some power or authority it

---

[38] See Lane (n 18) 1083–105.

asserts".[39] Given the 'waxing and waning' characteristic of the defence power, the application of the power was dependent upon facts. Thus, 'as those facts change so may its actual operation as a power enabling the legislature to make a particular law'.[40] The relevant facts are those facts which pertain to the exigency or danger which calls for the exercise of the defence power. Kitto J in the *Communist Party Case* elaborated:

> ...the "exigency" and "the danger" by reference to which the reach of the power is to be determined are objective facts, which the tribunal which has the constitutional duty of comparing challenged legislation with the power must be able to perceive.[41]

For these facts, 'the Court must depend upon matters of general knowledge'. In *Holland v. Jones*,[42] Isaacs J said:

> Whenever a fact is so generally known that every ordinary person may be reasonably presumed to be aware of it, the Court "notices" it, either simpliciter if it is at once satisfied of the fact without more, or after such information or investigation as it considers reliable and necessary in order to eliminate any reasonable doubt.[43]

In the *Communist Party Case*, Fullagar J provided a most lucid analysis of the scope of the defence power. Fullagar J distinguished two aspects of the defence power. The 'primary' aspect concerns the making of laws which have as their 'direct and immediate object' the naval and military defence of the Commonwealth and the several States. He instanced this by pointing to such matters as the enlistment and training and equipment of personnel in the navy, army and air force, the provision of ships and munitions, the manufacture of weapons and the erection of fortifications. The Commonwealth can undertake all these things in both peace and war because they were *ex facie* connected with 'naval and military defence'. The primary aspect of the defence power also included a power to make laws for the prevention or prohibition and punishment of activities obstructive of the preparation by such means of the nation for war.

In its 'secondary' aspect, the power extended to an infinite variety of matters which could not have been regarded in the normal conditions of

---

[39] Ibid 1084.
[40] *Andrews v. Howell* (1941) 65 CLR 255, 278.
[41] (1951) 83 CLR 1, 274.
[42] (1917) 23 CLR 149.
[43] Ibid 153.

national life as having any connection with defence. Fullagar J pointed to 'familiar' examples such as the prices of goods, the rationing of goods, rents and eviction of tenants, the transfer of interests in land and the conditions of employment in industry generally. Once the basic fact of war was established, two stages were involved in determining the validity of an impugned law. At the first stage, the existence of war or national emergency was recognised as bringing into play the secondary or extended aspect of the defence power. 'This is done simply as a matter of judicial notice, and it provides the justification for a presumption of validity which might not otherwise exist in the case of an enactment which on its face bore no relation to any constitutional power'. At its second stage, the enactment in question was examined with regard to its character as a step to assist with the emergency. The question arising at the second stage might turn on particular facts as distinct from the overriding general fact of war or national emergency. Fullagar J said that such facts might relate to the operation of the law in question or to a state of affairs which called for its enactment and that whether any and what evidence of such facts was admissible must depend on the circumstances of each particular case.

The majority judges took strong objection to the extraordinary nature of the Act. They emphasised that there was an essential difference between, on the one hand, a law providing for the dissolution of associations as to which specified facts existed and, on the other hand, a law providing specially for the dissolution of a particular association. The first law might be supportable under the defence power, but the other law could not be upheld because the operation of the law was independent of any facts peculiar to the association, and a consideration of its legal effects did not disclose any relevance to the subject of the power.

As far as the recitals were concerned, they were regarded as containing Parliament's reasons for passing the Act. The recitals were in no way decisive of the question whether the Act was valid or invalid. For the Commonwealth Parliament, being a parliament of limited competence which exercises powers which are conferred by the Constitution, the 'critical question' which has to be considered is: 'who decides whether or not the power exercised has been conferred?'[44] The answer was obvious, as succinctly pointed out by Professor Winterton: 'the judiciary,

---

[44] Winterton (n 37) 108, 127.

ultimately the High Court'.[45] That answer was bolstered by various judicial statements in the cases. McTiernan J said: 'The Constitution does not allow the judicature to concede the principle that the Parliament can conclusively "recite itself" into power'.[46] Likewise, Fullagar J said: 'Parliament cannot recite itself into a field the gates of which are locked against it by superior law'.[47] Fullagar J articulated the doctrine encapsulated in a maxim that 'a stream cannot rise higher than its source'.[48] He elaborated on the meaning of this doctrine:

> The validity of a law or of an administrative act done under a law cannot be made to depend on the opinion of the law-maker, or the person who is to do the act, that the law or the consequence of the act is within the constitutional power upon which the law in question itself depends for its validity. A power to make laws with respect to lighthouses does not authorize the making of a law with respect to anything which is, in the opinion of the law-maker, a lighthouse. A power to make a proclamation carrying legal consequences with respect to a lighthouse is one thing: a power to make a similar proclamation with respect to anything which in the opinion of the Governor-General is a lighthouse is another thing.[49]

Dixon J also provided other neat examples to illustrate the doctrine that 'a stream cannot rise higher than its source' when he said:

> It would ...be impossible for the parliament by reciting that a society for research in radio physics planned or carried on experiments causing or likely to cause an interference with wireless transmission to bring within s 51(v) (postal, telegraphic, etc. services) an enactment naming the society and dissolving it brevi manu. It would be impossible to bring under s 51 (xviii) (patents) a direct grant of a monopoly for a specified manufacturing process by reciting that it was an invention.[50]

Dixon J remarked that the elaborate recitals supported the observation that the difficulty in relating the Act to the defence power had not escaped the notice of the legislature itself. In his examination of the recitals, he could not find any direct allusion to any apprehension of external danger. In testing the validity of the Act at the date of the royal

---

[45] Ibid.
[46] (1951) 83 CLR 1, 205–06.
[47] Ibid 263.
[48] Ibid 258.
[49] Ibid.; See James Stellios, 'The Stream Cannot Rise Above Its Source": The Doctrine in the Communist Party Case', in *Zines's The High Court and the Constitution* (6th edn, Federation Press 2015) 332–67.
[50] (1951) 83 CLR 1, 200.

assent (20 October 1950), he could not find the prevailing situation sufficient to support its validity. The other majority judges also felt that to accede to the recitals would amount to an abdication by the Court of its duty under the Constitution. The majority judges were not denying the validity of the impugned Act under all circumstances. There were sufficient indications that the Act could be validated 'in the case of an actual or threatened outburst of violence or the like',[51] or in time of 'a clear and great national danger'.[52]

In the case, Dixon J described the Australian Constitution as an instrument framed in accordance with many traditional conceptions and said: 'Among these I think that it may fairly be said that the rule of law forms an assumption.'[53] Dixon J also 'explicitly warned of the danger of subversion of liberty by the Government itself'[54] and proceeded to caution:

> History and not only ancient history shows that in countries where democratic institutions have been unconstitutionally superseded, it has been done not seldom by those holding the executive power. Forms of government may need protection from dangers likely to arise from within institutions to be protected. In point of constitutional theory the power to legislate for the protection of an existing form of government ought not to be based on a conception, if otherwise adequate, adequate only to assist those holding power to resist or suppress obstruction or opposition or attempts to displace them or the form of government they defend.[55]

2.2.4 Marcus Clark & Co Ltd v. Commonwealth

The fear that the High Court's decision in the *Communist Party Case* would inhibit the Commonwealth from putting the country on a

---

[51] Ibid 194 (Dixon J).
[52] Ibid 268 (Fullagar J). Even then, Williams J was not prepared to concede parliamentary competence to legislate for the absolute forfeiture of the property of proscribed individuals or associations. If it was necessary for the Commonwealth to acquire property it could do so subject to s 51(xxxi) of the Constitution: ibid 229–30.
[53] (1951) 83 CLR 1, 193.
[54] Winterton (n 37) 132. Professor Winterton observed: 'If the *Communist Party* case were litigated today, the Act would probably be invalid on the grounds not only that the Commonwealth lacked power to enact it, but also that it breached two implied prohibitions: the implied freedom of political communication (probably including an incidental freedom of association for political purposes), and the separation of judicial power.' (ibid).
[55] (1951) 83 CLR 1, 188.

'preparation for war' footing was dispelled a year later by its decision in *Marcus Clark & Co Ltd* v. *Commonwealth*.[56]

The plaintiff company (Marcus Clark & Co Ltd) commenced action upon the refusal by the Treasurer to consent to the plaintiff company's proposals to borrow money and to issue new shares. The plaintiff company sought declarations that the Defence Preparations Act 1951 and the Defence Preparations (Capital Issues) Regulations were void and, alternatively, that the Treasurer's refusal of consent to certain applications of the plaintiff company were contrary to the regulations.

The Defence Preparations Act 1951 contained a preamble which consisted of eight recitals. The recitals stated, *inter alia*, the existence of a state of international emergency, the necessity of providing for the raising, equipping and provisioning of armed forces, that the defence preparations of Australia included the adoption of measures to secure the maintenance and sustenance of the people of Australia, etc., and the expansion of the capacity to produce and manufacture goods, and to provide services for the purpose of enabling the Australian economy to meet the probable demands upon it in the event of war. The sixth recital stated that defence preparations required the diversion of certain resources (including money, materials and facilities), for use in defence preparations.

The key provision of the Act was s 4, which empowered the Governor-General to make regulations, *inter alia*, for, or in relation to, '(a) the expansion of the capacity of Australia to produce or manufacture goods, or to provide services, for the purposes of defence preparations or for the purpose of enabling the economy of Australia to meet the probable demands upon it in the event of war; (b) the diversion and control of resources . . . for the purposes of defence preparations; (c) the adjustment of the economy of Australia to meet the threat of war or the avoidance or reduction of economic dislocation or instability caused by, or impeding, defence preparations; and (d) measures to secure the maintenance and sustenance of the people of Australia in the event of war or to contribute towards the maintenance and sustenance of the people of countries associated with Australia in defence preparations'.

---

[56] (1952) 87 CLR 177. See Sawer (n 37) 221–23; George Masterman, 'Defence Power: Tension Short of War' (1953–55) 1 Syd L Rev 266; Ross Anderson, 'Constitutional and Administrative Law' (1952) 2 UQLJ 159; Leslie Zines, 'Executive Discretion and the Adequacy of Judicial Remedies to Uphold the Constitution' (1971) 4 Fed L Rev 236, 246–51.

2.2 PRE-*THOMAS V. MOWBRAY* PHASE

On 1 August 1951, the Governor-General, purporting to act under s 4, made the Defence Preparations (Capital Issues) Regulations. The regulations prohibited, *inter alia*, certain borrowings by companies and certain share issues by companies unless the consent in writing of the Treasurer of the Commonwealth were first obtained. Regulation 16 provided that, where application was made for the consent of the Treasurer, the Treasurer might, subject to reg 17, grant the consent (either unconditionally or on terms), or refuse to grant the consent. Regulation 17 provided that the Treasurer should not refuse consent or impose a condition 'except for purposes of or in relation to defence preparations'. An aggrieved person could apply to the court for an order directing the Treasurer to state in writing the facts and matters by reason of which the refusal of consent or imposition of the condition was for purposes of, or in relation to, defence preparations. The court was empowered to make such an order.

Marcus Clark &Co Ltd commenced action upon the refusal by the Treasurer to consent to its proposals to borrow money and to issue new shares. The High Court (Dixon CJ, McTiernan, Webb and Fullagar JJ; Williams and Kitto JJ dissenting) upheld the validity of s 4 of the Defence Preparations Act 1951 and the Defence Preparations (Capital Issues) Regulations by holding them to be laws with respect to defence within s 51(vi) of the Constitution.

In establishing the connection between the impugned Act and the purpose of defence, Fullagar J found that the existence of a state of international tension as expressed in the preamble was supported by facts which were judicially noticed.[57] Webb J said that at the time of the enactment of the impugned Act it was a notorious and judicially noticed fact that there had been for some time considerable international tension and a distinct possibility of another world war.[58] McTiernan J, in agreement with Dixon J on the validity of the Act, applied the judicial notice doctrine and found that the impugned law would 'conduce to making the country ready for war, if it should come'.[59]

Williams and Kitto JJ, who dissented, had a different view of the international situation. They said: 'It could not be said in August 1951 that there was "an immediate apprehension of war". The danger

---

[57] (1952) 87 CLR 177, 255.
[58] Ibid 245.
[59] Ibid 227.

of war was no greater than the danger which existed in October 1950 when the *Communist Party Dissolution Act* 1950 came into force'.[60]

Professor Geoffrey Sawer observed that the Act and regulations had been drafted with 'the utmost care and art' in order to overcome the judicial obstacle encountered in the *Communist Party Case*.[61] He said that the art of the impugned regulations consisted in 'concentrating attention on what had appeared to be the main vice of the Communist Party legislation – namely the extent to which it elevated the opinion of Parliament and the Executive at the expense of judicial control'.[62] Indeed, Fullagar J remarked:' The Act and the regulations which are in question in the present case do not possess the exceptional character which belonged to ss 4, 5 and 9 of the Communist Party Dissolution Act'.[63] The majority judges distinguished the *Communist Party Case* on the basis that in *Marcus Clark* objective tests were provided in the regulations by which the 'connection, or want of connection, with the defence power'[64] could be seen or ascertained. However, according to Professor Sawer, the majority judges 'fell into a trap'. He found the stance of Williams and Kitto JJ very persuasive. However, he said:

> The procedures provided by the regulations for informing the Court as to the grounds on which the Treasurer had acted fell far short of vesting the Court with the power to decide the sufficiency of the connection between a particular refusal of additional capital and the expansion of the armed forces. The most that this procedure could do was to satisfy the Court that the Treasurer was bona fide of the opinion that the connection existed, and had acted on relevant considerations.[65]

2.3 The Variable Scope of the Defence Power

The generally accepted feature of the defence power is that it has a variable scope of application, encapsulated in descriptions as a power that 'ebbs and flows', or a power that 'waxes and wanes'. 'It is a fixed concept with a changing content because its scope depends on Australia's defence needs at any given time, and as these needs fluctuate, so does the scope of the power'.[66]

---

[60] Ibid 239–40.
[61] Sawer (n 37) 214.
[62] Ibid 222.
[63] (1952) 87 CLR 177, 253. Cited in Stellios (n 49) 340.
[64] (1952) 87 CLR 177, 215–16.
[65] Sawer (n 37) 214, 223.
[66] George Williams, 'Defence Power' in Anthony Blackshield, Michael Coper and George Williams (eds), *The Oxford Companion to the High Court of Australia* (OUP 2001) 200.

Professor Howard's observation reflected the Commonwealth's experience as an active participant in both World Wars. The range of laws which were passed and upheld by the Court or enforced without challenge encompassed the economic, commercial and industrial facets of life in Australia. Many of these laws would clearly, under peacetime conditions, have been outside the legislative competence of the Commonwealth Parliament.

2.3.1 The Wartime Phase of the Defence Power

During the actual course of war, the defence power empowers extensive control of the community by the Commonwealth in relation not only to war service and war supplies, but also to industry in general, food, clothing, housing, and financial, economic and social conditions.

In the First World War, s 4 of the War Precautions Act 1914–1915 empowered the Governor-General to make regulations for securing the public safety and defence of the Commonwealth. In *Lloyd v. Wallach*,[67] the High Court upheld the validity of a regulation (reg 55) made under s 4. The impugned regulation provided for a power of detention in military control of naturalised persons when there was reason to believe they were disaffected or disloyal. In *Pankhurst v. Kiernan*,[68] the High Court upheld the validity of s 4 of the Unlawful Associations Act 1916. The impugned section rendered it an offence for any person who 'advocates or encourages, or incites or instigates to the taking or endangering of human life, or the destruction or injury of property'. The High Court said that Parliament was competent to 'pass such legislation as may prevent any hampering or dislocation of the work of effectively prosecuting the war, that is, the defence of the country'.[69] Other legislative measures in the First World War which were upheld by the High Court included the deportation of aliens,[70] the control of enemy properties,[71] and the recruitment for service overseas.[72]

In the context of the Second World War, Professor Sawer noted 17 major cases in which the High Court was called upon to interpret

---

[67] (1915) 20 CLR 299.
[68] (1917) 24 CLR 120.
[69] Ibid 129 (Barton J).
[70] *Ferrando v. Pearce* (1918) 25 CLR 241.
[71] *Burkard v. Oakley* (1918) 25 CLR 422.
[72] *Sickerdick v. Ashton* (1918) 25 CLR 506.

the scope of the defence power.[73] In these cases, the High Court upheld a spectrum of laws providing for: the setting up of a marketing board for the purpose of disposing apples and pears grown in the Commonwealth to counter the disruption of shipping by the war;[74] the Commonwealth to direct any person to work for any employer, under pain of penalty if that person refused;[75] the Commonwealth to take over State income tax departments;[76] the imposition of price control;[77] the registration of alien doctors;[78] the controlling of the sale of alcohol;[79] the controlling of essential materials;[80] restricting Christmas advertising;[81] regulating industrial conditions.[82] Professor Sawer concluded that the High Court 'can claim with justice that...its decisions have shown a statesmanlike approach to the problems of total war'.[83]

2.3.2 The Post-War Phase of the Defence Power

It would be difficult to expect that upon the cessation of war there would be an instant reversal to the conditions which had prevailed before the outbreak of war. Parliament must be able to confer ample powers on the Commonwealth government to deal with the upheavals thrown up by wartime conditions in various spheres: industrial, social and economic. At the same time, various legislative measures introduced during a war would have to be carefully wound back.

The scope of the defence power in the transition from wartime to peacetime conditions was elucidated by the decision in *R v. Foster*.[84] Could the defence power sustain the validity of certain regulations even

---

[73] Geoffrey Sawer, 'The Defence Power of the Commonwealth in Time of War' (1946) 20 Australian Law Journal 295.
[74] *Andrews v. Howell* (1941) 65 CLR 255 – the impugned regulations were made pursuant to the National Security Act 1939–1940 (Cth).
[75] *Reid v. Sindberry* (1944) 68 CLR 504 – the National Security (Man Power) Regulations were made pursuant to the National Security Act 1939–1943 (Cth).
[76] *South Australia v. Commonwealth (First Uniform Tax Case)* (1942) 65 CLR 373.
[77] *Victorian Chamber of Manufactures v. Commonwealth* (1943) 67 CLR 335.
[78] *Gonzwa v. Commonwealth* (1944) 68 CLR 469.
[79] *De Mestre v. Chisholm* (1944) 69 CLR 51.
[80] *Stenhouse v. Coleman* (1944) 69 CLR 457.
[81] *Ferguson v. Commonwealth* (1943) 66 CLR 432.
[82] *Australian Woollen Mills v. Commonwealth* (1944) 69 CLR 476.
[83] Sawer (n 73) 296.
[84] (1949) 79 CLR 43.

2.3 THE VARIABLE SCOPE OF THE DEFENCE POWER

though the fighting in the Second World War had ceased for over three years?[85] After acknowledging that the scope of the defence power must necessarily diminish given the cessation of hostilities, the High Court noted that to permit the defence power to justify the validity of any legislation at any time to deal with any matter the character of which had been changed by the war would be contrary to the federal basis of the Constitution.[86] Latham CJ, Rich, Dixon, McTiernan, Williams and Webb JJ said:

> In winding up the arrangements made for war and restoring a community organized for war to a state in which it can resume peaceful courses the legislature may continue for a space this or that war-time control. For it may be incidental to defence to continue the control and regulation of a particular subject matter for a time after the cessation of hostilities and also to maintain such control while legislative provision is being made for the necessary re-adjustment. The sudden removal of all controls is not demanded by the collapse of enemy resistance. Given regulations or controls may no longer find a justification in the considerations which the active prosecution of the war supplied. Yet the very fact that the controls or regulations have been established may create a situation which must be maintained for a reasonable time while some other legislative provision is made'.[87]

The Court proceeded to expound some general principles: (i) that the Court should not take a narrow view of the problems which the Commonwealth has to deal with when it is entrusted with the supreme responsibility of the defence of the country; (ii) that the mere continued existence of a formal state of war is not enough in itself, after the enemy has surrendered, to bring within the defence power the same wide field of civil regulation and control as fell within it when the country was engaged in a conflict with powerful enemies; (iii) that the legislature should be able to continue regulating a particular subject matter for a time after the cessation of hostilities and also while legislation is being made for the necessary re-adjustment. In relation to (iii), if the Court is unable to see with reasonable clearness how it is incidental to the defence

---

[85] The impugned regulations were: Women's Employment Regulations 1946; National Security (Liquid Fuel) Regulations (S.R. 1940 No. 293 – 1944 No. 113), reg. 51; National Security (War Service Moratorium) Regulations (S.R. 1942 No. 437 – 1948 No. 109). The High Court held that the validity of these regulations could not be sustained by the incidental power.
[86] (1949) 79 CLR 43, 83.
[87] Ibid 84.

power to prolong a particular war measure dealing with a subject matter otherwise falling within the exclusive province of the States, it would be the duty of the Court to pronounce the legislation invalid.[88]

2.3.3 The Peacetime Phase of the Defence Power

In a period of profound peace, the defence power is at its narrowest width. In the *Communist Party Case*, Williams J said: 'The defence power in peace time authorizes any legislation which is reasonably necessary to prepare for war'.[89] He added: 'Any conduct which is reasonably capable of delaying or of otherwise being prejudicial to the Commonwealth preparing for war would be conduct which could be prevented or prohibited or regulated under the defence power'.[90]

It would authorise the enactment of legislation pertaining to the 'primary aspect' of the power: the enlistment and training and equipment of men and women in the navy, army and air force, the provision of ships and munitions, the manufacture of weapons and the erection of fortifications. In *Attorney-General (Vic) v. Commonwealth*,[91] a majority of the High Court held that the operation of a Commonwealth-owned clothing factory in relation to its sales of clothing to bodies outside the regular naval and military forces was authorised by the Defence Act, and was within the defence power. The sales to outside entities were to counteract the contracting requirement of the naval and military forces during peace-time and this was deemed by the Governor-General to be necessary in order to maintain intact the trained complement of the factory, so as to be prepared to meet the demands upon the factory in the event of war. On the other hand, in *Commonwealth v. Australian Commonwealth Shipping Board*,[92] an agreement by the Australian Commonwealth Shipping Board to supply, erect and maintain six turbo-alternators for the Municipal Council of Sydney was not authorised by the defence power as this was for the purpose of trade and wholly unconnected with any purpose of naval and military defence. In *Illawarra District County Council v. Wickham*,[93] the extension of

---

[88] Ibid.
[89] (1951) 83 CLR 1, 225 (cited in Callinan J in *Thomas v. Mowbray* [2007] HCA 33, [585]).
[90] Ibid.
[91] (1935) 52 CLR 533.
[92] (1926) 39 CLR 1. See JC Morris, 'Some Aspects of the Commonwealth Parliament's Defence Power under the Constitution' (1939–1941) 2 Res Jud 221; Sawer (n 37) 214.
[93] (1959) 101 CLR 467.

legislation into the thirteenth year after the cessation of hostilities giving preference in employment to discharged members of the armed services could not be sustained by the defence power.[94]

2.3.4 The Preparation for War Phase of the Defence Power

A situation falling short of war may so expand the scope of the defence power as to enable the Commonwealth to legislate on matters which *ex facie* have no relation to naval and military defence. 'It is no doubt true', Dixon J said 'that a mounting danger of hostilities before any actual outbreak of war will suffice to extend the actual operation of the defence power as circumstances may appear to demand'.[95] Judicial dicta support enabling the Commonwealth Parliament to legislate on a wide range of subject-matters to put the nation on a war footing, if the Court accepts the need for the preparation.

2.4 The Defence Power Post-*Thomas* v. *Mowbray*

The contemporary High Court jurisprudence on the defence power has been shaped by the decision in *Thomas* v. *Mowbray*.[96] A significant constitutional aspect of the case was put in context by Professor Lindell: '[T]he assumption made about the defence power before the decision in *Thomas* v. *Mowbray* was that that power was confined to dealing with Australia's external threats or enemies...'[97] That case poses the question whether the defence power can only be invoked in the context of *external* threats. It requires a new exposition of the scope of the defence power in the modern era of the 'war on terror'.[98] In the pre-*Thomas* phase, the orthodox jurisprudence views the power as fluctuating through four main stages, from its widest scope during wartime to its narrowest during a period of 'profound' peace, with the spectrum

---

[94] See Lane (n 18) 135–36. The validity of the preference law was assumed in *Wenn v. Attorney-General (Victoria)* (1948) 77 CLR 84, a case decided shortly after the war had ended.
[95] (1951) 83 CLR 1, 195.
[96] [2007] HCA 33; (2007) 233 CLR 307. See Oscar I Roos, 'Alarmed, but not Alert in the "War on Terror"?: The High Court, *Thomas* v. *Mowbray* and the Defence Power' (2008) 15 James Cook U L Rev 169.
[97] Geoffrey Lindell, 'The Scope of the Defence Power and Other Powers in the Light of *Thomas* v. *Mowbray*' (2008) 10(3) Constitutional Law and Policy Review 42, 43.
[98] Ibid 42; Roos (n 96).

punctuated by a post-war period and a period for the preparation for war. Professor Colin Howard said:

> It is a matter of convenience only that four main phases of the defence power are identified. They do not correspond precisely to any state of affairs. The question in any given case remains whether, having regard to the facts of which the court will take judicial notice or allow to be proved before it, the legislation is reasonably referable to defence or properly incidental thereto. In a state of limited or de facto war it is to be anticipated that the court will find a smaller class of legislation justified by the defence power than during times of greater national emergency.[99]

Hayne J in *Thomas* v. *Mowbray* remarked:

> The line between war and peace may once have been clear and defined by the declared state of relations between nations. But ... that line is now frequently blurred. The increasing capacity of small groups to carry out threats of widespread harm to persons and property may further obscure the distinction between war and peace if those terms are to be defined primarily by reference to dealings between nation states.[100]

In *Thomas* v. *Mowbray*, an interim control order was issued against Thomas (the plaintiff) by a Federal Magistrate under div 104 (s 104.4) of the Criminal Code (Cth). The object of div 104 is 'to allow obligations, prohibitions and restrictions to be imposed on a person by a control order for the purpose of protecting the public from a terrorist act'. Under the Code, to be a 'terrorist act', the 'action must be done, or the threat made, with the intention of advancing a political, religious or ideological cause, and the action must be done, or the threat made, with the intention of coercing or influencing by intimidation "the government of the Commonwealth or a State, Territory or foreign country' (or part of a State, Territory or foreign country) or with the intention of 'intimidating the public or a section of the public'": s 100.1. The Act sets out provisions relating to the application for an interim control order, the making of such an order, the procedure to be followed in confirming an interim control order and the obligations, prohibitions and restrictions that may be imposed on a person by virtue of a control order.

Under the interim control order made by the Federal Magistrate, Thomas was required, among other things, 'to remain at his residence...between midnight and 5 am each day' and 'to report to the police

---

[99] Howard (n 18) 429.
[100] [2007] HCA 33, [439].

three times each week'; prohibited 'from acquiring or manufacturing explosives, from communicating with certain named individuals, and from using certain communications technology' (para 2).

The Federal Magistrate based the making of the order on a number of grounds specified in the order, such as that there was admission by Thomas that he had 'trained with Al Qa'ida in 2001' and that he had undertaken 'weapons training, including the use of explosives and learned how to assemble and shoot various automatic weapons' (para. 1).

Division 104, under which the control order was made, was challenged on a number of grounds. First, it was asserted that div 104 conferred non-judicial power on a federal judicial court contrary to Ch III of the Australian Constitution. Secondly, even if the power conferred on a federal court was judicial in nature, nevertheless it was authorising the court to exercise the power in a manner contrary to Ch III. Thirdly, it was asserted that the impugned div 104 lacked a head of power to justify its validity.[101]

In relation to the third assertion, the defence power in s 51(vi) and the external affairs power in s 51(xxix) were among the heads of power invoked by the impugned legislation itself to support the validity of the law. Reliance was also placed on s 51(xxxvi) under which the States had referred to the Commonwealth Parliament matters to sustain a national framework of anti-terrorism legislation.

Gleeson CJ agreed with Gummow and Crennan JJ that the legislation was supported by the defence power and the external affairs power. Callinan and Heydon JJ upheld the validity of Division 104 of the Code under the defence power and felt it unnecessary to consider other heads of power advanced in argument before the High Court. Hayne J, dissenting, agreed that the impugned legislation fell within the defence power but found that 'the jurisdiction it purports to give to federal courts is not

---

[101] Another line of attack in *Thomas v. Mowbray* was that the legislation conferred non-judicial power and was therefore repugnant to Ch III of the Constitution. Gleeson CJ, Gummow and Crennan, Callinan and Heydon JJ rejected the argument. Gleeson CJ said the power was a judicial power. He rejected the argument that the power was exercised in a manner inconsistent with 'the essential character of a court' or inconsistent with the nature of judicial power (ibid [30]). Kirby J and Hayne J dissented. Kirby J held that s 104.4 did not afford 'an ascertainable test or standard' and that the test of reasonable necessity or appropriate or adapted amounted to criteria that attempted to confer powers that are 'unchecked and unguided' (ibid [321]–[322]). They were also of 'nebulous generality' (ibid [322]). Hayne J, who held that the impugned legislation was supported by the defence power, held that it was invalid because the power conferred was non-judicial (ibid [517]).

jurisdiction in a matter'[102] and was therefore in contravention of Ch III of the Constitution.[103] The other dissenting judge, Kirby J, held that Division 104 was not supported by the defence power because of its 'overreach' and was in breach of Ch III.[104]

The plaintiff's main submissions were succinctly summarised by Hayne J:

> The plaintiff submitted, first, that actual or threatened aggression from a foreign nation is a circumstance that is essential to the proper application of the defence power. Secondly, the plaintiff submitted that the power is with respect to the defence of the Commonwealth and the several bodies politic, not the defence of citizens or inhabitants of the Commonwealth or the States in their "individual capacities as such, or their property".[105]

Clearly, the majority judges took judicial notice of the prevailing threat of international terrorism. Gleeson CJ quoted Professor Greenwood who had said that the events of 11 September showed that 'a terrorist organization operating outside the control of any state is capable of causing death and destruction on a scale comparable with that of regular military action by a state'.[106] Professor Greenwood had also said: '[I]t would be a strange formalism which regarded the right to take military action

---

[102] [2007] HCA 33, [406].
[103] Hayne J, in addition to the defence power, relied on the reference power to support the validity of the impugned provisions and said that it was not necessary consider whether the external affairs power or an 'implied power to protect the nation' supported the impugned provisions: ibid [407]. Hayne J said that the exercise of judicial power must pertain to 'matters' as prescribed by ss 75 and 76 of the Constitution. If the exercise of the power given to a federal court is not governed by a 'defined or definable, ascertained or ascertainable' standard, it would not be a power to decide a 'matter': what it amounts to is 'a legal proceeding' and not 'arbitrament upon a question as to whether a right or obligation in law exists': ibid [474].
[104] Kirby J held that div 104 'lacks an established source in federal constitutional power' and was also in breach of Ch III of the Constitution: [2007] HCA 33, [157]. He accepted that the threat need not be 'external' but it must be directed at 'the bodies politic' (ibid [251]) as contrasted with being directed at 'the protection of people and property within the bodies politic' (ibid [252]). He said that he was 'not convinced' that the actual provisions were 'appropriate and adapted (that is, proportionate) to such a threat' (ibid [259]).
[105] [2007] HCA 33, [424]. The plaintiff further submitted 'that, if the defence power were not understood in this way, and in particular, if a threat from what was described as a "private group or organization" were sufficient to engage the power, it is a power which should still be understood as extending only to defence of the polities that make up the Australian federation, not the protection of the public, property, or "infrastructure systems" from aggression or violence.'
[106] Christopher Greenwood, 'International Law and the "War against Terrorism"' (2002) 78 International Affairs 301, 307–08, as cited in *Thomas v. Mowbray* [2007] HCA 33, [7].

2.4 THE DEFENCE POWER POST-*THOMAS V. MOWBRAY* 45

against those who caused or threatened such consequences as dependent upon whether their acts would somehow be imputed to a state'.[107]

Gummow and Crennan JJ rejected outright the submissions of the plaintiff.[108] They referred to comments regarding the defence power in a 2006 High Court decision[109] as indicating lack of support for a limited view of the defence power.[110] They also pointed to the 'long history in English law before the adoption of the Constitution which concerned defence of the realm against threats posed internally as well as by invasion from abroad by force of arms'.[111] They highlighted that an aspect of the law of treason involved the levying of war in the realm which 'required an insurrection accompanied by force, for an object of a public or general nature'.[112] They held that the notion of a 'body politic' could not 'sensibly be treated apart from those who are bound together by that body politic'.[113] They concluded that 'protection from a "terrorist act" as defined' would necessarily engage the defence power.[114]

Gleeson CJ expressed agreement with the joint judgment of Gummow and Crennan JJ. His conclusion encapsulated the approach of the majority judges: that the defence power 'is not limited to defence against aggression from a foreign nation; it is not limited to external threats; it is not confined to waging war in a conventional sense of combat between forces of nations; and it is not limited to protection of bodies politic as distinct from the public, or sections of the public'.[115]

---

[107] Greenwood (n 106).
[108] Gummow and Crennan JJ ([2007] HCA 33, [145]) found it was not necessary to consider the scope of the 'nationhood' power (per Mason CJ, Deane and Gaudron JJ in *Davis v. Commonwealth* [1988] HCA 63; (1988) 166 CLR 79) nor a power to legislate to protect the Parliament and the Commonwealth from domestic attacks arising from an interplay of ss 61 and 51(xxxix) (per Fullagar J in the *Communist Party Case* (1951) 83 CLR 1, 259).
[109] *NSW v. Commonwealth* [2006] HCA 52; (2006) 229 CLR 1, 127 [212].
[110] The High Court said at ibid: 'One arm of the defence power conferred by s 51(vi) is the control of the forces to "execute and maintain the laws of the Commonwealth"; on the application of the Executive Government of a State, the Commonwealth should protect the State "against domestic violence" (s 119). In their work, Quick and Garran discussed the concept of 'domestic violence' in s 119 with detailed reference to the decision of the Supreme Court of the United States in *In re Debs* [1895] USSC 177; 158 US 564, 582 (1895), which supported the intervention of the federal government in the Pullman Strike to break the strike by force'.
[111] [2007] HCA 33, [145].
[112] Ibid.
[113] Ibid [142].
[114] Ibid [146].
[115] Ibid [7].

Hayne J rejected the contentions of the plaintiff, saying that the propositions 'cast in the absolute terms advanced by the plaintiff'[116] were supported by neither the words of s 51(vi) nor the history of its application. He observed that the enemies of the Commonwealth are not 'necessarily confined to nation states' and that power which was once 'the exclusive province of large military forces of nation states may now be exerted in pursuit of political aims by groups that do not constitute a nation state'.[117]

Hayne J pointed out that most of the decisions rendered by the High Court on the defence power related to either the First or Second World War[118] and both wars were between nation states. Each of these conflicts had 'an identifiable commencement and an identifiable cessation of hostilities'.[119] He said those cases, however, do not necessarily determine the boundaries of the defence power, with terrorism posing 'new and different issues about legislative power'.[120] He added: 'The increasing capacity of small groups to carry out threats of widespread harm to persons and property may further obscure the distinction between war and peace if those terms are to be defined primarily by reference to dealings between nation states'.[121] He also rejected the dichotomy drawn by the plaintiff between 'bodies politic' and 'individual capacities as such, or their property' as 'unhelpful'.[122]

Hayne J held that the central concern of the defence power was focused on the 'defence against the imposition of political objectives on [the Australian bodies politic] by external force'.[123] The impugned laws accordingly came within the defence power because 'they provide measures directed to preventing the application of force to persons or property in Australia that is sought to be applied for the purpose of changing the federal polity's foreign policies'.[124] Hayne J made an interesting observation:

> There is, however, a related distinction that should be made. It may be drawn between the application of force by individuals whose motives for

---

[116] Ibid [435].
[117] Ibid [438].
[118] Ibid [411].
[119] Ibid [411].
[120] Ibid [417].
[121] Ibid [439].
[122] Ibid [441].
[123] Ibid [442].
[124] Ibid [444].

2.4 THE DEFENCE POWER POST-*THOMAS V. MOWBRAY*

doing so are not to further any international political aim and the application of force in furtherance of international political objectives. The latter kind of case, in which there are international political objectives, may engage the defence power; the former would seem unlikely to do so. Of course, it must be recognised that the distinction just described may be more difficult to draw in some cases than others, especially if the aim pursued is evidently not capable of fulfilment. And religious and ideological motives may present their own particular difficulties in that respect, especially if the aims being pursued were to be seen as utopian rather than practical.[125]

An interesting aspect of the case was an exchange between Callinan J and Kirby J in relation to the *Communist Party Case*. Callinan J said:

> I have commented on aspects of the judgment of Dixon J in the *Communist Party Case* which time, to say the least, as well as the facts proved here, make questionable: the drawing by his Honour of a distinction, as if there were a clear line between them for constitutional and all practical purposes, between times of peace and serious armed conflict, and internal and external threats. Perhaps it was the country's recent emergence from a prolonged and costly declared war during which liberties had been curtailed and rights suspended, that influenced his Honour's responses to the CPA. Latham CJ, although in dissent, was in a sense more perceptive and alive to the gravity of direct and indirect internal threats inspired externally, and the different manifestations of war and warfare in an unsettled and dangerous world. To regard war as a declared war only, to assume that a nation's foes would all identify themselves, and rarely act covertly, that they would act logically, and that they would not be people drawn from the Australian community was even then however to be somewhat naïve.[126]

Kirby J lamented: 'I did not expect that, during my service, I would see the *Communist Party Case* sidelined, minimised, doubted and even criticised and denigrated in this Court'.[127] He added: 'Given the reasoning expressed by the majority in these proceedings, it appears likely that, had the Dissolution Act of 1950 been challenged today, its constitutional validity would have been upheld'.[128] Kirby J responded to Callinan J's views with the following retort:

---

[125] Ibid [442].
[126] Ibid [589].
[127] Ibid [386].
[128] Ibid.

With all respect, I do not accept that Latham CJ's dissent in the *Communist Party Case* gains latter day authority because his political and diplomatic experience exceeded that of his colleagues. Dixon J too had very considerable diplomatic experience both during and after the War, working in wartime in close collaboration with Allied war leaders. He was to prove more aware of the lessons of history involving the misuse of executive powers. He also proved more capable of approaching the issue, as this Court should, as a legal and constitutional one – as guardian of the abiding values that lie at the heart of the Constitution.[129]

2.5 The Proportionality Principle and the Defence Power

The defence power being a purposive power is subject to the proportionality principle in determining the validity of impugned legislation purportedly enacted under that power. McTiernan J in *Marcus Clark* said:

> The defence power authorises the Parliament to take such measures as are appropriate to the end for which the constitution created the defence power. The end is the protection of Australia against invasion and the dangers of war.[130]

In the *Communist Party Case*, Williams J said that the impugned legislation would have to define the 'nature of the conduct and the means' adopted to combat it 'so that the Court would be in a position to judge whether it was reasonably necessary to legislate with respect to such conduct in the interests of defence and whether such means were reasonably appropriate for the purpose'.[131] Kitto J, also in the *Communist Party Case*, after explaining that the word 'purpose' had nothing to do with the motives or the policy lying behind the legislation, said: 'It refers to an end or object which legislation may serve; and the consequence which follows from the recognition of defence as a "purpose" in this sense of the word is that the relevance to defence which stamps a measure with the character of a law with respect to defence is to be found in a capacity to assist that purpose'.[132]

Dr Oscar Roos claimed that in *Thomas v. Mowbray* the High Court failed properly to apply a principle of proportionality in its assessment of the constitutionality of the impugned legislation. He said that the 'most striking example of this failure' appeared in the joint judgment of

---

[129] Ibid [244].
[130] (1952) 87 CLR 177, 226.
[131] (1951) 83 CLR 1, 225.
[132] Ibid 273.

Gummow and Crennan JJ, adding that these two judges had 'sweepingly' concluded, in relation to the critical definition of 'terrorist act' contained in the impugned law, that what was proscribed by that definition fell within 'a central conception of the defence power', and that protection from a 'terrorist act" as defined must necessarily engage the defence power. According to Dr Roos, 'these are extraordinary assertions, given the breadth of the activities encompassed in the definition of "terrorist act" in the Code'.[133]

2.6 The Limits of the Defence Power

In *Farey* v. *Burvett*, Isaacs J, while stating that the limits of the defence power at a time of war imperilling the nation's existence are 'bound only by the requirements of self-preservation',[134] did hint that even s 92 (which guarantees absolute freedom of interstate trade, commerce and intercourse) could not act as a restraint on the power. Griffith CJ in the same case described the defence power as 'a paramount power' and that if it conflicted with any reserved state rights the latter must give way.[135] Subsequent cases have indicated a retreat from this expansive approach in defining the scope of the defence power. Latham CJ, in *R* v. *Commonwealth Court of Conciliation and Arbitration; Ex parte State of Victoria*,[136] said that the most complete recognition of the power and responsibility of Parliament and of the Government in relation to defence would not lead to the conclusion that the 'defence power is without any limits whatever'.[137] He added:

> The Constitution cannot be made to disappear because a particular power conferred by the Constitution upon the Commonwealth Parliament is exercised by that Parliament. Indeed, the grant of the power to legislate with respect to defence is made expressly 'subject to this Constitution'...[138]

---

[133] Roos (n 96). See also Anne Twomey, 'Review of High Court Constitutional Cases 2007' (2008) 31(1) UNSWLJ 215, 223, wherein she said that Gummow and Crennan JJ, while accepting the purposive nature of the defence power, 'did not appear to apply a proportionality test to decide whether a law that provided for the abridgement of freedom by the imposition of control orders was proportionate to the defence interest to be serve'. She added: 'Only Kirby J expressly applied a proportionality test.'
[134] (1916) 21 CLR 433, 453.
[135] Ibid 441.
[136] (1942) 66 CLR 488.
[137] Ibid.
[138] Ibid.

Thus, even at the height of hostilities when the power was at its maximum reach, the High Court invalidated certain impugned legislation: *R* v. *Commonwealth Court of Conciliation and Arbitration; Ex parte State of Victoria*[139] (portions of reg. 29 of the National Security (Supplementary) Regulations); *R* v. *University of Sydney*[140] (reg. 16 of the National Security (Universities Commission) Regulations); *Adelaide Company of Jehovah's Witnesses Inc* v. *Commonwealth*[141] (certain of the National Security (Subversive Associations) Regulations); *Victorian Chamber of Manufactures* v. *Commonwealth*[142] (National Security (Industrial Lighting) Regulations); *R* v. *Commonwealth Court of Conciliation and Arbitration; Ex parte Victoria (sub nom Victoria* v. *Foster)*[143] (Women's Employment Regulations in relation to State employees employed on purely governmental activities).

On a textual interpretation of the Constitution, it is not difficult to see why the defence power cannot be given an unlimited scope. In the first place, it is one of 39 paragraphs or heads of legislative power in s 51. Higgins J in *Farey* v. *Burvett* remarked: 'There is no hierarchy in the powers, with the power as to defence on the top'.[144] Unlike s 51, some sections such as s 92 and s 116 (which prohibits the Commonwealth from legislating in respect of religion) are not stated to be subject to the Constitution. This does not mean that in the case of the defence power, the Commonwealth is totally precluded from infringing other provisions of the Constitution under all circumstances. Starke J in *Andrews* v. *Howell* acknowledged: 'Actual war operations and military necessity may require further consideration...'[145]

In *Andrews* v. *Howell*, the High Court held that the National Security (Apple and Pear Acquisition) Regulations did not contravene s 92. Thus, the Court did not have to decide whether the Regulations would have been covered by the defence power even though there was a contravention. However, it has been suggested that 'however much the defence power may be subject to s 92, it should not be beyond the skill of a draftsman to frame most genuine defence measures in such a way that they would avoid the operation of s 92 and would be slightly affected in

---

[139] (1942) 66 CLR 488.
[140] (1943) 67 CLR 95.
[141] (1943) 67 CLR 116.
[142] (1943) 67 CLR 413.
[143] (1944) 68 CLR 485.
[144] (1916) 21 CLR 433, 457.
[145] (1941) 65 CLR 255, 268.

2.6 THE LIMITS OF THE DEFENCE POWER

the achievement of their purposes by that section'.[146] However, it was held in *Gratwick v. Johnson*[147] that the defence power is subject to the limitations imposed by s 92 as 'the defence measure directly prohibited inter-State travel as such and therefore went to the very heart of s 92'.[148] It has also been determined that the defence power does not embrace the compulsory acquisition of property on terms which are not just and thus contrary to s 51(xxxi) of the Constitution.[149]

The relationship between s 116 and the defence power featured in *Adelaide Company of Jehovah's Witnesses Inc v. Commonwealth*.[150] The case arose from an action of trespass initiated by the plaintiff company against the Commonwealth as a result of the entry of Commonwealth officers into certain premises belonging to the plaintiff company. The Commonwealth invoked the National Security Act 1939–1940, the National Security (Subversive Associations) Regulations, and an Order in Council and directions of the Attorney-General made thereunder, for justification. The case was concerned with the validity of certain provisions of the Regulations. The Regulations provided that any body, corporate or unincorporated, the existence of which the Governor-General declares to be in his opinion prejudicial to the defence of the Commonwealth or the efficient prosecution of the war 'is hereby declared to be unlawful'. Any body in respect of which a declaration is made is, by force of the declaration, dissolved. Furthermore, any person, including a bank, having in his possession or custody any property which immediately prior to the dissolution belonged to, or was used by or on behalf of that body, shall on demand deliver that property to a person authorised by the Minister. Any person, not below the rank of sergeant, may by notice in writing served on any person, declare that any persons specified in the notice are, with respect to any account so specified in the notice, trustees for any such body, and that declaration is conclusive evidence that those persons are trustees of the body with respect to any moneys standing on the credit of the account. Any property taken possession of or delivered to a person authorised by the Minister is forfeited to the King for the use of the Commonwealth. Any house, premises, or place or part thereof

---

[146] Derham (n 10) 187.
[147] (1945) 70 CLR 1.
[148] Derham (n 10) 187.
[149] *Johnston, Fear & Kingham v. The Commonwealth* (1943) 67 CLR 314; *Minister for the Army v. Dalziel* (1944) 68 CLR 261.
[150] (1943) 67 CLR 116.

occupied by a body prior to its declaration may, if the Minister so orders, be occupied so long as there is in the house, premises or place or part thereof any property which the Minister is satisfied belonged to or was used by or on behalf of, or in the interest of, the body.

The whole Court held that there was no infringement of s 116 by the Regulations or by their application to a religious group, the Jehovah Witnesses. The Court concluded that s 116 does not prevent the Commonwealth Parliament from making laws prohibiting the advocacy of doctrines or principles which, though advocated in pursuance of religious convictions, are prejudicial to the prosecution of a war in which the Commonwealth is engaged. Rich J said that freedom of religion is not absolute and that it is 'subject to powers and restrictions of government essential to the preservation of the community'.[151] Williams J said that the meaning and scope of s 116 must be determined 'as one of a number of sections intended to provide in their inter-relation a practical instrument of government'.[152] Latham CJ observed that the maintenance of religious liberty assumed the continued existence of the community. These sentiments appeared to suggest that the prohibition is not that absolute in the face of a law which is designed to uphold the paramount interests of the community. Although the court held that the impugned regulations had not infringed s 116, it invalidated the impugned Regulations on the basis that the Commonwealth failed to establish a 'real connection' with defence.

2.7 Conclusion

In *The Federalist*, Alexander Hamilton observed:

> [I]t is impossible to foresee or define the extent and variety of national emergencies, or the correspondent extent and variety of the means which may be necessary to satisfy them. The circumstances that endanger the safety of nations are infinite, and for this reason no constitutional shackles can wisely be imposed on the power to which the care of it is committed.[153]

---

[151] Ibid 149.
[152] Ibid 159.
[153] Hamilton, Madison and Jay, in Benjamin F Wright (ed), *The Federalist* (HUP 1961) 200 (original emphasis); cited in *Thomas v. Mowbray* [2007] HCA 33, [136] (Gummow and Crennan J).

2.7 CONCLUSION

In its life span, Australia has faced wartime emergencies, and the defence power has mainly provided the constitutional anchorage for the extensive panoply of legislation to enable it to prosecute the wars effectively. As a result of that experience, the propositions regarding the scope of the defence power are well settled.

First, unlike most of the other powers enumerated in s 51, the defence power is purposive in nature. For a law to obtain validity under the defence power, some real connection between the law and the power must be established. The purpose of the law must be conducive to the efficient prosecution of war or the defence of the Commonwealth. The power expands and contracts or 'ebbs and flows' according to the prevailing circumstances calling forth the power. Those circumstances can be determined by the operation of the judicial notice doctrine. The courts will not, as a general rule, inquire into the desirability of a proposed measure, but it will not tolerate a measure which 'ousts' the courts from their role as arbiters of the constitutionality of the measure. Some limits in the form of the express constitutional prohibitions exist to qualify the power.

The traditional jurisprudence developed against the backdrop of the two World Wars viewed the defence power as one operating in relation to enemies of the Commonwealth who were state polities, and that there was a clear dividing line between wartime and peacetime. The activities of global terrorist organisations and governmental legislation to counter them led to an expansive construction of the defence power to justify the validity of such legislation. *Thomas* v. *Mowbray* enables the defence power to operate expansively even though Australia is not engaged in a formally declared war.

Overall, the defence power as interpreted by the High Court provides the Commonwealth with an ample source of legislative authority to secure the security of the nation and the safety of its populace.

3

The Executive, the Prerogative and Emergencies

> *'Once the constitution is removed as the frame of reference for the lawful exercise of authority, the only substitute is the balance of political – and, ultimately, military – power in the nation.'*
>
> George Winterton, 'Extra-Constitutional Notions in Australian Constitutional Law' (1986) 16 *Federal Law Review* 223, 238–29.

3.1 Introduction

One hallmark of the traditional conception of the executive government is that it has a special responsibility, indeed a duty, to respond to circumstances of emergency. The capacity to wage war and make peace is a paradigm in this respect.[1] However, the very same features of the executive which imbue it with the capacity to discharge this duty – its control of the administrative, policing and military capacities of the state – give rise to the risk that it may use those capacities to establish tyranny. As Dixon J said in the *Communist Party Case*,

> History and not only ancient history, shows that in countries where democratic institutions have been unconstitutionally superseded, it has been done not seldom by those holding the executive power.[2]

This chapter will discuss the executive powers of the Australian government that are of particular relevance in emergency contexts. In so doing, it will keep in mind this observation by Dixon J, and also his remark in the same case that the Australian Constitution is an instrument 'framed in accordance with many traditional conceptions ... Among these

---

[1] That these are incidents of executive power in Australia, as in many other constitutional orders, is undoubted: see, e.g. James Stellios, *Zines's The High Court and the Constitution* (6th edn, Federation Press 2015) 371, 375.
[2] *Australian Communist Party* v. *Commonwealth* (1951) 83 CLR 1, 187.

I think it may fairly be said that the rule of law forms an assumption.'[3] A principal contention of this chapter is that that assumption, which necessarily informs our understanding of the Australian constitutional order, leads to the conclusion that the emergency powers of the executive are limited because they are subject to law.

3.2 The Nature and Source of Executive Power

The Australian legal and governmental system has its origins in British legal and political tradition, reflecting the origins of the contemporary Australian state as a colony of the United Kingdom established in 1788. However, there are significant differences between Australia and the United Kingdom as far as the nature and source of executive power are concerned, and the recognition of these differences has increased over time.

3.2.1 The United Kingdom

In the British constitutional context, the inherent powers of the executive (or *the Crown*) fall into two broad categories: those powers and entitlements that the Crown enjoys in common with its 'subjects' (i.e., with ordinary juridical persons); and those special powers and entitlements that are unique to the Crown in virtue of its status as sovereign.[4] The latter can be described as the *royal prerogative*, or the prerogative powers of the Crown – Blackstone described these 'rights and capacities' as a 'special pre-eminence' consequent on the monarch's 'regal dignity' which 'the king enjoys alone, in contradistinction to others'.[5] (What these rights and capacities actually encompass will be discussed in due course.)

There is a usage of 'prerogative' which differs from Blackstone's, and includes both categories of power and entitlement mentioned: Dicey, for instance, described the prerogative as 'the residue of discretionary or arbitrary authority, which at any given time is legally left in the hands of

---

[3] Ibid 193.
[4] For judicial discussion of the concept of 'the Crown', and the various ways in which it can refer to the government, the body politic, and elements thereof, see *Sue v. Hill* (1999) 199 CLR 462, 496–502 [79]–[93] (Gleeson CJ, Gummow and Hayne JJ), 525–26 [165]–[166] (Gaudron J).
[5] Edward Blackstone, *Commentaries on the Law of England* (1765, ed Robert Malcolm Kerr, London, John Murray 1857), Book 1, 234.

the Crown'.[6] There is a certain appeal to this alternative formulation: it crisply reflects the subordination, in British and hence Australian constitutional tradition, of the executive to the law-making body. Parliament, by making laws, can deprive the executive of its power, or control the manner of its exercise. In the United Kingdom, this is the legal expression of the political developments that culminated in the great conflicts of the seventeenth century. In its recent exposition of this British constitutional history and its legal significance, the Supreme Court of the United Kingdom described the sovereignty of parliament as 'a fundamental principle of the UK constitution', and as having been 'conclusively established' by 'a series of statutes enacted in the twenty years between 1688 and 1707', including the Bill of Rights 1688/89 and the Act of Settlement 1701.[7]

3.2.2 Australia

In Australia, the relationship between political history and legal consequence is mediated via a written constitution. Thus, the subordination of the Commonwealth (i.e., national) government to the Australian parliament is secured by a range of constitutional provisions: for instance, section 62 provides that the Governor-General, as the Queen's representative, is to be advised by a Federal Executive Council, while section 64 provides that the Queen's Ministers of State for the Commonwealth, who are to be members of that Executive Council, must sit in the national parliament;[8] and section 51(xxxix) gives the parliament the power to legislate with respect to matters 'incidental to the execution of any power vested by this Constitution ... in the Government of the Commonwealth'.[9] As this chapter will argue, this subordination of the executive

---

[6] Albert Venn Dicey, *Introduction to the Study of the Law of the Constitution* (8th edn, London, Macmillan and Co., Ltd. 1915). This understanding of the prerogative has on occasion been adopted by justices of the High Court of Australia: for instance, Mason J has referred to 'the prerogative powers of the Crown, that is, the powers accorded to the Crown by the common law': *Barton v. Commonwealth* (1974) 131 CLR 477, 498.

[7] *R (on the application of Miller and another) v. Secretary of State for Exiting the European Union* [2017] UKSC 5, [41], [43].

[8] For a discussion of whether the responsible government to which these provisions give rise should be seen as a matter of constitutional convention or as a legal requirement, see Stellios (n 1) 369–70. Stellios tentatively concludes that the basic principles of responsible government should be considered constitutionally-mandated rules of law.

[9] For a full discussion of this point, see Ibid 401–16. See also *Plaintiff M68/2015 v. Minister for Immigration and Border Protection* (2016) 257 CLR 42, 93 [121]–[122] (Gageler J).

3.2 THE NATURE AND SOURCE OF EXECUTIVE POWER

to the law-making authority is important for understanding the nature and scope of any emergency powers enjoyed by the executive in Australia.

Just as the existence of a written constitution affects our understanding of how the principle of executive subordination to the parliament is given effect in Australian law, so it affects our understanding of the source of executive power. As will become clear below, and despite the appeal of Dicey's formulation, one consequence of this is that when discussing executive power in the Australian constitutional context, and especially the context of emergency powers, there is reason to favour Blackstone's more narrow usage of the term 'prerogative'.

Section 61 of the Australian Constitution provides that:

> The executive power of the Commonwealth is vested in the Queen and is exercisable by the Governor-General as the Queen's representative, and extends to the execution and maintenance of this Constitution, and of the laws of the Commonwealth.

It is now generally accepted that section 61 is the ultimate source of all national executive power in Australia.[10] In one of the most important recent cases on the nature and scope of this power, French CJ explained that:

> [T]he executive power referred to in s 61 extends to:
> - powers necessary or incidental to the execution and maintenance of a law of the Commonwealth;
> - powers conferred by statute;
> - powers defined by reference to such of the prerogatives of the Crown as are properly attributable to the Commonwealth;
> - powers defined by the capacities of the Commonwealth common to legal persons;
> - inherent authority derived from the character and status of the Commonwealth as the national government.[11]

---

[10] See for instance, *Barton v. Commonwealth* (1974) 131 CLR 477, 498 (Mason J); *Davis v. Commonwealth* (1988) 166 CLR 79, 93 (Mason CJ, Deane and Gaudron JJ); *Cadia Holdings Pty Ltd v. New South Wales* (2010) 242 CLR 195, 226 [86] (Gummow, Hayne, Heydon and Crennan JJ). For discussion of this point, see Stellios (n 1) 370–73.

[11] *Williams v. Commonwealth* (2012) 248 CLR 156, 184–85 [22]; see also at 342 [484] (Crennan J).

The relationship between section 61 as the source of power, and the categories by reference to which its content is elucidated, was explained by his Honour in an earlier judgment:

> Section 61 is the primary source of executive power. ... Other provisions of the Constitution vesting powers in the Governor-General [such as the power to appoint federal judges conferred by section 72] may be seen as distinct sources of executive power on their specific topics and as giving content to the power conferred by s 61. ... The use of the "prerogative" to describe such a power may properly acknowledge its historical antecedents but not adequately illuminate its origins in s 61 of the Constitution.[12]

Thus, the two categories of executive power in the British constitutional system – the prerogative (in Blackstone's narrower sense) and the ordinary juristic capacities of a legal person – have, in the Australian constitutional context, a single source: section 61. We also see one reason for using the term 'prerogative' in Blackstone's sense: it assists us in discerning and describing the various historical strands that have been woven together in section 61's conferral of power.[13]

French CJ's reference to *such of the prerogatives of the Crown as are properly attributable to the Commonwealth* gives recognition to the fact that Australia is a federal nation, and hence has executive governments operating at the State (sub-federal) level as well as at the national level. The constitutional analysis of executive power at the State level is somewhat different from its analysis in relation to the Commonwealth. This is in part a reflection of the fact that, at the time of federation – when the Constitution came into force – the self-governing colonies which were transformed thereby into the States of Australia were already in existence, with Governors and Executive Councils carrying out executive functions in accordance with established colonial practice.[14] This practice included

---

[12] *Ruddock v. Vadarlis* (2001) 110 FCR 491, 538 [176], [179].

[13] Earlier reflections on the Australian Constitution had suggested that some elements of prerogative power may have been conferred upon the Governor-General not pursuant to s 61, but either as a result of broader changes in the relationship between the United Kingdom and its former dominions, or pursuant to distinct grants of power made by the Queen under section 2 of the Constitution, which provides that the Governor-General 'shall have and may exercise ... such powers and functions of the Queen as Her Majesty may be pleased to assign him': see, e.g., *Commonwealth v. Tasmania* (1983) 158 CLR 1, 298–99 (Dawson J). For discussion of this view, now superseded, see Stellios (n 1) 371–72.

[14] See the discussion in *Plaintiff M68/2015 v. Minister for Immigration and Border Protection* (2016) 257 CLR 42, 91 [116]–[117] (Gageler J), which draws extensively upon Paul Finn, *Law and Government in Colonial Australia* (OUP 1987).

3.2 THE NATURE AND SOURCE OF EXECUTIVE POWER 59

an understanding that many of the prerogative powers that were enjoyed by the Crown in its government of Britain likewise were enjoyed by the governments that had arisen in the colonies.[15] The constitutions of the colonies were continued in force upon federation by section 106 of the Constitution; however, the constitutions of the Australian States are themselves ordinary legislation enacted by those States' parliaments, and lack any status as entrenched or 'superior' law.[16] Hence they do not serve as the foundation of the exercise of government in the States, but rather presuppose such a foundation.[17] The prerogative powers of the State executives, and the other capacities that they enjoy as juridical persons, are therefore matters primarily of common law (just as is the case in the United Kingdom). However, the prerogative power of State governments is not entirely a matter of common law (as modified by the enactment of legislation by State parliaments); it is also modified by the Constitution and other superior law. Of particular relevance to the topic of emergency

---

[15] For judicial discussion of the reception of the prerogative into the law of the Australian colonies, see *Cadia Holdings Pty Ltd v. New South Wales* (2010) 242 CLR 195, 206–09 [21]–[29] (French CJ).

[16] Pursuant to section 6 of the Australia Acts 1986 (Cth and Imp), those parliaments do enjoy a limited capacity to impose constraints on the amendment of certain parts of their constitutions (such as referendum or special majority requirements), but that limited capacity is not relevant to an understanding of the States' executive power.

[17] The State constitutions take varying approaches to the matter of executive power. Part 4 of the Constitution Act 1902 (NSW), which is entitled 'The Executive', provides that 'There shall continue to be an Executive Council to advise the Governor in the government of the State' (section 35B), but the Act does not establish or define the office of Governor. Part 3 of the Constitution Act 1934 (SA), entitled 'The Executive', confers certain powers upon the Governor, and establishes the rules for payment of a salary to him or her, but does not address the office per se. Part II of the Constitution Act 1934 (Tas) is entitled 'The Crown', but does not deal with the office of Governor at all. Part I of the Constitution Act 1975 (Vic) is entitled 'The Crown', but section 6(1) within that Part simply provides that 'There shall be a Governor of the State of Victoria', without defining the powers of that office. Part IIIA of the Constitution Act 1889 (WA) is entitled 'The Governor' and provides (section 50(1)) that 'The Queen's representative in Western Australia is the Governor', but the office is not further defined. Most expansive in this respect is Queensland: Part 3 of the Constitution Act 1867 (Qld), entitled 'The Governor', provides that 'The Queen's representative in Queensland is the Governor' (section 11A), while Part 2 of Chapter 3 of the Constitution of Queensland 2001 (Qld), entitled 'Governor', provides that 'There must be a Governor of Queensland' who 'is authorised and required to do all things that belong to the Governor's office under any law' (sections 29(1), 33). Several sections of the Constitution confer functions upon State Governors (e.g., sections 7, 12, 15, 21). Section 110 provides that such provisions 'extend and apply to the Governor for the time being of the State, or other chief executive officer or administrator of the government of the State.'

60   THE EXECUTIVE, THE PREROGATIVE AND EMERGENCIES

powers are section 114 of the Constitution, which provides that 'A State shall not, without the consent of the Parliament of the Commonwealth, raise or maintain any naval or military force', and section 2(2) of the Australia Acts 1986 (Cth & Imp),[18] which confers power upon State parliaments to legislate with extraterritorial effect but also provides that 'nothing in this subsection confers on a State any capacity that the State did not have ... to engage in relations with countries outside Australia'. As Australian States have never enjoyed any such capacity – at the time of federation it was the United Kingdom which managed Australia's foreign relations, and it is the national government which has since acquired that capacity as Australia has become an independent nation[19] – the combined effect of those two provisions means that the prerogative power enjoyed by Australian State governments does not extend to the declaring of war or the making of treaties.

The prerogatives of the Crown can be divided into three general classes:[20] *powers* in the strict sense, such as that to declare wars and to make treaties; *privileges and immunities*, such as the Crown's priorities in relation to the payment of debts and immunity from being sued; and *property rights*, such as the Crown's right to gold and silver mines. In the Australian context, prerogative entitlements in the nature of property are taken to have remained with the States which (as colonies) enjoyed them prior to federation, unless the property in question has been transferred to the Commonwealth;[21] but these entitlements have little relevance to the law of emergency powers. The Crown's privileges and immunities are, as a rule, enjoyed by governments at both levels;[22] in the context of

---

[18] The Australia Act 1986 was enacted by both the Commonwealth Parliament at the request of all State parliaments, and by the parliament of the United Kingdom (i.e., exercising its capacity as the Imperial Parliament within the Australian constitutional framework), to bring an end to remaining constitutional connections between Australia and the United Kingdom.

[19] For further discussion, see Stellios (n 1) 376, 417–18.

[20] See HV Evatt, *The Royal Prerogative* (Law Book Co 1987) 30–31. This analysis was reiterated by Evatt J in his judicial capacity: *Federal Commissioner of Taxation* v. *Official Liquidator of EO Farley Ltd* (1940) 63 CLR 278, 320–21.

[21] *Federal Commissioner of Taxation* v. *Official Liquidator of EO Farley Ltd* (1940) 63 CLR 278, 322 (Evatt J); *Cadia Holdings Pty Ltd* v. *New South Wales* (2010) 242 CLR 195, 210–11 [32–34] (French CJ), 226–27 [88] (Gummow, Hayne, Heydon and Crennan JJ).

[22] In *Federal Commissioner of Taxation* v. *Official Liquidator of EO Farley Ltd* (1940) 63 CLR 278, the High Court held that if both a State and the Commonwealth are creditors of a particular debtor, then their entitlement to priority is equal, and thus – if the debtor has insufficient funds to satisfy both debts – they are entitled to share in proportion to their overall claims. This need to analyse competing claims of governments

emergency powers, the most significant of these is any limits on the liability of the government to be sued. However, section 75 of the Constitution, which confers original jurisdiction upon the High Court of Australia in relation to certain matters involving the Commonwealth or a State as a party, makes it plain that there is no general assumption of government immunity in Australian law, and judicial decisions have rejected any general doctrine of Crown immunity as an element of Australian law.[23] The extent of prerogative powers in the strict sense, insofar as they pertain to emergency powers, will be subsequently discussed; but for the reasons already seen these pertain primarily to the Commonwealth executive, and hence it will be the focus of the ensuing discussion.[24]

In addition to powers connected to the execution and maintenance of the law, conferred by statute, or having their historical antecedents in the British constitutional conception of the executive power, it is noteworthy that French CJ included the *inherent authority derived from the character and status of the Commonwealth as the national government*. This is a somewhat contentious element of the power conferred by section 61, in

---

(both of which may be described as 'the Crown'), which arises in the Australian federal system, led Dixon J to emphasise the distinction between the monarch as a person, and the various governments as organised bodies politic:

> The Constitution sweeps aside the difficulties which might be thought to arise in a federation from the traditional distinction between, on the one hand the position of the Sovereign as the representative of the State in a monarchy, and the other hand the State as a legal person ... [I]t treats the Commonwealth and the States as organisations or institutions of government possessing distinct individualities.

Bank of NSW v. Commonwealth (1948) 76 CLR 1, 363. For similar reasons, Dixon CJ (as he went on to become) suggested that the priority of the Commonwealth over ordinary creditors in relation to payment of a debt, which 'arose from the sovereignty of the Crown and was accordingly' characterised as 'one of the prerogatives of the Crown in right of the Commonwealth', is 'in modern times' better described 'as a fiscal right belonging to the Commonwealth as a government and affecting its Treasury.' *The Commonwealth v. Cigamatic Pty Ltd (in liq)* (1962) 108 CLR 372, 376–78.

[23] *R v. Toohey; Ex parte Northern Land Council* (1981) 151 CLR 170; *Minister for Arts, Heritage and Environment v. Peko-Wallsend Ltd* (1987) 15 FCR 274. For a discussion of judicial oversight of emergency powers, see Chapter 8 in this volume.

[24] For a recent judicial reference to 'the responsibility of the Commonwealth for Australia's external affairs and the security of the nation' which ensures that State government unfolds 'within the relatively benign environment guaranteed by membership of the federation', see *Murphy v. Electoral Commissioner* (2016) 90 ALJR 1027, 1064–65 [216] (Keane J).

particular because of its role as a possible source of emergency powers. Before turning to the emergency powers of the Australian executive, however, it will be helpful to consider the role of the executive in relation to emergencies in more general terms.

3.3 Emergencies and the Executive – General Considerations

Following the September 11, 2001, terrorist attacks upon the United States, there has been a rekindled interest in the place of emergency powers within a liberal democratic conception of government and constitutionalism. This section will not purport to survey the extensive literature, but rather will make some general points that are of particular relevance to the legal analysis of emergency powers in Australia.

In the immediate aftermath of the attacks, Scheuerman identified three main trends in the American debate.[25] One such trend broadly accepts the claim of the German theorist Carl Schmitt,[26] that executive responses to emergencies cannot be contained within a contemporary legal order, because the demands of emergencies are in principle unforeseeable, and hence cannot be accommodated within a rule-of-law compliant framework of legal and constitutional norms. Given the (purported) ubiquity of emergencies in the modern era, any attempt to confine the response to them within such a framework of norms will inevitably bring about the collapse of that framework. Schmitt himself regards this as a refutation of the feasibility of constitutional government, but the contemporary scholars whom Scheuerman discusses offer an alternative view, namely, that the ordinary legal order should be preserved by locating governmental responses to emergency outside the law.[27] It follows that the monitoring and disciplining of exercises of emergency powers would also, necessarily, fall outside the legal order:[28] Tushnet, for instance, suggests that it is a 'mobilised citizenry', analogous to the American

---

[25] William E Scheuerman, 'Survey Article: Emergency Powers and the Rule of Law after 9/11' (2006) 14(1) JPP 61.
[26] Scheuerman describes Schmitt as 'twentieth-century Germany's most impressive authoritarian right-wing political thinker': Ibid 61. The best-known exposition of Schmitt's claim is in Schmitt, *Political Theology* (1922), trans. George Schwab (University of Chicago Press 2005).
[27] Scheuerman (n 25) 69–74.
[28] Ibid 73.

Revolutionaries, that ultimately must undertake this task.[29] There are echoes of Locke in this way of thinking about emergency power: Locke characterises the prerogative as a power enjoyed by the executive to respond to unforeseen needs and emergencies, even where this means breaking established law;[30] and the ultimate remedy for abuse of the prerogative is for the people to 'appeal to heaven',[31] that is, to resist the government.[32]

The other two trends reject Schmitt, but advocate different approaches to ensuring the conformity of emergency powers with legal requirements.[33] One such approach is to favour legislative control over the executive's use of emergency powers by requiring the legislature to confer such powers, and imposing strong constraints upon that legislative process so as to attempt to prevent abuse. An example is provided by the South African constitution, which permits the legislature to confer emergency powers upon the executive, but also requires (*i*) that the conferral be prospective, (*ii*) a strict time limit of no more than 21 days and (*iii*) a special majority to extend the emergency powers.[34] The other approach favours treating emergency powers as ordinary law, subject to ordinary oversight by the judiciary, including the application of interpretive principles such as the principle of legality, according to which a statute that is open to a rights-violating interpretation should be given such an interpretation only if a rights-violating intention is manifested in in unambiguous language indicating a deliberate legislative decision to interfere with the rights in question.[35] One motivating concern of this approach is that, if emergencies (or the perception of them) really are

---

[29] Mark Tushnet, 'Emergencies and the Idea of Constitutionalism' in Mark Tushnet (ed), *The Constitution in Wartime: Beyond Alarmism and Complacency* (Duke University Press 2005) 46, 50.

[30] John Locke, *Second Treatise of Civil Government* (6th edn, 1764, eBooks@Adelaide 2014) ch 14, ss 159–60.

[31] Ibid ch 14, s 168.

[32] For Locke's account of legitimate resistance to government, see ibid ch 19, ss 221–42. Locke denies that such resistance is rebellion, on the grounds that it is the government which is the rebel in such a case, by having exercised force and set itself up against the people: ibid ch 19, s 226–27, and see also ss 240–42.

[33] Scheuerman (n 25) 74–79.

[34] Constitution of the Republic of South Africa (1996), s 37. The first extension requires an absolute majority, and subsequent extensions a three-fifths majority: s 37(2)(b). The predominant feature of such emergency powers is to permit derogations from certain constitutionally-protected rights.

[35] David Dyzenhaus is a leading proponent of this view: see, for instance, David Dyzenhaus 'Humpty Dumpty Rules or the Rule of Law: Legal Theory and the Adjudication of

ubiquitous, then special regimes of emergency law, if allowed at all, may become normalised, with the result that ordinary understandings of legality and constitutional value become eroded.[36] Tushnet also expresses doubts that legislative oversight of emergency regimes is likely to have the same degree of effectiveness in systems of parliamentary government, in which the executive and legislature may be expected to demonstrate a relatively high degree of unity, as it may have in the United States.[37]

The Australian constitutional order implicitly repudiates the first of the three approaches just canvassed. Inherent to that order, and captured in Dixon J's remark (quoted in the opening of this chapter) that the rule of law forms an assumption that lies behind it, is the idea that all power is sourced in law, with the highest law being the Constitution. The Constitution expressly provides that it, and all laws made under it, 'shall be binding on the courts, judges and people of every State and of every part of the Commonwealth'.[38] We have already seen that executive power is sourced either in the common law (at the State level, as continued in force by section 106 of the Constitution) or section 61 of the Constitution

---

National Security' (2003) 28 AJLP1; David Dyzenhaus and Rayner Thwaites, 'Legality and Emergency – The Judiciary in a Time of Terror' in Andrew Lynch, Edwina MacDonald and George Williams (eds), *Law and Liberty in the War on Terror* (Federation Press 2007). For a clear judicial exposition of the principal of legality in the context of the interpretation of legislation permitting executive detention of non-citizens, see *Al-Kateb v. Godwin* (2004) 219 CLR 562, 577–79 [19]–[25] (Gleeson CJ). Identifying precisely which rights it is that the principle of legality is concerned with is an important matter, but will not be taken up in this chapter.

[36] For concern that the ostensibly emergency regime introduced in the United States following the events of 2001 is becoming normality rather than an exception, see e.g., Oren Gross, 'What 'Emergency' Regime?' (2006) 13(1) Constellations 74–88.

[37] Mark Tushnet, 'The Political Constitution of Emergency Powers: Parliamentary and Separation-of-Powers Regulation', (2007) 3(4) IJLC 275–88, 277, although Tushnet does go on to give examples (drawn from the United Kingdom and Canada) of political control of emergency powers occurring within parliamentary systems of government. For Tushnet's account of the relevant political processes in the United States, see Mark Tushnet, 'The Political Constitution of Emergency Powers: Some Lessons From *Hamdan*' (2007) 91 Minn LR 1451–72.

[38] This provision is found in covering clause 5, that is, section 5 of the Commonwealth of Australia Constitution Act 1900 (Imp). The text of the Constitution itself is set out in section 9 of that Imperial Act. In a formal sense, it is the legal paramountcy of that Imperial legislation that renders Australian governmental actors bound by it and unable to amend it (except as authorised by section 15 of the Australia Acts 1986 (Cth & Imp)). For an alternative conceptualisation of the law-constrained nature of Australian government, with the Constitution itself at the apex of the legal structure, see Lisa Burton Crawford, *The Rule of Law and the Australian Constitution* (Federation Press 2017) 200–02.

(at the Commonwealth level). There is no extra-legal source of executive power in the Australian framework of government.

Nor do Australian parliaments have special procedures to confer or constrain emergency powers: State parliaments are, within their States and subject to limits established by the Constitution, fully plenary;[39] the Commonwealth Parliament is not, being a parliament of enumerated powers,[40] but the Constitution makes no provision for special procedures in relation to particular categories of legislation other than that dealing with taxation and appropriations.[41] Thus, there is no distinctive constitutional category of 'emergency' legislation subject to special rules for its valid enactment.[42] In the Australian constitutional order, therefore, the establishment, exercise and control of executive responses to emergencies unfold in accordance with the ordinary framework of law.

3.4 Australian Emergency Powers

As we saw, French CJ elucidated the executive power conferred by section 61 of the Constitution in terms of five categories reflecting the historical background that conditions our understanding of them. This section will address these in turn.

---

[39] Australia Acts 1986 (Cth & Imp), s 2(1). An example of a constitutionally-imposed limit upon this plenary power is section 90, which makes the power to impose duties of customs and excise exclusive to the Commonwealth. As noted previously (n 16), State parliaments also enjoy a limited power to make amendment of certain elements of State constitutions subject to special requirements.

[40] See especially sections 51 and 52 of the Constitution.

[41] Sections 53–56 of the Constitution establish a superior role for the lower house in relation to such legislation, in accordance with Westminster conventions, and also establish procedural requirements to ensure that this superior role is not abused.

[42] It might be argued that the power to legislate for the 'defence of the Commonwealth of the several States' (section 51(vi) of the Constitution) is a de facto instance of such a power, for – as is discussed in Chapter 2 – it is well understood that the scope of this legislative power is much wider in times of warfare than in times of peace. Tushnet argues that framing responses to emergencies in this way – as manifestations of general constitutional principle, which yield a different from normal result only because the circumstances of its application are different – is misleading, and that such responses are better recognised as extra-legal exercises of power: 'Emergencies and the Idea of Constitutionalism' in Mark Tushnet (ed) (n 29) 39–40, 45–49. However, there is no space for such a conceptualisation within the Australian constitutional order.

3.4.1 Powers Arising under Statute

The first two of French CJ's categories – powers conferred by statute, or necessary or incidental to the execution and maintenance of a law of the Commonwealth – are not *inherent* powers of the executive. They are conferred by Parliament, or are the consequences of such conferrals. They will therefore not be discussed in this chapter, except to make some general points.[43]

Because the Commonwealth Parliament enjoys legislative power only with respect to particular enumerated subject matters, any statutory conferral of power upon the executive must fall under one or more of those heads of power. This necessarily conditions the nature of statutory conferrals of executive power. This was discussed by Dixon J in the *Communist Party Case*;[44] although the principal legal effect of the legislation at issue in that case was not to confer a power upon the executive, but rather to dissolve a named organisation (the Australian Communist Party) by direct force of the enactment,[45] the principles would apply in the same fashion to a purported conferral of executive power. One argument in favour of the validity of the legislation at issue in that case was that the dissolution of the Communist Party was incidental to the power of the executive government to execute and maintain the Constitution and the laws of the Commonwealth.[46] In response to this argument, and immediately following the remark quoted above about the rule of law, Dixon J stated that

> In such a system [of government, that takes the rule of law as an assumption] I think it would be impossible to say of a law of the character described, which depends for its supposed connection with the [legislative] power upon the conclusion of the legislature concerning the doings and the designs of the bodies or person to be affected and affords no objective test of the applicability of the power, that it is a law upon a matter incidental to the execution and maintenance of the Constitution and the laws of the Commonwealth. Indeed, upon the very matters upon

---

[43] A fuller discussion of particular statutory conferrals of emergency powers can be found in Chapters 4, 5, 6 and 7 of this volume.

[44] *Australian Communist Party v. Commonwealth* (1951) 83 CLR 1.

[45] Communist Party Dissolution Act 1950 (Cth), s 4(1).

[46] As noted previously, the relevant head of legislative power is s 51(xxxix), which permits the Commonwealth Parliament to legislate with respect to matters 'incidental to the execution of any power vested by this Constitution ... in the Government of the Commonwealth'; and the executive power conferred by section 61 'extends to the execution and maintenance of this Constitution, and of the laws of the Commonwealth'.

which the question whether the bodies or persons have brought themselves within a possible exercise of the power depends, it may be said that the Act would have the effect of making the conclusion of the legislature final and so the measure of the operation of its own power.[47]

A similar idea was articulated by Fullagar J by way of the metaphor that 'a stream cannot rise higher than its source.... Parliament cannot recite itself into a field the gates of which are locked against it by superior law'.[48] In other words, the Commonwealth Parliament cannot enact legislation which depends for its connection to some constitutionally-conferred head of legislative power upon the mere assertion of such a connection by the Parliament itself (such as that the Australian Communist Party is a revolutionary threat to the constitutional order of the nation). The legislation must itself, in virtue of the terms of its operation, exhibit such a connection, the adequacy of which is then amenable to adjudication, as to its constitutional validity, by the Australian courts. It is noteworthy that contemporary statutes permitting executive proscription of organisations for various purposes do establish criteria for such proscription, which criteria exhibit (or at least purport to exhibit) the requisite connection to legislative power.[49]

Another general point of some importance pertains to the operation of constitutional guarantees. The Constitution contains no general

---

[47] *Australian Communist Party* v. *Commonwealth* (1951) 83 CLR 1, 193.
[48] Ibid 258, 263.
[49] See, e.g., Charter of the United Nations Act 1945 (Cth), ss 15, 18; Criminal Code (Cth), s 102.1. The former provisions permit the Commonwealth executive to give effect to requirements established by the United Nations for the freezing of assets connected to terrorism, but require the decision 'to give effect to a decision' of the United Nations, thus establishing an objective criterion of legislative validity under s 51 (xxix), which permits the Commonwealth Parliament to legislate with respect to external affairs. The latter provision permits the Commonwealth executive to specify organisations as 'terrorist organisations', with such specification then activating further statutory provisions, including the criminalisation of various dealings with such organisations and their members (see, e.g., Criminal Code (Cth), ss 102.5(2), 102.8); but the grounds on which an organisation may be listed are (broadly speaking) its connection to political violence either in Australia or abroad, which establishes objective criteria of legislative validity under s 51(xxix) and also s 51(vi) (the defence power): see the discussion in *Thomas* v. *Mowbray* (2007) 233 CLR 307, 324–26 [6]–[9] (Gleeson CJ), 363–65 [141]–[151], [153] (Gummow and Crennan JJ). For further discussion of the defence power, see Chapter 2 in this volume. For a fuller discussion of the limits upon the scope of statutorily conferred executive power that result from the need for such conferrals to be valid under a head of legislative power, see Lisa Burton Crawford, 'Can Parliament Confer Plenary Executive Power? The Limitations Imposed by Sections 51 and 52 of the Australian Constitution' (2016) 44 FLR 287.

individual rights protections of the sort found in most contemporary constitutions. Therefore, statutory conferrals of emergency powers are not amenable to challenge on the basis that they infringe human rights. However, Commonwealth legislation is subject to various other constitutionally-generated constraints which may be relevant in the area of emergency powers. Three will be briefly mentioned at this point; a fourth, namely, the constitutional guarantee that compulsory acquisitions of property must take place upon just terms,[50] will be discussed in relation to the issue of requisitions. First, the Constitution guarantees that 'trade, commerce, and intercourse among the States ... shall be absolutely free'.[51] This provision may limit the capacity of Parliament to confer emergency powers that regulate commerce, or that create general prohibitions on the movement of person. Second, and as is discussed more fully in Chapter 5 of this volume, legislation which purports to confer executive power that, in virtue of its content or the proscribed manner of its performance, would interfere with the constitutional separation of judicial from executive power, will be invalid. Finally, legislation which purports to confer executive power that would, in its exercise, unjustifiably interfere with or undermine the constitutionally-prescribed system of representative government, according to which the members of the Commonwealth Parliament are to be 'directly chosen by the people' and the government is to answer to that Parliament,[52] will also be invalid.[53] In a case that was focused on the scope of the law of defamation in light of this constitutional requirement, a unanimous High Court explained that the Constitution imposes:

> a limitation on legislative and executive power to deny the electors and their representatives information concerning the conduct of the executive branch of government throughout the life of a federal Parliament.[54]

While the focus in that case was on access to information and free political communication, which are necessary concomitants of 'direct choice' in conditions of modern mass democracy,[55] the same logic would apply to other exercises of power which were apt to interfere with the system of government grounded in direct choice by the people. The

---

[50] Constitution, s 51(xxxi).
[51] Constitution, s 92.
[52] Constitution, ss 7, 24, 64.
[53] *Lange v. Australian Broadcasting Corporation* (1997) 189 CLR 520.
[54] Ibid, 561.
[55] Ibid 565.

extent of these limitations has not been explored in the context of emergency powers, and a relevant consideration would undoubtedly be that some exercises of emergency power may be *necessary* to preserve the constitutionally-prescribed system of government, in which case any burden upon political communication or participation may be more than warranted by the end served.[56] Nevertheless, and particularly when one keeps in mind Dixon J's remarks concerning the lessons of history quoted in the opening paragraph of this chapter, this is not an insignificant constitutional limitation on the conferral of emergency powers.

3.4.2 The Capacities of a Legal Person

Although the Commonwealth executive enjoys certain capacities in common with ordinary juridical persons, these powers are not as extensive as those of a natural person. As well as trite examples of this point, such as the inability of the Commonwealth to marry, there are important limitations on the power of the Commonwealth to enter into contracts and to expend public moneys. These limitations result from the status of the Commonwealth government as simply one component within a federal system governed along Westminster lines.

The High Court declared these limits in the case of *Williams* v. *Commonwealth*.[57] The most fundamental is this: as a general rule, the Commonwealth may not enter into contracts, or otherwise pay out or commit to pay out public moneys, without the authority of validly enacted legislation. There is an exception to this general rule: the Commonwealth may, without such authorisation, pay out moneys in the ordinary course of government; but a proper understanding of that latter notion must take account of the place of the Commonwealth as a national government within a federation that also contains state governments. The case itself concerned a contract that the Commonwealth had purported to enter into with a non-governmental religious organisation, for the provision of 'chaplaincy services' in a school administered by the government of the State of Queensland. The moneys in question had

---

[56] The relationship between legislative means and constitutionally permissible or mandated ends in this field of jurisprudence is a hotly debated topic. For recent demonstrations of divergent judicial approaches, see *Monis* v. *The Queen* (2013) 249 CLR 92; *McCloy* v. *New South Wales* (2015) 257 CLR 178.
[57] *Williams* v. *Commonwealth* [2012] HCA 23, (2012) 248 CLR 156; see also *Williams* v. *Commonwealth [No 2]* [2014] HCA 23, (2014) 252 CLR 416.

been appropriated by law,[58] but no statute otherwise authorised the contract or expenditure. While the Court did not explain in great detail what sorts of contracts and expenditure might fall within the scope of the exception to the general rule, it held that this contract did not, and hence that the contract itself, as well as payments purportedly made under it, were invalid.[59] The constitutional basis for these limits upon the Commonwealth government's capacities, which resulted in this finding of invalidity, is the federal nature of the Australian constitutional order. First, while the Commonwealth executive has responsibility for matters that are distinctively national, it does not – in the absence of valid legislation – have responsibility for matters that fall into the remit of State executives.[60] Second, the Commonwealth Parliament is a bicameral one. However, the upper house is not established on a straightforwardly national basis. While members of the upper house – Senators – are directly elected, just as are members of the House of Representatives, the seats in the chamber, and the franchise according to which Senators are chosen, are allocated on a federal (i.e., State-by-State) basis, similar to the Senate of the United States.[61] In Australia, therefore, the fundamental constitutional principle inherited from Westminster, that executive expenditure of public moneys must be subject to parliamentary control, has a distinctively federalist aspect to it: unless expenditure is occurring

---

[58] As sections 81 and 83 of the Constitution require.

[59] The plaintiff in the case had sought to contest the expenditure primarily on the ground that it infringed the constitutional prohibition on the establishment of any religion by the Commonwealth: the Constitution, s 116. The Court's treatment of that argument confirmed the established, and narrow, limits of Australian non-establishment doctrine; but, as discussed in the text, the Court revealed a new and unanticipated constraint on executive power.

[60] *Williams v. Commonwealth* [2012] HCA 23, (2012) 248 CLR 156, 179–80 [4], 192 [36], 193 [38], 216–17 [83] (French CJ), 235 [146] (Gummow and Bell JJ), 346–47 [499], 348 [503] (Crennan J). See also 250–51 [196], 252 [198], 281 [288] (Hayne J, also making the federalist point but declining to decide the larger issue as to the limits of Commonwealth executive power).

[61] Constitution, ss 7–12, 14–15, 21. It is noteworthy that the direct election of Senators has been a feature of the Australian system of government since Federation in 1901, and thus predates the 17th Amendment of the *United States* Constitution, which established direct election of the United States Senate in 1913. For discussion of the idea of the Senate as a democratic chamber elected by way of a federal franchise, see Brian Galligan, *A Federal Republic: Australia's Constitutional System of Government* (CUP 1995).

in the ordinary course of government, it must be sourced in a valid statute which, therefore, will have passed *both* houses of Parliament.[62]

Thus, the inherent juridical capacities of the Commonwealth executive, in the absence of any statutory conferral of power, are quite limited in their capacity to respond to emergencies. As Gageler J has stated, whatever effects such an exercise of power might have 'on legal rights or juridical relations [would] result not from the act being uniquely that of the Executive Government but from the application to the act of the same substantive law as would be applicable in respect of the act had it been done by any other actor.'[63] The most generic such exercise of power is the power to enter into a contract, and thereby establish rights and obligations; but as we have just seen, the Commonwealth executive's power in this respect is also quite limited. It could even be argued that, of necessity, responding to emergencies (for instance, by acquiring large stocks of emergency supplies) is not action undertaken in the ordinary course of government.

To ascertain the non-statutory emergency powers of the Commonwealth executive, it is therefore necessary to consider the remaining two of French CJ's categories.

3.4.3 Executive Power Appropriate to a National Government

The executive power of the Commonwealth is not confined to statutorily conferred power, and the capacities enjoyed by a legal person. There is also a further bundle of inherent powers – an analogue of what Blackstone called 'the prerogative', and which was described by French CJ as encompassing both 'powers defined by reference to such of the prerogatives of the Crown as are properly attributable to the Commonwealth' and the 'inherent authority derived from the character and status of the Commonwealth as the national government'.[64] For a number of reasons, this bundle of powers must be considered together.

---

[62] *Williams v. Commonwealth* [2012] HCA 23, (2012) 248 CLR 156, 205–06 [60]–[61] (French CJ), 232–33 [136], 235 [145] (Gummow and Bell JJ), 351–52 [516], 354–55 [532], 358 [544] (Crennan J). The mere fact that moneys have been validly appropriated will not be sufficient to answer these concerns, because – consistent with Westminster tradition, and as briefly noted in the previous section – the power of the upper house in relation to appropriation laws is limited by sections 53 and 56 of the Constitution.

[63] *Plaintiff M68/2015 v. Minister for Immigration and Border Protection* [2016] HCA 1; (2016) 257 CLR 42, 98 [135].

[64] *Williams v. Commonwealth* [2012] HCA 23, (2012) 248 CLR 156, 184–85 [22].

The first such reason is that, as put forward by French CJ, both elements of the bundle are characterised by reference to the Commonwealth's status as a national government. This is self-evident in his characterisation of the second element; but it is also implicit in his characterisation of the first, for – as was explained in sub-section 3.2.2 – to ascertain what prerogative powers are attributable to the Commonwealth requires understanding the Commonwealth as a national government, and hence as enjoying (for instance) such powers as those to declare war and enter into treaties, which the States (and the colonies that were their predecessors) do not, and never did, enjoy.

The second reason builds upon the first. It is generally accepted that the scope of the prerogative is vague,[65] as it is (to use Dicey's term) a 'residue' of power that has been gradually transformed and reduced by way of the historical and political processes described earlier in this chapter. The powers that are attributable to the status of the Commonwealth as a national government likewise are vague.[66] Hence, attempting to distinguish between prerogative powers associated with nationhood, such as the power to declare war, and whatever other powers might be appropriate to a national government, seems an ultimately pointless endeavour. This is particularly so in relation to emergency powers, where novel demands may be particularly apt to arise.

An example of such novel demands is illustrated by the case of *Pape v. Federal Commissioner of Taxation*.[67] The case concerned the validity of legislation enacted by the Commonwealth Parliament in response to the global financial crisis that began in 2007. The effect of the legislation was to entitle those who had lodged tax returns in the relevant year, and had a taxable income of no more than $100,000, to a cash payment from the Commonwealth Treasury. Although the law operated by reference to a person's participation in the tax system, and the payments were administered by the Commissioner of Taxation, the law could not be straightforwardly characterised as one with respect to taxation, and hence as valid under section 51(ii) of the Constitution, because the entitlement to payment did not correlate in any fashion to the actual amount of tax

---

[65] See, for instance, S Markesinis, 'The Royal Prerogative Re-visited' (1973) 32(2) CLJ 287, 308. George Winterton more optimistically describes the prerogative as being 'occasionally difficult to determine' and as uncertain 'in marginal cases': 'The Limits and Use of Executive Power by Government' (2003) 31 FLR 421, 432–33.

[66] Winterton makes this point in criticising the notion of 'national government' as a touchstone for the content of executive power: George Winterton (n 65) 430–33.

[67] [2009] HCA 23; (2009) 238 CLR 1.

3.4 AUSTRALIAN EMERGENCY POWERS

paid, and could indeed be greater than that amount. Hence the payment could not (for instance) be characterised as a tax refund.[68] The majority of the High Court nevertheless upheld the validity of the legislation, on the following grounds: first, the Commonwealth executive enjoyed, under section 61 of the Constitution, the power to respond to the national emergency to which the global financial crisis had given rise; and second, the Parliament could thus enact the legislation pursuant to section 51(xxxix) of the Constitution, as being incidental to that executive response.[69]

The need to analyse the legislation's validity in this fashion arises from the fact that the Commonwealth Parliament is a legislature of enumerated powers. The question of legislative invalidity for want of a head of power cannot arise in the case of the Westminster parliament; hence, in the United Kingdom there also does not arise the need to ascertain whether or not the inherent executive power extends – by way of the prerogative or otherwise – to making decisions about emergency fiscal policy. Little would seem to be gained in the Australian context by insisting that the analysis identify with precision some boundary between powers apt to be described as prerogative, and some other category of power whose source consists in some alternative notion of national government.

The third reason for considering this bundle of powers to be all of one piece emerges from the majority judgments in *Pape*. Thus, in that case French CJ says that:

> The collection of statutory and prerogative powers and non-prerogative capacities form part of, but do not complete, the executive power. They lie within the scope of s 61, which is informed by history and the common law relevant to the relationship between the Crown and the Parliament. That history and common law emerged from what might be called an organic evolution. Section 61 is an important element of a written constitution for the government of an independent nation. While history and the common law inform its content, it is not a locked display cabinet in a constitutional museum. It is not limited to statutory powers and the prerogative. It has to be capable of serving the proper purposes of a national government. . . . The executive power extends, in my opinion, to short-term fiscal measures to meet adverse economic conditions affecting the nation as a whole,

---

[68] *Pape v. Federal Commissioner of Taxation* [2009] HCA 23; (2009) 238 CLR 1, 92, 94, [246], [252] (Gummow, Crennan and Bell JJ), 129–33 [379]–[393] (Hayne and Kiefel JJ).
[69] Ibid 23, 60, 63–64 [8], [127], [133]–[134] (French CJ), 83, 87–89, 91–92 [213], [215], [227]–[228], [232]–[233], [241], [243], [245] (Gummow, Crennan and Bell JJ).

where such measures are on their face peculiarly within the capacity and resources of the Commonwealth Government.[70]

Similarly, Gummow, Crennan and Bell JJ say that:

> The conduct of the executive branch of government includes, but involves much more than, enjoyment of the benefit of those preferences, immunities and exceptions which are denied to the citizen and are commonly identified with "the prerogative"; the executive power of the Commonwealth enables the undertaking of action appropriate to the position of the Commonwealth as a polity created by the Constitution and having regard to the spheres of responsibility vested in it.... [T]he phrase "maintenance of this Constitution" in s 61 imports more than a species of what is identified as "the prerogative" in constitutional theory. It conveys the idea of the protection of the body politic or nation of Australia...
>
> Determining that there is the need for an immediate fiscal stimulus to the national economy in the circumstances set out above is somewhat analogous to determining a state of emergency in circumstances of a natural disaster. The Executive Government is the arm of government capable of and empowered to respond to a crisis be it war, natural disaster or a financial crisis on the scale here. This power has its roots in the executive power exercised in the United Kingdom up to the time of the adoption of the Constitution but in form today in Australia it is a power to act on behalf of the federal polity.... The present is an example of the engagement by the Executive Government in activities peculiarly adapted to the government of the country and which otherwise could not be carried on for the public benefit.[71]

These passages make it clear that the members of the majority in *Pape* see the idea of executive powers that are 'proper' or 'peculiar' to the national government and its role in ensuring the wellbeing of the country not as standing in contrast to the traditional conception of the prerogative powers, but as of a piece with and building upon that traditional conception. The power to formulate emergency fiscal policy is not to be contrasted with the power to declare war or to make treaties, but rather is to be seen as having a common source in section 61's conferral of executive power upon the national government.[72]

---

[70] Ibid 60, 63 [127], [133].
[71] Ibid 83, 89, 91–92 [214]–[215], [233], [242].
[72] Hayne and Kiefel JJ, ibid 122 [347], were critical of the majority on this point:

> Words like 'crisis' or 'emergency' do not readily yield criteria of constitutional validity. It may be accepted ... that there is shown to be a national crisis to which a national response is required ... It does not

Consistently with the decision in *Williams*, this executive power must be understood to be limited on federal grounds. French CJ makes the importance of such limits plain when he describes the emergency fiscal response at issue in *Pape* as 'peculiarly within the capacity and resources of the Commonwealth Government'. Gummow, Crennan and Bell JJ likewise acknowledge such limits:

> [T]he polity which the Constitution established and maintains is an independent nation state with a federal system of government.... [W]hile s 51(xxxix) authorises the Parliament to legislate in aid of the executive power, that does not mean that it may do so in aid of any subject which the Executive Government regards as of national interest and concern.[73]

> [I]t is only by some constraint having its source in the position of the Executive Governments of the States that the government of the Commonwealth is denied the power, after appropriation by the Parliament, of expenditure of moneys raised by taxation imposed by the Parliament. Otherwise there appears no good reason to treat the executive power recognised in s 61 of the Constitution as being, in matters of the raising and expenditure of public moneys, any less than that of the executive in the United Kingdom ...[74]

Thus, for emergency powers of the sort considered in *Pape* to be enlivened, the emergency – like the global financial crisis – must threaten the nation as a whole, and must be one to which only the Commonwealth has the capacity to adequately respond.

In addition to these federal limits, other important limits apply to this power. These pertain to the capacity of the executive to impose duties and to interfere with rights.

It is a basic premise of the Australian constitutional order that the executive government is bound by the law. This proposition has what could be described as a 'formal' dimension: as has already been discussed in this chapter, all executive power must flow from, and hence is limited by, law (with the Constitution as the highest source of law). But of particular importance in trying to understand the limits of the executive power to take action for the good of the nation, this proposition

---

follow, however, that the Commonwealth's executive power to respond to such circumstances by spending money is a power that is unbounded. Were it so, the extensive litigation about the ambit of the defence power during World War II was beside the point.

[73] Ibid 84, 87–88 [217], [228].
[74] Ibid 85 [220].

also has a 'substantive' dimension: there are particular legal rights that the executive lacks the power to infringe, and particular legal relationships that it lacks the power to alter.

One of the most important of these limits was stated in *Chu Kheng Lim v. Minister for Immigration, Local Government and Ethnic Affairs*: 'the common law knows neither lettre de cachet nor other executive warrant authorizing arbitrary arrest or detention,'[75] and hence section 61, with its content informed by the common law tradition inherited from the United Kingdom, does not permit the exercise of any such power. Gageler J puts the matter thus:

> The inability of the Executive Government of the Commonwealth to authorise or enforce a deprivation of liberty is... the consequence of an inherent constitutional incapacity which is commensurate with the availability, long settled at the time of the establishment of the Commonwealth, of habeas corpus to compel release from any executive detention not affirmatively authorised by statute.[76]

Another such limitation is the inability of the executive to change the law of the land. The executive cannot create new entitlements (except by exercising its ordinary capacities to do so, such as by entering into a contract) – hence the need for legislation in *Pape*, to establish legal entitlements to the statutory payments.[77] Nor can it create new criminal offences; legislation is necessary for this.[78] Nor can it dispense with the operation of the law and seek, thereby, to immunise itself and those who act on its behalf from the legal consequences of (including criminal liability for) their actions.[79] As Brennan J explained it, '[t]he

---

[75] (1992) 176 CLR 1, 19 (Brennan, Deane and Dawson JJ).
[76] *Plaintiff M68/2015* v. *Minister for Immigration and Border Protection* (2016) 257 CLR 42, 105 [159].
[77] *Pape* v. *Federal Commissioner of Taxation* [2009] HCA 23; (2009) 238 CLR 1, 92 [243].
[78] *Davis* v. *The Commonwealth* (1998) 166 CLR 79, 112–13; *Pape* v. *Federal Commissioner of Taxation* [2009] HCA 23; (2009) 238 CLR 1, 92 [244]–[245] (Gummow, Crennan and Bell JJ). For this reason, section 51(xxxix) cannot be used to enact a new criminal provision simply because the Commonwealth executive would endorse it as a matter of policy; offences created pursuant to that head of power must be purely incidental to the carrying out of an independently permissible executive policy (for instance, penalties for the wrongful expenditure of money): *Attorney-General (Vic); Ex rel Dale* v. *Commonwealth* (1945) 71 CLR 237, esp. 258 (Latham CJ); and see also *R* v. *Hughes* (2000) 202 CLR 535, 555 [39] (Gleeson CJ, Gaudron, McHugh, Gummow, Hayne and Callinan JJ).
[79] *Clough* v. *Leahy* (1904) 2 CLR 139, 155–56 (Griffith CJ); *Pirrie* v. *McFarlane* (1925) 36 CLR 170; *A* v. *Hayden* (1984) 156 CLR 532; *Re Residential Tenancies Tribunal (NSW)*

incapacity of the executive government to dispense its servants from obedience to laws made by Parliament is the cornerstone of a parliamentary democracy'.[80]

The exercise of inherent executive power can, however, on occasion interfere with the legal rights of others.[81] An important question, therefore, is *when is this so*? Some answers to this question are conceptually straightforward: a declaration of war may change the status of certain persons, for instance rendering them liable to be killed (as enemy soldiers) without such killings constituting crimes. But other suggested answers have provoked controversy. In the case of *Ruddock* v. *Vadarlis*, French J (as he then was) held that:

> the Executive power of the Commonwealth, absent statutory extinguishment or abridgement, would extend to a power to prevent the entry of non-citizens and to do such things as are necessary to effect such exclusion.... The power to determine who may come into Australia is so central to its sovereignty that it is not to be supposed that the Government of the nation would lack under the power conferred upon it directly by the Constitution, the ability to prevent people not part of the Australia community, from entering.[82]

On this basis, his Honour therefore concluded that the Australian government's use of military personnel to prevent the landing, in Australia, of a vessel carrying aliens seeking asylum but lacking entry permits, and the government's subsequent use of naval vessels to take those asylum seekers to third countries in the Pacific region, was lawful. French J took the view that these actions did not constitute detention of a sort lying beyond the inherent powers of the executive, as:

> the actions of the Commonwealth were properly incidental to preventing the [aliens] from landing in Australian territory where they had no right to go.... [N]othing done by the Commonwealth amounted to a restraint upon their freedom, they having neither right nor freedom to travel to Australia.[83]

---

v. *Henderson; Ex parte Defence Housing Authority* (1997) 190 CLR 410, 427–28 (Brennan CJ), 442–44 (Dawson, Toohey and Gaudron JJ); *Plaintiff M68/2015* v. *Minister for Immigration and Border Protection* (2016) 257 CLR 42, 91 [135]–[136] (Gageler J).

[80] *A* v. *Hayden* (1984) 156 CLR 532, 580.
[81] *Plaintiff M68/2015* v. *Minister for Immigration and Border Protection* (2016) 257 CLR 42, 91 [135] (Gageler J).
[82] (2001) 110 FCR 491, 543 [193].
[83] *Ruddock* v. *Vadarlis* (2001) 110 FCR 491, 548 [213]–[214].

This judgment has been subject to criticism. In a subsequent case also dealing with the Australian government's interdiction of asylum seekers to prevent them entering Australia, Hayne and Bell JJ reiterated the importance of the principle stated in *Chu Kheng Lim* and went on to ask the rhetorical question

> [W]hy should an Australian court hold that an officer of the Commonwealth Executive who purports to authorise or enforce the detention in custody of an alien without judicial mandate can do so outside the territorial boundaries of Australia without any statutory authority? Reference to the so-called non-statutory executive power of the Commonwealth provides no answer to that question. Reference to the royal prerogative provides no answer. Reference to "the defence and protection of the nation" is irrelevant, especially if it is intended to evoke echoes of the power to declare war and engage in war-like operations. Reference to an implied executive "nationhood power" to respond to national emergencies is likewise irrelevant. Powers of those kinds are not engaged in this case. To hold that the Executive can act outside Australia's borders in a way that it cannot lawfully act within Australia would stand legal principle on its head.[84]

Given the inherent vagueness and risk of expansion in the concept of power appropriate to a national government, it is suggested that these criticisms of French J's judgment are sound.[85]

3.4.4 Requisitions in Times of War

In *Madzimbamuto* v. *Lardner-Burke*, a case concerning executive detention without valid statutory authorisation, the Privy Council held that '[u]nder pressure of necessity the lawful Sovereign and his forces may be justified in taking action which infringes the ordinary rights of his subjects'.[86] At least as far as detention is concerned, however, this is not the case in Australia, for the reasons just considered.

---

[84] *CPCF* v. *Minister for Immigration* (2015) 255 CLR 514, 568 [150]; see also at 600 [276] (Kiefel J).

[85] Stellios agrees: see Stellios (n 1) 401. For criticism of French J's judgment on the basis that there is no prerogative power to expel friendly aliens, see *Ruddock* v. *Vadarlis* (2001) 110 FCR 491, 495–501 [9]–[29] (Black CJ); *CPCF* v. *Minister for Immigration* (2015) 255 CLR 514, 596–98 [261]–[269] (Kiefel J).

[86] [1969] 1 AC 645, 726 (Lord Reid for the majority). As the detainee in that case was being held by the Smith government in Southern Rhodesia, which was (the Privy Council held) *not* the lawful government, this principle did not apply to the circumstances of the case. For a critical discussion of a contemporary application of the 'necessity' doctrine, see

3.4 AUSTRALIAN EMERGENCY POWERS

It has also been held that the Australian executive cannot conscript citizens for military service without statutory authorisation.[87] But what is the status of property in wartime? In argument in *Madzimbamuto*, counsel pointed to *Burmah Oil Co Ltd* v. *Lord Advocate*[88] as authority for the proposition that principle of 'necessity' formed part of the law of the United Kingdom.[89] That latter case concerned the deliberate destruction by the armed forces of the United Kingdom, in 1942, of property owned by a group of British-registered companies – oil wells, refineries, stores of petroleum and the like – in order to prevent the assets falling into the hands of the Japanese. A majority in the House of Lords held that the government of the United Kingdom did enjoy a prerogative power to take or destroy property in time of war, but also held that the exercise of that power brought with it a duty to pay compensation. (It was not disputed that had the damage occurred actually in the course of conducting military operations, no compensation would have been payable.[90])

As far as legislative power is concerned, the Constitution empowers the Commonwealth Parliament to make law with respect to 'the acquisition of property ... for any purpose in respect of which the Parliament has power to make laws'.[91] However, such acquisition must be on just terms, and this requirement of just terms operates as a limit upon other heads of power. This limit on the legislative power applies even when the legislatively authorised acquisition of the property occurs pursuant to the defence power,[92] and even if the Commonwealth's acquisition of property does not involve permanent acquisition of a recognised class of property right but only, for instance, a temporary entitlement to possession.[93] On the other hand, if no right or interest in the property is

---

Michael Head, 'A Victory for Democracy? An Alternative Assessment of *Republic of Fiji v Prasad*' (2001) 2(2) Melb J Int'l L 535.

[87] *Marks* v. *The Commonwealth* (1964) 111 CLR 549, 573–74, 587 (Windeyer J).
[88] [1965] AC 75.
[89] *Madzimbamuto* v. *Lardner-Burke* [1969] 1 AC 645, 681–82, 709 (arguments from counsel for the appellant), 698 (arguments from the amicus curiae).
[90] See also *Shaw Savill and Albion Co Ltd* v. *The Commonwealth* (1940) 66 CLR 344; *Groves* v. *Commonwealth* (1982) 150 CLR 113.
[91] Section 51(xxxi).
[92] *Johnston Fear & Kingham & the Offset Printing Co Pty Ltd* v. *The Commonwealth* (1943) 67 CLR 314.
[93] *Minister of State for the Army* v. *Dalziel* (1944) 68 CLR 261.

acquired then the just terms requirement does not apply.[94] Thus, while legislation authorising the requisition of assets for defence or other emergency purposes would enliven the just terms requirement, it seems that a law which permitted the Commonwealth executive to undertake activities which simply destroyed property, but did not involve an acquisition of any sort of interest in the property, would be valid.

When it comes to inherent executive power, the situation in Australia is not clear. In a case decided prior to *Burmah Oil Co Ltd*, Latham CJ and Starke J suggested that the requirement of just terms may not apply to the executive power of the Commonwealth used to requisition property for war purposes.[95] However, more recent judicial remarks on the topic appear to incline the other way. In *Clunies-Ross v. The Commonwealth*, a majority of the High Court, in the course of explaining why executive powers of compulsory acquisition should be narrowly construed, cited *Burmah Oil Co Ltd* with approval.[96] And in 2008 a unanimous High Court appeared to express at least some doubt about the existence of a 'war prerogative' with respect to property.[97] The better view, therefore, seems to be that while there probably is an executive power of requisition under section 61, it requires the paying of compensation. This is also consistent with broader principle – it would be anomalous for the executive, which is subordinate to, and subject to regulation by, the Parliament, to enjoy a more expansive power of acquiring or destroying property for its military purposes than the legislative power found in section 51(xxxi).

3.5 Conclusion

As was foreshadowed at the outset of this chapter, the emergency powers of the Australian executive are limited because they are subject to law. The executive power is grounded in law – there are no extra-legal emergency powers known to Australian law. And just as importantly, while the executive power to take actions appropriate to a national

---

[94] *Commonwealth v. Tasmania* (1983) 158 CLR 1, 145 (Mason J); *JT International SA v. Commonwealth* (2012) 250 CLR 1, 34–35 (French CJ), 59–60, 63–64 (Gummow J), 72–73 (Hayne and Bell JJ), 110 (Crennan J), 130–32 (Kiefel J).
[95] *Johnston Fear & Kingham & the Offset Printing Co Pty Ltd v. The Commonwealth* (1943) 67 CLR 314, 318–19 (Latham CJ), 325 (Starke J).
[96] (1984) 155 CLR 193, 201 (Gibbs CJ, Mason, Wilson, Brennan, Deane and Dawson JJ).
[97] *Walker Corporation Pty Ltd v. Sydney Harbour Foreshore Authority* (2008) 233 CLR 259, 269 [29] (Gleeson CJ, Gummow, Hayne, Heydon and Crennan JJ).

3.5 CONCLUSION

government is undoubtedly vague, and perhaps in some respects more extensive than a more traditional conception of the prerogative, it is also limited by substantive considerations of legality: there is no power of arbitrary executive detention, and the executive has no power to change or dispense with the law of the land. The inherent powers of the executive clearly extend to the carrying out of military operations, and to responding in non-coercive ways to other crises and emergencies. It seems likely that they also extend to the requisition of property during wartime, provided that compensation is provided. But these are limited powers. The bulk of the emergency powers enjoyed by the Australian executive are those that have been conferred by statute.

4

Maintenance of Public Order

> The object of [public order] legislation is generally the same: the preservation of order in public places in the interests of the amenity and security of citizens, and so that they may exercise, without undue disturbance, the rights and freedoms involved in the use and enjoyment of such places. . . . The right of one person to ventilate personal grievances may collide with the right of others to a peaceful enjoyment of public space...it is often the case that one person's freedom ends where another person's right begins.
>
> Chief Justice Gleeson, *Coleman v. Power* (2004) 220 CLR 1, 12 [32].

4.1 Introduction

In 1817, the British Parliament passed legislation suspending the writ of *habeas corpus* in order to suppress British revolutionary sentiment in the aftermath of the French and American republican revolutions.[1] During the parliamentary debates on the law, the Marquess Wellesley observed that

> The wisest patriots had ever felt, that true liberty has its basis in public order – *pax est tranquilla libertas*. The most arduous struggles for independence, the most furious civil wars, all concluded in establishing this maxim – that whatever was inconsistent with the tranquillity of a state could not be consistent with liberty. But although that principle was true, it was not on every allegation of public disturbance, it was not on every ebullition, even of a treasonable tendency, even though the branches of that treason spread far and deep, that the parliament should be called upon to alter the existing laws of the land, or suspend for a moment the great bulwarks of the constitution.[2]

---

[1] Habeas Corpus Suspension Act 1817 (57 Geo. III, c. 3). See also Thomas Erskine May, *The Constitutional History of England since the Accession of George III, 1760–1860* (W. J. Widdleton 1866) 257.

[2] Parl Debs, HL, vol. 35, *col. 559*, 24 February 1817.

Marquess Wellesley's observations are echoed today, in all constitutional democracies that purport to defend the rule of law. Governments generally have a broad spectrum of powers with which to suppress public disturbances, but, in democratic societies, are charged with responding in a way that preserves the people's liberty to protest and resist government action that they oppose, and this gives rise to a tension between the measures adopted and fundamental freedoms.

This chapter will consider the way this tension has been managed in Australian law, focusing in particular on the role of the 'implied freedom of political communication', a constitutional doctrine that limits the power of government to restrict political speech. The chapter also raises the question as to what role the concept of emergency actually plays in enabling the police and other government authorities to respond to public disorder in a way they could not otherwise do.

The powers of the police to control public spaces are now so broad that it is arguable that the concept of 'emergency powers' is a redundancy in this area insofar as the phrase suggests, as Marquess Wellesley did, that emergency powers are constitutionally exceptional. If there is a serious difference, it may lie in the fact that non-emergency public disorder powers must be sensitive to the constitutional importance of assembly and association for political purposes. In other words, the distinguishing characteristic of emergency public disorder powers may be that they displace the already-limited guarantees the Australian Constitution provides for political expression.

4.2 Australia's Public Order Framework

Australia has seen the full spectrum of protest and unrest across its history. The Eureka Rebellion and Stockade, involving charges of sedition and treason, is one of the most famous historical instances of public disorder in the Australian collective memory. The control of public disorder was of concern to pre-federation State governments,[3] enough to justify the creation of statutory schemes: section 34 of the original Police Act 1892 (WA), for example, permitted a magistrate to appoint special constables 'upon the oath of any credible person that any tumult, riot, or felony has taken place, or may be reasonably apprehended'.

---

[3] Manning Clark, *History of Australia* (MUP 1993) 27–28.

At the time of Federation, it was concluded that the principal responsibility for maintaining internal order would lie with the States in exercise of their police powers. Drawing upon a line of authority derived from the United States' Supreme Court's decision in *In re Debs*,[4] Quick and Garran observed that '[t]he maintenance of order in a State is primarily the concern of the State, for which the police powers of the State are ordinarily adequate'.[5] Accordingly, after Federation, the power to respond to public disorder remained with the States: none of the Commonwealth's enumerated powers in section 51 expressly 'relate to public order, to the control of what is written, spoken or published, to the limits upon freedom of expression, to the maintenance of the King's peace or to social order', and section 119 of the Constitution, which permits the Commonwealth to intervene in domestic violence upon application by a State executive government, reinforces the primary responsibility of the States for guaranteeing public order.[6]

Over time, traditional public order offences have been supplemented, indeed replaced, by far-reaching powers that enable the police to control and prevent threats to public order. This is in part a response to developments across the late twentieth and early twenty-first centuries, which have in many respects been a time of mass social protest. Protest has been driven by concerns about the environment, economic globalisation and inequality, war, institutional racism, and, on the other end of the spectrum, by opposition to multiculturalism and immigration.

Perhaps the most infamous recent instance of violent unrest was the so-called 'Cronulla Riots', which occurred in Cronulla, Sydney, in December 2005. After a fight between a group of life-savers and Lebanese-Australian youths, more than 5,000 people rioted on Cronulla Beach. The riots had arguably been encouraged by talkback radio hosts.[7] The Cronulla Riots were somewhat of a turning point for the development of the law of public order in Australia. Chris Cuneen observes, for example, that '[f]ollowing the riots at Cronulla and other Sydney beaches,

---

[4] 158 US 564 (1895).
[5] John Quick and Robert Garran, *Annotated Constitution of the Australian Commonwealth* (Angus and Robertson 1901) 965. See also *R v. Sharkey* (1949) 79 CLR 121, 151 (Dixon J, dissenting).
[6] *R v. Sharkey* (1949) 79 CLR 121, 151 (Dixon J, dissenting). See also *Attorney-General for the Commonwealth v. Colonial Sugar Refining Co. Ltd.* [1914] AC 237, 255.
[7] 'Mob Violence Envelops Cronulla' *Sydney Morning Herald* (11 December 2005); 'Jones Makes Apology on Air over Lebanese Comments' *Sydney Morning Herald* (19 December 2012).

the NSW Government introduced a raft of legislative amendments with the expressed aim of preventing and controlling large-scale public disorder incidents'.[8]

As a consequence of events like Cronulla, in Australia the powers of government to address public disorder have become extremely broad, even in the absence of a declared state of emergency. Australian governments, often following developments in the United Kingdom, have granted the police the power to 'move on' persons from a public place based on the anxiety they may cause to others, and some jurisdictions have introduced entire systems of warrantless search and seizure of property based on the potential for public disorder. These powers are designed to be preventative, in the sense that they are directed at defusing or reducing the potential for serious public disorder.

4.2.1 Constitutional Protections for Political Assembly

One of the reasons why powers to control public disorder have become so broad is because the Constitution provides no explicit protections to freedom of non-political speech, assembly and association.[9] As a form of statutory protection, many public order laws make the powers they confer non-applicable to authorised public assemblies. Other laws that do not so provide should be read in light of longstanding common law principles, such as the principle of legality. As Isaacs J observed in *Melbourne Corporation* v. *Barry*,[10] unless legislatures are forced to restrain the right to protest in public places using very explicit language, 'how are individuals to attempt to conform to law without a total surrender of their right ... on occasions that frequently represent great and important national, political, social, religious or industrial movements or opinions?'[11] This observation is doubly relevant in jurisdictions that have a statutory charter of human rights, such as Victoria and the Australian Capital Territory, where the principle of legality is applied

---

[8] 'Law, Policing and Public Order: The Aftermath of Cronulla' in Noble (ed) *Lines in the Sand. The Cronulla Riots, Multiculturalism and National Belonging* (ICP 2009) 220–31.
[9] See, e.g., *Mulholland* v. *Australian Electoral Commission* (2004) 220 CLR 181, 234 [148] (Gummow and Hayne JJ); *Wainohu* v. *New South Wales* (2011) 243 CLR 181, 220 [72] (French CJ and Kiefel J), 230 [112] (Gummow, Hayne, Crennan and Bell JJ), [186] (Heydon J); *Tajjour* v. *New South Wales* (2014) 254 CLR 508, 566 [95] (Hayne J).
[10] (1922) 31 CLR 174.
[11] Ibid 197.

with amplified force to construe laws constraining public assembly as being compatible with human rights.[12]

In *Lange v. Australian Broadcasting Corporation*,[13] the High Court held that 'ss 7 and 24 and the related sections of the [Australian] Constitution necessarily protect that freedom of communication between the people concerning political or government matters which enables the people to exercise a free and informed choice as electors'.[14] Traditionally, this implied freedom of political communication has required the application of a two-step test. First, it must be determined whether a burden has actually been imposed on political communication, while the second step requires the government to justify its ends and means; the burden must serve a legitimate end compatible with representative government, and achieve that end in a 'reasonably appropriate and adapted' way.[15]

The second step has increasingly taken on the form of German- and Canadian-style proportionality analysis,[16] involving consideration of the restriction's rational connection to the law's underlying purpose; whether it is the least restrictive means of achieving that purpose; and its proportionality *stricto sensu*, a 'result-oriented test'[17] that 'places the proper purpose of the limiting law on one side of the scales and the limited constitutional right on the other, while balancing the benefit gained by the proper purpose with the harm it causes to the right'.[18] In *McCloy v. New South Wales*,[19] the majority of the High Court used a similar test, adapted to the Australian constitutional context,[20] although that approach was resisted by Gageler J, who preferred a 'levels of scrutiny' approach that former Chief Justice Sir Anthony Mason had previously

---

[12] See Charter of Human Rights and Responsibilities 2006 (Vic), s 32; Human Rights Act 2004 (ACT), s 30. See also *Momcilovic v. The Queen* (2011) 245 CLR 1.
[13] (1997) 189 CLR 520.
[14] Ibid 560.
[15] See, e.g., *Lange v. Australian Broadcasting Corporation* (1997) 189 CLR 520, 567–68.
[16] As described by Aharon Barak in *Proportionality, Constitutional Rights and Their Limitations* (CUP 2012).
[17] Ibid 342.
[18] Ibid 343.
[19] (2015) 257 CLR 178.
[20] Ibid 195–96 [3]–[4] (French CJ, Kiefel, Bell and Keane JJ); see also *Brown v. Tasmania* [2017] HCA 43, [278] (Nettle J).

described as 'somewhat similar to the approach adopted by the Supreme Court of the United States'.[21]

The courts protect the implied freedom of political communication through legal interpretation as well. This involves 'reading down' laws to restrain only political communication that poses a serious public danger. This approach is apparent from two of the High Court's earlier decisions on the implied freedom of political communication, both dealing with protest actions: *Levy v. Victoria*[22] and *Coleman v. Power*.[23] Both decisions involved protests that threatened to undermine public order or safety; in *Levy*, because the protest took place on a duck hunting site, and in *Coleman*, because it involved insulting a police officer in public. Taken together, and read in light of later decisions, these cases establish the propositions that the implied freedom extends to 'any form of expressive conduct... capable of communicating a political or government message to those who witness it',[24] and that statutes that prohibit such expressive conduct will be read to do so only to the extent necessary to prohibit serious threats to public order.[25]

Those propositions were the subject of debate in a later decision, *Monis v. The Queen*,[26] where the High Court split on whether 471.12 of the Criminal Code (Cth), which prohibits the use of a postal service in a way that reasonable persons would regard as being, in all the circumstances, 'offensive', should be struck down entirely as serving a purpose incompatible with the maintenance of representative government[27] or, alternatively, read as only prohibiting seriously offensive communications.[28] Courts have also been willing, on multiple occasions, to read broad discretions as subject to the implied freedom.[29] These

---

[21] Sir Anthony Mason, *Sir Anthony Mason Honorary Lecture: Proportionality and Its Use in Australian Constitutional Law* (2015). Gordon J also resisted the approach adopted by the majority in *McCloy*, stating at (2015) 257 CLR 178, [311] that '[t]he method or structure of reasoning to which the plurality refres does not yield in this case an answer any different from that reached by the accepted modes of reasoning'.
[22] (1997) 189 CLR 579.
[23] (2004) 220 CLR 1.
[24] *Levy v. Victoria* (1997) 189 CLR 579, 623.
[25] *Coleman v. Power* (2004) 220 CLR 1, 6 [14] (Gleeson CJ), 52–57 (Gummow and Hayne JJ), 87 [226] (Kirby J).
[26] (2013) 249 CLR 92.
[27] Ibid 134 [75]–[76] (French CJ), 174 [220]–[221] (Hayne J), 178 [236] (Heydon J).
[28] Ibid 210 [333] (Crennan, Kiefel and Bell JJ).
[29] *Wotton v. Queensland* (2012) 246 CLR 1, 9 [9]–[10] (French CJ, Gummow, Hayne, Crennan and Bell JJ), citing *Miller v. TCN Channel Nine Pty Ltd* (1986) 161 CLR 556, 613–14 (Brennan J).

principles have consequences for the exercise of public disorder powers, particularly when they are used to disperse public assemblies.

The point is moot for many State public disorder laws, however, which are not targeted at political speech and so do not attract the protection of the implied freedom. For example, so-called 'anti bikie laws' permit State executive governments to prohibit biker organisations from gathering on the basis that they pose a threat of lawless behaviour. The principal instrument of the anti-bikie law is the 'control order', which prohibits members of biker gangs from gathering with each other, regardless of whether they have committed a criminal offence.

Control orders are also relevant to the Commonwealth's anti-terrorism laws. However, unlike at the Commonwealth level, where the constitutional separation of powers prohibits executive detention absent conviction,[30] the only constitutional limitation on such State powers is the State separation of powers principle expressed in *Kable* v. *Director of Public Prosecutions (NSW)*.[31] This principle is understood to hold that by permitting the vesting of federal jurisdiction in State courts, and establishing a pathway of judicial review from State Supreme Courts to the High Court in section 73, Chapter III of the Constitution 'assumes and requires ... an institutional integrity of the State court structure' and 'necessarily impl[ies] that there be in each State a body answering the constitutional description of the Supreme Court of that State'.[32]

As later decisions have shown, this principle operates as a constitutional guarantee of a State court's independence and impartiality, prohibiting the legislature or executive from directing a State court in the exercise of its functions or vesting a power in it that is incompatible with or detracts from the exercise of judicial power.[33] The *Kable* principle has been applied in a number of decisions to prevent State governments from using the courts as a 'rubber stamp' to impose control orders

---

[30] See, e.g., *Chu Kheng Lim* v. *Minister for Immigration Local Government and Ethnic Affairs* (1992) 176 CLR 1.
[31] (1996) 189 CLR 51.
[32] Ibid 127, 139 (Gummow J). See also *Kirk* v. *Industrial Court of New South Wales* (2010) 239 CLR 531; Enid Campbell and HP Lee, *The Australian Judiciary* (2nd edn, CUP 2013) 64.
[33] See, e.g., *Gypsy Jokers Motorcycle Club Inc* v. *Commissioner of Police* (2008) 234 CLR 532; *South Australia* v. *Totani* (2010) 242 CLR 1; *Wainohu* v. *New South Wales* (2011) 243 CLR 181; *Momcilovic* v. *The Queen* (2011) 245 CLR 1; *Condon* v. *Pompano* (2013) 252 CLR 38; *Attorney-General (NT)* v. *Emmerson* (2014) 253 CLR 393; *North Australian Aboriginal Justice Agency Ltd* v. *Northern Territory* (2015) 256 CLR 569.

without providing that person with a degree of process befitting an Australian court (such as holding hearings in open court, or providing an opportunity to address the reasons given for making a control order). However, these principles are more about the integrity of the separation of powers within the various branches of government as opposed to its ability to exercise such powers in the interests of public order.

This chapter will reference but not focus upon these principles. A great deal has been written elsewhere about these regimes.[34] Instead, this chapter focuses on the tools that governments use to regulate public assembly and prevent or punish unlawful assembly, and examines the way those powers change when the assembly is political in character and thus attracts the protection of the implied freedom of political communication.

4.3 Regulating Public Assembly

The phrase 'public assembly' invokes the notion of an organised public gathering for the purposes of common association, potentially of a political nature. The protest or demonstration is the most iconic image associated with the idea of an assembly. The phrase shall generally be taken to refer to gatherings in open public places that potentially impact, impede or obstruct other members of the public from movement.

4.3.1 Unlawful Assembly and Obstruction Offences

Traditionally, at common law '[a]s long as all is done peaceably and in good order, without threats or incitement to violence or obstruction to traffic, [assembly] is not prohibited'.[35] In Australia, that common law rule has been protected through the application of the principle of

---

[34] See, e.g., HP Lee and Michael Adams, 'Defining Characteristics of "Judicial Power" and "Court": Global Lessons from Australia' (2013) 21 Asia Pacific L Rev 167; Gabrielle Appleby, 'The High Court and *Kable*: A Study in Federalism and Rights Protection' (2014) 40(3) Mon LR 673; Fiona Wheeler, 'Constitutional Limits on Extra-Judicial Activity by State Judges: *Wainohu* and Conundrums of Incompatibility' (2015) 37(3) Syd L Rev 301; Rebecca Ananian-Welsh, 'Preventative Detention Orders and the Separation of Judicial Power' (2015) 38(2) UNSWLJ 756.

[35] *Hubbard* v. *Pitt* [1976] QB 142, 178 (Lord Denning M.R.), citing *Beatty* v. *Gillbanks* (1882) 9 QBD 308.

legality by courts to public order offences.[36] A public assembly becomes 'unlawful assembly' when three or more persons gather together either (i) for the purpose of committing, or preparing to commit, a crime involving the use of violence, or (ii) for any purpose, whether lawful or unlawful, in such a manner as to give firm and courageous persons in the neighbourhood reasonable grounds to fear a breach of the peace.[37]

An unlawful assembly may also involve other common law offences such as affray (violence or a threat of violence in a public place), and may become a rout (an assembly that takes steps towards becoming a riot) or riot (where a group of people collaborate to threaten or commit violence). The unifying principle underlying these offences is that they punish behaviour that raises a level of 'public alarm because they are currently or potentially dangerous'.[38]

Unlawful assembly is now also provided for in statute in almost every Australian jurisdiction,[39] except South Australia, which has abolished it entirely,[40] and New South Wales, which only uses the common law offence.[41] These statutes modify the law in various ways; some statutes elaborate on elements of the offence,[42] or the number of persons who must be involved before the acts associated with unlawful assembly attract punishment.[43]

---

[36] The principle that an intention to interfere with fundamental rights must be clearly manifested by unmistakable and unambiguous language: see *Somerset* v. *Stewart* (1772) 98 ER 499; *Potter* v. *Minahan* (1908) 7 CLR 277, 304; *Bropho* v. *Western Australia* (1990) 171 CLR 1, 18; *Coco* v. *The Queen* (1994) 179 CLR 427.

[37] *R* v. *Vincent* (1839) 173 ER 754; *R* v. *Neale* (1839) 173 ER 899; *R* v. *Graham and Burns* (1888) 16 Cox CC 420. See also *Melbourne* v. *Barry* (1922) 31 CLR 174.

[38] *R* v. *McCormack* [1981] VR 104, 108 (Young CJ, Kaye and McGarvie JJ).

[39] Public Order (Protection of Persons and Property) Act 1971 (Cth), s 6(1) (applicable in the ACT and the NT by virtue of s 4); Summary Offences Act 2005 (Qld), s 10A(1); Criminal Code Act 1924 (Tas), s 73; Unlawful Assemblies and Processions Act 1958 (Vic), s 5 (see also Crimes Act 1958 (Vic), s 320); Criminal Code Act Compilation Act 1913 (WA), s 63; Criminal Code (NT), s 63(1)–(3).

[40] Criminal Law Consolidation Act 1935 (SA), sch 11 s 1. See also Nick O'Neill, Simon Rice, Roger Douglas, *Retreat from Injustice: Human Rights Law in Australia* (Federation Press 2004) 322.

[41] O'Neill, Rice and Douglas (n 40) 320, citing *Black* v. *Corkery* (1988) 33 A Crim R 134, 138 (Young J).

[42] See, e.g., Criminal Code Act 1924 (Tas), s 73(1)(b) (requiring that persons assembled for a common purpose must have 'an intent to assist each other in resisting any person opposing the execution of the common purpose').

[43] See, e.g., Crimes Act 1900 (NSW), s 545C (providing, in the context of the crime of knowingly joining or participating in an unlawful assembly, that an unlawful assembly is 'any assembly of five or more persons whose common object is by means of intimidation

4.3 REGULATING PUBLIC ASSEMBLY

Similarly, the common law offences of riot, rout and affray have been abolished[44] or provided for in statute[45] in some jurisdictions, and almost every State has introduced replacement crimes called 'violent disorder' or 'out of control gathering', which punish people gathered together who engage in violent acts or conduct.[46]

The common law also contains a number of summary offences that have traditionally been used to preserve the public peace, and which have now also been incorporated into statute, including 'obstruction offences', such as offences concerning hindering, assaulting and obstructing the police or other public officers in the execution of their duty[47] and

---

or injury to compel any person to do what the person is not legally bound to do or to abstain from doing what the person is legally entitled to do').

[44] Crimes Act 1900 (NSW), sch 3 s 3 (abolishing common law riot, rout and affray); Criminal Law Consolidation Act 1935 (SA), sch 11 s 1 (abolishing common law riot, rout and affray); Criminal Code Act 1924 (Tas), s 6 (abolishing non-code offences); Crimes Act 1958 (Vic), s 195G.

[45] Public Order (Protection of Persons and Property) Act 1971 (Cth), ss 6, 8; Crimes Act 1900 (NSW), ss 93B (riot), 93C (affray); Criminal Code Act 1899 (Qld), sch 1 ss 61 (riot), 71 (affray); Criminal Code Act 1924 (Tas), ss 75 (riot), 80 (affray); Criminal Code Act Compilation Act 1913 (WA), ss 65 (riot), 67 (rioters causing damage); Crimes Act 1900 (ACT), s 35A (affray); Criminal Code (NT), s 63(4) (riot).

[46] Summary Offences Act 1988 (NSW), s 11A; Summary Offences Act 1953 (SA), s 6A; Criminal Code Act Compilation Act 1913 (WA), s 75A (out-of-control gathering); Summary Offences Act (NT), s 47AA. The Crimes Legislation Amendment (Public Order) Act 2017 (Vic), s 8 introduces a new Division 2C into pt I of the Crimes Act 1958 (Vic) that abolishes the common law offences of affray, rout and riot (in new s 195G) and which imposes 5 years' maximum imprisonment on a person who commits affray because he or she 'uses or threatens unlawful violence and whose conduct would cause a person of reasonable firmness present at the scene to be terrified'. The legislation also introduces a crime of 'violent disorder' into new s 195I, which 'occurs where 6 or more persons (the participants) who are present together use or threaten unlawful violence with a common goal or intention and the conduct of them, taken together, causes injury to another person or causes damage to property'. See also Summary Offences Act 2005 (Qld), s 6(2)(a)(iv) (defining as a 'public nuisance offence' violent behaviour that prevents peaceful passage in a public place).

[47] Criminal Code Act 1899 (Qld), sch 1 ss 199, 340(2AA) (defining a 'serious assault' as including a person who 'resists or wilfully obstructs' a public officer while performing a function of office); Summary Offences Act 1953 (SA), s 6; Police Offences Act 1935 (Tas), s 34B; Summary Offences Act 1966 (Vic), s 51 (relating to the assault of 'emergency workers', including police as defined under s 10AA(8) of the Sentencing Act 1991 (Vic)); Criminal Code Act Compilation Act 1913 (WA), s 172.

obstructing persons or traffic from accessing public places,[48] trespass,[49] and other 'public nuisance offences' such as the use of indecent, profane and obscene language, images or behaviour,[50] as well as vagrancy and loitering.[51] Some of these laws particularise the offences in some way, or expand their field of operation. Section 18A of the Summary Offences Act 1953 (SA), for example, not only prohibits disorderly or offensive conduct or language in a public place but also prohibits, and applies the same penalty to, 'disorderly, indecent, offensive, threatening or insulting' behaviour or 'threatening, abusive or insulting' language 'at or near a place where a public meeting is being held' or, more generally, attempts to obstruct or interfere with such meetings. The purpose of the prohibition appears to be to create a system by which persons meeting in public may enlist the police in protecting them from being disrupted by others.[52]

Prohibitions on offensive conduct, images, or language, if applied to such actions of a political nature, would seem to raise implied freedom of political communication issues – namely, the issue raised in *Coleman v. Power*, that such prohibitions are compatible with the freedom only to the extent that it is necessary to prevent retaliation and thus a public disturbance.[53] Indeed, courts, on the very few occasions that they have considered this tension, have generally downplayed the issue by using statutory interpretation to limit the prohibition's operation to conduct of

---

[48] Summary Offences Act 1988 (NSW), s 6; Criminal Code Act 1899 (Qld), sch 1 s 230; Summary Offences Act 2005 (Qld), s 6; Summary Offences Act 1953 (SA), s 58; Summary Offences Act 1966 (Vic), ss 4(e) and 5, 52(1A) (relating to besetting premises); Police Offences Act 1935 (Tas), s 13 (dealing with public annoyance generally).

[49] Summary Offences Act 2005 (Qld), s 11; Summary Offences Act 1953 (SA), ss 17A, 17AB; Police Offences Act 1935 (Tas), pt 2 div 1A; Summary Offences Act 1966 (Vic), s 9; Criminal Code Act Compilation Act 1913 (WA), s 70A; Trespass Act 1987 (NT) ss 5 and 6.

[50] Summary Offences Act 1988 (NSW), ss 4 and 4A; Summary Offences Act 2005 (Qld), s 6; Summary Offences Act 1953 (SA), s 7; Police Offences Act 1935 (Tas), s 12; Summary Offences Act 1966 (Vic), ss 17, 17A; Criminal Code Act Compilation Act 1913 (WA), s 74A.

[51] Summary Offences Act 1953 (SA), s 18 (loitering); Police Offences Act 1935 (Tas), s 7 (loitering).

[52] See, e.g., Summary Offences Act 1953 (SA), ss 18A(2) and (3) (requiring the police to remove persons disrupting or obstructing the meeting at the request of the person presiding over the meeting). See also Summary Offences Act 1966 (Vic), s 17(2).

[53] Julia Quilter, Luke McNamara, 'Time to Define the 'Cornerstone of Public Order Legislation:' The Elements of Offensive Conduct and Language under the Summary Offences Act 1988 (NSW)' (2013) 36(2) UNSWLJ 534, 540–41.

4.3 REGULATING PUBLIC ASSEMBLY

this kind. For example, in *Fraser* v. *County Court of Victoria*, Emerton J of the Supreme Court of Victoria interpreted the prohibition against showing obscene images in s 17(1)(b) of the Summary Offences Act 1966 (Vic) as prohibiting only images 'that are of the most seriously shocking type'.[54] It remains to be seen, however, how some of the broader prohibitions such as s 18A of the the Summary Offences Act 1953 (SA), which does not contain restraining concepts such as 'obscenity', fare under such scrutiny.

The Public Order (Protection of Persons and Property) Act 1971 (Cth) proscribes unlawful assembly in the Australian Capital Territory and the Northern Territory[55] as well as on certain 'Commonwealth Premises',[56] including the Parliamentary Precincts.[57] Section 6(1) of the Act provides that:

> Where persons taking part in an assembly that is in a Territory or is wholly or partly on Commonwealth premises conduct themselves, in the Territory or on the Commonwealth premises, in a way that gives rise to a reasonable apprehension that the assembly will be carried on in a manner involving unlawful physical violence to persons or unlawful damage to property, each of those persons commits an offence, punishable on conviction by a fine of not more than 20 penalty units.

An 'assembly' is defined in section 4 of the Act as 'not less than three persons ... assembled for a common purpose'. The penalties escalate to a maximum of twelve months' imprisonment where a person 'intentionally does an act of physical violence to another person, or an act that results in damage to property'.[58] A similar offence applies where the assembly takes place on 'protected premises',[59] which are premises used for diplomatic, special or consular purposes.[60] Evan Smith observes that the Public Order (Protection of Persons and Property) Act 1971 was used to suppress the infamous 'Day of Rage' and anti-apartheid protests that

---

[54] [2017] VSC 83, paras [45] and [71].
[55] Public Order (Protection of Persons and Property) Act 1971 (Cth), s 4.
[56] This being 'premises, whether in a State or in a Territory, occupied by the Commonwealth or by a public authority under the Commonwealth:' Public Order (Protection of Persons and Property) Act 1971 (Cth), s 4.
[57] Parliamentary Precincts Act 1988 (Cth), s 11.
[58] Public Order (Protection of Persons and Property) Act 1971 (Cth), s 6(2). For both of these offences, absolute liability applies to the physical element of presence in the Territory or on Commonwealth premises: Public Order (Protection of Persons and Property) Act 1971 (Cth), ss 6(1A), (3).
[59] Public Order (Protection of Persons and Property) Act 1971 (Cth), s 15(1).
[60] Public Order (Protection of Persons and Property) Act 1971 (Cth), s 4.

occurred in the early 1970s.[61] After protestors began to adapt their tactics away from confrontation, the Act began to fall into disuse.[62]

4.3.2 Permission Systems

In practice, the bulk of public assembly is largely managed through regulation; in particular, through the use of what Roger Douglas has described as 'modern permission systems' designed to map out the way a public assembly will be carried out, and which set out the consequences for a breach of the permission system's terms and conditions.[63] These regimes generally work by providing an indemnification against obstruction offences where those who wish to assemble apply to do so in conformity with the requirements of the law.

In 1999, the Victorian Parliament's Scrutiny of Acts and Regulations Committee's *Review of Redundant and Unclear Legislation* classified the various permission systems. There are three models: the 'Delegated Control Model', which confers the authority upon local councils to make by-laws that regulate public assembly;[64] the 'Notification Model', which confers some measure of immunity in respect of obstruction offences if prior notice of the assembly is given to the police;[65] and the 'Permit Model', which reverses the onus of the notification model by requiring the police to grant a permit before a measure of immunity is granted.[66] These permission systems have largely supplanted the older, common law rule as expressed in *Melbourne v. Barry* and are likely to be one of the reasons why the '[u]se of unlawful assembly laws is rare' in Australia.[67]

---

[61] Evan Smith, 'Policing Protest in the Australian Capital Territory: The Introduction and Use of the Public Order Act 1971' (2016) 40 J Australian Studies 92, 101–02.

[62] Ibid 106. Instead, the federal government began to use other strategies to prevent demonstrations from interfering with public events, such as the Public Assemblies Ordinance 1982 (ACT) passed by the Fraser government to stop the 'Women against Rape' protestors from interrupting an Anzac Day parade.

[63] Roger Douglas, *Dealing with Demonstrations: The Law of Public Protest and Its Enforcement* (Federation Press 2004) 62.

[64] Scrutiny of Acts and Regulations Committee, *Report on the Review of the Unlawful Assemblies and Processions Act 1958* (1999) 36.

[65] Ibid 38.

[66] Ibid 36.

[67] Douglas (n 63) 55. Indeed, one Member of the Victorian Legislative Council, in 2012, observed of the Victorian law proscribing unlawful assembly that he 'did not even know we had such a thing as the Unlawful Assemblies and Processions Act 1958'. Vic Parl Debs, LC, 7 June 2012, 2944.

4.3.2.1 Notification Models

Queensland's notification model as set out in the Peaceful Assembly Act 1992 (Qld), described elsewhere as the most 'liberal' system,[68] guarantees persons the right to assemble peacefully with others in public.[69] Indemnity from civil or criminal liability is extended to those who cause obstruction in a public place where they are part of an 'authorised public assembly' where notice is given in the prescribed form with the prescribed particulars,[70] as long as it is 'peaceful' and held in accordance with the particulars and conditions in respect of notice given under ss 7–10 of the Act.[71]

To prohibit the assembly, the Commissioner or local authority must apply to the Magistrates Court outside of five business days before the date of the assembly for an order to refuse the holding of a public assembly or apply specific conditions to that assembly.[72] Before making such an application, the Commissioner or local authority must have regard to the objects of the Act and consider, on reasonable grounds, the assembly's potential impact on public safety, public disorder and the rights and freedoms of others.[73] Furthermore, they cannot apply unless they have consulted and participated in a mediation process with those affected.[74]

By contrast, there is an absence of criteria involved in decision making under the notification model set out in Part 4 of the Summary Offences Act 1988 (NSW). To hold an 'authorised public assembly' in New South Wales, it is necessary to obtain permission in the form set out in section 23.[75] Section 23(1)(e) also requires a person to take responsibility for the assembly, and provide the police with their address so that a process may be served on them for the purposes of the Part. If all of these conditions are met, the assembly may proceed if the Commissioner does not object[76]

---

[68] Douglas (n 63) 62.
[69] Peaceful Assembly Act 1992 (Qld), s 5(1).
[70] The particulars are set out in Peaceful Assembly Act 1992 (Qld), s 9.
[71] Peaceful Assembly Act 1992 (Qld), s 6(1).
[72] Peaceful Assembly Act 1992 (Qld), s 12.
[73] Peaceful Assembly Act 1992 (Qld), s 13(1)(a), (b)(i)–(iii).
[74] Peaceful Assembly Act 1992 (Qld), s 13(1)(c), (d).
[75] Section 23 provides that an 'authorised public assembly' is one in which notice has been given to the Commissioner of Police setting out the date upon which the assembly is proposed to be held; its time and place; its purpose; 'such other particulars as may be prescribed'; and the number of persons expected to participate in the assembly. See generally Summary Offences Act 1988 (NSW), s 23(1)(a)–(d).
[76] Summary Offences Act 1988 (NSW), s 23(1)(f).

and it is not 'prohibited' by a court under section 25, which provides the Commissioner with a means of applying to the Court for the assembly to be prohibited after conferring with the protest organiser. If the application was made less than seven days from the date of the assembly, the organiser must also seek an order from the court authorising the assembly in addition to the Commissioner's permission. Once a public assembly is authorised, by virtue of section 24 'a person is not, by reason of any thing done or omitted to be done by the person for the purpose only of participating in that public assembly, guilty of any offence relating to participating in an unlawful assembly or the obstruction of any person, vehicle or vessel in a public place'.

These notification systems are generally designed to strike a balance between the right to assembly, particularly politically motivated assembly, on the one hand, and the right to enjoy public space, on the other.[77]

The Australian Capital Territory sets out explicit guidelines for those who wish to conduct a protest.[78] Those guidelines state that no official approval is required to protest, unless it involves the erection of structures. The most important exception to this rule is when the protest is to take place within the Parliamentary Precincts,[79] in which case permission must be sought from the President of the Senate and the Speaker of the House of Representatives in their capacity as Presiding Officers under the Parliamentary Precincts Act 1988 (Cth).[80]

In South Australia, the Public Assemblies Act 1972 (SA) allows an assembly to take place when the organiser serves notice with the prescribed details on the Chief Secretary, the Commissioner of Police or the clerk of the local council in which the assembly is to be held.[81]

---

[77] For example, in Queensland, the right to assemble peacefully is subject to restrictions 'necessary and reasonable in a democratic society' to achieve public safety, public order or the protection of others' rights and freedoms: Peaceful Assembly Act 1992 (Qld), sub-ss 5(2)(a)–(c), (4). See also *Commissioner of Police v. Rintoul* [2003] NSWSC 662, [5].

[78] National Capital Authority, *The Right to Protest Guidelines* (2008).

[79] These essentially being the areas inside the 'retaining wall' a 'wall of varying height that partly surrounds the perimeter of the site of Parliament House and is near the inner kerb of Capital Circle': Parliamentary Precincts Act 1988 (Cth), s 4(2), (3). It also includes 'property that is owned or held under lease by the Commonwealth and is not within the Parliamentary precincts defined by section 4:' Parliamentary Precincts Act 1988 (Cth), s 5(1), as well as property certified by the Presiding Officers to be 'required for purposes of the Parliament' as declared by the regulation: Parliamentary Precincts Act 1988 (Cth), s 5(2).

[80] National Capital Authority, *The Right to Protest Guidelines* (2008), 3. See also Parliamentary Precincts Act 1988 (Cth), s 6.

[81] Public Assemblies Act 1972 (SA), s 4(4)(a)(c).

The recipient of the notice may raise an objection to the assembly on the grounds that it may 'unduly prejudice any public interest', which must be served on the person who gave notice at least two days before the date of the assembly.[82] A participant in the assembly then gains the right to apply to a judge for a determination, and the judge may quash the objection or approve an alternative proposal.[83] Once notice is served, or a judge approves a proposal to assemble, the proposed assembly becomes known as an 'approved proposal'.[84] Like other systems, an indemnity is gained in respect of actions undertaken pursuant to an approved proposal, 'notwithstanding the provisions of any other Act or law regulating the movement of traffic or pedestrians, or relating to the use or obstruction of a public place'.[85]

4.3.2.2 Permit Models

The permit models in place in Western Australia and Tasmania are notionally more restrictive than notification models, because indemnification is conditional both upon a permit being issued by the relevant authority and compliance with the specific terms of a given permit. For example, section 4(1) of the Public Order in Streets Act 1984 (WA) indemnifies any person participating in a 'public meeting'[86] or a 'procession'[87] who abides by the conditions set out in a permit issued under the Act. Should a person wish to obtain a permit, they must provide notice to the Commissioner of Police more than four days from the date of the proposed assembly.[88]

---

[82] Public Assemblies Act 1972 (SA), s 4(6).
[83] Public Assemblies Act 1972 (SA), s 5(1), (2).
[84] Public Assemblies Act 1972 (SA), s 3.
[85] Public Assemblies Act 1972 (SA), s 6(2).
[86] Defined by s 4(3)(a) of the Public Order in Streets Act 1984 (WA) as an assembly that '(i)... comprises 3 or more persons; (ii)... is held for the purpose of communicating or expressing any view to, or of ascertaining the view of, the public or any section of the public (whether or not an organization or body of persons having requirements for membership), or of demonstrating, as to any matter; and (iii) [where] members of the public in general are invited, induced or permitted to attend'.
[87] Defined by s 4(4) of the Public Order in Streets Act 1984 (WA) as an assembly that '(a)... comprises 3 or more persons'; who are '(b)... assembled with the intent of moving, or move, from the place of assembly by means of any street as, or substantially as, a body of persons in orderly succession proceeding by a common route'.
[88] Public Order in Streets Act 1984 (WA), s 5(3)(a).

Once notice is received, the Commissioner or an 'authorised officer'[89] must expeditiously review[90] the notice and decide whether to grant a permit under section 7 of the Act. The decision-maker may grant the permit, grant the permit subject to conditions, or refuse it.[91] They may refuse the permit if they decide on reasonable grounds that the public meeting or procession would cause 'serious public disorder' or cause 'damage to public or private property';[92] cause public nuisance;[93] obstruct the street in a way that is 'too great or too prolonged in the circumstances';[94] or jeopardise the safety of any person.[95]

Even once a permit is granted, the indemnity does not apply where 'it is proved that the act was done, or ordered or authorised to be done, maliciously and without reasonable and probable cause'.[96] The Commissioner of Police may give instructions for the regulation of an authorised public meeting or procession, including the regulation of traffic and the maintenance of 'order in streets'. However, an instruction may not be given with the purpose of 'frustrating' that public meeting or procession.[97] Police officers may give 'reasonable directions' pursuant to the Commissioner's instructions, and it is an offence to knowingly not comply with those directions.[98] If a person 'acts in a disorderly manner for the purpose of preventing the transaction of the business for which the meeting or procession assembled', obstructs the passage of emergency vehicles, or impedes pedestrians on the street in a way that falls outside of the terms of the permit or incites others to do these things, then he or she has committed an offence.[99]

Part 2 div IIIAA of the Police Offences Act 1935 (Tas) deals with 'activities on public streets'. Section 49AB(1)(a) prohibits the organisation of a 'demonstration' – defined by section 49AA as a 'march, rally or

---

[89] This being a police officer conferred with responsibility pursuant to the Public Order in Streets Act 1984 (WA), s 6.
[90] Public Order in Streets Act 1984 (WA), s 5(4).
[91] Public Order in Streets Act 1984 (WA), s 7(1)(a)(i) & (ii), (b).
[92] Public Order in Streets Act 1984 (WA), s 7(2)(a).
[93] Public Order in Streets Act 1984 (WA), s 7(2)(b).
[94] Public Order in Streets Act 1984 (WA), s 7(2)(c).
[95] Public Order in Streets Act 1984 (WA), s 7(2)(d).
[96] Public Order in Streets Act 1984 (WA), s 10.
[97] Public Order in Streets Act 1984 (WA), s 9(1), (2).
[98] Public Order in Streets Act 1984 (WA), s 9(3), (4).
[99] Public Order in Streets Act 1984 (WA), s 9.

other kind of political demonstration' – on a public street[100] without a permit issued by a 'senior police officer'.[101] The matters to be taken into account when deciding whether to issue the permit are public safety and convenience, and the arrangements made to protect the safety and convenience of assembly participants,[102] as well as 'such other considerations as appear relevant having regard to the time and nature of the proposed activity and its location or, if applicable, its route'.[103] The senior police officer may apply any conditions he or she deems 'necessary or expedient for the safety and convenience of participants and the public'.[104] It is an offence punishable by a fine of 10 penalty units for the holder of the permit not to comply with its conditions or fail to immediately produce it upon the demand of a police officer.[105]

4.3.2.3 Delegated Control Models

In practice, every State government allows local governments to exercise a form of 'delegated control' over public assembly by exercising their powers to ensure public safety and convenience in the areas they administer.[106] Some jurisdictions, however, rely almost entirely on the discretion of local governments to regulate public assembly.

The Victorian permission system builds upon the relatively broad powers conferred upon local governments by the Local Government Act 1989 (Vic). Council functions include 'any other function relating to the peace, order and good government of the municipal district'.[107] Under section 111(1), 'A Council may make local laws for or with respect to any act, matter or thing in respect of which the Council has a function

---

[100] A 'public street' being defined in s 3 of the Traffic Act 1925 (Tas) as 'any street, road, lane, thoroughfare, footpath, bridge, or place open to or used by the public, or to which the public have or are permitted to have access, whether on payment of a fee or otherwise'. See also Police Offences Act 1935 (Tas), s 3.
[101] Police Offences Act 1935 (Tas), s 49AB(2). A 'senior police officer' is the Commissioner of Police, the Deputy Commissioner or an Assistant Commissioner, or a police officer of or above the rank of inspector: Police Offences Act 1935 (Tas), s 3.
[102] Police Offences Act 1935 (Tas), s 49AB(4)(a), (b).
[103] Police Offences Act 1935 (Tas), s 49AB(4)(c).
[104] Police Offences Act 1935 (Tas), s 49AB(5)(b).
[105] Police Offences Act 1935 (Tas), s 49AB(8)(a), (b).
[106] The full list of local government powers in this regard may be found in Bligh Grant, Joseph Drew, *Local Government in Australia: History, Theory and Public Policy* (Springer 2017) 191.
[107] See generally Local Government Act 1989 (Vic), s 3E(1)(a)–(h).

or power under this or any other Act'. From 2017, Victorian councils will have to consult with the police before authorising a protest.[108]

The Northern Territory's system is similar to Victoria's. The Alice Springs (Management of Public Places) By-Laws 2009, made under the Local Government Act 2008 (NT), provide that 'a permit may be granted by council to a person on the application of that person for an activity in a public place that would otherwise be unlawful under these By-laws'.[109] Section 33 makes it an offence to '[o]rganise or lead a demonstration or protest in a public place without a permit'.

4.3.3 Protest and the Implied Freedom of Political Communication

The permission systems described in Section 4.3.2 are important in that they require both protestors and the police to engage in a kind of balancing exercise; a balance between the right to engage in political communication and the public safety concerns associated with that communication.

The decision of *NSW Commissioner of Police* v. *Folkes* is instructive in that it shows how assemblies that are threats to public order but involve political speech are dealt with through negotiation and engagement. It involved a notice submitted by the chairman of the 'Party for Freedom', Mr Folkes, who wished to hold a public assembly at Cronulla Beach in commemoration of the 10-year anniversary of the Cronulla Riots. The Commissioner applied to the Supreme Court under section 25 of the Summary Offences Act, on the basis that the assembly posed a 'substantial risk' of inciting violence between the supporters of the Party for Freedom's anti-Muslim immigration views and their opponents.[110]

In applying section 25, Adamson J gave close attention to the series of notices that had been supplied to the police by Mr. Folkes. The Second Notice, provided after further details were requested by the police, indicated that a hearse with a coffin would be used in the protest, and that a number of guest speakers would attend. After a number of community representatives expressed their concerns, the Superintendent requested that the rally be held elsewhere, suggesting the place of Captain

---

[108] Crimes Legislation Amendment (Public Order) Act 2017 (Vic).
[109] In s 8(1).
[110] [2015] NSWSC 1887, [2].

4.3 REGULATING PUBLIC ASSEMBLY

Cook's landing in Australia, or a local hall using a Q&A format where the Party for Freedom's 'views could be tested'.[111]

Subsequently, a third notice was submitted by Mr. Folkes, which claimed the assembly would 'celebrate [the] democratic right to assembly, and the valued right to dissent by commemorating the tenth anniversary of Cronulla victims who stood up and fought back against the criminal anti-social wave to highlight the media bias against Cronulla and double standards prejudice'.[112] The organisers again met with the police to discuss who was attending and their political allegiances. The police criticised the slogans on the clothing produced by the Party for Freedom, saying it suggested they condoned violence.[113]

Eventually, the police issued a notice to Mr. Folkes per section 25(2)(a) of the Act, requesting a formal conference and in effect initiating the procedure by which the police could apply for a prohibition under section 25(1). At this formal conference, the superintendent expressed concern that Mr Folkes had no experience of managing the relatively large numbers of people – around 400 – who were expected to attend the protest. The Party for Freedom also began to advertise the assembly, inviting the Socialist Alliance (which had deeply opposing views) to attend and celebrating the assembly as an opportunity to engage with Cronulla residents who had been affected by 'the devastating and brutal cover-up perpetrated by the state and federal governments' regarding so-called 'Islamic gangs'.[114]

Before the hearing for the superintendent's section 25 application, a deposition was given by a chief inspector of police expressing his views that those in attendance would ignore police directions and commit offences, as well as actively attempt to undermine the police's arrest of individuals in attendance. Because a counter-rally was expected, the police would be placed in between the rallies, which could 'degenerate into serious public disorder'. To prevent this, the police would need to divert significant resources from their ordinary policing duties. The chief inspector concluded that '[t]he risk of conflict, injuries, property damage and significant public disorder is HIGH and cannot

---

[111] Ibid [18]–[21].
[112] Ibid [25].
[113] Ibid [32].
[114] Ibid [40].

be mitigated due to the geography, topography and demographics of the proposed assembly'.[115]

As Adamson J had suggested earlier in her judgment, the question before her was not whether the rally could go ahead. It was whether those assembled were entitled to protection under section 24. Adamson J noted that the Party for Freedom's literature was 'provocative, if not inflammatory' and that their invitation to the Socialist Alliance was 'nothing short of a challenge'.[116] Even if the two groups did not come to violence, it was 'fanciful' to suggest that others associated with their views would 'resolve their differences by discussion and debate'.[117] In granting the prohibition, Adamson J ensured that 'the police have available to them all relevant powers and are not inhibited in exercising those powers'.[118] Accordingly, it was not to the point, as Folkes had submitted, that the assembly would proceed regardless of whether it was prohibited.

Decisions to permit or disallow a protest must also be exercised compatibly with the implied freedom. Many of the modern cases dealing with political communication tend to focus on the exercise of delegated control by local councils, which pose a particular problem in this respect because they are so broad and it can be difficult to tell whether the discretion is appropriately balancing the public safety objective against the implied freedom. In *Attorney-General (SA) v. Corporation of the City of Adelaide*, the High Court upheld an Adelaide City Council by-law prohibiting persons from preaching, canvassing, haranguing, touting for business or conducting surveys or polls, or from handing out printer literature, on any road without permission, on the basis that it was an appropriate and adapted use of the Council's power to make by-laws for 'convenience, comfort and safety'.[119] In so deciding the High Court, following its previous decision in *Wotton v. Queensland*,[120] considered the Adelaide City Council's discretion to be 'circumscribed by the purposes of the by-law'.[121]

This feature of *Adelaide Corporation* points to the importance of the statutory or regulatory permission systems that burden political speech. In particular, those systems should ensure such decisions are made only

---

[115] Ibid [51].
[116] Ibid [56].
[117] Ibid.
[118] Ibid [57].
[119] (2013) 249 CLR 1.
[120] (2012) 246 CLR 1.
[121] *Adelaide Corporation* (2013) 249 CLR 1, 87 [213] (Crennan and Kiefel JJ).

when they are rationally connected to, and necessary to achieve, public safety. That is not to say, however, that a statutory or regulatory regime must closely guide the decision-maker in this regard. That idea is demonstrated in the '*Occupy* cases',[122] in which the Federal Court accepted that local councils could use a broad discretion to order Occupy tent installations to be removed from public gardens because it was not practicable to confine the discretion, given the range of potential threats to public amenity,[123] and the use of that discretion was necessary to prevent the specific harm to public safety and amenity the camping, if permitted, would cause.[124]

4.4 Anti-Assembly Powers

A number of jurisdictions have experimented with powers aimed at preventing public assembly altogether in certain circumstances. Here, they are described as 'anti-assembly powers', because they are preemptive: they are directed at attacking the characteristics or qualities of particular assemblies that endanger public order before the threat emerges.

4.4.1 Move-On Powers

One controversial development in the law of public order, relating to the powers of the police to disperse such assemblies, is the advent of 'move-on powers'. In short, move-on powers grant the police the discretion to order people to disperse even if their behaviour falls short of unlawful assembly as defined under the common law, because their presence is causing anxiety or concern.[125] These powers are inspired by the common law power authorising the police to take all reasonable steps necessary to prevent the breach of the peace. Move-on powers are sometimes justified

---

[122] *Muldoon* v. *Melbourne City Council* (2013) 217 FCR 450, appealed in *Kerrison* v. *Melbourne City Council* (2014) 228 FCR 87; *O'Flaherty* v. *City of Sydney City Council* (2013) 210 FCR 484; the appeal is reported at (2014) 221 FCR 382.
[123] *Muldoon* v. *Melbourne City Council* (2013) 217 FCR 450, 533 [411].
[124] *Kerrison* v. *Melbourne City Council* (2014) 228 FCR 87, 140 [235]-[236]; *O'Flaherty* v. *City of Sydney City Council* (2013) 210 FCR 484, 499-500 [71]-[77].
[125] Tamara Walsh and Monica Taylor, '"You're Not Welcome Here:" Police Move-On Powers and Discrimination Law', (2007) 30(1) UNSWLJ 151, 157-58.

as important contributors to public safety.[126] However, the reason why move-on powers are controversial is precisely because they go beyond the common law and extend even further into people's entitlement to assemble in public.[127]

Versions of these powers have been enacted in all States and Territories.[128] As discussed in this section, there are differences between these laws, but their exercise tends to be predicated on the police officer's apprehension or suspicion that a person or persons in a public place is breaching or is likely to breach the peace, endanger the safety of others, or, perhaps most controversially, to cause anxiety to others.

The powers are balanced differently. Generally speaking, the Australian Capital Territory is the most restrictive, allowing move-on powers to be used against violent behaviour; South Australia and Western Australia allow move-on powers to be used based on an offence or where a person has been threatened; and New South Wales, Queensland and the Northern Territory allow move-on directions to be given to a person causing 'anxiety' or interfering with others' enjoyment of a public space.[129] Victoria's law is similar to those of South Australia and Western Australia in that it is designed to prevent a breach of the peace or the endangerment of public safety.[130]

Move-on powers may only be exercised once the police officer forms a 'reasonable suspicion' that the person poses the requisite threat to the peace, an assessment that must be 'based on facts which would create a reasonable suspicion in the mind of a reasonable person'.[131] Some States and Territories simply state that move-on directions must or may require

---

[126] Dan Rogers, 'Crime and Misconduct Commission: Review of Police Move-On Powers' (2011) 31 QLD Lawyer 31, 32–33.

[127] Simon Bronitt, 'The New Public Disorder Laws: The Rise of Move-On Powers' (2011) LegalDate, 5–6.

[128] Law Enforcement (Powers and Responsibilities) Act 2002 (NSW), pt 14; Police Powers and Responsibilities Act 2000 (Qld), Ch 2 pt 5; Summary Offences Act 1953 (SA), s 18; Police Offences Act 1935 (Tas), s 15B; Summary Offences Act 1966 (Vic), pt 1 div 1A; Criminal Investigation Act 2006 (WA), s 27; Crimes Act 1900 (ACT), pt 9; Summary Offences Act (NT) s 47A.

[129] Ibid.

[130] Summary Offences Act 1966 (Vic), s 6(1).

[131] *Rowe v. Kemper* [2008] QCA 175, [6] (McMurdo P), citing *Tucs v. Manley* (1985) 62 ALR 460. It may also mean, per s 4 of the Criminal Investigation Act 2006 (WA), that a person 'personally has grounds at the time for suspecting the thing and those grounds (even if they are subsequently found to be false or non-existent), when judged objectively, are reasonable'.

the person to leave for a period of time,[132] but New South Wales and Queensland allow any move-on direction to be given as long as it is reasonable,[133] meaning that the exact direction given must be 'judged in light of the reasonable suspicion that is held'.[134]

A comparison of some of these move-on powers reveals the different degrees to which they allow police officers to interfere with public assembly. Section 48(1) of the Police Powers and Responsibilities Act 2000 (Qld) authorises a police officer to 'give to a person or group of persons doing a relevant act any direction that is reasonable in the circumstances'. Section 46(1) further provides that a police officer may give the direction if he or she reasonably suspects the person's behaviour has been:

(a) causing anxiety to a person entering, at or leaving the place, reasonably arising in all the circumstances; or
(b) interfering with trade or business at the place by unnecessarily obstructing, hindering or impeding someone entering, at or leaving the place; or
(c) disorderly, indecent, offensive, or threatening to someone entering, at or leaving the place; or
(d) disrupting the peaceable and orderly conduct of any event, entertainment or gathering at the place.[135]

In 2010, the Queensland Crime and Misconduct Commission (CMC) undertook a substantial review of Queensland's move-on law. In its review, the CMC recognised that move-on powers required a 'delicate balancing exercise that police must undertake in maintaining public order and safety, while respecting the rights of all people to use and access public space'.[136] The CMC noted that move-on powers are not designed to enable police to impose a 'biased or subjective conception of

---

[132] Police Offences Act 1935 (Tas), s 15B(1); Summary Offences Act 1966 (Vic), s 6(4); Criminal Investigation Act 2006 (WA), s 27(2)(b); Crimes Act 1900 (ACT), s 175(3)(b).
[133] Law Enforcement (Powers and Responsibilities) Act 2002 (NSW), s 197(2); Police Powers and Responsibilities Act 2000 (Qld), s 48(1).
[134] *Rowe v. Kemper* [2008] QCA 175, [91] (McMurdo P).
[135] Similarly, s 47(1) of the Police Powers and Responsibilities Act 2000 (Qld) provides that a move-on direction may be given where a person's 'presence' causes (a) anxiety, (b) interferes with trade or business or (c) disrupts the peaceable or orderly conduct of an event, entertainment or gathering.
[136] Queensland Crime and Misconduct Commission, *Police Move-on Powers: A CMC Review of Their Use* (2010) v.

socially acceptable behaviour that may marginalise, and even criminalise, disadvantaged individuals who exhibit challenging characteristics or behaviours that otherwise do not cause harm, much less pose a threat to social order or community safety'.[137] Rather, the purpose of move-on powers was to deal with behaviour that might 'actually compromise public order' by de-escalating the situation.[138]

The 'anxiety' ground in sections 46(1)(a) and 47(1)(a) of the Act was noted by the CMC to give the police 'a high level of discretionary power' to determine 'the impact of the behaviour or presence on another person's psychological state'.[139] Accordingly, the CMC recommended the repeal of the anxiety ground as it applies to presence and, insofar as the ground relates to behaviour, be amended to require the behaviour cause fear to a reasonable person and that the police receive a complaint about the person's behaviour before they exercise the move-on direction.[140] In rejecting the recommendation, the Queensland Government stressed that it was 'important that all persons in the community feel safe and that public order is able to be maintained in circumstances where the presence and the mannerism or conduct of a person cause another member of the community anxiety'.[141]

The CMC also focused upon the level of belief a police officer had to have about a person's actions before they could order a person to move on from a public area. The CMC recommended that the requirement that a police officer form a 'reasonable suspicion' before giving a move-on direction be heightened to a 'reasonable belief' standard.[142] This was rejected by the Queensland Government, which argued that the heightened standard would prevent police from acting to de-escalate a person's behaviour before it became necessary to arrest that person.[143] Although the CMC considered police discretion a vital aspect of such powers, it recognised that police might exercise that discretion in light of their subjective, pre-existing views about particular groups of people.[144] Indeed, the empirical evidence has tended to show that these move-on

---

[137] Ibid 8.
[138] Ibid.
[139] Ibid 36.
[140] Ibid 39.
[141] Queensland Government, *Response to the CMC Report* (2011) 2.
[142] Queensland Crime and Misconduct Commission, *Police Move-on Powers: A CMC Review of Their Use* (December 2010) 39–40.
[143] Queensland Government, *Response to the CMC Report* (2011) 3.
[144] Ibid 12.

powers are used disproportionately against vulnerable sections of the population, such as Aboriginal Australians.[145]

The Queensland law may be contrasted with the move-on powers set out in part 1 div 1A of the Summary Offences Act 1966 (Vic). Section 6(1) provides that a police officer, or an on-duty protective services officer, may give a direction to leave a public place if they suspect on reasonable grounds that:

(a) the person is or persons are breaching, or likely to breach, the peace; or
(b) the person is or persons are endangering, or likely to endanger, the safety of any other person; or
(c) the behaviour of the person or persons is likely to cause injury to a person or damage to property or is otherwise a risk to public safety.

The bases upon which a person might be directed to move on are tied closely to the concept of breach of the peace at common law, or otherwise to grounds of public safety (as opposed to 'anxiety'). The person may be prohibited from returning to the public place for 24 hours,[146] and those given a direction must not, 'without reasonable excuse', contravene a move-on direction they have been given.[147]

Some States and Territories have sought to offset the potentially detrimental effect that move-on powers could have upon political communication, either by prohibiting their use against apparently legitimate protests entirely,[148] permitting the use of move-on powers against protests only to ensure the public safety,[149] and/or tying the use of move-on powers to violations of the permission systems discussed in Section 4.3.2.[150] For instance, by virtue of the Police Powers and Responsibilities Act 2000 (Qld), a direction does not apply to an 'authorised public

---

[145] See, e.g., Paul Spooner, 'Moving in the Wrong Direction: An Analysis of Police Move-On Powers in Queensland' (2001) 20(1) Youth St Aus 27; Tamara Walsh and Monica Taylor, '"You're not Welcome Here:" Police Move-On Powers and Discrimination Law' (2007) 30(1) UNSWLJ 151, 152; Dan Rogers, 'Crime and Misconduct Commission: Review of Police Move-On Powers' (2011) 31 QLD Lawyer 31.
[146] Summary Offences Act 1966 (Vic), s 6(3).
[147] Summary Offences Act 1966 (Vic), s 6(4).
[148] Summary Offences Act 1966 (Vic), s 6(5); Crimes Act 1900 (ACT), s 175(2).
[149] Law Enforcement (Powers and Responsibilities) Act 2002 (NSW), s 200(3);
[150] See Law Enforcement (Powers and Responsibilities) Act 2002 (NSW), s 200(4); Police Powers and Responsibilities Act 2000 (Qld), s 45. The Criminal Investigation Act 2006 (WA), s 27(3) requires the police officer giving the order to 'take into account the likely effect of the order on the person'.

assembly' under the Peaceful Assembly Act 1992 (Qld).[151] Moreover, section 48(2) provides that the officer may not give a move-on direction 'that interferes with a person's right of peaceful assembly unless it is reasonably necessary in the interests of (a) public safety; or (b) public order; or (c) the protection of the rights and freedoms of other persons'. Section 48(2) lists examples of the kinds of rights and freedoms that might justify the making of a move-on direction, these including the right of the public to enjoy a place, and the right of persons to conduct lawful business in or 'in association with' the place.

The Law Enforcement (Powers and Responsibilities) Act 2002 (NSW) also prohibits police from issuing a move-on direction in respect of 'an apparently genuine demonstration or protest', a 'procession' or 'organised assembly', except where the police officer forms a belief on reasonable grounds 'that the direction is necessary to deal with a serious risk to the safety of the person to whom the direction is given or to any other person' or where the public assembly has not been authorised under the Summary Offences Act 1988 (NSW) or is being conducted outside of the terms of that authorisation.[152]

The Summary Offences Act 1966 (Vic), by contrast, imposes absolute constraints on issuing move-on directions to political protesters – it does not permit the police officer to engage in *ad hoc* balancing against competing rights and interests. Move-on directions may not be given to persons involved in industrial picketing of their place of employment, or who are 'demonstrating or protesting about a particular issue', or who are 'speaking, bearing or otherwise identifying with a banner, placard or sign or otherwise behaving in a way that is apparently intended to publicise the person's view about a particular issue'.[153]

In 2014, the Napthine Liberal Government of Victoria had introduced a suite of powers enabling the police to use move-on powers during protests and industrial action.[154] With the election of the Andrews Labor Government in 2015, these amendments were repealed and the present restraints were introduced into the Summary Offences Act 1966 (Vic) by the Summary Offences Amendment (Move-on Laws) Act 2015 (Vic). Minister Paukla explained in his second reading speech that the Government opposed the use of these laws on lawful protest and that part 1 div

---

[151] Police Powers and Responsibilities Act 2000 (Qld), s 45.
[152] See Law Enforcement (Powers and Responsibilities) Act 2002 (NSW), s 200(3), (4).
[153] Summary Offences Act 1966 (Vic), s 6(5).
[154] Summary Offences and Sentencing Amendment Act 2014 (Vic).

4.4 ANTI-ASSEMBLY POWERS

1A as it stands was a 'more appropriate balance between the use of move-on powers to maintain public order and the protection of the fundamental right of all Victorians to move freely, express their views and associate with whomever they choose'.[155]

There are three observations that may be made about these laws. First, it is important to recognise that the police already have a system with which to determine whether a protest or other assembly needs to be dispersed in the interests of public order. These are the public order and unlawful assembly offences, and the various permission systems, described in Section 4.3 of this chapter. An additional layer of dispersal powers is unhelpful because protestors should be able to understand the point at which their assembly will transition into unlawfulness. This is important not only for protestors who wish to avoid breaking the law, but also for protestors who wish to commit civil disobedience to make their point.

Second, for that reason, move-on powers should not be used against protests. Where a lawful protest is to be broken up, it should be done according to prescribed criteria or thresholds set out by law that can be comprehended by the protestors before they commence their unlawful actions, and not based on an inherently opaque and subjective police discretion. This is necessary not merely because of the inherent importance of political protest in a democratic society, but because the implied freedom of political communication attaches itself to structured discretions that transparently serve the achievement of public order. To this end, Victoria's current absolute restraints are preferable to the balancing exercise contemplated in the Queensland legislation. Without doubting the capacity of the police to make *ad hoc* assessments about competing rights and interests, it is very difficult to assess whether the correct balance has been struck in a particular case. In any case, these assessments will tend to take place after the fact, in the course of some general review of their use, and by that time the damage has been done to those protests subjected to the move-on powers. In any case, absolute rules, in very difficult situations, are easier to apply and provide a clear standard against which the use of these directions by the police may be assessed.

Third, and building upon the previous point, absolute prohibitions of the kind contained in the Victorian law more fully preserve the 'right' to assembly. The absolute prohibition prevents the use of move-on powers

---

[155] Vic Parl Debs, LA, 11 February 2015, 174.

in respect of any apparently legitimate demonstration, whereas Queensland's framework only prohibits outright the use of these powers against 'authorised assemblies' as provided for by the Peaceful Assemblies Act 1992 (Qld). This means that the Victorian police cannot disperse protests using move-on powers. Although it is important to indemnify participants in peaceful assembly against certain criminal laws, it is equally important to recognise that un-indemnified, but peaceful, protests should not be disbanded simply because they cause another person anxiety.

4.4.2 Anti-Protest Laws

Move-on powers tend to contain explicit or implicit mechanisms to avoid breaking up political assemblies. A more direct challenge to political communication has arrived in the form of laws that prohibit or severely restrain protest in particular areas used for particular purposes. They are sometimes described, pejoratively, as 'anti-protest laws'.[156]

Anti-protest laws are used for a variety of purposes, to protect interests that the government considers to be vital or particularly vulnerable to protest and demonstration. Increasingly, these interests include corporate interests or important industries that have attracted the ire of the environmental movement. Many of these laws outright prohibit protest activity in designated spaces. Generally speaking, they are designed to prevent what is sometimes described as direct action – a protest strategy that is designed to interrupt or prevent the activity that is being protested against. Direct action has been famously used by environmental protestors in the Tasmanian forests to prevent logging activities from taking place. Protestors would lock themselves to machinery to prevent their use, and build blockades to prevent loggers from entering logging coupes. Direct action tactics have also been used by environmental protestors in New South Wales, to prevent coal-seam gas extraction.

One *ad hoc* application of these anti-protest laws can be seen in Queensland's securing of the G20 summit using the G20 (Safety and Security) Act 2013 (Qld). As enacted, the Act created 'security areas', 'restricted areas' and 'motorcade areas' to which particular rights and prohibitions attached.[157] The Act provided for lawful assemblies in

---

[156] See, e.g., Hugh de Kretser, 'NSW Anti-Protest Laws are Part of a Corrosive National Trend' *Sydney Morning Herald* (22 March 2016). See also Emily Howie, 'Anti-Protest Legislation and the Chilling of Free Speech' (2016) 136 Precedent 26.

[157] G20 (Safety and Security) Act 2013 (Qld), pt 2 div 1.

4.4 ANTI-ASSEMBLY POWERS

'declared areas', but prohibited the disruption of the G20[158] and provided that the Peaceful Assembly Act 1992 (Qld) did not apply in security areas.[159] Special requirements were imposed requiring organisers of proposed assemblies to give 48 hours' notice.[160]

Special powers were conferred allowing police officers and other appointed persons to, inter alia, conduct search and seizure, give directions preventing entry or removing persons from security areas, and to give general directions for the safety and security of the G20 meeting.[161] Of particular note was the power for the Commissioner of Police to place persons on a list and thereby prohibit them entry to security areas, if he or she was satisfied that the person would pose a 'serious threat to the safety or security of persons or property in a security area'; '... cause injury to persons or damage to property outside a security area' due to their opposition to the G20; or 'may disrupt any part of the G20 meeting'.[162]

Anti-protest laws have been described as 'shaking the core' of the Australian legal system.[163] Several UN Special Rapporteurs have described one proposed anti-protest law, the Criminal Code Amendment (Prevention of Lawful Activity) Bill 2015 (WA), as being 'against Australia's international obligations under international human rights law', as having 'the chilling effect of silencing dissenters' and as 'disproportionately criminali[sing] legitimate protest actions'.[164] Because these laws tend to impose outright prohibitions on protest in a particular area, and apply severe penalties to breaches of the prohibitions they impose, their constitutionality is open to serious question.

Recently, the High Court of Australia struck down one such law as applied to forestry operations, the Workplaces (Protection from Protesters) Act 2014 (Tas), in *Brown v. Tasmania*.[165] However, *Brown* does not necessarily spell the end of anti-protest laws altogether. Rather, what it

---

[158] G20 (Safety and Security) Act 2013 (Qld), s 18.
[159] G20 (Safety and Security) Act 2013 (Qld), s 17.
[160] G20 (Safety and Security) Act 2013 (Qld), s 19.
[161] G20 (Safety and Security) Act 2013 (Qld), pt 4.
[162] G20 (Safety and Security) Act 2013 (Qld), s 50(2)(a)–(c).
[163] Sunili Govinnage and Nick Duff, 'WA Anti-Protest Laws Shake the Core of our Legal System' *The Sydney Morning Herald* (24 March 2015).
[164] United Nations, 'UN Human Rights Experts Urge Western Australia's Parliament not to Pass Proposed Anti-Protest Law' (15 February 2016) www.ohchr.org/EN/NewsEvents/Pages/DisplayNews.aspx?NewsID=17047.
[165] [2017] HCA 43.

requires lawmakers to do is confine the operation of the law in a sensible and comprehensible way that is rationally connected and necessary to achieving the asserted purpose of the law. Other courts that have considered such questions have focused on whether a particular burden on political communication is justified by its purpose in the circumstances of the case;[166] an approach that, as indicated in *McCloy*, and as *Brown* confirms,[167] appears to be increasingly favoured by a majority of the High Court.

4.4.2.1 Preventing Protests at Businesses

Some States have enacted, or attempted to enact, anti-protest laws that essentially prohibit protest action at business premises. What makes these acts unusual and novel, from a constitutional perspective, is that they are addressed at protecting private property, or private businesses conducting their activities on public land, from direct action tactics adopted by protestors. This raises a series of questions around the relationship between the implied freedom of political communication and the activities of private enterprise.[168]

These Acts have as their purpose the protection of important industries: for example, the Workplaces (Protection from Protesters) Act 2014 (Tas) was intended to 'ensure that protesters do not damage business premises or business-related objects, or prevent, impede or obstruct the

---

[166] See, e.g., *RJR-MacDonald Inc.* v. *Canada* [1994] 1 SCR 311, [133]; see also Paul Yowell, 'Proportionality in US Constitutional Law' in Liora Lazarus, Christopher McCrudden, Nigel Bowles (eds), *Reasoning Rights: Comparative Judicial Engagement* (Hart Publishing 2014) 111.

[167] Ibid [123]–[129] (Kiefel CJ, Bell and Keane JJ), [236] (Nettle J). Gageler and Gordon JJ did not accept, to varying degrees, that proportionality analysis was entirely reconcilable within or comprehensible to the judicial function because it required value judgments to be made: as Gageler J noted, '*McCloy* does not elevate three-staged proportionality testing to the level of constitutional principle; and *McCloy* does not endow it with precedential status. The point is one of emphasising that the tool is, at best, a tool. For my own part, I have never considered it to be a particularly useful tool.' (ibid [159]; see also [428]–[438] (Gordon J).

[168] For example, whether the 'the proprietary rights of the Crown or the operation of the general law' are affected by the implied freedom of political communication: see *Levy* v. *Victoria* (1997) 189 CLR 579, 626 (McHugh J), and, moreover, whether anti-protest laws merely augment the existing general law relating to the exclusion of trespassers or nuisances from private property or represent a separate burden entirely due to the nature and breadth of the powers to exclude granted by anti-protest laws. See also *Brown* v. *Tasmania* [2017] HCA 43, [108]–[118] (Kiefel CJ, Bell and Keane JJ), [186]–[190] (Gageler J), [259] (Nettle J), cf [391]–[393] (Gordon J), [490]–[491], [557]–[563] (Edelman J).

carrying out of business activities on business premises'.[169] The Act is designed in part to protect forestry land.[170] Similarly, the Inclosed Lands, Crimes and Law Enforcement Legislation Amendment (Interference) Act 2016 (NSW) amended various legislation[171] and is designed to prevent protestors from hindering coal seam gas operations.[172] The stated purpose of these new prohibitions is to prevent the kinds of protests that put police at risk and cost businesses 'hundreds of thousands of dollars in direct costs, such as making repairs and hiring rescue equipment as well as productivity losses'.[173] The Minister introducing the New South Wales scheme flagged alternative avenues of protest that protestors could use to 'lawfully voice their concerns', such as letter and email writing and 'peaceful protest', and explained that it was necessary to deter protestors from entering mining areas without authorisation because they endangered themselves, other members of the public, and members of the police and rescue services.[174]

The Tasmanian Act, which was found to be invalid as applied to forestry land in *Brown*, requires protestors,[175] under s 11, to comply with a direction given by a police officer to leave a 'business premises', a term which is broadly defined but which includes forestry land,[176] or a 'business access area'.[177] The police officer may issue a direction to leave a business premises where he or she reasonably believes that a person 'has committed, is committing, or is about to commit' an offence under

---

[169] Workplaces (Protection from Protesters) Act 2014 (Tas) (long title).
[170] Workplaces (Protection from Protesters) Act 2014 (Tas), s 5.
[171] The Act amended the Inclosed Lands Protection Act 1901 (NSW); the Crimes Act 1900 (NSW); and the Law Enforcement (Powers and Responsibilities) Act 2002 (NSW).
[172] Vic Parl Debs, LA, 8 March 2016, 2595.
[173] NSW Parl Debs, LA, 8 March 2016, 7029.
[174] Ibid.
[175] The Act defines a 'protestor' as a person who engages in 'protest activity', this being activity that '(a) takes place on business premises or a business access area in relation to business premises; and (b) is (i) in furtherance of; or (ii) for the purposes of promoting awareness of or support for, an opinion, or belief, in respect of a political, environmental, social, cultural or economic issue'. Workplaces (Protection from Protesters) Act 2014 (Tas), s 4(2).
[176] Workplaces (Protection from Protesters) Act 2014 (Tas), s 5(1)(a)-(e) defines a range of 'business premises', specifically mining, mining operations, or mineral exploration as defined by the Mineral Resources Development Act 1995 (Tas); forestry land; 'premises used for agriculture, horticulture, viticulture, aquaculture, commercial food production or commercial food packaging, or as an abattoir, or for any associated purpose'; manufacturing, building or construction premises; shops, markets or warehouses.
[177] Workplaces (Protection from Protesters) Act 2014 (Tas), s 3 (definition of 'business access area').

the Act or contravene section 6 of the Act.[178] Section 6 then prohibits protestors from entering into or acting on business premises or business access areas in ways that prevent, hinder or obstruct business activity.[179] A failure to comply with the direction is an offence[180] that attracts a penalty of $10,000.[181] Greater penalties apply where the protestor causes damage to business premises or a 'business-related object'[182] being taken to or from the premises; a body corporate may be fined $250,000, whereas individuals may be fined $50,000 and sentenced to a maximum of five years' imprisonment.[183] The Act confers powers upon police to arrest and remove persons without a warrant,[184] and they may use reasonable force necessary to exercise powers under the Act.[185]

Brown concerned a challenge by former Australian Greens party leader Dr Bob Brown and another protestor against directions by police to leave the Lapoinya Forest. The case largely turned upon the majority's concern that as a matter of practice police officers would give a direction that were reasonable but mistaken, because it was difficult to determine whether a protestor was actually in a business premises or business access area as defined by the Workplaces (Protection from Protesters) Act.[186] The plurality were concerned that this would discourage protestors from being in forestry areas, to which the Act arguably did not apply, even where their presence did not affect forestry operations and was not otherwise prohibited.[187] Ultimately, this meant that the Act's prohibitions were not reasonably necessary, and were 'likely to deter protest of all kinds and that is too high a cost to the freedom given the limited purpose of the Protesters Act'.[188]

---

[178] Workplaces (Protection from Protesters) Act 2014 (Tas), s 11(1).
[179] Workplaces (Protection from Protesters) Act 2014 (Tas), s 6(1)–(3).
[180] Workplaces (Protection from Protesters) Act 2014 (Tas), s 6(4).
[181] Workplaces (Protection from Protesters) Act 2014 (Tas), s 8(1).
[182] A 'business-related object' is 'an object that belongs to, is in the possession of, or is to be used by, a business occupier in relation to the business premises'. Workplaces (Protection from Protesters) Act 2014 (Tas), s 3.
[183] Workplaces (Protection from Protesters) Act 2014 (Tas), ss 7(1)(a), (b); 7(2)(a), (b).
[184] Workplaces (Protection from Protesters) Act 2014 (Tas), s 13.
[185] Workplaces (Protection from Protesters) Act 2014 (Tas), s 14.
[186] Brown v. Tasmania [2017] HCA 43, [77] (Kiefel CJ, Bell and Keane JJ). See also [226]–[230] (Gageler J), [292] (Nettle J).
[187] Ibid [84]–[85] (Kiefel CJ, Bell and Keane JJ). See also [203] (Gageler J).
[188] Ibid [145] (Kiefel CJ, Bell and Keane JJ). Similarly, Nettle J found that the provisions were necessary but "grossly disproportionate" when balanced against the Act's purpose: ibid [282]–[295].

4.4 ANTI-ASSEMBLY POWERS

Brown may call into question the constitutionality of the Inclosed Lands, Crimes and Law Enforcement Legislation Amendment (Interference) Act 2016 (NSW). The Act introduced an offence into the Inclosed Lands Protection Act 1901 (NSW), of 'aggravated unlawful entry on inclosed lands', which a person commits if he or she 'interferes with, or attempts or intends to interfere with, the conduct of the business or undertaking' while unlawfully on inclosed lands.[189] The Act introduced provisions into the Crimes Act 1900 (NSW) that impose seven years' imprisonment on people who, inter alia, intentionally or recklessly '[hinder] the working of equipment belonging to, or associated with, a mine'.[190] The Act also amended the Law Enforcement (Powers and Responsibilities) Act 2002 (NSW), allowing police to 'stop, search and detain' persons, vehicles, vessels or aircraft without a warrant if they reasonably suspect the person or transport they have stopped has or contains 'anything that is intended to be used to lock-on or secure a person to any plant, equipment or structure for the purpose of interfering with the conduct of a business or undertaking and that is likely to be used in a manner that will give rise to a serious risk to the safety of any person'.[191]

It should be noted that the New South Wales anti-protest scheme is somewhat more narrowly tailored than its Tasmanian equivalent. It punishes protestors, albeit severely, for a specific set of actions associated with the hindering of or damage to mine equipment. The seizure and detention powers are designed to be used to offset serious risks to public safety. It does not make use of the broad and unstructured directions impugned in *Brown*. It did introduce move-on powers into the Law Enforcement (Powers and Responsibilities) Act 2002, which may not

---

[189] Inclosed Lands Protection Act 1901 (NSW), ss 4 and 4B. 'Inclosed lands' includes certain 'prescribed lands' as well as 'any land, either public or private, inclosed or surrounded by any fence, wall or other erection, or partly by a fence, wall or other erection and partly by a canal or by some natural feature such as a river or cliff by which its boundaries may be known or recognised, including the whole or part of any building or structure and any land occupied or used in connection with the whole or part of any building or structure': s 3.

[190] Crimes Act 1900 (NSW), s 201(1)(d). Section 201(1) also makes it an offence for a person to intentionally or recklessly (a) cause water to run into a mine or any subterranean channel connected to it; (b) destroy, damage or obstruct any shaft, passage, pit, airway, waterway or drain of, or associated with, a mine; (c) destroy, damage or render useless any equipment, structure, building, road or bridge belonging to, or associated with, a mine.

[191] Law Enforcement (Powers and Responsibilities) Act 2002 (NSW), ss 45A and 45B.

be used against protestors, as described in Section 4.4.1. The other offences the scheme introduces are tied to an actual or attempted interference with business operations as opposed to any beliefs formed by a police officer about the intentions of a protestor. However, *Brown* illustrates that what is important is how these laws are applied in practice; and, even if the scheme is capable of clear application, it may be that the heavy penalties it imposes then become more relevant to the proportionality of this scheme.[192]

4.4.2.2 Preventing Protests at Abortion Clinics

Tasmania, Victoria and the Australian Capital Territory have also enacted anti-protest laws to protect abortion clinics from being interfered with by anti-abortion protestors.[193] These laws create 'safe zones', excluding protestors from coming within a certain distance of abortion clinics and intimidating or preventing women seeking abortions from accessing the clinic.

The restrictions and penalties applied by these laws are also fairly serious. The Victorian Public Health and Wellbeing Act 2008 (Vic), for example, not only essentially prohibits a person from interfering, intimidating or otherwise 'impeding by any means' a person from entering an abortion clinic, but prohibits 'communicating by any means in relation to abortions in a manner that is able to be seen or heard' to a person entering an abortion clinic in a way that is 'reasonably likely to cause distress or anxiety'. It also prohibits interfering with the footpath or road in front of an abortion clinic, and intentionally recording another person attempting to access or leave an abortion clinic.[194] The punishment is '120 penalty units or imprisonment for a term not exceeding 12 months'.[195]

One commentator on the Tasmanian law has questioned whether the tactics of anti-abortion protestors, which tend to be personal and focused upon deterring the individual woman from obtaining an abortion, in fact

---

[192] See, e.g., *Brown v. Tasmania* [2017] HCA 43, [87] (Kiefel CJ, Bell and Keane JJ).
[193] These being pt 9A of the Public Health and Wellbeing Act 2008 (Vic), as introduced by the Public Health and Wellbeing Amendment (Safe Access Zones) Act 2015 (Vic); the Reproductive Health (Access to Terminations) Act 2013 (Tas); and pt 6 div 6.2 of the Health Act 1993 (ACT), as introduced by the Health (Patient Privacy) Amendment Act 2015 (ACT).
[194] Public Health and Wellbeing Act 2008 (Vic), ss 185B, 185D.
[195] Public Health and Wellbeing Act 2008 (Vic), s 185D.

constitute 'political communication'.[196] Nonetheless, she concludes that the Tasmanian law would most likely not survive constitutional scrutiny. Section 9(1), like its Victorian equivalent, prohibits anti-abortion protests that are 'able to be seen or heard' by the patient, and she argues the penalties are too severe to be considered appropriate and adapted to the purpose of public order and public safety; up to $9750 or 12 months' imprisonment.[197]

4.4.3 Anti-Association Measures

State governments have passed laws that prohibit association or assembly altogether, where the group that proposes to associate or assemble is deemed to pose a threat to public order. Almost every State and Territory provides for a statutory regime of 'control orders' by which individuals may be prohibited from associating with each other.[198] Control orders have also been used in the context of counter-terrorism, as is discussed in Chapter 5.

These measures have been controversial because they target certain organisations and prohibit them from associating based upon a projection of future criminality, and the effectiveness and constitutionality of these regimes has repeatedly been called into question.[199] The greatest point of controversy from a constitutional perspective has been the recruitment of the courts into the process of applying control orders to members of criminal organisations declared under the legislation. A control order is not necessarily contingent upon a finding of criminal guilt or conviction, which is somewhat antithetical to the role of a court. Moreover, courts have been expected to make control orders with a certain absence of process, such as not being required to give reasons for a decision, which detracts from the perception that courts are exercising their functions openly, fairly and with impartiality, and

---

[196] Eleanor Jones, 'Comment: Implementing Protest-Free Zones Around Abortion Clinics in Australia' (2014) 36 Syd L Rev 169, 177–78.
[197] Ibid 182–83.
[198] See, e.g., the Crimes (Criminal Organisations Control) Act 2012 (NSW); Crimes (Serious Crime Prevention Orders) Act 2016 (NSW); Penalties and Sentences Act 1992 (Qld), pt 9D; Serious and Organised Crime (Control) Act 2008 (SA); Criminal Organisations Control Act 2012 (Vic); Criminal Organisations Control Act 2012 (WA); Crimes (Sentencing) Act 2005 (ACT), pt 3.4; Serious Crime Control Act 2009 (NT).
[199] See, e.g., George Williams, 'The Legal Assault on Australian Democracy' (2016) 16 QUT L Rev 19, 32–33.

which have been deemed in some instances to undermine the courts' institutional integrity.[200]

Another issue that has been raised pertains to the workability of the control order regimes. Workability concerns ultimately led to the repeal of Queensland's Criminal Organisation Act 2009 (Qld) and its accompanying Vicious Lawless Association Disestablishment Act 2013 (Qld),[201] a regime that was held to be compatible with the *Kable* principle by the High Court in *Condon* v. *Pompano*[202] and *Kuczborski* v. *Queensland*,[203] and which served as the model for certain versions of the New South Wales and South Australian regimes.[204] A new regime was also introduced into div 3 of pt 9D Penalties and Sentences Act 1992 (Qld), predicated substantially upon a finding of criminal responsibility.

The December 2015 *Review of the Criminal Organisation Act 2009* by Alan Wilson SC criticised the control order regime provided for in the repealed Act as unworkable:

> Queensland is not alone in experiencing difficulties with control orders which hinge upon declarations. None of the five other Australian jurisdictions with similar legislation has succeeded in obtaining a valid declaration-based control order, notwithstanding significant political will and the allocation of substantial public resources. It is thus reasonably clear that Parts 2 and 3 are unlikely to be effective in their current form.[205]

The South Australian police had reported that obtaining a control order 'required significant police resources, involving 18 months' police work, 21 police witnesses, nine civilian witnesses, a large volume of sworn affidavits and evidence, and 12 appearances before the Magistrate'.[206] The system is burdensome because of the secretive nature of the activity involved and the fact that it operates as an 'alternative', not an 'adjunct' to the criminal justice system.[207]

---

[200] In particular, in *South Australia* v. *Totani* (2010) 242 CLR 1 and *Wainohu* v. *New South Wales* (2011) 243 CLR 181; see also Fiona Wheeler, 'Constitutional Limits on Extra-Judicial Activity by State Judges: Wainohu and Conundrums of Incompatibility' (2015) 37(3) Syd L Rev 301, 313–14.
[201] Serious and Organised Crime Legislation Amendment Act 2016 (Qld), s 492.
[202] (2013) 252 CLR 38.
[203] (2014) 254 CLR 51.
[204] Alan Wilson SC, Department of Justice and Attorney-General, *Review of the Criminal Organisation Act 2009* (2015) 144 and 156.
[205] Ibid 213.
[206] Ibid 215.
[207] Ibid.

4.4 ANTI-ASSEMBLY POWERS

Instead, Wilson suggested, as one of a suite of options, that a control regime approaching the Serious Crimes Act 2007 (UK) could be used. In the United Kingdom,

> ...the control order regime is enlivened if a person is convicted of a serious offence or (effectively, the same thing) they are proved beyond a reasonable doubt to have engaged in serious criminal activity. The court may then impose a control order if satisfied on the balance of probabilities that 'the order would protect the public by preventing, restricting or disrupting involvement by the person in serious crime'. Conditions can then be tailored to the offender's particular circumstances and risk factors. Unlike in Australia, this version has found frequent use, albeit reserved for serious offenders due to the cost involved in monitoring compliance with the orders.[208]

Wilson's initial recommendations in this respect were supported by the Taskforce on Organised Crime Legislation's 31 March 2016 Report on Queensland's Organised Crime Legislation.[209] The Taskforce considered the United Kingdom's approach to be superior because it better managed the tensions between public order and freedom of association and assembly. It acknowledged criticisms that the present regime, and by implication regimes like it, 'punishes individuals on the basis of their associations with others, rather than on the basis of their actual criminal behaviour; and [so is] fundamentally at odds with the principles of a liberal democracy (and, historically-entrenched approaches to crime in our criminal justice system)'.[210]

A regime that relies on convictions, by contrast, provides a more narrowly tailored and evidentially compelling basis upon which to restrain a person's freedom of association. The burden involved in obtaining a control order, as well as the use of criminal intelligence and the procedures associated with it, could be avoided because the information used to make the order would have been used to convict the person subject to the order.[211] Ultimately, a new regime was introduced into div 3 of pt 9D of the Penalties and Sentences Act 1992 (Qld) that reflects the approach of the Serious Crimes Act 2007 (UK).

---

[208] Ibid (citations omitted).
[209] Taskforce on Organised Crime Legislation, Department of Justice and Attorney-General, Report (2016).
[210] Ibid 254.
[211] Ibid.

The Taskforce's recommendations were also made in light of the adoption by New South Wales, in the Crimes (Serious Crime Prevention Orders) Act 2016 (NSW), of a post-conviction regime similar to that used in the United Kingdom. Under the NSW regime, the District Court or the Supreme Court of New South Wales may make a 'serious crime prevention order' against a person who has been convicted of a 'serious criminal offence'.[212] The new regime still provides for pre-conviction control orders to be made; the Supreme Court may make such an order where the person has been involved in 'serious crime related activity'[213] and is satisfied that there are 'reasonable grounds to believe that the making of the order would protect the public by preventing, restricting or disrupting involvement by the person in serious crime related activities'.[214] It appears that, at least in NSW, the new regime is intended to operate in tandem with the more traditional control order regime set out in the Crimes (Criminal Organisations Control) Act 2012 (NSW).[215]

4.4.3.1 Anti-Consorting Laws

A close relative of the anti-association control order regimes described in Section 4.4.3 is the 'anti-consorting law', which prohibits persons from 'habitually consorting' with convicted offenders outside of specified circumstances.[216] These laws, like the anti-association laws described in the previous section, are designed to combat organised crime. Anti-consorting laws have been enacted in Queensland,[217] Victoria,[218] South

---

[212] Crimes (Serious Crime Prevention Orders) Act 2016 (NSW), s 5(1)(b)(i). A 'serious criminal offence' is defined in s 6(2) the Criminal Assets Recovery Act 1990 (NSW).
[213] This meaning 'anything done by a person that is or was at the time a serious criminal offence, whether or not: (a) the person has been charged with the offence, or (b) if charged, the person: (i) has been tried, or (ii) has been tried and acquitted, or (iii) has been convicted (even if the conviction has been quashed or set aside):' Crimes (Serious Crime Prevention Orders) Act 2016 (NSW), s 3.
[214] Crimes (Serious Crime Prevention Orders) Act 2016 (NSW), s 5(1)(b)(ii), (1)(c). See also Taskforce on Organised Crime Legislation, Department of Justice and Attorney-General, Report (2016) 258.
[215] NSW Parliamentary Research Service, Serious Crime Prevention Orders (April 2016) 6.
[216] Police Offences Act 1935 (Tas), s 6 (prohibiting a person from habitually consorting with 'reputed thieves');
[217] Criminal Code Act 1899 (Qld), sch 1 pt 9A.
[218] Criminal Organisations Control Act 2012 (Vic), pt 5A.

Australia,[219] New South Wales,[220] and the Northern Territory.[221] These laws have an antecedence in vagrancy laws.[222] So, for example, section 6(1) of the Vagrancy Act 1966 (Vic) made it an offence to 'habitually consort' with 'reputed thieves or known prostitutes' unless the person could give a 'good account of his lawful means of support and also of this so consorting'.[223] Such laws still exist in some jurisdictions.[224]

The purpose behind anti-consorting laws is to clarify the procedural requirements that must be followed by police when deciding that a person's consorting is 'habitual;' to formalise the kind of notice that is due to persons before they may be convicted of an offence; and to extend the meaning of 'consorting' to electronic and other modern kinds of communication.[225]

4.5 Special Public Disorder Emergency Powers

As will be discussed in Chapter 6, States and Territories have emergency special powers frameworks that are designed to coordinate the executive government's response to a state of emergency. In the context of civil emergency, States and Territories provide that emergencies be dealt with under the oversight of senior public servants or ministers in the executive government and tend to concentrate emergency powers in emergency management commissioners, councils and advisory bodies who are responsible for planning and executing the response to an emergency. Although some of those frameworks define 'emergency' as including a

---

[219] Summary Offences Act 1953 (SA), s 13.
[220] Crimes Act 1900 (NSW), s 93X. This section survived a constitutional challenge in *Tajjour v. New South Wales* (2014) 254 CLR 508. There was little question that the law could burden political communication. In their majority judgment, Crennan, Kiefel and Bell JJ decided that it employed a means appropriate and adapted to the end of preventing convicted offenders from consorting. Proportionality analysis was used to resolve this question, which was framed as whether 'the means chosen by the legislature are proportionate to the purpose pursued'. The judges tested this proposition in part by considering whether the means adopted by the anti-consorting law were 'reasonably necessary' to achieving this purpose: [116].
[221] Summary Offences Act 1923 (NT), s 55A.
[222] Andrew McLeod, 'On the origins of consorting laws' (2013) 37(1) MULR 103.
[223] See also *Johanson v. Dixon* (1979) 143 CLR 376.
[224] See, e.g., Summary Offences Act 1923 (NT), s 56(1)(e)(i), which prohibits a person from habitually consorting with 'reputed criminals'.
[225] See, e.g., Cth Parl Debs, LA, 14 February 2012, 8131–32.

riot or civil disturbance,[226] many jurisdictions provide that these special powers are not to be used to quell an industrial dispute, or riots, civil disorders, disturbances and the like, unless they occur during an emergency declared for the reasons defined in the legislation.[227]

One part of Queensland's emergency framework, as provided for in the Public Safety Preservation Act 1986 (Qld), confers special powers to address various kinds of emergency, including terrorism and public disorder.[228] This framework will be discussed in more detail in Chapter 6 in the context of civil emergencies generally.

In response to the Cronulla Riots, New South Wales has also provided for special powers that are specifically designed to be used by the police to deal with a state of emergency arising from public disorder. New South Wales' emergency public disorder framework is primarily contained in Part 6A of the Law Enforcement (Powers and Responsibilities) Act 2002 (NSW). The framework permits a range of emergency powers to be exercised by senior police officers in response to a 'public disorder' defined in section 87A(1) as 'a riot or other civil disturbance that gives rise to a serious risk to public safety, whether at a single location or resulting from a series of incidents in the same or different locations'. Many of these emergency powers are based on reforms that took place in the United Kingdom in 1994 and 2000.[229] They are targeted at the kind of behaviour that escalated the Cronulla Riots, in particular the use of mobile phones by the rioters to communicate gathering points and identify targets.[230] These special powers have been invoked to quell several instances of public disorder.[231]

These emergency powers may be activated as a matter of police discretion. The Act tends to predicate the exercise of these powers on

---

[226] Emergency Management Act 2004 (SA), s 3 (defining an 'emergency' as including 'riots'); Emergency Management Act 2013 (Vic), s 3 (defining an 'emergency' and a 'class 2 emergency' as including 'a hi-jack, siege or riot').

[227] State Emergency and Rescue Management Act 1989 (NSW), s 4(1); Disaster Management Act 2003 (Qld), s 10; Emergency Management Act 2004 (SA), s 4(2); State Emergency and Rescue Management Act 1989 (NSW), s 7; Emergency Management Act 2006 (Tas), s 4; Emergency Management Act 2005 (WA) s 9(b); Emergencies Act 2004 (ACT), s 150(3); Emergency Management Act 2013 (NT), s 4.

[228] Public Safety Preservation Act 1986 (Qld), pt 2A (providing for 'terrorist emergency').

[229] Office of Police Integrity, Victoria Police, Review of Victoria Police Use of 'Stop and Search' Powers (2012) 12–15.

[230] Ibid 15.

[231] NSW Ombudsman, Review of Emergency Powers to Prevent or Control Disorder (2007) 5–6.

4.5 SPECIAL PUBLIC DISORDER EMERGENCY POWERS

the occurrence of public disorder of 'large scale', although that phrase is not defined by the Act. A police officer of the rank of Superintendent or higher may order the closure of premises licensed to sell liquor,[232] or establish 'emergency alcohol-free zones',[233] in areas in the vicinity of a large-scale public disorder for up to forty-eight hours. The Commissioner of Police or the Deputy or Assistant Commissioner of Police may also authorise the use of 'special powers' for forty-eight hours in respect of a particular area or road that is a public place.[234] An authorisation may only be given if the officer has reasonable grounds for believing there is a large-scale public disorder occurring, or a risk of one occurring in the near future, and that an authorisation is 'reasonably necessary to prevent or control the public disorder'.[235]

Within the authorised area or road, police officers may establish roadblocks or cordons;[236] stop and search vehicles[237] and persons[238] without a warrant, and detain vehicles or persons to give effect to a search;[239] require a person to disclose his or her identity if the police officer reasonably suspects the person has been or is likely to be involved in the public disorder;[240] seize and detain vehicles, mobile phones or other things for seven days for the purposes of preventing or controlling public disorder[241] or without a time limit if the thing may provide evidence of a serious indictable offence;[242] and may order groups of persons within the authorised area to immediately disperse.[243]

This is not to say that police in the other States and Territories lack the powers of their counterparts in New South Wales. To the contrary, NSW's emergency powers are exceptional because they are formalised as emergency powers, in the sense that their exercise is predicated on the existence of a large-scale public disorder and must be formally invoked.

---

[232] Law Enforcement (Powers and Responsibilities) Act 2002 (NSW), s 87B.
[233] Law Enforcement (Powers and Responsibilities) Act 2002 (NSW), s 87C.
[234] Law Enforcement (Powers and Responsibilities) Act 2002 (NSW), ss 87F(1), G(2).
[235] Law Enforcement (Powers and Responsibilities) Act 2002 (NSW), s 87D(1)(a) and (b).
[236] Law Enforcement (Powers and Responsibilities) Act 2002 (NSW), s 87I.
[237] Law Enforcement (Powers and Responsibilities) Act 2002 (NSW), s 87J.
[238] Law Enforcement (Powers and Responsibilities) Act 2002 (NSW), s 87K(1).
[239] Law Enforcement (Powers and Responsibilities) Act 2002 (NSW), ss 87J(2), 87K(3).
[240] Law Enforcement (Powers and Responsibilities) Act 2002 (NSW), s 87L.
[241] Law Enforcement (Powers and Responsibilities) Act 2002 (NSW), s 87M(1)(a).
[242] Law Enforcement (Powers and Responsibilities) Act 2002 (NSW), s 87M(1)(b).
[243] Law Enforcement (Powers and Responsibilities) Act 2002 (NSW), s 87MA.

A number of Australian police forces have similar powers.[244] These powers tend to be narrower than New South Wales' special powers, focusing more on search and seizure of dangerous objects, and do not come as part of a suite of powers that may be used with the objective of quelling a large-scale public disorder.

The other frameworks are also different because they generally require that there must be some reasonable basis for exercising specific powers.[245] For example, section 10 of the Control of Weapons Act 1990 (Vic) empowers the Victorian police to search a person or a vehicle without a warrant, and detain a person to that end, where they have 'reasonable grounds for suspecting that a person is carrying or has in his or her possession in a public place a weapon contrary to this Act'. By contrast, New South Wales', South Australia's and Queensland's legislation simply require that the initial invocation of special powers be reasonable: that it is reasonable to believe that serious public disorder could occur.[246]

Another relevant difference is in the range of objects that may be targeted by non-emergency laws for search and seizure.[247] Unlike the 'things' that may be seized in order to prevent or control a public disorder using the equivalent powers in section 87M of the Law Enforcement (Powers and Responsibilities) Act 2002 (NSW), the 'weapons' that may be seized in the Control of Weapons Act 1990 (Vic) refers to specific items that are prohibited, controlled or otherwise deemed weapons.[248]

An exception to this rule is in Western Australia, where the warrantless search and seizure provisions are equally as broad as their emergency equivalent in NSW. The Criminal Investigation Act 2006 (WA) does not

---

[244] Police Powers and Responsibilities Act 2000 (Qld), pt 2 divs 2. 3 and 4; Summary Offences Act 1953 (SA), s 72B; Control of Weapons Act 1990 (Vic), s 10; Criminal Investigation Act 2006 (WA), pt 8 div 2.

[245] Police Powers and Responsibilities Act 2000 (Qld), ss 29(1), 31(1); Summary Offences Act 1953 (SA), s 72B(3).

[246] Law Enforcement (Powers and Responsibilities) Act 2002 (NSW), ss 87D(1)(a), (b); Public Safety Preservation Act 1986 (Qld), s 5(1); Summary Offences Act 1953 (SA), s 72B(3).

[247] See also Police Powers and Responsibilities Act 2000 (Qld), s 29.

[248] Control of Weapons Act 1990 (Vic), s 10(7), referring to 'prohibited weapons' and 'controlled weapons' as prescribed in the Control of Weapons Regulations 2011 (Vic), as well as 'dangerous articles' as defined in s 3(1) of the Control of Weapons Act 1990 (Vic) as '(b) an article which has been adapted or modified so as to be capable of being used as a weapon; or (c) any other article which is carried with the intention of being used as a weapon'.

4.5 SPECIAL PUBLIC DISORDER EMERGENCY POWERS 125

require a police officer to have a warrant in order to, inter alia, strip search a person whom he or she reasonably suspects 'has in his or her possession or under his or her control any thing relevant to an offence'.[249] By requiring reasonable suspicion, the formulation is mildly more restrictive than the equivalent warrantless search and seizure power in the Law Enforcement (Powers and Responsibilities) Act 2002 (NSW), but the Criminal Investigation Act 2006 (WA) defines 'thing relevant to an offence' expansively, as something that 'may afford evidence relevant to proving the commission of an offence or who committed an offence', which can be 'non-material'.[250]

The most significant difference is that the other frameworks, other than the aforementioned Public Safety Preservation Act 1986 (Qld),[251] do not confer a blanket power to disperse groups equivalent to section 87MA of the Law Enforcement (Powers and Responsibilities) Act 2002 (NSW). The only condition on the use of that power is the one mentioned previously – that it be reasonable to believe that serious public disorder could occur and that, in the case of New South Wales, it will be reasonably necessary to exercise such powers.

One can imagine a number of legitimate reasons why police officers may form the belief that it will be reasonably necessary to disperse a non-violent political protest during a large-scale public disorder. They may be concerned that any protest will be targeted by violent rioters, or itself become violent. It may be that they have no specific concerns about non-violent protest at all: the requirement of reasonableness only attaches to the authorisation of emergency powers, not to the exercise of individual powers.

The nature of these special powers, and in particular the power to disperse, raise some interesting questions about their relationship with the implied freedom of political communication. Does the implied freedom apply in an emergency context and, if so, does the proportionality analysis it requires apply in the same way? As will be discussed later on in this book, one of the core characteristics of an emergency is its insusceptibility to judicial analysis and scrutiny. This reflects a deeper conceptual argument about whether emergency powers represent some extra-constitutional state of affairs in which the ordinary rules do not apply

---

[249] Criminal Investigation Act 2006 (WA), s 68.
[250] Criminal Investigation Act 2006 (WA), s 68(1)(d)(i) and (2): the example of non-material things being the 'distance between two things or the visibility from a window'.
[251] Public Safety Preservation Act 1986 (Qld), s 8(1)(d),(e).

because law and order has broken down.[252] Although the decision of *Wotton v. State of Queensland (No. 5)*,[253] discussed in Chapter 6, suggests otherwise, it may be that constitutional limits on legislative power such as the implied freedom of political communication doctrine do not apply to these special powers.

In the case of the Law Enforcement (Powers and Responsibilities) Act 2002 (NSW), an implied condition of reasonableness or proportionality could require that an order for a political assembly to disperse not only be underpinned by a reasonable apprehension of serious public disorder, but that the immediate order *itself* be reasonable; requiring the court to consider whether the police officer had a reasonably less restrictive means of achieving the objectives in section 87D(1) and – applying proportionality analysis – whether the specific order to disperse went too far in the circumstances, given the situation that confronted the police at the time the order was made.

However, it would be profoundly difficult for a court to decide, for example, whether the police or governmental authorities could have used a less restrictive alternative to dispersing a political gathering when there has been a total breakdown of law and order. Moreover, because the purposes of the legislation are so broad and urgent, and so clearly directed at securing public safety in the face of a serious threat, it would be difficult to constrain the exercise of the dispersal power by requiring it to be exercised consistently with those purposes.

Still, with regard to the principle that 'a discretion must be exercised by the repository of a power in accordance with any applicable law', including any relevant constitutional limitation,[254] there are two alternative possibilities; either these special powers are subject to constitutional restraints such as the implied freedom, with all the difficulty that entails, or the Constitution limits and defines what may be an 'emergency' for the purposes of creating exceptions to these constitutional restraints.

With respect to the latter approach: It is possible that the Constitution itself recognises that an invocation of emergency powers signals a State's need to be freed from ordinary constitutional constraints during public

---

[252] See, e.g., David Dyzenhaus, *The Constitution of Law: Legality in a Time of Emergency* (CUP 2006); Victor Ramraj (ed), *Emergencies and the Limits of Legality* (CUP 2008).
[253] [2016] FCA 1457.
[254] *Miller v. TCN Channel Nine Pty Ltd* (1986) 161 CLR 556, 613–14 (Brennan J); see also *Wilcox Mofflin Ltd v. New South Wales* (1952) 85 CLR 488, 522 (Dixon, McTiernan and Fullagar JJ).

disorder. What is troubling about this line of reasoning is that it suggests a State Parliament can recite the executive or the police into freedom from the constraints imposed by the Constitution using the rubric of emergency. Assuming this argument is plausible at all, it must follow that there is some further rule defining when a declaration of emergency powers is recognised as setting aside the Constitution. Such a rule would necessarily require some definition of emergency, one potentially embedded within or implied from the Constitution itself.

4.6 Offences against the State: Sedition

One of the most prominent developments in the law relating to public order is in relation to the crime of sedition and, to some extent, treason. Sedition has a long and storied relationship with the suppression of threats to public order, real and imagined. It sits alongside other offences against the government associated with insurrection that remain prohibited in Australian law, such as treason,[255] treachery,[256] sabotage[257] and mutiny.[258] Unlike crimes like treason, however, sedition has been periodically used by Australian governments as a way of punishing what they consider to be behaviour threatening the government or public order generally.

Although crimes like sedition are not exclusively federal,[259] they pose a particular problem when one considers the limited powers of the Commonwealth. Unlike the States, the Commonwealth Parliament is one of enumerated powers. It may only pass legislation with respect to the matters described in section 51 of the Constitution. However, judges have increasingly recognised the existence of an implied nationhood power to address emergencies or matters that are particular to 'the character and status of the Commonwealth as a national government', including the matter of its protection.[260]

---

[255] Criminal Code 1995 (Cth), ss 80.1, 80.1AA.
[256] Crimes Act 1914 (Cth), s 24AA.
[257] Crimes Act 1914 (Cth), s 24AB.
[258] Crimes Act 1914 (Cth), s 25.
[259] Criminal Code Act 1899 (Qld), ch 7 sch 1 pt 2; Criminal Code Act 1924 (Tas), sch 1 pt 2 ch 6; Criminal Code Act Compilation Act 1913 (WA), sch 1 pt 2 ch 7.
[260] See, e.g., *R v. Sharkey* (1949) 79 CLR 121; *Victoria v. Commonwealth (AAP Case)* (1975) 134 CLR 338, 379 (Mason J); *Pape v. Federal Commissioner of Taxation* (2009) 238 CLR 1, 83 [215] (Gummow, Crennan and Bell JJ). See also Nicholas Aroney, Peter Gerangelos,

Even that power has limits, however, which is illustrated in the field of public disorder by the decision of *Australian Communist Party v. Commonwealth*.[261] In that decision, a majority of the High Court rejected the constitutionality of the Communist Party Dissolution Act 1950 (Cth) on the basis that it did not fall within the Commonwealth's legislative competence. Accordingly, there have always been questions around the scope of the Commonwealth's authority to provide for such crimes.

There has long been a sense that the offence of sedition is incompatible with the maintenance of a representative democracy. One of the most famous British seditionists sentenced to transportation in Australia, the Scottish republican Thomas Muir, described the crime at his trial:

> Sedition. Is there a term so vague and so undefined, so familiar to power, so familiar to corruption. All who ever dared to oppose ARBITRARY POWER, and who in the hour of danger came forward to save their country, have been branded by the epithet of sedition. The term is therefore no longer a term of opprobrium. In one age, it has been applied to men rejected by society, whose names were honoured by after times, and upon whose virtues, and upon whose sufferings, the succeeding age reared the majestic pillar of the constitution ... I know for what I am brought to this bar, it is for having strenuously and actively engaged in the cause of Parliamentary Reform; for having exerted every effort, by constitutional measures, to procure an equal representation of the people, in the House of the People.[262]

Sir James Stephen's oft-cited definition of sedition, as incorporated into the English common law in *R v. Burns*,[263] focuses upon the intention of the words expressed or literature used. In his *Digest of the Criminal Law*, he stated:

> Every one commits a misdemeanour who publishes verbally or otherwise any words or any document with a seditious intention. If the matter so published consists of words spoken, the offence is called the speaking of seditious words. If the matter so published is contained in anything capable of being a libel, the offence is called the publication of a seditious libel. Every one commits a misdemeanour who agrees with any other

---

Sarah Murray and James Stellios, *The Constitution of the Commonwealth of Australia: History, Principle and Interpretation* (CUP 2015) 196–98; and Chapter 3 of this book.

[261] (1951) 83 CLR 1.
[262] *An Account of the Trial of Thomas Muir, Esq. Younger, of Huntershill, before the High Court of Justiciary, at Edinburgh, on the 30th and 31st days of August, 1793, for Sedition*, (J Robertson 1793) 79–80.
[263] (1886) 16 Cox CC 355.

person or persons to do any act for the furtherance of any seditious intention common to both or all of them. Such an offence is called a seditious conspiracy.

In Sir James' original definition, it was not seditious to make observations about deficiencies in the laws, the government or the constitution with the view to reforming them, or to encourage English subjects to reform or change the laws, or to identify matters that were producing hatred and ill-will between classes of British subjects. The key element to the intention is that it be directed at change through *unlawful* means. The question in *Burns* was whether the accused did 'intentionally incite ill-will between different classes in such a way as to be likely to lead to a disturbance of the public peace'.[264]

4.6.1 The Australian Sedition Cases

The Australian cases departed from this aspect of the formulation in *Burns*. The high-water mark for Australian sedition was in the first half of the twentieth century. In 1920, the Commonwealth Parliament introduced a crime of sedition into the Crimes Act 1914 (Cth). Section 24D of this law punished persons who wrote, printed, uttered or published seditious words, and other provisions punished seditious enterprises conducted pursuant to a range of seditious intentions. Section 24B(2) provided that seditious words were words expressive of a seditious intention. A range of seditious intentions were defined by section 24A(1) of the Crimes Act, but they included, relevantly, words calculated '(b) to excite disaffection against the Sovereign or the Government or Constitution of the United Kingdom or against either House of Parliament of the United Kingdom; (c) to excite disaffection against the Government or Constitution of any of the Queen's dominions; (d) to excite disaffection against the Government or Constitution of the Commonwealth or against either House of the Parliament of the Commonwealth ... (g) to promote feelings of ill-will and hostility between different classes of Her Majesty's subjects so as to endanger the peace, order or good government of the Commonwealth'.

This law was at issue in the 'sedition cases', *Burns* v. *Ransley*[265] and *R* v. *Sharkey*.[266] These cases involved members of the Australian

---

[264] (1886) 16 Cox CC 355, 366.
[265] (1949) 79 CLR 101.
[266] (1949) 79 CLR 121.

Communist Party who were accused of speaking seditious words at public meetings. In *Burns* v. *Ransley,* the appellant had been convicted for stating at a public debate that, in the event of a third world war between Soviet Russia and the Western powers, the Communist Party would side with the Soviets. In *R* v. *Sharkey,* the accused was charged with having uttered seditious words when he made a statement to a newspaper reporter that Australian workers would 'welcome' Soviet forces who entered Australia, 'as the workers welcomed them throughout Europe, when the Red troops liberated the people from the power of the Nazis ... The job of the Communists is to struggle to prevent war and to educate the mass of people against the idea of war. The Communist Party also wants to bring the working class to power but if Fascists in Australia use force to prevent the workers gaining that power Communists will advise the worker to meet force with force'.

In both cases, a majority held that the notion of exciting disaffection did not necessarily involve an intention to incite violence. In *Burns* v. *Ransley,* the Chief Justice, whose judgment resolved the case in the face of an equally split court, defined 'disaffection' as involving

> ... not merely the absence of affection and regard, but disloyalty, enmity and hostility ... [it] refers to the implanting or arousing or stimulating in the minds of people a feeling or view or opinion that the Sovereign and Government should not be supported ... but they should be opposed, and when the question is made in relation to a war it means that they should, if possible, be destroyed. Such advocacy is encouragement of and incitement to active disloyalty.[267]

The sedition cases also touched upon the idea of an implied nationhood power. In *Burns* v. *Ransley,* for example, Latham CJ justified the function of sedition laws as 'protection against fifth column activities and subversive propaganda' which was 'desirable or even necessary for the purpose of preserving the constitutional powers and operations of governmental agencies and the existence of government itself'.[268] Similarly, Dixon J wrote that

> Our institutions may be changed by laws adopted peaceably by the appropriate legislative authority. It follows almost necessarily from their existence that to preserve them from violent subversion is a matter within the legislative power. But ... I am able to see why it should

---

[267] (1949) 79 CLR 101, 108.
[268] Ibid 110.

not include the suppression of actual incitements to an antagonism to constitutional government, although the antagonism is not, and may never be, manifested by any overt acts of resistance or by any resort to violence.[269]

This reasoning supplies some sense of the public purpose that is served by these laws. However, by focusing on the intention or purpose of the person expressing seditious words, as opposed to the probable objective effect of those words, it is open to question whether sedition as applied in *Burns* v. *Ransley* and *R* v. *Sharkey* would today survive scrutiny under the implied freedom.

It is worth noting in this respect Gaudron J's *obiter* comment in *Cunliffe* v. *Commonwealth* that the prohibition of sedition does not violate the implied freedom of political communication because it 'operates in an area in which discussion has traditionally been curtailed in the public interest'.[270] But, as noted in Section 4.2.1, courts have sometimes interpreted statutes to require that political communication involve a serious risk of public disorder before their prohibition may serve a legitimate end compatible with the maintenance of representative government. By contrast, the effect of the High Court's decisions was to send men to prison 'for doing no more than expressing highly unpopular political opinions – the former in an orderly public debate and the latter in a series of telephone conversations with a journalist'.[271]

4.6.2 Subsequent Reforms

The law of sedition fell into obsolescence and disuse after the cases described in Section 4.6.1. It was used again in 1960, for the trial of Brian Cooper.[272] In 1986, minor amendments were made to the Crimes Act 1914 (Cth) in relation to the burden of proof, consistently with the recommendations of the Royal Commission on Australia's Security and Intelligence Agencies.

In 1991, the Committee of Review of Commonwealth Criminal Law, under the chairmanship of Sir Harry Gibbs, a former Chief Justice of

---

[269] Ibid 116.
[270] (1994) 182 CLR 272, 389. See also *Coleman* v. *Power* (2004) 220 CLR 1, 102 [327] (Heydon J).
[271] Laurence Maher, 'The Use and Abuse of Sedition' (1992) 14 Syd L Rev 287, 288.
[272] *Cooper* v. *The Queen* (1961) 105 CLR 177.

Australia, issued a series of reports that characterised the laws such as sedition, treason and the like as redundant and archaic.[273] The 'Gibbs Committee' noted that the definition of 'seditious intention' was 'misleadingly wide', but recommended that a version of the offence be retained that emphasised an intention to overthrow the Commonwealth by force or violence.[274]

In 2005, the Howard Government, ostensibly acting on the Gibbs Committee's recommendations,[275] repealed the sedition offences in the Crimes Act 1914 (Cth) and introduced new sedition offences into schedule 7 of the Criminal Code 1995 (Cth) as a part of its overall counter-terrorism law reform. A number of new offences were introduced, which extended to the urging for the overthrow of federal, State or Territory governments, as well as 'the lawful authority of the Government of the Commonwealth'.[276]

Another new provision, section 80.2(5), made it an offence to 'urge violence within the community' by urging a group or groups, 'whether distinguished by race, religion, nationality or political opinion', to use force or violence against other groups so distinguished, where 'the use of the force or violence would threaten the peace, order and good government of the Commonwealth'. All the new offences were punishable by seven years' imprisonment. A prosecution under the Division could not proceed without the written consent of the Attorney-General.[277]

The sedition offences were subject to the defence of good faith, set out in section 80.3 of the Criminal Code. Arguably, this defence attempted to strike the same balance struck in *Burns,* in that a person who had a bona fide desire to bring change through constitutional and legal means, as opposed to unlawful means, should not be considered to have seditious intentions. For example, a person charged with sedition had a defence where they were trying in good faith to show that the government or the Constitution, legislation, or administration of justice had 'errors or defects ... with a view to reforming those errors or defects'.[278] Similarly,

---

[273] Ben Saul, 'Speaking of Terror: Criminalising Incitement to Violence' (2005) 28(3) UNSWLJ 868, 872.
[274] Harry Gibbs, Ray Watson and Andrew Menzies, *Review of Commonwealth Criminal Law: Fifth Interim Report* (1991) para [32.13], as reported by the Australian Law Reform Commission in *Review of Sedition Laws, Discussion Paper* (2006) 37 para [2.21].
[275] Explanatory Notes to the Anti-Terrorism Bill (No 2) 2005 (Cth), 88.
[276] Anti-Terrorism Act 2005 [No.2] (Cth), sch 7 (Criminal Code 1995 (Cth), s 80.2).
[277] Anti-Terrorism Act 2005 [No.2] (Cth), sch 7 (Criminal Code 1995 (Cth), s 80.5).
[278] Anti-Terrorism Act 2005 [No.2] (Cth), sch 7 (Criminal Code 1995 (Cth), s 80.3(1)(b)).

4.6 OFFENCES AGAINST THE STATE: SEDITION   133

it was a defence to point out in good faith 'any matters that are producing, or have a tendency to produce, feelings of ill-will or hostility between different groups, in order to bring about the removal of those matters'.[279]

Those good faith defences were, however, qualified by a series of considerations to which the court could have regard. These considerations included whether the acts were done for a purpose 'intended to be prejudicial to the safety or defence of the Commonwealth;'[280] or whether it was intended to assist an enemy at war with the Commonwealth or engaged in armed hostilities against the Australian Defence Force,[281] or that had the intention of assisting the enemies of countries proclaimed under section 24AA of the Crimes Act 1914 (Cth) or treacherous persons as proscribed in sections 24AA(2)(a) and (b);[282] or that had the 'intention of causing violence or creating public disorder or a public disturbance'.[283]

As Simon Bronitt has pointed out, by focusing on trying to prevent forms of expression directed at the overthrow of the government by force or violence the purpose of these laws was to tie the crime even more closely to the security of the Commonwealth.[284] Yet he, and others, criticised the laws on the basis that they were too broad.[285] In a submission to the Senate Legal and Constitutional Legislation Committee in a review it conducted of the Bill, a group of Australian newspapers described the provisions as 'the gravest threat to publication imposed by the Government in the history of the Commonwealth'.[286] They noted that there was no media reporting defence, as appeared in the Trade

---

[279] Anti-Terrorism Act 2005 [No.2] (Cth), sch 7 (Criminal Code 1995 (Cth), s 80.3(1)(d)).
[280] Anti-Terrorism Act 2005 [No.2] (Cth), sch 7 (Criminal Code 1995 (Cth), s 80.3(2)(a).
[281] Anti-Terrorism Act 2005 [No.2] (Cth), sch 7 (Criminal Code 1995 (Cth), s 80.3(2)(b), (c).
[282] Anti-Terrorism Act 2005 [No.2] (Cth), sch 7 (Criminal Code 1995 (Cth), s 80.3(2)(d), (e).
[283] Anti-Terrorism Act 2005 [No.2] (Cth), sch 7 (Criminal Code 1995 (Cth), s 80.3(2)(f).
[284] Simon Bronitt, 'Hate Speech, sedition and the War on Terror', Katherine Gelber and Adrienne Stone (eds) *Hate Speech and Freedom of Speech in Australia* (Federation Press 2007) 134–35.
[285] Simon Bronitt and James Stellios, 'Sedition, Security and Human Rights: 'Unbalanced' law reform in the 'War on Terror'' (2006) 30(3) MULR 923.
[286] John Fairfax Holdings Limited, News Limited, West Australian Newspapers Limited, Australian Press Council, AAP, *Submission to the Senate Legal and Constitutional Legislation Committee on Anti Terrorism Bill No. 2 2005* (2005) 6.

Practices Act 1974 (Cth) and the Privacy Act 1988 (Cth), nor was there an exemption for artistic expression.[287]

Others supported the requirement that the urging be for the use of force and violence as opposed to the incitement of 'disaffection' or 'ill-will' as proscribed in previous laws.[288] But the need for these laws was repeatedly questioned. It was pointed out in several submissions that the law as framed was redundant because the conduct it proscribed would fall within 'incitement to violence'.[289] The only difference between the new laws and the incitement to violence offence was a disturbing one – that the new offence of sedition was easier to prove because it was unnecessary to show that the person urging the commission of an offence intended that offence to be carried out.[290] Ultimately, the Senate Legal and Constitutional Legislation Committee recommended that the sedition offences in schedule 7 be removed 'pending a full and independent review' by the Australian Law Reform Commission.[291]

Schedule 7 was enacted regardless. In 2006, however, Attorney-General Ruddock referred schedule 7 to the Australian Law Reform Commission (ALRC), stating in the terms of reference that the ALRC should inquire and report on whether the sedition law would effectively proscribe urging the use of force or violence. ALRC made a number of recommendations designed to improve the law's operation. Most importantly, the ALRC recommended that section 80.2 of the Criminal Code 1995 (Cth) be reformed to require a specific intention that force or violence be used by others to achieve the ends that the accused has urged.[292] The Commission was not of the view that the laws as phrased breached the implied freedom of political communication, but recognised that the laws would probably be read narrowly to avoid unconstitutionality.[293] Eventually, these reforms were enacted by the Parliament during the tenure of the Gillard Labor Government in 2010, and the

---

[287] Ibid 12.
[288] Senate Legal and Constitutional Legislation Committee, Provisions of the Anti-Terrorism Bill (No. 2) 2005 (2005) 191 para [7.64.]
[289] Ibid 86 para [5.56].
[290] Ibid 86–87 paras [5.59]–[5.60].
[291] Ibid 114 paras [5.168]–[5.171].
[292] Australian Law Reform Commission, *Fighting Words: A Review of Sedition Laws in Australia*, (ALRC Report 104, 2006) 14.
[293] Ibid 118 para [7.20].

crime was renamed 'Urging the overthrow of the Constitution or Government by force or violence.'[294]

In 2014, however, the Counter-Terrorism Legislation Amendment (Foreign Fighters) Act 2014 (Cth) was passed in the federal Parliament. The Act introduced a new section 80.2C into the Criminal Code 1995 (Cth), which creates the offence of 'advocating terrorism'. Section 80.2C provides that it is an offence for a person to advocate for 'the doing of a terrorist act' or for the commission of a 'terrorism offence' as defined in sub-section (2).[295] To 'advocate' for a terrorist act or terrorism offence is to 'counsel, promote, encourage or urge' the doing of those acts.[296] Section 80.2C has been, perhaps improperly, 'consciously analogised to treason and sedition'.[297] The difference between section 80.2C and offences such as sedition is that the advocacy of terrorism does not necessarily entail an act of disloyalty against the Australian state because, by definition, terrorism might in fact be directed at a foreign government or public and not concern Australia at all.[298] The effect of this, it has been argued, is to 'conflate disobedience with disloyalty'.[299]

---

[294] National Security Legislation Amendment Act 2010 (Cth).
[295] That being a terrorism offence set out in the Crimes Act 1914 (Cth), s 3(1), where '(a) the offence is punishable on conviction by imprisonment for 5 years or more; and (b) the offence is not: (i) an offence against section 11.1 (attempt), 11.4 (incitement) or 11.5 (conspiracy) to the extent that it relates to a terrorism offence; or (ii) a terrorism offence that a person is taken to have committed because of section 11.2 (complicity and common purpose), 11.2A (joint commission) or 11.3 (commission by proxy)'. Criminal Code 1995 (Cth), s 80.2C(3).
[296] Criminal Code 1995 (Cth), s 80.2C(3) (definition of 'advocates').
[297] Benjamin Brooks, 'Treason, Terrorism and Imprecision: Locating s 80.2C of the Criminal Code (Cth) in the Taxonomy of Crimes against the State' (2016) 38(1) Syd L Rev 121, 122.
[298] Ibid at 135, 138.
[299] Ibid at 139.

5

Public Safety and the War on Terror

> *'My Lords, indefinite imprisonment without charge or trial is anathema in any country which observes the rule of law. It deprives the detained person of the protection a criminal trial is intended to afford. Wholly exceptional circumstances must exist before this extreme step can be justified'.*
>
> Lord Nicholls in A and Others v. Secretary of State for the Home Department [2005] 2 AC 68, 127.

5.1 Introduction

In Australia, federal and State legislatures responded to the horrific 9/11 attacks in the US, and the many bombing tragedies in cities in a number of other countries, by passing many pieces of new legislation to better empower the authorities 'to deal with terrorist events and, hopefully, to prevent such events happening'.[1] The anti-terrorism legislation defines a 'terrorist act' as referring to an action which causes harm or death to a person, or serious damage to property or endangers people's lives (other than the life of the person taking 'the action').[2] Such an action or threat of action is effected with the 'intention of advancing a political, religious or ideological cause'. There must also be an intention to coerce or intimidate the government of the Commonwealth or a State, Territory or foreign country or a part thereof. This is the basic thrust of the definition of 'terrorist act' adopted by Commonwealth and State legislation.[3]

Australia's counter-terrorism framework is the product of agreement between the federal government and its State counterparts.[4] Clause 2.4

---

[1] M Kirby, 'Terrorism and the Democratic Response 2004' (2005) UNSWLJ 221, 225.
[2] Security Legislation Amendment (Terrorism) Act 2002 (Cth), Sch. 1.
[3] See B Golder and G Williams, 'What is "Terrorism"? Problems of Legal Definition' (2004) 27(2) UNSWLJ 270, 275–77.
[4] See Council of Australian Governments, *Agreement on Australia's National Counter-Terrorism Arrangements 2002.*

5.1 INTRODUCTION

of the *Agreement on Australia's National Counter-Terrorism Arrangements 2002* confers primary responsibility for dealing with terrorist incidents on State and Territory governments, and places the Commonwealth in a supporting role. The need to ensure consistency within the federal system has given rise to a number of intergovernmental agreements and policies aimed at streamlining and harmonising anti-terrorism laws.[5]

Given their front-line position, States and Territories perform functions that are operationally beyond Commonwealth responsibility. For example, special command structures within the State and Territory police forces take the operational lead in responding to terrorist threats, such as during the infamous 'Sydney Siege', in which Man Haron Monis took hostages at the Martin Place Lindt café in Sydney.[6] Threats such as these more closely resemble threats to public order, which are traditionally the responsibility of the States. Given that traditional primary role, and the logistical and operational considerations involved, it is not unsurprising that the front-line response for dealing with terrorist threats would also fall to the states, as it does in the United States.[7]

It is not the aim of this chapter to analyse in detail the minutiae of the spectrum of federal and State anti-terrorism legislation and policy. The special powers available to police dealing with terrorism resemble the special powers described in Chapters 4 and 6, raise the same constitutional and interpretive questions, and can be subjected to similar criticisms.[8] The focus of the chapter is on the constitutionality of two special statutory measures that are peculiar to terrorist emergencies:

---

[5] See, e.g., the *Australia New Zealand Guidelines for Deployment of Police to High Risk Situations 2013*; the *National Counter-Terrorism Plan 2012*.

[6] See State Coroner of NSW, *Inquest into the Deaths Arising from the Lindt Café Siege: Findings and Recommendations* (2017), 107–08.

[7] See, e.g., MC Waxman, 'Police and National Security: American Local Law Enforcement and Counterterrorism After 9/11' (2009) JNSLP 377, 386.

[8] See Terrorism (Police Powers) Act 2002 (NSW); Terrorism (Police Powers) Act 2005 (SA); Police Powers (Public Safety) Act 2005 (Tas); Terrorism (Community Protection) Act 2003 (Vic), pt 3A; Terrorism (Extraordinary Powers) Act 2005 (WA); Terrorism (Extraordinary Temporary Powers) Act 2006 (ACT); Terrorism (Emergency Powers) Act (NT). Queensland has amended its general special powers statute, the Public Safety Preservation Act 1986 (Qld), to permit a 'terrorist emergency forward commander', who is a police official, to declare an area to have a 'terrorist emergency' and oversee the exercise of special powers within that area: see pt 2A.

preventative detention orders and control orders. It examines how the constitutionality issue pertaining to these two statutory powers has been dealt with by the High Court and whether it has done this in a manner which reconciles the protection of public safety with the rule of law.

The power to order 'preventative' (or 'preventive') detention and the power to issue 'control orders' are now among the most potent elements of the legal armoury made available to the authorities to combat terrorism. There are a number of differences between the two, which go mainly to the restraints imposed on the person subject to the order. A control order places restrictions on one's movement and association, whereas a preventative detention order entails a person being taken into custody. Preventative detention orders are in theory more invasive because they involve the actual detention of the person, and have a more targeted purpose; they are designed not only to prevent terrorist attacks, but preserve evidence before formal charges are laid against the detainee in the event that a terrorist attack has occurred.[9]

As the Commonwealth Parliament is a parliament of enumerated powers or one of limited competence, a question at the outset is the source of law-making power to enact legislation providing for the power of preventative detention and the power to make control orders. In the context of federal legislation to combat terrorism, heads of legislative power of relevance, and which were invoked in *Thomas* v. *Mowbray*,[10] are the defence power in section 51(vi) and the external affairs power in section 51(xxix). Another potential source of federal power to deal with terrorism generally, and engage in preventative detention specifically, is the possible existence of an implied power to protect the nation. This implied power is said to arise from the fact of nationhood or from an interplay of the executive power in section 61 and the express incidental power in section 51(xxxix).[11] Attention has been also been drawn to section 119 of the Australian Constitution, which mandates the federal government to protect every State against 'invasion' or, on the application of the State executive government, 'against domestic violence'.[12] Such powers might be considered to underpin Part IIIA of the *Defence*

---

[9] P Fairall and W Lacey, 'Preventative Detention and Control Orders under Federal Law: The Case for a Bill of Rights' (2007) 31 MULR 1072, 1076–77, 1079–80.
[10] [2007] HCA 33; (2007) 233 CLR 307.
[11] See *Pape* v. *Federal Commissioner of Taxation* (2009) 238 CLR 1; see also Chapter 3.
[12] See Peta Stephenson, 'Fertile Ground for Federalism: Internal Security, the States and Section 119 of the Constitution' (2015) 43 FLR 289.

5.1 INTRODUCTION

Act 1903 (Cth), which sets out the conditions in which the Australian Defence Force may be used to defend Commonwealth, State, and self-governing Territory interests.

Before *Thomas* v. *Mowbray*, it might have been argued that, considered together, these sources of power would not give the Commonwealth the power to deal with any and all terrorist threats, let alone authorise the preventative detention of an individual in any but the most extraordinary circumstances. Those powers appear to contemplate threats of such a scale that they overwhelm the States to the point where only the federal government can respond, a fact that is established by the failure of a State government to resolve the threat itself and its request of federal help.[13] As is discussed in Chapter 2 and, here, at Section 5.4, however, the High Court appears to have accepted in *Thomas* v. *Mowbray* that even smaller-scale, internal threats to life and property can be the subject of the defence power. This means that the Commonwealth may legislate to address such threats, notwithstanding whether the State is capable of dealing with the threat itself. That reasoning has implications not only for the distribution of constitutional responsibility for addressing terrorism, but for the Commonwealth's power to deal with threats to public order generally.

Because of the ongoing uncertainty surrounding the constitutionality of preventative detention by the Commonwealth, the most effective way of ensuring the validity of the legislation is to anchor the legislation to the power to make laws with respect to matters referred to the Commonwealth Parliament by the legislatures of the States.[14] The States did in fact refer the power to make laws with respect to a range of terrorism related matters in 2002 and 2003.[15] In addition, the Commonwealth has employed the States to engage in preventative detention and use control orders in a way which it cannot because it would potentially breach the federal separation of powers.

For example, under the State and Territory preventative detention frameworks, individuals may be detained for far longer than they can

---

[13] Ibid. See also Defence Act 1903 (Cth), s 51B(1)(a) (permitting the Commonwealth to protect a State against domestic violence only where 'the State is not, or is unlikely to be, able to protect itself against the domestic violence'.)

[14] This being a head of legislative power under s 51(xxxvii) of the Australian Constitution, which provides that the Commonwealth Parliament may enact laws with respect to "matters referred to the Parliament of the Commonwealth by the Parliament or Parliaments of any State or States."

[15] See the Terrorism (Commonwealth Powers) Act passed in every State.

be detained under the Commonwealth law; fourteen days, as opposed to twenty-four hours (or forty-eight hours in certain circumstances).[16] This reflects the fact that State governments, unlike their federal counterpart, have no limits on their legislative power apart from any inconsistencies arising from Commonwealth legislation, or limitations expressly imposed by or implied from the Constitution. To that end, and as the discussion at Section 5.6 makes clear, there are open questions as to how these State preventative detention frameworks are affected by the doctrine expressed in Kable v. Director of Public Prosecutions (NSW).[17] In any case, State governments have still provided for protections in their preventative detention legislation substantially equivalent to the protections provided at the federal level; although some jurisdictions allow police officers to issue twenty-four-hour preventative detention orders.[18] All jurisdictions require a preventative detention order of more than twenty-four hours' duration to be issued by a judge.[19]

The nature of counter-terrorist detention is still developing at both the State and federal level. New South Wales and the Commonwealth have recently enacted laws directed at the 'continuing detention' of 'high risk terrorist offenders'.[20] The New South Wales law states that it is designed to enable 'the extended supervision and continuing detention of certain offenders posing an unacceptable risk of committing serious terrorism offences so as to ensure the safety and protection of the community'.[21]

---

[16] See generally: Terrorism (Police Powers) Act 2002 (NSW), pt 2A; Terrorism (Preventative Detention) Act 2005 (Qld); Terrorism (Preventative Detention) Act 2005 (SA); Terrorism (Preventative Detention) Act 2005 (Tas); Terrorism (Community Protection) Act 2003 (Vic); Terrorism (Preventative Detention) Act 2006 (WA); Terrorism (Extraordinary Temporary Powers) Act 2006 (ACT), pt 2; Terrorism (Emergency Powers) Act (NT), pt 2B. See also S Tyulkina and G Williams, 'Preventative Detention Orders in Australia' (2015) 38 UNSWLJ 738, 748–49.

[17] (1996) 189 CLR 51.

[18] See, e.g., the Terrorism (Preventative Detention) Act 2005 (Qld), s 8 of which permits a police officer to apply to an 'issuing authority', defined in s 7 as a senior police officer, for an 'initial order', which per s 17(5) must not be more than 24 hours. See also Terrorism (Preventative Detention) Act 2005 (Tas), s 5(3) (permitting a senior police officer to issue a preventative detention order if the applicant considers there is an 'urgent need for the order' and it is not practicable to apply to the Supreme Court. Under s 9(4), an order made in this way must also be made to the Supreme Court as soon as practicable).

[19] Tyulkina and Williams (n 16) 748–49.

[20] See the Terrorism (High Risk Offenders) Act 2017 (NSW); Criminal Code Amendment (High Risk Terrorist Offenders) Act 2016 (introducing div 105A into the Criminal Code 1995 (Cth)).

[21] Terrorism (High Risk Offenders) Act 2017 (NSW), s 3(1).

Interestingly, the federal legislation vests the power to make these orders in the Supreme Courts of the States and Territories, as opposed to the federal courts – a point that shall be returned to at the end of this chapter.[22] The key difference between this legislation and the preventative detention regime is that it targets convicted 'terrorist offenders',[23] and imposes special supervision or extended detention measures based on the Supreme Court's assessment of the risk that the offender will commit further terrorist-related offences if the order is not made.[24]

5.2 Preventative Detention Orders and Control Orders

The preventative detention power is controversial, for it empowers the authorities to incarcerate a person – such as a suspected terrorist who is planning to launch attacks on the public – who poses a danger to the community. Bearing in mind that Australia is a signatory to the International Covenant on Civil and Political Rights ('ICCPR'), the concern about this power is that the detainee has not been charged and tried in a court of law. The detention is based simply on the belief that such a person, if unconstrained, would commit a terrorist act. There has been much debate about whether the invocation of a preventative detention power in the fight against terrorism is a constitutionally valid means

---

[22] See, e.g., Criminal Code 1995 (Cth), div 105A.7(1) (authorising a 'Supreme Court of a State or Territory' to make a continuing detention order).

[23] Defined in div 1.3 of the Terrorism (High Risk Offenders) Act 2017 (NSW) as certain 'eligible' offenders, defined by s 7 as offenders who have been convicted and sentenced to imprisonment for an indictable offence. For the purposes of applying the Act, eligible offenders are sorted into those who engaged in activities as defined under s 8 ('Convicted NSW terrorist offenders' who were convicted for being a member of a terrorist organisation under Crimes Act 1900 (NSW), s 310J); under s 9 ('Convicted NSW underlying terrorism offenders' who had committed certain defined serious offences such as firearms offences or offences concerning damage to life, property, public safety or infrastructure in a 'terrorist context', meaning they had an intention to take, or were reckless in taking, actions to advance a 'political, religious or ideological cause' with the objective of coercing a government or the public); and s 10 ('Convicted NSW terrorism activity offenders' who had at any time been subject to a control order, had been a member of a terrorist organisation, or otherwise been involved in advocating for terrorist acts).

[24] See, e.g., Terrorism (High Risk Offenders) Act 2017 (NSW), pt 2 (allowing the Supreme Court to make 'extended supervision orders' to be made for up to a 3-year limit as imposed by s 26(6)), pt 3 (allowing the Supreme Court to make 'continuing detention orders' over a detained or supervised offender up to a 3-year limit as imposed by s 40(1); see also, e.g., Criminal Code 1995 (Cth), div 105A subdiv B (permitting 'continuing detention orders' to be made in respect of certain terrorist offences under the Criminal Code).

in a liberal democracy.[25] Both preventative detention orders and control orders impact adversely on a broad spectrum of fundamental human rights: right to liberty, presumption of innocence, right to privacy, freedom of association, freedom of expression and freedom of movement.[26]

5.3 Preventative Detention in Wartime

The power of preventative detention had been resorted to in Australia during wartime. The British and Australian governments have used such a power in both World Wars. The Australian wartime experience indicated the judiciary adopting a deferential role in relation to the exercise of such a power.

During the First World War, the War Precautions Act 1914, as amended by the Act of 1915, empowered the Governor-General to make regulations for 'securing the public safety and the defence of the Commonwealth' in relation to a number of enumerated objects. Pursuant to this power reg 55(1) of the War Precautions Regulations 1915 was made. It provided that where the Minister 'has reason to believe that any naturalized person is disaffected or disloyal', he may order that person to be detained in military custody in such place as he thinks fit during the continuance of the war. In response to a writ of habeas corpus issued out of the Supreme Court of Victoria, a warrant was returned under the hand of the Minister of Defence which recited that the Minister did believe that Wallach was disaffected or disloyal.

In *Lloyd v. Wallach*,[27] the Supreme Court of Victoria, by a majority, ordered that Wallach be discharged because they found the impugned regulation was invalid. However, this decision was reversed by the High

---

[25] See, e.g., Kate Chetty, '*Persona Designata*, Punitive Purposes and the Issue of Preventative Detention Orders: All Roads Lead to Infringement of the Separation of Judicial Power' (2016) 40(1) MULR 87; Andrew Lynch, Edwina MacDonald, George Williams, *Law and Liberty in the War on Terror* (Federation Press 2007).

[26] In *A v. Secretary of State for the Home Department* [2005] 2 AC 68 (the Belmarsh Case), Lord Walker said that the detention without trial of terrorist suspects is 'a crucial instance – probably the most crucial instance of all – of the problems of reconciling individual human rights with the interests of the community, and of determining the proper functions, in this process, of different arms of government' (ibid 160). See also Tyulkina and Williams (n 16) 746–48.

[27] (1915) 20 CLR 299. See HP Lee, '*Salus Populi Suprema Lex Esto*: Constitutional Fidelity in Troubled Times' in HP Lee and Peter Gerangelos (eds), *Constitutional Advancement in a Frozen Continent* (Federation Press 2009) 53, 64.

5.3 PREVENTATIVE DETENTION IN WARTIME

Court of Australia. In the wartime cases of both the First and Second World Wars pertaining to preventative detention, the focus was on the extent to which the court could inquire into the fact of the Minister's belief that a detainee merited preventative detention. In brief the choice was between applying a 'subjective' or an 'objective' test. In *Lloyd v. Wallach*, Griffith CJ in the High Court expressed the view that the Minster's belief 'is the sole condition of his authority, and that he is the sole judge of the sufficiency of the materials on which he forms it'.[28] But, what if the Minister had in fact not formed any such belief? Griffith CJ proffered the opinion that if this could be established '*aliunde* in other proceedings', the person aggrieved 'might perhaps have other means of redress'.[29]

During the Second World War, reg 26(1)(c) of the National Security (General) Regulations enacted pursuant to the National Security Act 1939–1940 empowered the Minister to order the detention of any person if the Minister was satisfied that it was necessary to do so with a view to preventing that person acting in any manner prejudicial to the public safety or the defence of the Commonwealth. In *Little v. Commonwealth*,[30] the plaintiff sued the Commonwealth for false imprisonment and sought damages on the basis that, in relation to his incarceration, the Minister, whose requisite opinion was recited in the order, 'did not in fact possess that opinion'. Counsel for the Commonwealth argued that the Minister's opinion or expression of opinion on these matters was not examinable.

Dixon J said:

> Courts have not always been at one on the question whether it is open to them to examine the truth of such a recital in an order of this character. . . . But, in any case, I do not think that the plaintiff has established that when he made the order the Minister did not entertain the opinion the recital ascribes to him . . .
>
> But I think it is right to say that his evidence raised a very strong presumption that the orders had been mistakenly made and had no real foundation in any acts, conduct or tendencies of the plaintiff. The law makes it unnecessary for the Commonwealth to disclose the information upon which the Minister acted and I am not aware of its nature. But it is also right to say that nothing has appeared in the proceedings before me which would justify any suggestion against the plaintiff's loyalty or

---

[28] (1915) 20 CLR 299, 304.
[29] Ibid 305.
[30] (1947) 75 CLR 94. See Lee (n 27) 65.

steadfastness to the allied cause. That, however, is beside the point which I have to decide, namely whether there is any ground for nullifying the Minister's order. That he was mistaken in his opinion is certainly not such a ground. Even if it were open to show that the recital that he entertained the opinion was wrong, that has not been shown. But I do not think the order is examinable upon any ground affecting the Minister's opinion short of bad faith.[31]

A few years prior to *Little* v. *Commonwealth*, the subjective test had been endorsed by a majority of the House of Lords in the famous case of *Liversidge* v. *Anderson*.[32] The case was concerned with the construction of reg 18B of the Defence (General) Regulations 1939, made pursuant to the Emergency Powers (Defence) Act 1939, which provided, inter alia, that, if the Secretary of State has reasonable cause to believe any person to be of hostile origin or associations and that by reason thereof it is necessary to exercise control over him, he may make an order against the person directing that he be detained. In the words of Lord Wright, all that it required was that the Secretary of State 'must be reasonably satisfied before he acts, but it is still his decision and not the decision of anyone else'.[33] Lord Maugham said that the regulation did not contemplate 'the possibility of the action of the Secretary of State being subject to the discussion, criticism and control of a judge in a court of law'[34]. Lord Macmillan said: 'The production by the Secretary of State of an order of detention by him ex facie regular and duly authenticated, such as the House has before it in this case, constitutes a peremptory defence to any action of false imprisonment and places on the plaintiff the burden of establishing that the order is unwarranted, defective or otherwise invalid'.[35]

Lord Atkin delivered a dissenting judgment which 'seized the imagination of lawyers and layman alike'.[36] He said:

> It is surely incapable of dispute that the words 'if A has X' constitute a condition the essence of which is the existence of X and having of it by A. ... 'If A has a broken ankle' does not mean and cannot mean 'if A thinks he has a broken ankle'. 'If A has a right of way' does not mean

---

[31] Ibid 103.
[32] [1942] AC 206. See HP Lee, 'Of Lions and Squeaking Mice in Anxious Times' (2016) Mon LR 1, 2–4.
[33] [1942] AC 206, 268.
[34] Ibid 220.
[35] Ibid 258.
[36] RFV Heuston, 'Liversidge v. Anderson in Retrospect' (1970) 86 LQR 33, 36.

5.4 THE HIGH COURT AND CONTROL ORDERS

and cannot mean that 'if A thinks that he has a right of way'. 'Reasonable cause' for an action or a belief is just as much a positive fact capable of determination by a third party as is a broken ankle or a legal right.[37]

He added that the application of a 'subjective' test 'would startle any judge versed in trying crimes'.[38] Lord Atkin also criticised the majority judges for being 'more executive minded than the executive'.[39] Subsequent decisions of the House of Lords have recognised that the majority decision in *Liversidge* v. *Anderson* was erroneous.[40] This has also cast doubt about the contemporary authoritative effect of *Lloyd* v. *Wallach* and *Little* v. *Commonwealth*.

5.4 The High Court and Control Orders

The defence power is 'fluid', in that its scope ebbs and flows depending on the ends for which it is to be used.[41] In the case of counter-terrorism, this creates an issue in deciding what are the powers of the government, because terrorism is not generally of the same nature or scale as war between territorial states. Moreover, even if federal legislation providing for indefinite preventative detention orders and control orders to counter terrorism could find justification for its validity under the defence power, it still has to confront another constitutional hurdle. Unlike the wartime regulations authorising a Minister to issue a preventative detention order, the authority to issue a preventative detention order or a control order for counter-terrorism purposes is vested in a judicial officer. In the case of federal legislation, it is often either a judge of the Federal Court or the Circuit Court. A possible impediment to the validity of the federal legislation providing for preventative detention orders or control orders is posed by the separation of judicial power doctrine.

In *Thomas* v. *Mowbray*, the power under challenge was not that of preventative detention, but the power to make a control order when that power is reposed in the hands of a federal judicial officer. Given the deep constitutional objections to federal detention by executive order, and that this is an important difference between control orders and preventative

---

[37] [1942] AC 206, 227–28.
[38] Ibid 231.
[39] Ibid 244.
[40] See *IRC* v. *Rossminster Ltd* [1980] AC 592.
[41] *Thomas* v. *Mowbray* (2007) 233 CLR 307, 359 [135] (Gummow and Crennan JJ).

detention orders, it is uncertain to what extent the reasoning is equally applicable to a preventative detention order.

Thomas v. *Mowbray* concerned a challenge to an interim control order made by a Federal Magistrate under Div 104 of the *Criminal Code* (Cth) against the plaintiff. In making an interim control order, the Federal Magistrate had to be satisfied on the 'balance of probabilities' that the order would substantially assist in preventing a terrorist act, or that the plaintiff had provided training to or received training from a listed terrorist organisation. The Federal Magistrate also had to be satisfied that 'each of the obligations, prohibitions and restrictions to be imposed' on the plaintiff was 'reasonably necessary, and reasonably appropriate and adapted, for the purpose of protecting the public from a terrorist act'.[42]

A majority of the High Court held that Div 104 of the *Criminal Code* (Cth) was within the scope of the defence power. As is discussed in Chapter 2 of this volume, Gummow and Crennan JJ, with whom Gleeson CJ and Heydon J relevantly agreed,[43] found that the control order regime was within the 'central conception of the defence power' because, in their view, there existed a historical analogy between the regime and attempts to levy war or foment insurrection against the English sovereign.[44] The limiting principle potentially implied by section 119 was not explicitly addressed.[45] Nor did the differentiating feature of federalism feature in Gummow and Crennan JJ's use of historical analogy with England; there was no real accounting for the fact that England is a unitary state, whereas Australia is a federation with co-sovereigns assigned different functions by virtue of their capacities and the process of constitutional interpretation. Touching on this point in his dissent, Kirby J observed:

> As drafted, Div 104 proceeds outside the proper concerns of s 51(vi) and into areas of ordinary civil government. The plaintiff was correct to say that, if the *Constitution* were intended to empower the Commonwealth to make laws for the general safety and protection of the Australian public, irrespective of the source of danger and its targets, it could readily have said so. These being within the essential "police powers" of the States, the

---

[42] *Thomas* v. *Mowbray* (2007) 233 CLR 307, 372 [177].
[43] Ibid 324 [6] (Gleeson CJ), 511 [611] (Heydon J).
[44] Ibid 361–63. See also Chapter 2 at 2.4.
[45] See also Kirby J at ibid 394, 389–90; s 119 provides that the Commonwealth shall protect every State 'against domestic violence' only 'on the application of the Executive Government of the State'.

rubric of "naval and military defence" is a singularly inapt expression to use to attribute such powers to the Commonwealth.[46]

After rejecting the submission that the defence power could not sustain the validity of the impugned legislation, the High Court went on to consider the invocation of Chapter III of the Australian Constitution as a basis for challenging the constitutional validity of the empowering legislation arising from the judicial involvement in the making of a control order. The High Court was required to consider the following questions: Did the impugned legislation confer a non-judicial power on a federal court contrary to Chapter III of the Commonwealth Constitution? Even if it did confer a judicial power, did it authorise the exercise of that power in a manner incompatible with Chapter III? The High Court's answers to these questions called into play the settled doctrine of separation of judicial powers.

5.4.1 The Separation of Judicial Powers

The Australian Constitution does not provide for an explicit recognition of a separation of powers doctrine. However, the constitutional framework compartmentalises the different categories of powers in three different chapters of the Constitution. Federal legislative power is vested by Chapter I in the federal or Commonwealth Parliament; the executive power is vested by Chapter II in the Sovereign and is exercisable by the Governor-General as the Sovereign's representative; and, the judicial power is vested by Chapter III in the High Court of Australia and in such other courts as the Commonwealth invests with federal jurisdiction. Section 71 in Chapter III states:

> The judicial power of the Commonwealth shall be vested in a Federal Supreme Court, to be called the High Court of Australia, and in such other federal courts as the Parliament creates, and in such other courts as it invests with federal jurisdiction.

The compartmentalisation of the three broad categories of powers and the different organs of government was regarded as reflecting a separation of powers.[47] However, because Australia has a Westminster system

---

[46] Ibid 401 [264].
[47] The Privy Council observed: 'In the absence of any contrary provisions the principle of the separation of powers is embodied in the Constitution'.

of government at both State and federal levels, there is no strict separation between the legislative and the executive power.

There is a strict separation of judicial power, and the doctrine as enunciated by the High Court in *R v. Kirby; Ex parte Boilermakers' Society of Australia* ('*Boilermakers*')[48] contains two main propositions: First, federal judicial power cannot be invested in a federal court that does not satisfy the requirements of Chapter III of the Constitution;[49] second, a non-judicial power, other than a power which is ancillary or incidental to the exercise of judicial power, cannot be invested in a Chapter III court. In consequence, the admixture of judicial and non-judicial functions in the same tribunal would contradict Chapter III of the Constitution.[50] To establish whether the *Boilermakers'* doctrine has been breached, it is necessary therefore to determine the true nature of the function which the impugned legislation has reposed in the federal judicial officer.

5.4.2 Definition of Judicial Power

The classic definition of judicial power was enunciated by Griffith CJ in *Huddart Parker and Co Pty Ltd v. Moorehead*:[51]

> [T]he words 'judicial power' as used in s 71 of the Constitution mean the power which every sovereign must of necessity have to decide controversies between its subjects, or between itself and its subjects, whether the rights relate to life, liberty or property. The exercise of this power does not begin until some tribunal which has power to give a binding and authoritative decision (whether subject to appeal or not) is called upon to take action.[52]

Some functions lie in a conceptual 'borderland' between the functions that can definitively be characterised as an exercise of either the judicial

---

[48] (1956) 94 CLR 254.
[49] *New South Wales v. Commonwealth* (the *Wheat* case) (1915) 20 CLR 54; *Waterside Workers' Federation v. J W Alexander* (the *Alexander* case) (1918) 25 CLR 434.
[50] *Attorney-General of the Commonwealth of Australia v. The Queen* (1957) 95 CLR 529, 540–41. The doctrine was endorsed by the Privy Council, which explained the underlying rationale: '[I]n a federal system the absolute independence of the judiciary is the bulwark of the constitution against encroachment whether by the legislature or the executive. To vest in the same body executive and judicial power is to remove a vital constitutional safeguard'.
[51] (1908) 8 CLR 330.
[52] Ibid 357.

5.4 THE HIGH COURT AND CONTROL ORDERS

or executive powers.[53] The difficulty in formulating a comprehensive definition of judicial power is amplified by the fact that the combination of relevant factors is not always the same, thus posing the difficulty of pointing to any essential or constant characteristic.[54] In some instances where a function lacks one or more of the characteristics of a judicial function, it may nevertheless be regarded as of a judicial nature as it is 'of a kind which had come by 1900 to be so consistently regarded as peculiarly appropriate for judicial performance that it then occupied an acknowledged place in the structure of the judicial system'.[55] The complexity in the task of identifying the nature of the function is also aggravated by the recognition of a 'chameleon' doctrine that a function 'may take its character from that of the tribunal in which it is reposed'.[56]

5.4.3 *The* Persona Designata *Doctrine*

However, the strict separation of federal judicial power does not preclude the conferral of a non-judicial function upon a federal judicial officer. This was made possible by a distinction drawn by the High Court between the conferral of a function *upon a court* as opposed to conferral upon a member of the federal judiciary *in his or her personal capacity*, that is, as *persona designata*. It becomes necessary to decide whether a power is or is not a judicial power, and whether the power was conferred *persona designata*.

The invocation of the *persona designata* exception is not, of itself, sufficient to render legitimate the vesting of a non-judicial function in a federal judge. The High Court of Australia, in *Grollo v. Palmer*,[57] held that even if the non-judicial power is determined to have been conferred upon a judge in a personal capacity, it is necessary to enquire whether the performance of the non-judicial function would be compatible with the

---

[53] R v. *Trade Practices Tribunal, Ex parte Tasmanian Breweries Pty Ltd* (1970) 123 CLR 361 at 394 (Windeyer J). See P Gerangelos, *The Separation of Powers and Legislative Interference in Judicial Process: Constitutional Principles and Limitations* (Oxford and Portland, Oregon: Hart Publishing, 2009) 3, wherein it was observed that 'judicial power' is a concept 'notoriously resistant to precise definition, and indeed to definition which may render it absolutely distinct from the non-judicial powers'.

[54] *Brandy* v. *Human Rights and Equal Opportunity Commission* (1995) 183 CLR 245, 267 (Deane, Dawson, Gaudron and McHugh JJ).

[55] R v. *Davison* (1954) 90 CLR 353, 382 (Kitto J).

[56] R v. *Hegarty; Ex parte City of Salisbury* (1981) 147 CLR 617, 628 (Mason J).

[57] (1995) 184 CLR 348.

performance of judicial functions.[58] The impugned legislation conferred power to issue interception of communications warrants on 'eligible' judges of courts created by the Commonwealth Parliament. Brennan CJ, Deane, Dawson and Toohey JJ, after stating that no non-judicial function that is not incidental to a judicial function can be conferred without the judge's consent, added 'no function can be conferred that is incompatible either with the judge's performance of his or her judicial functions or with the proper discharge by the judiciary of its responsibilities as an institution exercising judicial power (the incompatibility condition)'.

The majority of the High Court in *Grollo* v. *Palmer* articulated three limbs in the incompatibility condition. They said:

> The incompatibility condition may arise in a number of different ways. Incompatibility might consist in so permanent and complete a commitment to the performance of non-judicial functions by a Judge that the further performance of substantial judicial functions by that Judge is not practicable. It might consist in the performance of non-judicial functions of such a nature that the capacity of the Judge to perform his or her judicial functions with integrity is compromised or impaired. Or it might consist in the performance of non-judicial functions of such a nature that public confidence in the integrity of the judiciary as an institution or in the capacity of the individual Judge to perform his or her judicial functions with integrity is diminished.[59]

The majority stressed that judges appointed to exercise the judicial power of the Commonwealth cannot be authorised to engage in the performance of non-judicial functions so as 'to prejudice the capacity either of the individual Judge or of the judiciary as an institution to discharge effectively the responsibilities of exercising the judicial power of the Commonwealth'.[60]

In *Wilson* v. *Minister for Aboriginal and Torres Strait Islander Affairs*,[61] the High Court elaborated on the third limb of the incompatibility test. Brennan CJ, Dawson, Toohey, McHugh and Gummow JJ, in a joint judgment, said that the function that had to be performed in exercise of the non-judicial power must be examined in order to ascertain

---

[58] It is said 'when that condition is satisfied, judges not only are, but are seen to be, independent of the other branches of government. The appearance of independence preserves public confidence in the judicial branch'. See Wilson v. Minister for *Aboriginal & Torres Strait Islander Affairs* (1996) 189 CLR 1, 14 (Brennan CJ, Dawson, Toohey, McHugh and Gummow JJ).

[59] (1995) 184 CLR 348, 365 (Brennan CJ, Deane, Dawson and Toohey JJ).

[60] Ibid.

[61] (1996) 189 CLR 1.

its compatibility with the exercise of judicial powers. They specified the following criteria for the consideration of the court:

> The statute or the measures taken pursuant to the statute must be examined in order to determine, first, whether the function is an integral part of, or is closely connected with, the functions of the Legislative or the Executive Government ... Next, an answer must be given to the question whether the function is required to be performed independently of an instruction, advice or wish of the Legislative or the Executive Government, other than a law or an instrument made under a law ... If the function is one which must be performed independently of any non-judicial instruction, advice or wish, a further question arises: Is any discretion purportedly possessed by the Chapter III judge to be exercised on political grounds – that is, on grounds that are not confined by factors expressly or impliedly prescribed by law? In considering these questions, it will often be relevant to note whether the function to be performed must be performed judicially, that is, without bias and by a procedure that gives each interested person an opportunity to be heard and to deal with any case presented by those with opposing interests.[62]

5.4.4 Thomas v. Mowbray

In *Thomas* v. *Mowbray*, the plaintiff was subjected to a number of controls prescribed under an interim control order. The order summarised the grounds on which it was made. These grounds stated, inter alia, that the plaintiff had admitted that he had trained with Al Qa'ida, a proscribed terrorist organization, and had weapons training with them; that as a result of that training, he has become 'an available resource that can be tapped into to commit terrorist acts on behalf of Al Qa'ida or related terrorist cells'; that he was susceptible to the views and beliefs of persons who would nurture him during his reintegration into the community; that by his association with senior Al Qa'ida figures and his training he has become 'attractive to aspirant extremists'. The order went on to state that the controls placed on the plaintiff would protect the public and 'substantially assist in preventing a terrorist act', and that without the controls, the plaintiff's knowledge and skills could provide a potential resource for the planning or preparation of a terrorist act'.[63] As a result of the order, the plaintiff was required: to remain at his residence between midnight and 5:00 AM each day unless he notified the Australian

---

[62] Ibid 17.
[63] (2007) 233 CLR 307 at 322 [1].

Federal Police ('AFP') of a change of address; to report to the police three times each week; and, to submit to having his fingerprints taken. Additionally, he was prohibited: from leaving Australia without the permission of the police; from acquiring or manufacturing explosives; from communicating with specified individuals; and, from using certain communications technology.

A majority of the High Court (Gleeson CJ, Gummow, Callinan, Heydon and Crennan JJ) upheld the validity of the impugned statutory regime on the basis that the power to make a control order was an exercise of judicial power. As they had when considering the defence power, the majority drew an analogy with various powers which, based on historical considerations, are regarded as judicial powers. Gleeson CJ cited two 'familiar' examples: bail and apprehended violence orders.[64] Gleeson CJ acknowledged that both examples were not 'exact' analogies. Both instances exemplify the judicial exercise of power to create new rights and obligations. Nevertheless, the example of bail illustrates that the imposition of restrictions under the control order 'is not foreign to judicial power'.[65] Gleeson CJ also pointed out that in the case of apprehended violence orders, they have 'many of the characteristics of control orders, including the fact they may restrain conduct that is not in itself unlawful'.[66] Kirby and Hayne JJ dissented on the basis that the standards prescribed for the exercise of the power were of 'nebulous generality'[67] or were too indeterminate.[68] *Thomas* v. *Mowbray* illustrates that the identification of a particular power as judicial or non-judicial can yield conflicting results.[69]

5.5 Judicially Authorised Warrants

In the fight against terrorism, Commonwealth legislation provides for a variety of warrants that may be issued by federal judges, including warrants authorising the interception of telecommunications and

---

[64] Ibid 328–29 [16].
[65] Ibid.
[66] Ibid.
[67] Ibid 418–19 [322].
[68] Ibid 468 [475].
[69] See: F Wheeler, 'The Separation of Judicial Power and Progressive Interpretation' in HP Lee and P Gerangelos (eds), *Constitutional Advancement in a Frozen Continent* (Federation Press 2009), 234; D Myerson, 'Using Judges to Manage Risk: The Case of *Thomas* v. *Mowbray*' (2008) 36 FLR 209, 228.

5.5 JUDICIALLY AUTHORISED WARRANTS 153

warrants authorising criminal investigators to use surveillance devices such as listening and tracking devices.[70] Federal Magistrates acting in a *persona designata* capacity under the *Crimes Act 1914* (Cth), may, on an application from the AFP, compel a third party to produce a range of documents that are 'relevant to, and will assist, the investigation' of any of a range of offences punishable by two or more years of imprisonment.[71] It is an offence for the third party to fail to comply with, or to disclose the existence or nature of, the notice.[72] The constitutionality of this regime has not been tested.

The Criminal Code (Cth) provides for a regime of preventative detention orders.[73] A senior member of the AFP may issue such an order upon the application of another member of the AFP, authorising the detention of a person for up to twenty-four hours, if (i) a terrorist act has occurred within the last twenty-eight days, and (ii) detaining the person is reasonably necessary in order to preserve evidence of, or relating to, the terrorist act. Alternatively, an order may be issued if the issuing AFP member is satisfied both that detaining the person is reasonably necessary in order to substantially assist in preventing a terrorist act occurring, and that there are reasonable grounds to suspect that the person to be detained either (i) will engage in a terrorist act, or (ii) possesses a thing connected with the preparation for, or the engagement of a person in, a terrorist act, or (iii) has done an act in preparation for or planning a terrorist act. In each of these latter three cases, reference to a 'terrorist act' is reference to a terrorist act that is imminent, and that is expected to occur at some time in the next fourteen days.[74] The *Criminal Code* further vests federal judges, acting in a *persona designata* capacity, with the power to extend a preventative detention order that has been issued and executed. The grounds for extension are the same as those on which

---

[70] Telecommunications (Interception and Access) Act 1979 (Cth); Surveillance Devices Act 2004 (Cth), ss 12, 14.
[71] Crimes Act 1914 (Cth), pt IAA, div 4B, subdiv C. This subdivision was introduced into the Crimes Act by the Anti-Terrorism Act (No. 2) 2005 (Cth).
[72] Crimes Act 1914 (Cth), ss 3ZQS, 3ZQT.
[73] Criminal Code (Cth), div 105. This division was introduced into the Criminal Code by the Anti Terrorism Act (No. 2) 2005 (Cth).
[74] Criminal Code (Cth), ss 105.4, 105.8. Under Australian law it is an offence to engage in a terrorist act, to possess a thing connected with the preparation for, or the engagement of a person in, a terrorist act while knowing of or being reckless as to that connection, or to do an act in preparation for or planning a terrorist act: Criminal Code (Cth), ss 101.1, 101.4, 101.6. The threshold for arrest without warrant is belief on reasonable grounds that a person has committed or is committing an offence: Crimes Act 1914 (Cth), s 3W.

an order may initially be issued, and the maximum duration of detention is forty-eight hours in total.[75]

While subject to preventative detention, a person is limited to communicating with his or her lawyer, certain public officials, and her family – but in the latter case, only to tell them that he or she is 'safe but unable to be contacted for the time being'.[76] A preventative detention order, whether issued by a police officer or a judge, may also prohibit contact with particular family members or lawyers if the AFP member who applies for the order seeks such an order, which may be issued on any of a number of grounds relating to the integrity of ongoing criminal investigations or the prevention of harm or risk.[77]

This regime of *executive* preventative detention may have to surmount another constitutional hurdle. The regime, it could be argued, amounts to an attempt to vest a purely judicial function in a non-judicial body. In *Chu Kheng Lim v. Minister for Immigration, Local Government and Ethnic Affairs*,[78] Brennan, Deane and Dawson JJ stated that 'the adjudgment and punishment of criminal guilt under a law of the Commonwealth' is 'essentially and exclusively judicial in character'.[79] They added that, part from exceptional cases, 'the involuntary detention of a citizen in custody by the State is penal or punitive in character ... and exists only as an incident of the exclusively judicial function of adjudging and punishing criminal guilt'.[80] They declared citizens 'enjoy, at least in times of peace ... a constitutional immunity from being imprisoned by Commonwealth authority except pursuant to an order by a court in the

---

[75] Criminal Code (Cth), ss 105.2, 105.12, 105.14, 105.18.
[76] Criminal Code (Cth), ss 105.34, 105.35, 105.36, 105.37, 105.41.
[77] Criminal Code (Cth), ss 105.14A, 105.15, 105.16, 105.40.
[78] (1992) 176 CLR 1. The High Court upheld the validity of impugned provisions of the Migration Act 1958 (Cth), which empowered the executive to detain a 'designated person'.
[79] Ibid 27.
[80] Ibid. The exceptional cases include 'the arrest and detention in custody, pursuant to executive warrant, of a person accused of crime to ensure that he or she is available to be dealt with by the courts', and 'involuntary detention in cases of mental illness or infectious disease'. Gaudron J remarked: 'Detention in custody in circumstances not involving some breach of the criminal law and not coming within well-accepted categories of the kind which Brennan, Deane and Dawson JJ refer is offensive to ordinary notions of what is involved in a just society. But I am not presently persuaded that legislation authorising detention in circumstances involving no breach of the criminal law and travelling beyond presently accepted categories is necessarily and inevitably offensive to Ch III'. (Ibid 55).

exercise of the judicial power of the Commonwealth'.[81] The crucial element underpinning validity of a preventative detention regime is how to determine whether the executive preventative detention is punitive.

The regime under the *Criminal Code* has features that appear to be intended to secure its constitutionality by distinguishing it from the paradigm of imprisonment in the course of criminal investigation and punishment. In particular, a person who is being detained under a preventative detention order may not be questioned except for the purposes of confirming that he or she is the person specified in the order, ensuring his or her safety and well-being, or otherwise allowing the questioning police officer to comply with a duty arising under the preventative detention regime. Similarly, identification material such as fingerprints or photographs may be taken from a detained person only for the purposes of confirming his or her identity.[82] Nevertheless, preventative detention is quite different from the other exceptions to the prohibition upon executive detention. Not only is it quite different from detention following arrest upon suspicion of having committed a crime, but there is also little resemblance to regimes of quarantine except perhaps in the most metaphorical of fashions. It may be questioned whether the Commonwealth Parliament has the power to enact a detention regime of this sort.

If preventative detention orders are nevertheless constitutional, then it is at least arguable that it is also constitutional to vest federal judges, acting in a *persona designata* capacity, with the power to extend such orders. Although these orders are not strictly analogous to

---

[81] Ibid 28-29. In *Al-Kateb v. Godwin* (2004) 219 CLR 562 and *Minister for Immigration and Multicultural Affairs v. Al Khafaji* (2004) 219 CLR 664, the High Court upheld the validity of indefinite detention without trials of aliens. Dan Meagher, 'The "Tragic" High Court Decisions in Al-Kateb and Al Khafaji: The Triumph of the "Plain Fact" Interpretive Approach and Constitutional Form over Substance' (2005) 7(4) CLPR 69, 77 said: 'The decisions in *Al-Kateb* and *Al Khafaji* confirm that the Commonwealth may detain an unlawful non-citizen until it becomes reasonably practicable to remove him from Australia. If that is unlikely to occur in the foreseeable future due to circumstances beyond the control of either party, the continued detention of the unlawful non-citizen remains lawful so long as removal from Australia is still sought by the Commonwealth. And, for as long as the purpose of the administrative detention is to effect removal, the Ch III limitation on legislative and executive power is not breached'. Cf Dennis Rose, 'The High Court Decisions in Al-Kateb and Al Khafaji—A Different Perspective' (2005) 8(3) CLPR 58.
[82] Criminal Code (Cth), ss 105.42, 105.43, 105.44.

telecommunications interception warrants, it seems likely that if the discretion involved in issuing such warrants is not excessively political, then neither should that be involved in deciding whether or not to extend a preventative detention order. Nor is the coercive and clandestine character of preventative detention, given the comparatively short duration of such detention, in any obvious way less compatible with the judicial function than the interference with privacy under a telecommunications interception warrant that may last for up to ninety days.[83]

A countervailing consideration is that a judge only becomes involved in the preventative detention regime once an order has already been issued by a senior member of the AFP and the person taken into custody. The legislative goal seems to be to interpose the judge between executive and detainee as an independent decision-maker, and (consistently with *Grollo*) this is suggestive of compatibility. But the regime creates the obvious possibility of a judge being requested to extend the duration of detention in circumstances where the judge suspects the existing detention to be improper or even unlawful, without giving the judge any power to respond to such circumstances (for example, by revoking the existing order[84]). The possibility of a judge being compromised in this way is compounded by the judge having only a limited power to request further information from the AFP member applying for the extension.[85] This possibility may have the potential to undermine public confidence in the integrity of the federal judiciary. No federal preventative detention order has yet been issued, and thus the constitutionality of the federal legislation has not been tested in the federal courts.

Under the Australian Security Intelligence Organisation Act 1979 (Cth), a federal judge acting as *persona designata* may, at the request of the director-general of ASIO, issue a warrant authorising the compulsory questioning of a person by ASIO. Such a warrant may also authorise the

---

[83] Telecommunications (Interception and Access) Act 1979 (Cth), s 49.

[84] Under the regime, a judge vested with the power to extend a preventative detention order has the power to revoke such extensions upon the application of a member of the AFP: Criminal Code (Cth), s 105.17. He or she has no power to revoke an order on his or her own motion, nor to revoke an order issued by a senior member of the AFP.

[85] Criminal Code (Cth), s 105.4(7) limits the judge to requesting information concerning the grounds on which the order is sought, and permits the AFP member to refuse to provide such information. This contrast with (for example) section 44 of the Telecommunications (Interception and Access) Act 1979 (Cth), which permits a judge to require that further information to be given in connection with an application for a telecommunications interception warrant.

5.5 JUDICIALLY AUTHORISED WARRANTS 157

detention of that person in custody for up to seven days, in order to enable that person to be questioned.[86] The grounds on which such a warrant may be issued are that the issuing judge 'is satisfied that there are reasonable grounds for believing that the warrant will substantially assist the collection of intelligence that is important in relation to' any of a range of offences defined by their connection (more or less proximate) to an actual or possible terrorist act.[87] Such a warrant may be sought only with the consent of the Commonwealth Attorney-General, who may grant that consent only if satisfied on reasonable grounds (*i*) in the same way as the issuing judge and (*ii*) that relying on other methods of collecting the intelligence would be ineffective. In addition, before authorising a request for a warrant that would permit detention, the Attorney-General must be satisfied on reasonable grounds that detention of the subject of the warrant is necessary in order either to compel the person's appearance for questioning, to prevent the person destroying, damaging or altering a record or thing that he or she may be requested to produce in accordance with the warrant, or to prevent that person alerting anyone else involved in a terrorism offence that that offence is being investigated.[88] Once a warrant is issued it is an offence to disclose its existence while it remains in force, and it is an offence to disclose what took place pursuant to the warrant for a further two years.[89] While being questioned or detained under a warrant, it is an offence for a person to speak to anyone but their lawyer or certain public officials.[90]

Issuing these warrants is a function closely connected to the executive government. Furthermore, given (i) the broad criteria governing the issue of these warrants, (ii) the character of ASIO as an agency quite unlike both State and federal police forces, being governed by more obviously political considerations and being ultimately under the direction of a federal cabinet minister (namely, the Minister for Home Affairs)[91] and (iii) the direct role played by the Attorney-General in the issuing of a warrant, it seems that this is a function that, in its political character, comes within the invalidating criteria stated in *Wilson*. Therefore, the

---

[86] Australian Security Intelligence Organisation Act 1979 (Cth), ss 34AB, 34E, 34G, 34L, 34S. This regime was introduced into the Act by the Australian Security Intelligence Organisation Legislation Amendment (Terrorism) Act 2003 (Cth).
[87] Australian Security Intelligence Organisation Act 1979 (Cth), ss 34E, 34G.
[88] Australian Security Intelligence Organisation Act 1979 (Cth), ss 34D, 34F.
[89] Australian Security Intelligence Organisation Act 1979 (Cth), s 34ZS.
[90] Australian Security Intelligence Organisation Act 1979 (Cth), s 34K.
[91] Australian Security Intelligence Organisation Act 1979 (Cth), s 8.

attempt to vest federal judges with the power to issue ASIO questioning and detention warrants most likely falls foul of the incompatibility doctrine.

The constitutionality of ASIO detention is also doubtful in itself, for much the same reasons as the preventative detention regime. Like that regime, ASIO detention can be distinguished from the paradigm of criminal imprisonment, on the grounds that there is no requirement that the subject of an ASIO detention warrant be the object of criminal suspicion or investigation.[92] But this very feature also establishes a clear distinction between ASIO detention and the ordinary regime of criminal investigation and punishment. Nor is ASIO detention analogous to quarantine. It is therefore doubtful that the Commonwealth Parliament has the power to establish this executive detention regime.[93] No ASIO detention warrant has yet been issued, however, and this question has therefore not been tested in the courts.

5.6 The *Kable* Principle and State Courts

Given that the constitutions of the Australian States do not establish a separation of judicial power comparable to that which obtains at the federal level, challenges to the validity of State legislation providing for a power to make a preventative detention order or a control order call into play a different route of reasoning.[94] Under Chapter III of the Commonwealth Constitution, State courts may be vested by the Commonwealth Parliament with the exercise of federal judicial power. *Kable v. Director of Public Prosecutions (NSW)*[95] established a constitutional principle that 'no State or federal parliament can legislate in a way that might undermine the role of those courts as repositories of federal judicial power'.[96]

---

[92] Proponents of the regime strongly emphasise this distinction between 'intelligence gathering' and criminal investigation: Parliamentary Joint Committee on ASIO, ASIS and DSD, *ASIO's Questioning and Detention Powers: Review of the operation, effectiveness and implications of Division 3 of Part III in the Australian Security Intelligence Organisation Act 1979* (Canberra, 2005) 24–25.

[93] For a fuller discussion of this issue, see G Carne, 'Detaining Questions or Compromising Constitutionality?: The ASIO Legislation Amendment (Terrorism) Act 2003 (Cth)' (2004) 27 UNSWLR 524.

[94] See Patrick Emerton and HP Lee, 'Judges and Non-Judicial Functions in Australia' in HP Lee (ed), *Judiciaries in Comparative Perspective* (CUP 2011) 422–26.

[95] (1996) 189 CLR 51. See HP Lee, 'The *Kable* Case: A Guard-Dog that Barked but Once?' in G Winterton (ed), *State Constitutional Landmarks* (Federation Press 2006) 390.

[96] *Kable* (1996) 189 CLR 51, 116 (McHugh J).

5.6 THE *KABLE* PRINCIPLE AND STATE COURTS

In *Attorney-General (NT) v. Emmerson*,[97] French CJ, Hayne, Crennan, Kiefel, Bell and Keane JJ elaborated on the meaning of the *Kable* principle:

> The principle for which *Kable* stands is that because the Constitution establishes an integrated court system, and contemplates the exercise of federal jurisdiction by State Supreme Courts, State legislation which purports to confer upon such a court a power or function which substantially impairs the court's institutional integrity, and which is therefore incompatible with that court's role as a repository of federal jurisdiction, is constitutionally invalid.[98]

Kable v. Director of Public Prosecutions (NSW)[99] concerned the Community Protection Act 1994 (NSW), an *ad hominem* enactment of the New South Wales parliament. Section 5(1) empowered the Supreme Court to order that Gregory Wayne Kable be detained in prison for a renewal period of six months if it was satisfied, on reasonable grounds: (a) that the person is more likely than not to commit a serious act of violence; and (b) that it is appropriate, for the protection of a particular person or persons or the community generally, that he be held in custody. The legislation was a response to the imminent release from custody of Kable, who had pleaded guilty to manslaughter of his wife, and his sending of threatening letters to his deceased wife's family members while he was in prison. This was essentially a prototypical form of preventative detention.

A majority of the High Court held the impugned legislation to be invalid. According to McHugh J, the Act made the Supreme Court 'the instrument of a legislative plan, initiated by the executive government, to imprison [Kable] by a process that is far removed from the judicial process that is ordinarily invoked when a court is asked to imprison a person'.[100] McHugh J concluded:

> At the time of its enactment, ordinary reasonable members of the public might reasonably have seen the Act as making the Supreme Court a party to and responsible for implementing the political decision of the executive government that the appellant should be imprisoned without the benefit of the ordinary process of law. Any person who reached that conclusion could justifiably draw the inference that the Supreme Court was an

---

[97] [2014] HCA 13; (2014 253 CLR 393).
[98] Ibid 424 [40].
[99] (1996) 189 CLR 51. See HP Lee (n 95) 390.
[100] (1996) 189 CLR 51, 122.

instrument of executive government policy. That being so, public confidence in the impartial administration of the judicial functions of the Supreme Court must inevitably be impaired. The Act therefore infringed Ch III of the Constitution and was and is invalid.[101]

Gaudron J concluded that the provisions of Chapter III of the Commonwealth Constitution 'clearly postulate an integrated Australian court system for the exercise of the judicial power of the Commonwealth'.[102] In exercising federal jurisdiction, the State courts have a role and existence 'transcending their status as State courts'.[103] Consequently, the Parliaments of the States cannot legislate to confer powers on State courts which are 'repugnant to or incompatible with' their exercise of federal judicial power. According to Gaudron J, this constraint on State legislative power is compelled by the necessity 'to ensure the integrity of the judicial process and the integrity' of the courts specified in section 71.[104] Gaudron J described the Act as 'making a mockery of the judicial process'.[105] Gummow J characterised the legislation as drawing in the Supreme Court of a State 'as an essential and determinative integer of a scheme whereby, by its order, an individual is incarcerated in a penal institution otherwise than for breach of the criminal law'.[106]

The essence of the *Kable* principle is that a court capable of exercising the judicial power of the Commonwealth, including a State court, must be and must appear to be an independent and impartial tribunal. In *Kable*, Gummow J referred in general terms to the importance of maintaining 'the efficacy of the exercise of the judicial power of the Commonwealth' without referring in particular to the need to maintain public confidence, and stressed later that '[p]erception as to the undermining of public confidence is an indicator, but not the touchstone, of invalidity; the touchstone concerns institutional integrity'.[107] In reaching this conclusion, three of the four *Kable* majority judges drew upon the *Grollo* incompatibility doctrine, and two emphasised in particular the third limb

---

[101] Ibid 124.
[102] Ibid 101.
[103] Ibid 103.
[104] Ibid 104.
[105] Ibid 108.
[106] Ibid 133. Toohey J, at 99, also stressed that the Act was 'expressed to operate in relation to one person only, the appellant, and has led to his detention without a determination of his guilt for any offence'.
[107] *Fardon* (2004) 223 CLR 575, 618.

5.6 THE KABLE PRINCIPLE AND STATE COURTS

of that doctrine.[108] Subsequent cases concerned with the application of the *Kable* principle have turned on the question as to whether the legislation whose validity is under challenge unduly subordinates the State court to the imperatives of the executive or the legislature.[109] To that end, cases have also focused on whether the law deprives a State court of one of its 'essential characteristics', such as the giving of reasons and the holding of proceedings in open court.[110] This is an idea also reflected in *Kirk v. Industrial Court (NSW)*,[111] which recognised that a defining characteristic of State Supreme Courts, protected by section 73

---

[108] (1996) 189 CLR 51, 96, 98 (Toohey J), 116 (McHugh J), 132 (Gummow J). Gaudron J, who stated that 'The limitation on State legislative power is more closely confined' than the *Grollo* incompatibility doctrine, nevertheless used the necessity to maintain public confidence in the courts, and in particular the criminal process, as a basis for holding the legislation invalid.

[109] Of particular recent concern have been provisions of State legislation apparently allowing the executive to direct the manner in which a State court is to exercise its powers. In *Gypsy Jokers Motorcycle Club Incorporated v. Commissioner of Police* (2008) 234 CLR 532 and *K-Generation Pty Ltd v. Liquor Licensing Court* (2009) 237 CLR 501 the High Court considered the validity of legislation (respectively the Corruption and Crime Commission Act 2003 (WA), s 76(2) and the Liquor Licensing Act 1997 (SA), s 28A) that appeared to give the Commissioner of Police the power to direct a State court to treat certain information as confidential. In each case the High Court upheld the validity of the legislation by interpreting it as in fact reserving to the court a discretion as to whether or not to accept the Commissioner's claim for confidentiality, consistently with the principle that legislation 'should be interpreted, so far as its words allow, to keep it within constitutional limits': *K-Generation* (2009) 237 CLR 501, 519 (French CJ). In *International Finance Trust Company Limited v. New South Wales Crime Commission* (2009) 240 CLR 319, the High Court invalidated s 10 of the Criminal Assets Recovery Act 1990 (NSW), which permitted the Crime Commission to apply *ex parte* for an order freezing certain assets, and which obliged the court to issue the order if the statutory grounds were made out. Procedural fairness or natural justice was described as lying at 'the heart of the judicial function' (ibid 354–55 [54]–[56]). Furthermore, requiring a court to hear and determine it *ex parte*, if the Executive so desired, was akin to directing the court as to the manner in which it exercises its jurisdiction. The High Court held that there was incompatibility with the judicial function of that Court.

[110] See, e.g., *Condon v. Pompano Pty Ltd* (2013) 252 CLR 38. French CJ described these essential characteristics as follows (at 72 [68]):

'The defining or essential characteristics of courts are not attributes plucked from a platonic universe of ideal forms. They are used to describe limits, deriving from Ch III of the *Constitution*, upon the functions which legislatures may confer upon State courts and the commands to which they may subject them. Those limits are rooted in the text and structure of the *Constitution* informed by the common law, which carries with it historically developed concepts of courts and the judicial function'.

[111] (2010) 239 CLR 531.

of the Constitution, was their supervisory jurisdiction over the executive and inferior courts.[112]

One important case, *Fardon v. Attorney-General (Qld)*,[113] represented an attempt to confine the *Kable* principle to extraordinary cases of preventative detention. *Fardon* concerned the Dangerous Prisoners (Sexual Offenders) Act 2003 (Qld), which was directed at all persons serving a period of imprisonment for a 'serious sexual offence'. The Act gave the Supreme Court the power to decide whether to preventatively detain the person in order to protect the public. The *Fardon* majority held the law to be consistent with the institutional integrity doctrine because, unlike *Kable*, it was a law of general application that granted the judiciary substantial discretion as to whether and what kind of order should be made against legally tangible criteria. In upholding the law's validity, Gleeson CJ observed:

> ...as Gaudron J pointed out in *Kable*:
> [T]here is nothing to prevent the Parliaments of the States from conferring powers on their courts which are wholly non-judicial, so long as they are not repugnant to or inconsistent with the exercise by those courts of the judicial power of the Commonwealth.
>
> Nor is there anything in the Constitution that would preclude the States from legislating so as to empower non-judicial tribunals to determine issues of criminal guilt or to sentence offenders for breaches of the law.[114]

With this approach in mind, Gleeson CJ also stated:

> It might be thought that, by conferring the powers in question on the Supreme Court of Queensland, the Queensland Parliament was attempting to ensure that the powers would be exercised independently, impartially, and judicially. Unless it can be said that there is something inherent in the making of an order for preventive, as distinct from

---

[112] Ibid 580–81 [98]. In *Kirk*, the majority (French CJ, Gummow, Hayne, Crennan, Kiefel and Bell JJ) observed (at 581 [99]) that:

> To deprive a State Supreme Court of its supervisory jurisdiction enforcing the limits on the exercise of State executive and judicial power by persons and bodies other than that Court would be to create islands of power immune from supervision and restraint. It would permit what Jaffe described as the development of "distorted positions" ... it would remove from the relevant State Supreme Court one of its defining characteristics.

See also Wendy Lacey, '*Kirk v. Industrial Court of New South Wales*: Breathing Life into *Kable*' (2010) 34(2) MULR 641.

[113] (2004) 223 CLR 575.

[114] Ibid 600 [40].

punitive, detention that compromises the institutional integrity of a court, then it is hard to see the foundation for the appellant's argument.[115]

Gummow J, also in the majority, adopted an approach that focused on the process that preceded the detention. He preferred

> a formulation of the principle derived from Ch III in terms that, the "exceptional cases" aside, the involuntary detention of a citizen in custody by the State is permissible only as a consequential step in the adjudication of criminal guilt of that citizen for past acts ... That formulation eschews the phrase "is penal or punitive in character". In doing so, the formulation emphasises that the concern is with the deprivation of liberty without adjudication of guilt rather than with the further question whether the deprivation is for a punitive purpose.[116]

5.6.1 Totani v. The State of South Australia

Cases like *Kable* and *Fardon* illustrate that the core tension in the *Kable* doctrine is the effect of a particular law on a State court's institutional standing in the overall Australian constitutional structure. This suggests, by implication, that detention or other forms of State control in terrorism cases may only be attacked when those processes undermine the institutional integrity of State courts. This can still result in such laws being held invalid. For example, *Totani v. The State of South Australia*[117] is a significant case as the focus of attention was on the validity of State legislation providing for a regime of control orders. A majority of the Full Court of the South Australian Supreme Court applied the *Kable* principle to strike down section 14(1) of the Serious and Organised Crime (Control) Act 2008 (SA), which permits the Police Commissioner to seek the imposition of control orders upon members of 'declared organisations', forbidding those subject to them from associating with specified persons, from entering or being in the vicinity of specified premises and from possessing specified sorts of items. The power to declare organisations is vested by the Act in the Attorney-General of South Australia, who may take into account a wide range of information

---

[115] Ibid 592 [20].
[116] Ibid 612 [80]–[81].
[117] [2009] SASC 301 ('*Totani* ').

pertaining to the criminal activity of the organisation and its members.[118] Under the Act, the Attorney-General's declaration is immune to review or challenge.[119]

The Supreme Court took the view that the control order regime, considered in isolation from the role of the Attorney-General in declaring organisations, would not fall foul of the *Kable* principle.[120] In the view of the majority, however, when the role of the Attorney-General in declaring organisations was taken into account, section 14(1) could be seen to establish a regime which was unconstitutional because it required the court 'to act on what was, in effect, the certificate of the Attorney-General ... [who] is not subject to or bound by the rules of evidence or any standard of proof'. The majority said:

> It is as though the legislation provided for the required elements to be proved on application to the Court, but that the Court was to refer the findings on the major elements to a non-judicial officer, acting without any judicial safeguards, whose decision would be final, not reviewable and binding on the Court. In a very real sense the Court is required to "[act] as an instrument of the Executive".[121]

The majority rejected a suggested analogy between the Attorney-General's role in the control order regime and the accepted role of the executive in determining prohibited substances for the purposes of drug laws, because the former role 'involves the assessment of and making a judgment about human behaviour and its effects'.[122] The majority did not refer to the principle that the adjudication and punishment of criminal guilt is a strictly judicial function, but their reasoning – that '[i]t is the integration of the administrative function with the judicial function to an unacceptable degree which compromises the institutional integrity of the Court'[123] – is consistent with that principle.

The High Court, by a 6–1 majority, dismissed the appeal against the decision of the South Australian Supreme Court.[124] The majority placed importance on the need to protect the 'institutional integrity' of State courts which are receptacles of federal jurisdiction.

---

[118] Serious and Organised Crime (Control) Act 2008 (SA), s 10.
[119] Serious and Organised Crime (Control) Act 2008 (SA), s 41.
[120] *Totani* [2009] SASC 301, [84]–[93], [120]–[122], [128]–[143] (Bleby J), [216]–[249], [251], [254], [272]–[275] (White J), [277] (Kelly J) (concurring with Bleby J).
[121] Ibid [155]–[156] (Bleby J).
[122] Ibid [158] (Bleby J).
[123] *Totani* at [157] (Bleby J) (Kelly J concurring).
[124] *State of South Australia v. Totani* (2010) 242 CLR 1.

5.6.2 Institutional Integrity and Preventative Detention

The *Kable* doctrine focuses on the way State courts are recruited into performing functions that degrade their independence, and whether their essential characteristics as courts have been impaired. It may follow that, unlike at the federal level of government, the doctrine as presently phrased does not seem to turn on whether detention is imposed by the executive or the Parliament in violation of the principle that detention must generally be authorised by a court unless it falls into the limited set of exceptional categories described in *Chu Kheng Lim*.[125] If this is all there is to the doctrine, it would follow that as long as courts are not involved, State executives and Parliaments may employ powers that are, at the federal level, reserved for the courts pursuant to the *Chu Kheng Lim* decision, including the power to detain.

This is a position that is confused by some inconsistencies between recent High Court and State Supreme court decisions. For example, *North Australian Aboriginal Justice Agency Ltd v. Northern Territory*[126] concerned div 4AA of pt VII of the Police Administration Act (NT), which permitted the police to arrest a person without a warrant and hold them in custody – for four hours, or longer if the person was intoxicated – in order to maintain public order and allow the police to decide how to proceed against the detained person. Courts were not involved in this initial decision to detain, but became involved after a decision was made to proceed with any charges. The power was argued to violate the *Kable* doctrine because it deprived the Territory courts of an essential characteristic, namely their supervision over the exercise of penal or punitive detention powers.[127]

---

[125] See also R Ananian-Welsh, 'Preventative Detention Orders and the Separation of Judicial Power' (2015) 38(2) UNSWLJ 756; J Stellios, 'Kable, Preventative Detention and the Dilemmas of Chapter III' (2014) 88 ALJ 52.

[126] (2015) 256 CLR 569, [2015] HCA 41.

[127] See also *North Australian Aboriginal Legal Aid Service Inc v. Bradley* (2004) 218 CLR 146. It was also argued that the federal separation of powers doctrine expressed by *Boilermakers* applied to the power to make laws with respect to the territories provided for in s 122 of the Constitution, and that it followed that the Territory legislature, which was created and granted powers by an Act of Parliament, was bound by *Boilermakers* as well. That argument was considered unnecessary to answer by French CJ, Kiefel, and Bell JJ, and Nettle and Gordon JJ, because they concluded the power was not punitive (at 593 [38] and 652 [237]), and other members of the Court determined it was not accurate to say that *Boilermakers* applied to the Northern Territory legislature in this way: at 613–14 [104]–[107] (Gageler J) and 636 [178] (Keane J).

In rejecting these arguments, a majority of the High Court adopted the position that the form of detention provided for in div 4AA was not punitive, treating it instead as a form of custody that either had to be temporary or result in the detained person being brought before a judge. This was considered by the majority to be similar to one of the exceptional categories identified in *Chu Kheng Lim*, being the detention of an accused in order to bring that person before the courts.[128] The only judge who considered the punitive question to be immaterial was Keane J.[129]

Depending on how they formulated *Kable*, members of the Court were more or less prepared to contemplate the idea that preventative detention by the executive could in principle violate the *Kable* doctrine if it deprived a State court of its supervisory authority. For example, French CJ, Kiefel and Bell JJ observed:

> It might be possible to envisage a scheme in which power was conferred on the executive in such a way as effectively to deprive the courts of supervision of its exercise. Such a scheme might on established principles, or some extension thereof, be impermissible.[130]

Gageler J, dissenting, focused instead on the more traditional formulation of *Kable* as directed towards protecting the court's institutional integrity. He found that the detention was punitive, because the decision to detain was based in part on the police officer's assessment that a person had committed or was about to commit an offence.[131] Accordingly, for judges to be involved in this process was to make them 'support players in a scheme the purpose of which is to facilitate punitive executive detention. They are made to stand in the wings during a period when arbitrary executive detention is being played out'.[132] Gageler J was well aware that this line of reasoning made it plausible that legislatures would remove judicial oversight entirely, noting in that event '[t]he political choice for the Legislative Assembly would be whether or not to enact a scheme providing for deprivation of liberty in that stark form' and that such a

---

[128] *North Australian Aboriginal Justice Agency Ltd v. Northern Territory* (2015) 256 CLR 569, 592–93 [37] (French CJ, Kiefel and Bell JJ); 651–52 [236]–[237] (Nettle and Gordon JJ).
[129] Ibid 625–26 [149], 639 [189].
[130] Ibid 596 [44].
[131] Ibid 612 [102].
[132] Ibid 621 [134].

5.6 THE *KABLE* PRINCIPLE AND STATE COURTS

choice could be resolved using the available methods of political accountability.[133]

Notwithstanding *North Australian Aboriginal Justice Agency Ltd*, some State courts have understood the High Court to be moving away from the idea that the *Kable* principle is concerned with the classification of detention as punitive as opposed to the way the detention scheme undermines the courts. In *Kamm v. State of New South Wales (No 4)*,[134] Beazley P of the New South Wales Court of Appeal considered whether the Crimes (High Risk Offenders) Act 2006 (NSW) violated the *Kable* principle. This was the act upon which the continuing detention regime in the Terrorism (High Risk Offenders) Act 2017 (NSW) was based, and it employs a materially similar process.[135] Considering the implications of *Fardon* for this legislation, Beazley P observed:

> There have been judicial observations eschewing or tending to doubt the relevance of characterising legislation by reference to whether it is penal or punitive. Gummow J referred to this in *Fardon* ... when he expressed a preference for a statement of the principle in terms that involuntary detention is permissible as a consequential step in the adjudication of criminal guilt ... Gleeson CJ's acceptance in *Fardon* that the legislation before the court validly authorised "preventive detention" also indicates that the characterisation of legislation as penal or punitive does not necessarily assist in determining whether such legislation is constitutionally valid.[136]

Similarly, Beazley P considered that the decisions of Kiefel J and Hayne J in *State of South Australia v. Totani* were in support of this view.[137] The President concluded that

> [a]s is apparent from *Fardon* and *Totani*, the preventive nature of the High Risk Offenders Act does not establish any constitutional invalidity. The legislation requires a judicial determination of the type that was upheld in *Fardon*, being a decision made in respect of the individual offender subject of the application in accordance with a proper judicial process.[138]

---

[133] Ibid 621 [135].
[134] [2017] NSWCA 189.
[135] Explanatory Notes to the Terrorism (High Risk Offenders) Bill 2017 (NSW), 1.
[136] [2017] NSWCA 189, [49].
[137] Ibid [51]–[53].
[138] Ibid [54].

Presumably, it is reasoning of this kind that informed the Commonwealth's decision to vest the power to continuously detain terrorist offenders under the *Criminal Code* in State and Territory courts, as opposed to federal courts; in justifying the legislation, the Attorney-General made reference to its compatibility with *Fardon*.[139] However, the Commonwealth Parliament is in a different position; it is not permitted to vest State courts with non-judicial power.[140] The question, therefore, again becomes about the nature of the power and the implications of *Thomas* v. *Mowbray* for preventative detention.

Returning to the State Parliaments, however; it must be said that if Beazley P is correct in respect of her reasoning about *Kable* and *Fardon*, then it would apply with amplified force to laws that are designed to prevent or respond to terrorism. Even if the position of the plurality in *North Australian Aboriginal Justice Agency Ltd* was accepted, and it is inherently important for State courts to be involved in the supervision of detention for all but the most exceptional cases, it would still be necessary to contend with the historical analogy presented in *Thomas* v. *Mowbray*.

According to that analogy, we should not deal with terrorists as if we were in a 'time of peace', to paraphrase *Chu Kheng Lim*. The terrorist – however that category is chosen to be defined – stands in for the insurrectionist and other groups of persons who levy war against the sovereign. On such logic, the terrorist is accordingly different to other criminals, in that there is a need to engage in formal defence against them. As Gummow and Crennan JJ noted in *Thomas* v. *Mowbray*, considering the scope of the defence power, 'restrictions aimed at anticipating and avoiding the infliction of the suffering which comes in the train of [terrorist attacks] are within the scope of federal legislative power',[141] and are, therefore, presumably, within the relatively unfettered scope of State legislative power. The reply to that argument is that the analogy is incorrect or incomplete; notwithstanding the threat posed by terrorism, Australia remains in a 'time of peace' and its civil liberties remain intact. Absent an emergency equivalent to war, preventative detention is inconsistent

---

[139] See, e.g., Monica Biddington's discussion in the *Parliamentary Library Bills Digest no. 48, 2016–17: Criminal Code Amendment (High Risk Terrorist Offenders) Bill 2016*, 3–4.
[140] *Queen Victoria Memorial Hospital* v. *Thornton* (1953) 87 CLR 144, 151–52; *Hilton* v. *Wells* (1985) 157 CLR 57, 67 (Gibbs CJ, Wilson and Dawson JJ).
[141] (2007) 233 CLR 307, 363 [145].

with the basic principles of fairness and process that animate Australian political life.

5.7 Conclusion

There is no end in sight in the current fight against terrorism. The federal and State governments in Australia, while resorting to legal weapons of an unprecedented nature, are conscious of the need to reconcile the protection of public safety with the preservation of fundamental freedoms. Ultimately, the reconciliation requires a judgment relating to a reasonable proportionality between the means and the desired ends. A proportionate response must take into account the fundamental values underpinning a democratic polity. The liberty of the person is one such value. President Barak of the Supreme Court of Israel said that a democracy 'does not see all means as acceptable', and that '[t]he rule of law and the liberty of an individual constitute important components in its understanding of security'.[142]

It has been said that amid the clash of arms the laws are not silent.[143] The experience so far is that courts in Australia have tended to err on the side of caution by adopting a deferential approach in the face of the ongoing terrorism emergency. The upholding by the High Court of the constitutional validity of legislation empowering judicial authorisation of telecommunications interception warrants in *Grollo* v. *Palmer* and of control orders legislation in *Thomas* v. *Mowbray* indicates a judicial acknowledgment of the need to accord priority to the imperative of *salus populi suprema lex esto*. However, there could be some doubt overhanging the validity of legislation empowering the issuance by the executive of preventative detention orders. It may ultimately be accepted that an essential characteristic of an Australian court is to supervise detention, and, when the executive purports to take that supervisory power away, or subordinate the courts to an executive detention regime, it undermines the constitutional stature of the judicial branch of government. Assuming Australia remains in a time of peace, this argument would have serious ramifications for Australia's counter-terrorism laws.

---

[142] A Barak, 'A Judge on Judging: The Role of a Supreme Court in a Democracy' (2002) 116 Harv LR 148. This view was endorsed by Lord Bingham in the *Belmarsh* case.
[143] *Liversidge* v. *Anderson* [1942] AC 206, 244.

6

Civil Emergencies and Special Powers Legislation

If a state decides that an emergency institution is to be provided for in law, then the purpose, powers, effects, and limitations of that institution ought to be clearly qualified ... no dictatorial institution should be adopted, no right invaded, no regular procedure altered any more than is absolutely necessary for the conquest of the particular crisis.

Clinton Rossiter, *Constitutional Dictatorship: Crisis Government in the Modern Democracies* (1979, original 1948) 302

6.1 Introduction

The term 'civil emergency' may be taken to include any emergency that, due to its size, scope, and destructive capacity, is sufficient to justify the exercise of special emergency powers by a government. Such emergencies can be natural or man-made. They include earthquakes, bushfires and floods; viral epidemics; or wide-spread disruptions of the public order.

In order to respond to or prevent civil emergencies, governments sometimes exercise 'special powers' granted to them by Parliament. Special powers can either be general or specific in nature. The older special powers frameworks tend to be general in nature, in the sense that they confer general powers to deal with a range of emergencies. These general powers tend to activate upon a declaration or proclamation being made to that effect. It has become increasingly common, however, for legislation to confer special powers to deal with specific types of emergency, such as an epidemic, that are tailored to that emergency: a 'sectoral approach' to emergency legislation.[1] This is intended to facilitate cooperation, and allocate responsibilities amongst the different departments of government in different fields of emergency.

---

[1] See also HP Lee, 'Constitutionalised Emergency Powers' in Victor Ramraj, Arun Thiruvengadam (eds), *Emergency Powers in Asia: Exploring the Limits of Legality* (OUP 2010) 401.

6.1 INTRODUCTION

Traditionally, the Commonwealth has tended to support the operation of State special powers frameworks financially and logistically, or legislate with respect to specific civil emergencies. Over time, an integrated framework has developed in which Commonwealth, State and local governments cooperate to respond to civil emergencies according to their respective capacities. Typically, the Commonwealth will provide financial and logistical aid to the affected State government, which has principal responsibility for managing the emergency.

Recently, however, the Commonwealth Parliament has passed laws that purport to give it significant control over the management of a certain type of civil emergency, a 'biosecurity emergency'. Indeed, the Commonwealth has increasingly asserted its constitutional responsibility as being to coordinate emergency action and, in some cases, to assert certain legislative and executive emergency powers to deal with emergencies of national significance. In so doing, the Commonwealth is drawing on rationales associated with the implied legislative 'nationhood power' alluded to in decisions such as the *Communist Party Case*[2] and *R v. Sharkey*[3] and the emergency executive power associated with *Pape v. Federal Commissioner of Taxation*,[4] rationales which recognise the Commonwealth's authority to exercise certain emergency powers associated with the national preservation and defence by virtue of its very 'existence and its character as a polity'.[5]

The question of whether the ordinary limits of constitutional law apply and, if so, how, is posed when special powers legislation is invoked in response to an emergency. Conceivably, constitutional limitations such as the implied freedom of political communication and the *Melbourne Corporation* doctrine of implied inter-governmental immunities[6] have less of a role to play when a civil emergency requiring the application of special powers arises. In such a case, the constitutional question would be whether these limitations frustrate the resolution of a declared emergency, and, if so, whether that matters. So conceived, special powers legislation has a constitutional significance as well; it signals the need to depart from the ordinary functioning of the Constitution in favour of

---

[2] *Australian Communist Party v. The Commonwealth* (1951) 83 CLR 1, 187–88 (Dixon J). (See Chapter 2.)
[3] (1949) 79 CLR 121, 148–49 (Dixon J). (See Chapter 4.)
[4] (2009) 238 CLR 1. (See Chapter 3.)
[5] *Victoria v. Commonwealth and Hayden (AAP Case)* (1975) 134 CLR 338, 397.
[6] *Melbourne Corporation v. Commonwealth* (1947) 74 CLR 31.

an alternative scheme of constitutional law appropriate and adapted to the circumstances of an emergency.

Similar questions may be asked about whether special powers must be exercised compatibly with human rights and anti-discrimination legislation, both at the federal level[7] and in certain States and Territories.[8] The interaction between constitutional law, rights, and emergency has been a vexing question in other constitutional democracies, such as the United States.[9] There, '[t]he constitutional question presented in the light of an emergency is whether the power possessed embraces the particular exercise of it in response to particular conditions'.[10] Another perspective was offered by the Reid Commission when it recommended a new Constitution for the new Federation of Malaya: that

> neither the existence of fundamental rights nor the division of powers ... ought to be permitted to imperil the safety of the State or the preservation of a democratic way of life. The Federation must have adequate power in the last resort to protect these essential national interests. But ... infringement of fundamental rights or of State rights is only justified to such an extent as may be necessary to meet any particular danger which threatens the nation.[11]

The character of these powers, and their consequences for Australia's constitutional system of government, are considered in this chapter. In particular, the extent to which these frameworks contribute to, or undermine, 'constitutional resilience' shall be considered. In short, constitutional resilience may be understood to refer to the strategies used to ensure that special powers do not permanently distort or undermine the stability of the Australian constitutional structure and the division of powers and responsibilities to which that structure gives effect.

---

[7] See, e.g., the Racial Discrimination Act 1975 (Cth); Sex Discrimination Act 1984 (Cth).
[8] See, e.g., the Charter of Human Rights and Responsibilities 2006 (Vic); Human Rights Act 2004 (ACT).
[9] Clinton Rossiter, *Constitutional Dictatorship: Crisis Government in the Modern Democracies* (first published 1948, Greenwood Press 1979); Bruce Ackerman, 'The Emergency Constitution', (2004) 113 YLJ 1029, 1030–31; David Dyzenhaus, 'Schmitt v. Dicey: Are States of Emergency Inside or Outside the Legal Order?' (2006) 27 Cardozo L Rev 2005, 2016–26.
[10] *Home Building & Loan Assn. v. Blaisdell* 290 U.S. 398, 426 (1934) (Hughes CJ).
[11] *Report of the Federation of Malaya Constitutional Commission* (HMSO 1957), para [172]. See also Kevin Tan, 'From Myanmar to Manila' in Victor Ramraj, Arun Thiruvengadam (eds) *Emergency Powers in Asia: Exploring the Limits of Legality* (CUP 2010) 158.

6.2 Civil Emergencies and the Australian Constitutional Structure

Australia has faced a number of natural or environmental emergencies. In 2017 alone, Cyclone Debbie caused widespread flooding and destruction in South East Queensland, causing $2.4 billion worth of damage and killing 14 people.[12] The increasing prevalence of civil emergencies of this scope and scale has led to major developments in Australian emergency law and policy. In 2008, then Prime Minister Kevin Rudd declared in his National Security Statement that 'climate change represents a most fundamental national security challenge for the long term future'.[13] Australia was subsequently faced with a series of natural disasters of substantial scale: most prominently, the 2009 Black Saturday bushfires, which killed over 173 people and caused over $4 billion in damage throughout Victoria,[14] and the Queensland floods of 2010–2011.

The *National Strategy for Disaster Resilience* published by the Council of Australian Governments sets out a strategy for responding to the impact of climate change on Australia.[15] The National Strategy reoriented policy to emphasise the need to plan and improve resilience, in the sense that communities would recover from the physical and economic effects of a natural disaster.[16] At the same time, the Council of Australian Governments began to treat emergency management as a responsibility that had to be shared, with roles that were defined and allocated between communities, local governments, the States, and the Commonwealth.[17]

These developments were accompanied by developments in the Australian national security framework and the increased role of Emergency Management Australia, an agency within the Commonwealth Attorney-General's department that is responsible for providing assistance to States and Territories facing a civil emergency beyond their capacity. Policy documents such as the *Model Arrangements for Leadership During Emergencies of National Consequence* sought to formalise intergovernmental responsibility by focusing the power to coordinate

---

[12] Aon Benfield, *Global Catastrophe Recap* (April 2017) 9.
[13] Prime Minister Kevin Rudd, *National Security Statement* (2008).
[14] Danuta Mendelson and Rachel Carter, 'Catastrophic Loss and the Law: A Comparison between 2009 Victorian Black Saturday Fires and 2011 Queensland Floods and Cyclone Yasi', (2012) 31(2) U Tas L Rev 32, 34.
[15] Council of Australian Governments, *National Strategy for Disaster Resilience* (2011), IV.
[16] Ibid 1–2.
[17] Ibid. See also Commonwealth of Australia, *Australian Emergency Management Arrangements* (2014), 3.

emergencies in the Prime Minister and the First Ministers of the States and Territories.[18] The *Model Arrangements* recognise that '[S]tates and [T]erritories have primary responsibility for the management of emergencies within the jurisdictions' and that the Commonwealth will provide 'certain forms of physical and financial assistance' as well as act upon obligations in areas such as national security, quarantine and international relations.[19]

Similar intergovernmental agreements and frameworks have been created in areas such as the environment,[20] energy security,[21] biosecurity,[22] and public health.[23] These inter-governmental agreements and frameworks contribute to constitutional resilience as well, because they attempt to preserve, or at least define, the federal character of the Australian constitutional state in the face of serious threats to life and property. A traditional division of constitutional responsibilities is achieved by some of these frameworks, which reinforce that the States are primarily responsible for exercising special powers in response to civil emergencies, whereas the responsibilities of the Commonwealth generally lie in providing logistical and financial support as required, using the grants power in section 96.[24]

What remains largely unresolved in these frameworks is what happens when a civil emergency is so great that it requires emergency powers to be centralised into a single, national hub; a situation in which a response to a crisis is 'peculiarly adapted to the government of a nation and which cannot otherwise be carried on for the benefit of the nation'.[25] The implications of the decision of *Pape* for the capacity of the executive power to support intervention by the national government in emergencies are discussed in Chapter 3. However, some recent special powers agreements and frameworks appear to concentrate power in the Commonwealth, which suggests that the Commonwealth is increasingly

---

[18] Ibid Appendix ('Model Arrangements for Leadership during Emergencies of National Consequence').
[19] Ibid 26.
[20] Council of Australian Governments, *Heads of Agreement on Commonwealth/State Roles and Responsibilities for the Environment* (1997).
[21] Council of Australian Governments, *Australian Energy Market Agreement* (2004).
[22] Council of Australian Governments, *National Health Security Agreement* (2007); Council of Australian Governments, *Intergovernmental Agreement on Biosecurity* (2012).
[23] Council of Australian Governments, *National Healthcare Agreement* (2012).
[24] Ibid [24].
[25] *AAP Case* (1975) 134 CLR 338, 397 (Mason J).

willing to assert the circumstances in which a civil emergency shall be peculiarly national in character.[26]

From a constitutional and practical perspective, it is not only desirable but necessary that Commonwealth and State governments cooperate to deal with civil emergencies. The Commonwealth does not have the logistical capacity, let alone the power, to deal with the contingencies of every emergency by itself. One of the advantages of the federal system is that there are State governments which, because of their political and operational proximity, are better positioned to respond to many emergencies. The political and organisational realities of federalism resonate with Hayne and Kiefel JJ's observation in their dissent in *Pape* that the expanded application of Commonwealth power beyond its ordinary constitutional competence, for the sake of emergency or otherwise, 'does not fit easily with the long-accepted understanding of the constitutional structure, expressed in *Melbourne Corporation v. The Commonwealth* or *R v. Kirby; Ex parte Boilermakers' Society of Australia*, of separate polities, separately organised, continuing to exist as such, in which the central polity is a government of limited and defined powers'.[27]

However, where a civil emergency is so serious that the Commonwealth is the only government capable of responding to it – because, for example, the emergency has disabled one or more State governments – it may well be that these objections necessarily fade and any constitutional restraints are considerably diminished.

6.3 Special Powers of General Application

Every State has a range of general special powers available to it in times of emergency. These general powers set aside the normal distribution of legislative and executive powers established by the State's Constitution[28] and instead tend to concentrate broad regulation-making power in an official of the executive government. The executive government is typically authorised to make regulations with respect to anything that it deems necessary to respond to the emergency that triggered the special powers.

---

[26] See, e.g., the biosecurity emergency laws discussed in Section 6.4.3.2.
[27] *Pape v. Federal Commissioner of Taxation* (2009) 238 CLR 1, 115 [325].
[28] An action which is entirely permitted, because State parliaments exercise plenary legislative power and are not bound to adhere to their own Constitutions: see *Union Steamship Co of Australia Pty Ltd v. King* (1988) 166 CLR 1, 10.

Some of these powers are specific, in the sense that they are directed at preserving essential services or particular resources such as food or fuel. What makes them 'general special powers', however, is the fact that the range of emergencies that justify their exercise is left unspecified and the concept of emergency tends to be defined generally.

General special powers are important because they give a government the powers it may need to cope with the general effects of an emergency. In a sense, these laws define an emergency by addressing their effects; an emergency, so conceived, involves an absence of resources, services, and law and order. However, there is a danger to enacting general special powers; they can establish a 'permanent legal institution of constitutional dictatorship',[29] the invocation and operation of which is not confined to a particular set of facts or events. It is important, therefore, to restrain and make accountable the exercise of general special powers.

6.3.1 Emergency Powers in the United Kingdom

The most immediate precursor to and influence on modern special powers legislation was the Emergency Powers Act 1920 (UK). The law as originally phrased provided that the King (now Queen) in Council may proclaim a state of emergency if it appears that:

> any action has been taken or is immediately threatened by any persons or body of persons of such a nature and on so extensive a scale as to be calculated, by interfering with the supply and distribution of food, water, fuel, or light, or with the means of locomotion, to deprive the community, or any substantial portion of the community, of the essentials of life.[30]

In 1964, the law was amended to extend to natural disasters, by substituting the phrase 'there have occurred, or are about to occur, events of such a nature' for the more public disorder-focused phrase 'immediately threatened by any persons or body of persons'.

Once an emergency is declared under the Act, the Queen in Council is empowered to make regulations for 'securing the essentials of life to the community' and for conferring on any person such powers and duties 'for the preservation of the peace, for securing and regulating the supply and distribution of food, water, fuel, light and other necessities, for

---

[29] Oren Gross and Fionnuala Ní Aoláin, *Law in Times of Crisis: Emergency Powers in Theory and Practice* (CUP 2006) 235.
[30] Emergency Powers Act 1920 (UK), s 1.

maintaining the means of transit or locomotion, and for any other purposes essential to the public safety and the life of the community and incidental matters'.[31] Additionally, the Queen in Council was granted the authority to make regulations providing for the trial by summary jurisdiction any offence against the regulations, punishable by a maximum of three months' imprisonment or a fine of $100.[32] The regulations could not be used to enforce compulsory military service or industrial conscription, and could not be used to prohibit persons from taking part in a strike.[33]

The Act also gave an oversight function to Parliament. Any regulations made under the Act had to be put before the Parliament, and they expired within seven days unless both Houses of Parliament passed a resolution allowing them to continue. The Act also gave both Houses of Parliament the authority to add to, alter, or revoke the regulations.[34]

6.3.1.1 The Civil Contingencies Act 2004 (UK)

The Emergency Powers Act 1920 (UK) was enacted largely to deal with industrial strikes and economic uncertainty that occurred during the 1920s and the 1930s.[35] It was inspired by the experiences of the British Government during World War I with the Defence of the Realm Act 1914 (UK). This Act, in the United Kingdom as elsewhere, 'established a precedent that became the benchmark for future emergency legislation not only in wartime but also in times of peace'.[36]

Over time, the framework in the United Kingdom has been amended, added to by supplementary legislation, and ultimately replaced by the Civil Contingencies Act 2004 (UK). This Act is designed to modernise the law of emergency by requiring, in Part 1, that all levels of government coordinate on the creation of contingency plans, and confers a regulation-making power to that end. Part 2 of the Act then allows the Queen in Council (or, in some instances, the Secretary of State) to make

---

[31] Emergency Powers Act 1920 (UK), s 2(1).
[32] Emergency Powers Act 1920 (UK), s 2(3).
[33] Emergency Powers Act 1920 (UK), s 2(1).
[34] Emergency Powers Act 1920 (UK), s 2(4): although, as the British Parliament cannot limit its own legislative power, it may be questioned as to whether this provision was necessary or effective.
[35] Gross and Ní Aoláin (n 29) 235.
[36] Ibid 234.

'emergency regulations' where an emergency has occurred and the creation of those regulations becomes both necessary and urgent.[37]

Under section 22, the regulations may contain 'any provision which the person making the regulations is satisfied is appropriate for the purpose of preventing, controlling or mitigating an aspect or effect of the emergency in respect of which the regulations are made'.[38] This includes the power to make provision of any kind that could be made by 'Act of Parliament or by the exercise of the Royal Prerogative'.[39] These powers have been described as 'Henry VIII' powers, in that they essentially allow the executive to promulgate laws.[40] Importantly, the emergency regulations include what are described in this Chapter as 'coordinative powers', in the sense that they are supposed to concentrate into the hands of a certain public officer, 'Emergency Coordinators', the power to direct the activities of government agencies in response to an emergency.[41]

In its First Report, the Joint Committee on the Draft Civil Contingencies Bill observed:

> Despite the severe challenges which have been faced in the 20th and the 21st centuries, including emergent threats of international terrorism, rogue and failed states, environmental change and other concerns identified in the Consultation Document, it should remain a constant that laws dealing with crises, disasters and threats must be focused upon resilience and restoration. This objective applies to the principles of

---

[37] Civil Contingencies Act 2004 (UK), ss 20, 21(1)–(4). Essentially, emergency regulations are 'necessary' where existing legislation cannot be relied on 'without the risk of serious delay' or would not be sufficiently effective: Civil Contingencies Act 2004 (UK), s 21(5), (6).

[38] Civil Contingencies Act 2004 (UK), s 22(1). Section 22(2) provides that the purposes include: (a) protecting human life, health or safety, (b) treating human illness or injury, (c) protecting or restoring property, (d) protecting or restoring a supply of money, food, water, energy or fuel, (e) protecting or restoring a system of communication, (f) protecting or restoring facilities for transport, (g) protecting or restoring the provision of services relating to health, (h) protecting or restoring the activities of banks or other financial institutions, (i) preventing, containing or reducing the contamination of land, water or air, (j) preventing, reducing or mitigating the effects of disruption or destruction of plant life or animal life, (k) protecting or restoring activities of Parliament, of the Scottish Parliament, of the Northern Ireland Assembly or of the National Assembly for Wales, or (l) protecting or restoring the performance of public functions.

[39] Civil Contingencies Act 2004 (UK), s 22(3).

[40] Mark Elliott, Robert Thomas, *Public Law* (3rd edn, OUP 2017) 144.

[41] Civil Contingencies Act 2004 (UK), s 24(3).

constitutionalism just as it applies to the lives of people affected or the physical environment.

> The rule of law demands that the courts and Parliament are not impotent in response to the might of executive power in an emergency.[42]

What this required, in the view of the Joint Committee, was that key terms had to be defined within the Bill, and there needed to be a 'clear and objective trigger for action under Part 1 and 2'.[43] In particular, the so-called 'triple lock' of 'seriousness, necessity and geographical proportionality' were reinforced in the Act to create a sense of the scale of an emergency that would justify the use of emergency powers.[44] The Act also established a mechanism for Parliamentary scrutiny of emergency regulations made under the Act.[45]

The concept of 'constitutional resilience' asserted by the Joint Committee is a useful one when considering special powers legislation. It could be defined in a number of ways; one definition describes a 'resilient constitution' as 'allowing core constitutional values to persist throughout the crisis and to play a role in the recovery process'.[46] Further and alternatively, constitutional resilience might be understood as describing the circuit-breakers preventing the rules and norms a constitution represents from being permanently usurped, even if constitutional rules and values break down during an emergency.

6.3.2 Civil Emergency and Special Powers Frameworks in Australia

Australian general special powers frameworks resemble, in some respects, their UK counterparts. This is appropriate in the case of the Australian States, which like the UK Parliament enjoy plenary legislative

---

[42] Joint Committee on Draft Civil Contingencies Bill, *Report and Evidence* (HL Paper 184 HC 1074, 2002–03) 47 paras [179]–[180].

[43] Ibid 7 para [8].

[44] Civil Contingencies Act 2004 (UK), s 19(1) (defining an 'emergency' as an event that 'threatens serious damage' to human welfare, the environment or security, s 21(3), (4) (permitting emergency regulations to be made only where it is necessary and urgent to do so) and s 23(1)(a), (b) (addressing the appropriateness and the proportionality of the emergency regulation). See also Clive Walker, James Broderick, *The Civil Contingencies Act 2004: Risk, Resilience, and the Law in the United Kingdom* (OUP 2006) 52, 72–73.

[45] Civil Contingencies Act 2004 (UK), s 27.

[46] Xenophon Contiades and Alkmene Fotiadou, 'The Resilient Constitution', in Alexia Herwig, Marta Simoncini (eds) *Law and the Management of Disasters: The Challenge of Resilience* (Routledge 2016) 196.

power, subject to the constraining effects of the Australian Constitution and the principle that they cannot bind themselves, except as to the manner and form by which legislation is passed, or permanently abdicate their legislative power.[47]

Traditionally, Australian special powers resembled the broad framework provided for by the Emergency Powers Act 1920 (UK). Acts in each State provided for the Governor in Council to proclaim a state of emergency, at which time the ordinary constitutional arrangements would be set aside and broad grants of power made to Ministers and other public officers.[48] Some of those powers remain.[49] Ancillary special powers address the control of essentials of life such as food and fuel during an emergency,[50] and, similarly, allow a responsible Minister to take control of essential public utilities and other services that are a key part of the state's infrastructure.[51] Some of these powers are the subject of inter-governmental agreements about their use and exercise.[52]

Increasingly however, special powers are exercised with the benefit of comprehensive frameworks of law and policy that are designed to guide the exercise of emergency powers by public officials. Over the past few decades, new, general civil emergency frameworks, generally described as Emergency Management Acts, have been passed in every State and Territory.[53] Like the Civil Contingencies Act 2004 (UK), these frameworks are

---

[47] *Attorney-General (NSW)* v. *Trethowan* (1931) 44 CLR 395; Jeffrey Goldsworthy, *Parliamentary Sovereignty: Contemporary Debates* (CUP 2010) 196.

[48] See, e.g., the repealed Emergency Powers Act 1949 (NSW); repealed Emergency Powers Act 1974 (SA); repealed Public Safety Preservation Act 1928 (Vic).

[49] Public Safety Preservation Act 1958 (Vic).

[50] See, e.g., Liquid Fuel Emergency Act 1984 (Cth), pt III; Energy and Utilities Administration Act 1987 (NSW), pt 6; Electricity Act 1994 (Qld), ch 5 pt 2; State Transport Act 1938 (Qld), s 2; Electricity Industry Act 2000 (Vic), pt 6; Fuel Emergency Act 1977 (Vic), s 3; Electricity Supply Industry Act 1995 (Tas), pt 6; Fuel, Energy and Power Resources Act 1972 (WA), pt III; Fuel Control Act 1979 (ACT), s 11.

[51] See, e.g., Essential Services Act 1988 (NSW), s 10; Essential Services Act 1981 (SA), s 3; Essential Services Act 1958 (Vic), s 4, Vital State Industries (Works and Services) Act 1992 (Vic), ss 4–8; Utilities Act 2000 (ACT), pt 9; Essential Goods and Services Act 1981 (NT), s 5.

[52] See, e.g., the *National Energy Market: Memorandum of Understanding on the Use of Emergency Powers* (2015).

[53] Disaster Management Act 2003 (Qld); Emergency Management Act 2004 (SA); Emergency Management Act 2006 (Tas); Emergency Management Act 1986 (Vic), Emergency Management Act 2013 (Vic); Emergency Management Act 2005 (WA); Emergencies Act 2004 (ACT); Emergency Management Act 2013 (NT). New South Wales' State Emergency and Rescue Management Act 1989 (NSW) is older but generally reflects the same principles and structure.

6.3 SPECIAL POWERS OF GENERAL APPLICATION

intended to standardise the bureaucratic management of emergencies and, to that end, create new advisory councils and agencies that are responsible for advising the responsible Minister in the event of an emergency. They implement what has been described as an 'all-hazards' approach, in that the framework is designed to be sufficiently flexible to adapt to different emergencies.[54] Many of these frameworks also concentrate power in particular individuals, and thereby effect a degree of change to the ordinary structure of government in the event of an emergency. It follows that, as in the United Kingdom, it is useful to understand why these special powers exist, and to consider the circuit-breakers that might be used to overcome them in the event that they are abused.

As is the case in the United Kingdom, the Australian frameworks put an emphasis on planning for emergencies. Where the Australian frameworks differ from, or perhaps go beyond, the Civil Contingencies Act 2004 (UK), however, is in the level of detail they dedicate to setting out in statute the way power is redistributed in an emergency. Every framework creates a dedicated Emergency Commissioner who is responsible for overseeing and coordinating agency functions.[55] These frameworks tend to require the creation of emergency management plans, which set out agency responsibilities and enable the Commissioner to oversee, coordinate and direct agencies to perform functions assigned to them by the plan in the event of an emergency.[56] The plans are intended to identify particular vulnerabilities, and this legislation confers functions on Ministers or advisory bodies requiring them to assess and develop plans to protect, for example, critical infrastructure.[57]

---

[54] Australian Institute for Disaster Resilience, *Emergency Management in Australia: Concepts and Principles* (2004) vii.

[55] State Emergency and Rescue Management Act 1989 (NSW), ss 18, 20A; Disaster Management Act 2003 (Qld), pt 2 div 1 subdiv. 2; Emergency Management Act 2004 (SA), pt 3; Emergency Management Act 2006 (Tas), s 10; Emergency Management Act 2013 (Vic), pt 4; Emergency Management Act 2005 (WA), pt 2 div 1; Emergencies Act 2004 (ACT), ch 2; Emergency Management Act 2013 (NT), pt 4 div 2.

[56] State Emergency and Rescue Management Act 1989 (NSW), pt 2 div 1 subdiv. 2; Disaster Management Act 2003 (Qld), pt 3; Emergency Management Act 2004 (SA), pt 1A; Emergency Management Act 2006 (Tas), pt 3; Emergency Management Act 2013 (Vic), s 12; Emergency Management Act 2005 (WA), s 18; Emergencies Act 2004 (ACT), Ch 7 pt 7.2; Emergency Management Act 2013 (NT), pt 2 div 1.

[57] State Emergency and Rescue Management Act 1989 (NSW), pt 2 div 1 subdiv. 3; Disaster Management Act 2003 (Qld), pt 2; Emergency Management Act 2004 (SA), pt 2; Emergency Management Act 2006 (Tas), s 7; Emergency Management Act 2013 (Vic), pt 2; Emergency Management Act 2005 (WA), pt 2 div 2.

Generally speaking, these new frameworks reflect a shift in priority, as well as in the nature of emergency. As emergencies have shifted from being man-made to natural in origin, or have developed the potential to involve the kind of extraordinary mass violence and destruction associated with terrorism, it has become important for government to plan its response in advance. Where, as is the case in some of these frameworks, emergency power is diffused throughout a group of responsible public officers, and a bureaucratic structure is created to facilitate its exercise, it promotes constitutional resilience by making it more difficult for one, or a small group of, those political officers to exceed the limits of their power or concentrate the exercise of that power to permanently weaken the State's democratic structure.

The problem, however, is that these frameworks standardise, and in some cases even automate, the activation of emergency powers (or, more accurately, they standardise and automate changes to the constitutional structure through which executive powers are conferred through relatively specific legislation passed by Parliament and exercised by administrative officers) to the point that they cease to be capable of characterisation as 'special powers'.

By 'automation', it is meant that the law operates to automatically engage special powers and emergency responsibilities in response to the fact of an emergency, or even its apprehension, as opposed to any formal declaration by a Minister or proclamation by a Governor. Automation does not necessarily pose an issue because, as yet, the new State frameworks do not automate the total redistribution of legislative power to the executive in times of emergency. A clause that did redistribute legislative power, automated in the style of some of this new emergency legislation, would potentially constitute an abdication of legislative power because the automation contributes to the scheme's significant, unreviewable or irrevocable character.[58]

It is not within the scope of this chapter to address every framework in detail: for present purposes, Victoria's framework is examined in detail, and then points of similarity and difference in other jurisdictions shall be raised.

---

[58] See generally Anthony J Connolly, *The Foundations of Australian Public Law: State, Power, Accountability*, (CUP 2017) 181; *Cobb and Co Ltd v. Kropp* (1967) 1 AC 141; cf. Greg Taylor, *The Constitution of Victoria* (Federation Press 2006) 218–19.

6.3.2.1 Victoria's Emergency Framework

Victoria has retained some of the general special powers that were based on the Emergency Powers Act 1920 (UK). Sections 3(1) and (2) of the Public Safety Preservation Act 1958 (Vic) provide that the Governor in Council may issue a 'proclamation of emergency' declaring a state of emergency of up to one month's duration. Where a proclamation of emergency has been made, the Governor in Council may issue regulations for the purpose of securing public safety or order, and may confer powers upon Ministers, officers or 'other persons' for that purpose.[59] The Act contemplates that such powers and functions are to be used for the purpose of preventing 'interference with or intimidation molestation or annoyance of' persons conducting lawful activity,[60] prohibiting or regulating liquor,[61] and 'to prevent the doing of any act or thing ... with the object of or which may have the effect of prejudicing the public safety or order'.[62] The Governor in Council is also empowered to create regulations with respect to securing the 'essentials of life' for the community.[63] The Act provides that any person who fails to comply with regulations made under the Act, or who assists in a failure to comply, is guilty of an offence punishable by a fine of $200 or three months' imprisonment.[64]

The Public Safety Preservation Act 1958 (Vic) is complemented by the Essential Services Act 1958 (Vic). The Essential Services Act 1958 repealed and replaced the Essential Services Act 1948, in the aftermath of serious industrial unrest in Victoria. Section 4(1) of the Act empowers the Governor in Council to proclaim a state of emergency where it appears 'that any action has been taken or is likely to be taken or has been threatened to be taken by any person or body of persons whereby any essential service is or is likely to be interrupted' and that action prejudices or threatens peoples' employment, public health or safety, or the maintenance of peace and good order in Australia.

The powers of the Minister to control industry are exceptionally broad: Under a state of emergency proclaimed under this Act, the

---

[59] Public Safety Preservation Act 1958 (Vic), s 4(a) and (b).
[60] Public Safety Preservation Act 1958 (Vic), s 4 (b)(i).
[61] Public Safety Preservation Act 1958 (Vic), s 4 (b)(ii).
[62] Public Safety Preservation Act 1958 (Vic), s 4 (b)(iii).
[63] Public Safety Preservation Act 1958 (Vic), s 5.
[64] Public Safety Preservation Act 1958 (Vic), s 9.

Minister 'may provide operate control regulate and direct any essential service'.[65] An 'essential service' includes transport, fuel, light, power, water, sewerage and other services specified in the *Government Gazette* by order of the Governor in Council, as provided to the public by a range of operators, including operators specified by the Governor in Council, or which are under the control of the Minister during an emergency.[66]

The Essential Services Act may be seen to have a narrower focus than the Public Safety Preservation Act 1958 (Vic); it is designed to ensure that essential services are protected even in the face of industrial unrest. Sections 11 and 12 of the Act make unlawful any strike held at an essential service unless its workers vote beforehand to strike in a secret ballot held at the Victorian Electoral Commission; section 13 prohibits lock-outs of essential services; section 14 prohibits, during an emergency, the intimidation, molestation or annoyance of employees or other persons in relation to the execution of duties in respect of an essential service; and section 15 provides that it is an offence not to comply with 'any direction prohibition or requisition or any Order in Council or regulation under this Act'.

An Act of similarly narrow focus is the Fuel Emergency Act 1977 (Vic), which was enacted following a tanker drivers' strike. The Act activates based on the Governor in Council's apprehension that an action taken or threatened by persons is likely to lead to a situation where a 'kind of fuel is or is likely to become unavailable to meet the reasonable requirements of the community'.[67] It provides similar powers to the Essential Services Act, allowing the Minister to 'provide operate control regulate and direct any service' in relation to the type of fuel that is the subject of the emergency.[68] Unlike the Essential Services Act, the Fuel Emergency Act does not contain provisions securing fuel from striking workers.

Practically speaking, however, these laws have been largely superseded by the Emergency Management Acts. The more recent Act, the Emergency Management Act 2013 (Vic), is to be read as one with the Emergency Management Act 1986 (Vic),[69] which was

---

[65] Essential Services Act 1958 (Vic), s 5(1).
[66] Essential Services Act 1958 (Vic), s 3 (definition of 'essential service').
[67] Fuel Emergency Act 1977 (Vic), s 3(1).
[68] Fuel Emergency Act 1977 (Vic), s 4(1).
[69] Emergency Management Act 2013 (Vic), s 4(1). Although this scheme is used for illustration, it is in the process of being refined and consolidated: see the Emergency Management Legislation Amendment Bill 2018 (Vic).

introduced to replace the State Disasters Act 1983 (Vic) after the 1983 Ash Wednesday bushfires.

Section 23(1) of the Emergency Management Act 1986 is consistent with the previous version of the power in section 4 of the State Disasters Act 1983 (Vic). It empowers the Premier to declare a 'state of disaster', this being 'an emergency which the Premier of Victoria after considering the advice of the Minister and the Emergency Management Commissioner is satisfied constitutes or is likely to constitute a significant and widespread danger to life or property in Victoria'. The term 'emergency' is defined in section 4 as:

(a) an earthquake, flood, wind-storm or other natural event; and
(b) a fire; and
(c) an explosion; and
(d) a road accident or any other accident; and
(e) a plague or an epidemic or contamination; and
(f) a warlike act or act of terrorism, whether directed at Victoria or a part of Victoria or at any other State or Territory of the Commonwealth; and
(g) a hi-jack, siege or riot; and
(h) a disruption to an essential service.[70]

Once a state of disaster is declared, the Minister is responsible for 'directing and co-ordinating the activities of all government agencies, and the allocation of all available resources of the Government, which the Minister considers necessary or desirable for responding to the disaster'.[71] The Minister must report on the exercise of these powers to both Houses of Parliament 'as soon as is practicable after the declaration'.[72]

The powers the Minister may exercise include the power to 'direct any government agency to do or refrain from doing any act, or to exercise or perform or refrain from exercising or performing any function, power, duty or responsibility';[73] Additional powers include the power to take possession of property as 'the Minister considers necessary or desirable for responding to the disaster',[74] as well as the powers to prevent entry

---

[70] See also Emergency Management Act 2013 (Vic), s 3 (definition of 'emergency').
[71] Emergency Management Act 1986 (Vic), s 24(1).
[72] Emergency Management Act 1986 (Vic), s 23(7).
[73] Emergency Management Act 1986 (Vic), s 24(2)(a).
[74] Emergency Management Act 1986 (Vic), s 24(2)(c).

into, and compel evacuation from, the disaster area.[75] Agencies are subordinate to the Minister's authority: they must comply with the Minister's directions,[76] which prevail over any contradictory Act,[77] and the Minister has the authority to suspend Acts of Parliament or regulations prescribing the agency's authority that in his or her opinion would prevent the Agency from responding to the disaster.[78]

Under section 23(1A) of the Emergency Management Act 1986, however, the Minister is not authorised to use these powers in a situation in respect of whom a proclamation may be made under section 4(1) of the Essential Services Act 1958 (Vic). It appears to be intended that a separate regime, the one provided for in the Essential Services Act, apply to situations where a state of emergency must be declared in order to secure essential services because of an 'action taken by any person or body of persons'. This does not prohibit the Minister from using these powers to take control of property or directing agencies in respect of essential services in the case of a natural disaster or similar emergency. It merely prevents the powers in the Act from being used in a situation to which the Essential Services Act applies.

The Emergency Management Act 2013 (Vic) was introduced in the aftermath of the 2009 'Black Saturday' bushfires and the 2010–11 and 2011–12 floods in regional Victoria.[79] The Royal Commission into the bushfires handed down a report recommending the creation of a new framework for dealing with natural disasters. The recommendations included, materially, that the Premier be required to consult with the Minister responsible for police and emergency services and the Chief Commissioner of Police should they become aware of a situation that would justify declaring a state of disaster;[80] introducing a graded scale for emergency declarations short of a state of disaster;[81] and enacting new legislation designed to increase the operational capability of the fire services.[82]

---

[75] Emergency Management Act 1986 (Vic), s 24(2)(d),(e).
[76] Emergency Management Act 1986 (Vic), s 24(3)(a).
[77] Emergency Management Act 1986 (Vic), s 24(3)(b).
[78] Emergency Management Act 1986 (Vic), s 24(2)(b).
[79] Vic Parl Debs, LC, 28 November 2013, 3902.
[80] Victorian Bushfires Royal Commission, *Summary of the Final Report* (2009) 26 (Recommendation 12).
[81] Ibid 26 (Recommendation 13).
[82] Ibid 36 (Recommendation 63). See the Fire Services Commissioner Act 2010 (Vic).

6.3 SPECIAL POWERS OF GENERAL APPLICATION

The need for reform was pressed home by the Review of the 2010–11 Flood Warnings and Response, which noted that '[t]he absence of any overarching policy framework or centralised operational control ... results in a siloed, uncoordinated structure that invariably breaks down in the face of a large scale or protracted emergency ... these shortcomings can only be overcome by the establishment of a central body that has the authority, capacity and capability to drive a program of major reform'.[83] The Review recommended the creation of a 'logical, hierarchical approach to all phases of emergency management'.[84] It noted that the special powers provided for in the 1986 Act, permitting the declaration of a state of disaster, had never been used in Victoria.[85]

These events were followed by a White Paper that sought to, inter alia, reform 'Victoria's emergency management governance arrangements ... to reflect the characteristics of contemporary emergencies'.[86] More concretely, the reforms aimed to encourage inter-agency cooperation, transparency and accountability. To this end, the White Paper identified a number of measures that are now implemented in the Emergency Management Act 2013 (Vic). This included the creation of a State Crisis and Resilience Council and subcommittees, responsible for advising government and creating overarching strategy for emergency management;[87] the creation of Emergency Management Victoria, responsible for coordinating and overseeing the roles, responsibilities and powers to be exercised by government agencies during emergencies;[88] and the Emergency Management Commissioner, a statutory appointment who is responsible for preparing State emergency response plans subject to review by the State Crisis and Resilience Council[89] and, during major emergencies, for exercising control over the response. The State emergency response plan is the scheme's principal instrument because it prescribes the roles and responsibilities of agencies, and the actions they must take, in an emergency.[90]

---

[83] Neil Comrie AO, *Review of the 2010–11 Flood Warnings and Response, Final Report* (2011) 4.
[84] Ibid.
[85] Ibid 173.
[86] Victorian Emergency Management Reform, *White Paper* (2012) 16.
[87] Ibid 18–19.
[88] Ibid 21.
[89] Emergency Management Act 2013 (Vic), s 53.
[90] Victorian Emergency Management Reform, *White Paper* (2012) 22.

These measures were considered necessary to cope with 'major emergencies', which the White Paper defined, drawing on previous definitions relating to, inter alia, fire safety,[91] as a 'large or complex emergency (regardless of how it is caused)' which:

> has the potential to cause loss of life and extensive damage to property, infrastructure or the environment;
>
> has the potential to have or is having significant adverse consequences for the Victorian community or a part of the Victorian community, and
>
> requires the involvement of two or more emergency agencies to respond to the emergency.[92]

The 2013 Act adopts this definition[93] and, for the purposes of coordinating the response to a major emergency, classifies them into Class 1 and Class 2 emergencies. Class 1 emergencies include a 'major fire' as well as other major emergencies for which the Metropolitan Fire and Emergency Services Board, the Country Fire Authority and the Victoria State Emergency Service Authority are designated by the State emergency response plan as 'control agencies'.[94] Class 2 emergencies are defined as all other major emergencies except for those that result from a warlike act or act of terrorism, or a hi-jack, siege or riot.[95] The latter are excluded from the Act as they are to be dealt with using Victoria Police's existing powers.[96]

The purpose of this classification is to activate particular sections of the Act that allocate responsibilities and powers. For example, in a Class 1 emergency, the Emergency Management Commissioner must appoint a State Response Controller to coordinate the planning for and response to that emergency.[97] In a Class 2 emergency, an agency has overall control of how the response is organised,[98] although the Emergency Management Commissioner may direct the senior officer of that agency in the performance of his or her functions.[99]

---

[91] Fire Services Commissioner Act 2010 (Vic), s 3 (definition of 'major emergency').
[92] Victorian Emergency Management Reform, *White Paper* (2012) 23.
[93] Emergency Management Act 2013 (Vic), s 3 (definition of 'major emergency').
[94] Emergency Management Act 2013 (Vic), s 3 (definition of 'Class 1 emergency').
[95] Emergency Management Act 2013 (Vic), s 3 (definition of 'Class 2 emergency').
[96] Explanatory Memorandum to the Emergency Management Bill 2013, 3. See also Emergency Management Act 2013 (Vic), s 45(2)(b).
[97] Emergency Management Act 2013 (Vic), s 37(1).
[98] Emergency Management Act 2013 (Vic), s 39(1).
[99] Emergency Management Act 2013 (Vic), s 40(b).

6.3 SPECIAL POWERS OF GENERAL APPLICATION

The Emergency Management Commissioner is an important figure generally in the scheme. He or she has several functions under section 32 of the Act, including, under sub-section (1)(a), to 'be responsible for the coordination of the activities of agencies having roles or responsibilities in relation to the response to Class 1 emergencies or Class 2 emergencies'. The Commissioner performs this function by allocating responsibilities to agencies under the State emergency response plan,[100] which he or she may direct them to follow.[101]

This account of the Emergency Management Act's structure, and the 'coordinative powers' it confers upon the Emergency Management Commissioner, raises the question of what role the formal act of declaring a state of disaster will play in Victoria's emergency framework going forward. Although the two Emergency Management Acts work concurrently, the 2013 Act is ultimately intended to replace the 1986 Act.[102] If this happens, the responsible Minister would potentially be armed in an emergency only with those special powers otherwise provided for in legislation such as the Public Safety Preservation Act 1958, which are typically directed to threats posed by persons as opposed to natural events.

As noted, the functions and powers provided for in the Emergency Management Act 2013 (Vic) do not rely on a formal determination or proclamation of a state of disaster by a responsible Minister.[103] Instead, many of the powers are intended to flow automatically from the coming into existence of an emergency, in accordance with the operational procedures set out in the State emergency response plan. For example, the responsibilities of the Commissioner to appoint a State Response Controller activate when a Class 1 emergency 'is occurring or has occurred'.[104]

This may not pose such a difficulty. Unlike the powers contained in section 24 of the Emergency Management Act 1986 (Vic), the Emergency Management Act 2013 (Vic) seems to be attempting to create an emergency framework that promotes constitutional resilience by ensuring

---

[100] Emergency Management Act 2013 (Vic), s 53(1)(a).
[101] Emergency Management Act 2013 (Vic), s 55A(1),(4).
[102] Explanatory Memorandum to the Emergency Management Bill 2013, 30 (cl. 78).
[103] It was recently observed by Emergency Management Victoria that '[i]t is a fundamental principle underling Victoria's emergency management arrangements, that normal emergency actions take place when the need is evident, and do not require special administrative decision or declaration. The declaration of a state of disaster creates a legal condition applying to a specified area only in extreme circumstances'. Emergency Management Victoria, *Emergency Management Manual* (2018) 19.
[104] Emergency Management Act 2013 (Vic), s 37(1)(b).

that, in an emergency, agencies cannot exercise arbitrary powers because they must adhere to the State emergency response plan prepared by the Commissioner.[105] Moreover, any duties the Commissioner's State emergency response plan confers upon agencies do not prevail over duties, powers or functions conferred upon them by the common law or an inconsistent Act, regulation or licence,[106] nor do they prevail over intergovernmental agreements or agency agreements that relate to the emergency.[107]

6.3.2.2 Points of Comparison and Difference

In this section, the approaches of other States and Territories shall be considered, and compared to the Victorian approach. What is fundamental is that the tools available to State and Territory legislatures and courts ensure constitutional resilience by restraining or controlling the redistribution of legislative power to the executive, or preventing the over-concentration of executive power into an individual. By way of taxonomy, these tools may be definitional, in the sense that they narrow what constitutes an emergency; or they may be procedural, in the sense that they apply formal conditions to the exercise of emergency powers and resist automating broad delegations of legislative power.

Queensland's framework is broadly similar to that of Victoria. The Public Safety Preservation Act 1986 (Qld) retains a set of broad special powers directed at emergencies generally, and an emergency management framework is provided for in the Disaster Management Act 2003 (Qld). The latter Act, like its Victorian and New South Wales equivalents, establishes a planning framework and creates an advisory body in the form of a Queensland Disaster Management Committee.[108]

As currently in force, section 5 of the Public Safety Preservation Act 1986 (Qld) empowers an 'emergency commander', defined by the section as a commissioned officer,[109] to declare the existence of an 'emergency situation' in an emergency area once he or she is satisfied on reasonable grounds that one has arisen. An 'emergency situation' is defined to include, inter alia, 'any' explosion, fire, chemical spill, escape of gas, accident involving an aircraft, train, vessel or vehicle, incident involving

---

[105] Emergency Management Act 2013 (Vic), s 55A(1).
[106] Emergency Management Act 2013 (Vic), s 55A(2)(a)–(c).
[107] Emergency Management Act 2013 (Vic), s 55A(d),(e).
[108] Disaster Management Act 2003 (Qld), pt 2 div 1.
[109] In other words, a police officer of the rank of Inspector or above.

6.3 SPECIAL POWERS OF GENERAL APPLICATION

a bomb or weapon, flood or landslide, and, in sub-section (g), other accident or incident, 'that causes or may cause a danger of death, injury or distress to any person, a loss of or damage to any property or pollution of the environment'.[110]

This definition is remarkably broad. It reflects some of the concerns raised in the context of the Civil Contingencies Act 2004 (UK), in the sense that allowing powers to be invoked to respond to an emergency that 'may cause a danger of death, injury or distress to any person' or damage 'any property' does not reflect a sense of scale, let alone the 'triple lock' of 'seriousness, necessity and geographical proportionality' that Act is understood to require before a state of emergency may be declared. Substantively, the emergency commander and other police officers may order persons to surrender resources or otherwise take control of resources in the area;[111] evacuate or exclude people from a premises and forcibly remove them if they refuse to leave;[112] close roads and other modes of access;[113] enter, search and remove things or animals from a premises;[114] or direct persons to operate resources or assist them,[115] as long as it does not put those persons in danger.[116] People ordered to surrender resources, operate resources or assist must do so unless they have a reasonable excuse, or be punished by one year's imprisonment.[117]

It is also worth noting that definitional or procedural safeguards are only effective insofar as they are enforceable. This raises the question posed earlier in the chapter and throughout this book: to what extent are emergency powers justiciable and their limits enforceable? The courts have recently showed themselves willing to constrain emergency powers to the strict terms in which they are conferred by statute. In 2016, a declaration under the Public Safety Preservation Act 1986 (Qld) was challenged in the Federal Court in *Wotton* v. *State of Queensland (No. 5)*.[118] Riots had erupted in response to the death of Mulrunji, an Aboriginal man, in police custody, which appeared to be

---

[110] Disaster Management Act 2003 (Qld), Dictionary Sch. 1 (definition of 'emergency situation').
[111] Public Safety Preservation Act 1986 (Qld), s 8(1)(a)–(c).
[112] Public Safety Preservation Act 1986 (Qld), s 8(1)(d).
[113] Public Safety Preservation Act 1986 (Qld), s 8(1)(e).
[114] Public Safety Preservation Act 1986 (Qld), s 8(1)(f)–(h).
[115] Public Safety Preservation Act 1986 (Qld), s 8(1)(c),(i).
[116] Public Safety Preservation Act 1986 (Qld), s 8(2).
[117] Public Safety Preservation Act 1986 (Qld), s 8(3).
[118] [2016] FCA 1457.

192   CIVIL EMERGENCIES & SPECIAL POWERS LEGISLATION

the result of an assault by the police.[119] Amongst other things, the local police station was burnt down.

In response to the riots, the police invoked the emergency powers provided for in section 5, and declared an emergency situation in the area. Between 88 and 111 police officers were stationed on Palm Island, including officers from the Special Emergency Response Team and the Public Safety Response Team.[120] Once emergency powers were invoked, these officers conducted searches in people's homes and arrested people, without warrants.[121] Air and ferry transport to the area ceased.[122]

Although the Act as in force at the time was slightly different, and has since been amended to address some of the court's holdings, Justice Mortimer's decision in *Wotton* is a rare example of the judicial review of emergency powers in Australia. It is useful for understanding the principles of interpretation that may be applied to emergency powers, the extent to which the exercise of emergency powers must be compatible with other laws, and in general serves as an example of how emergency powers may be judicially reviewed.

Justice Mortimer observed that the emergency declaration was justified by the fire at the police station, because it fell within the definition of an emergency situation given by the Act.[123] However, Mortimer J also found that the police officer had failed to revoke the emergency declaration after the fire had been put out, and the Act as in force at the time had provided him with no alternative basis with which to support the emergency declaration.[124]

The judge's reasoning in this regard discloses a careful attention to language and an attitude of strict and literal construction, one that is inconsistent with some of the general assumptions about the deferential approach judges should take to emergency legislation. Mortimer J's finding that there was no basis for the emergency declaration was based on her reading of the then-in-force version of section 5(g), which read only to include other 'accidents' as opposed to 'incidents' and so did not

---

[119] Ibid [318]–[327].
[120] Ibid [1239].
[121] Ibid [348]–[362].
[122] Ibid [1141].
[123] Ibid [1125].
[124] Ibid [1139].

6.3 SPECIAL POWERS OF GENERAL APPLICATION

cover deliberate actions such as 'throwing rocks, yelling abuse, engaging in protest and causing property damage'.[125]

Moreover, the decision to continue and not revoke the emergency declaration was one of several actions held to be in violation of section 9(1) of the Racial Discrimination Act 1975 (Cth).[126] As Mortimer J noted, 'A [S]tate law cannot authorise conduct which contravenes s 9 of the [Racial Discrimination Act]. Insofar as the [S]tate law had such an effect, it would be invalid by reason of the operation of s 109 of the Constitution'.[127]

In other words, Mortimer J did not accept, or acknowledge, that State legislation dealing with a situation of emergency, or which involves a declaration of emergency, should be subject to a different set of constitutional limits or be interpreted according to different rules. Such reasoning is to be lauded. Moreover, Mortimer J's approach treats a decision to declare a state of emergency as something that is justiciable, which paints a different picture of some of the procedurally weak frameworks described in this chapter. Public officers who have the power to declare a state of emergency – and thereby grant themselves emergency powers – will have to do it according to the strict terms of the statutory grant of authority and, in particular, with close attention as to whether an emergency exists as it is defined in the relevant legislation, as well as any relevant constitutional limitations.

Mortimer J's approach to the justiciability and interpretation of the Public Safety Preservation Act 1986 (Qld) has ramifications for the other States' and Territories' emergency legislation. It enjoins the observer to read the language of the statute carefully and consider the procedural conditions it imposes on the exercise of emergency powers, as well as the relationship between those procedural conditions and the nature of the power being exercised.

New South Wales provides in the State Emergency and Rescue Management Act 1989 (NSW) that 'an actual or imminent occurrence' that endangers or threatens to endanger human or animal life, or which

---

[125] Ibid [1127]–[1128].
[126] Section 9(1) prohibits an action involving a distinction, exclusion, restriction or preference based on race, colour, descent or national or ethnic origin which has the purpose or effect of nullifying or impairing the recognition, enjoyment or exercise, on an equal footing, of any human right or fundamental freedom in the political, economic, social, cultural or any other field of public life.
[127] [2016] FCA 1457, [146].

destroys or threatens to destroy property or the environment,[128] must require a 'significant and coordinated response' to qualify as an emergency.[129] This definition ties the definition of an emergency to the required response, which does not necessarily provide a sense of scale. By contrast, Western Australia's Emergency Management Act 2005 (WA) provides that to be an emergency 'extraordinary measures are required to prevent or minimise' the loss of or harm to the life, safety or health of persons or animals; or damage or destruction to property or the environment.[130] The Western Australian Act implies, moreover, that scale is relevant in the definition of emergency provided in section 3, which must be 'of such a nature or magnitude that it requires a significant and coordinated response'.

The emergency legislation is also not uniform in terms of the procedural requirements that condition the formal vesting of emergency powers into emergency officers. Some frameworks allow the police or emergency officers to essentially invoke emergency powers on their own initiative.[131] For example, Queensland's Public Safety Preservation Act, which confers broad special powers, is missing the requirement that a state of emergency be formally declared by a senior officer or Minister, instead permitting it to be declared by the police. As Mortimer J's decision in *Wotton (No. 5)*[132] shows, this procedural requirement is important because it imposes an additional layer of accountability and transparency on a decision to activate emergency powers and can potentially prevent their abuse.

Other frameworks apply a procedure that requires a responsible Minister, the Premier, or the Governor to issue a declaration or proclamation.[133]

---

[128] The term 'property' including the environment: see State Emergency and Rescue Management Act 1989 (NSW), s 4(2).
[129] State Emergency and Rescue Management Act 1989 (NSW), s 4(1). See also the Emergency Management Act 2013 (NT), s 8, defining an 'emergency' as an 'event that requires a significant coordinated response using the combined resources of the Territory and non-government entities within the Territory'.
[130] Emergency Management Act 2005 (WA), s 56(2)(c).
[131] See, e.g., Public Safety Preservation Act 1986 (Qld), s 5 (allowing an emergency commander—a senior police officer—to declare an emergency situation exists).
[132] [2016] FCA 1457.
[133] See, e.g., State Emergency and Rescue Management Act 1989 (NSW), s 33; Public Safety Preservation Act 1958 (Vic), s 3(1); ; Emergencies Act 2004 (ACT), ss 150A–C (allowing the Chief Minister to appoint officers to declare emergency powers without declaring a 'state of emergency'), 151 (allowing the responsible Minister to declare a 'state of alert'), 156 (allowing the Chief Minister to declare a 'state of emergency'); Emergency

6.3 SPECIAL POWERS OF GENERAL APPLICATION 195

Sometimes, where a framework provides for tiers of emergency powers of differing scope and application, both approaches are used.[134]

Queensland's own Disaster Management Act 2003 (Qld) takes a far more robust approach than the Public Safety Preservation Act, both in the definitional and procedural sense. Under that scheme, special 'declared disaster powers' are activated and may be exercised by certain authorised public officers once a 'disaster situation' is declared.[135] Such a declaration may be made either by the responsible Minister and the Premier[136] or the chairperson of a District Disaster Management Group, who is a 'disaster district coordinator' and the repository of emergency powers, with the approval of the responsible Minister.[137]

When a disaster district coordinator proposes to declare a disaster situation, they must also try to consult with the district group for the

---

Management Act 2013 (NT), ss 19 (allowing the responsible Minister to declare a 'state of emergency'), 21 (allowing the Administrator to declare a 'state of disaster').

[134] See, e.g., Emergency Management Act 2004 (SA), ss 22 and 23 (allowing the State Co-Ordinator to declare an 'identified major incident' or a 'major emergency'), 24 (allowing the Governor to declare a 'disaster'); Emergency Management Act 1986 (Vic), s 23(1) (allowing the Premier to declare a state of disaster); 36A (allowing a police officer to declare an emergency area); Emergency Management Act 2005 (WA), ss 50 (allowing the State Emergency Coordinator to declare the existence of an emergency situation), 56 (allowing the Minister to declare a state of emergency).

[135] Disaster Management Act 2003 (Qld), s 75. Members of the emergency services are eligible for appointment, as well as 'persons whom the appointor is satisfied has the necessary expertise or experience to exercise the powers:' sub-s (1)(d). Section 77(1) provides a significant list of powers: being to '(a) control the movement of persons, animals or vehicles within, into, out of or around the declared area for the disaster situation; (b) give a direction to a person to regulate the movement of the person, an animal or a vehicle within, into, out of or around the declared area; (c) evacuate persons or animals from the declared area or a part of the area; (d) enter a place in the declared area; (e) take into a place in the declared area the equipment, persons or materials the officer reasonably requires for exercising a power under this subdivision; (f) contain an animal or substance within the declared area; (g) remove or destroy an animal, vegetation or substance within the declared area; (h) remove, dismantle, demolish or destroy a vehicle, or a building or other structure, in the declared area; (i) use, close off or block a facility for drainage; (j) shut off or disconnect a supply of fuel, gas, electricity or water, and take and use the fuel, gas, electricity or water; (k) turn off, disconnect or shut down any motor or equipment; (l) open a container or other thing, or dismantle equipment; (m) excavate land or form tunnels; (n) build earthworks or temporary structures, or erect barriers; (o) close to traffic any road; (p) maintain, restore, or prevent destruction of, essential services; (q) require a person to give the relevant district disaster coordinator or declared disaster officer reasonable help to exercise the coordinator's or officer's powers under this subdivision'.

[136] Disaster Management Act 2003 (Qld), s 69.
[137] Disaster Management Act 2003 (Qld), s 64(a),(b).

disaster district and the local government affected, although a failure to do so will not affect the declaration's validity.[138] The declarant must be satisfied that 'disaster has happened, is happening or is likely to happen, in the State' and that 'it is necessary, or reasonably likely to be necessary', for district disaster coordinators and declared disaster officers to exercise 'declared disaster powers' in order to minimise the loss of human life; illness or injury to humans; property loss or damage; or damage to the environment.[139] 'Disaster' is relevantly defined in section 13(1) of the Act as a 'serious disruption in a community, caused by the impact of an event, that requires a significant coordinated response by the State and other entities to help the community recover from the disruption'. 'Serious disruption' is defined by section 13(2)(a)–(c) as 'loss of human life, or illness or injury to humans', 'widespread or severe property loss or damage', or 'widespread or severe damage to the environment'.

Some of the frameworks previously described in this Section create tiers of emergency with accompanying powers and attach specific procedural conditions to the invocation and exercise of those powers.[140] The procedural requirements for invoking a particular tier of emergency powers appear, in some cases, to have some correlative relationship with the relative invasiveness and breadth of the emergency powers they activate. If this is the objective, however, it should be considered what these distinctions achieve in terms of improving constitutional resilience.

Some frameworks that take this approach are flawed in that they pose no formal barrier to or oversight over the exercise of powers that nonetheless set aside the ordinary structure of government because they enable the individual vested with coordinative powers to determine the conditions in which special powers that displace the operation of the law should be exercised. For example, the Emergency Management Act 2004 (SA) permits its equivalent advisory body, the State Emergency Management Committee, to publish guidelines setting out the circumstances in which an 'emergency' should be declared to be 'an identified major incident', a 'major emergency' or a 'disaster'.[141] The power to declare an emergency an 'identified major incident' or a 'major emergency' is vested in the State Co-ordinator, the functional equivalent of the

---

[138] Disaster Management Act 2003 (Qld), s 69(2),(3).
[139] Disaster Management Act 2003 (Qld), s 69(a),(b).
[140] See the examples given in footnotes 133 and 134.
[141] Emergency Management Act 2004 (SA), s 21.

6.3 SPECIAL POWERS OF GENERAL APPLICATION

Victorian Emergency Management Commissioner.[142] The power to declare a 'disaster', by contrast, remains with the Governor.[143]

Moreover, section 25 of the Emergency Management Act 2004 (SA) confers a broad range of powers that the State Co-ordinator may exercise during an emergency if 'of the opinion that it is necessary to do so',[144] and does not generally distinguish between these types of emergency. In other words, the Act confers upon an agency the power to define the categories of emergency and grants the State Co-ordinator, who is the Commissioner of Police,[145] the power to invoke on his or her own initiative a broad range of special powers, which are generally equal to the powers available were the Governor to declare a state of disaster.

The only new power available when a major emergency or disaster is declared is provided for in section 25(2)(n), which permits the State Co-ordinator to 'give directions to any control agency or person whose responsibilities require him or her to engage in response or recovery operations, or who is so engaged' only 'in the case of a major emergency or disaster'.[146] Nonetheless, because the State Co-ordinator has the power to declare a major emergency, he or she may invoke these coordinative powers without any formal oversight by the Minister.

In Tasmania, the State Controller, who is either appointed by the responsible Minister or the head of the responsible agency,[147] has the power to authorise the use of the emergency powers provided for in Schedule 1 of the Emergency Management Act 2006 (Tas) even without a state of emergency being declared.[148] He or she may do so if satisfied that:

---

[142] Emergency Management Act 2004 (SA), ss 22 and 23.
[143] Emergency Management Act 2004 (SA), s 24.
[144] Including the power to 'take possession of, protect or assume control over any land, body of water, building, structure, vehicle or other thing' (Emergency Management Act 2004 (SA), s 25(2)(b)); 'direct the owner of, or the person for the time being in charge of, any real or personal property to place it under the control or at the disposition of a specified person' (s 25(2)(d)); 'direct a person to remain isolated or segregated from other persons or to take other measures to prevent the transmission of a disease or condition to other persons' (s. 25(2)(fb)); 'remove to such place as he or she thinks fit any person who obstructs or threatens to obstruct response or recovery operations' (s. 25(2)(l)).
[145] Emergency Management Act 2004 (SA), s 14.
[146] Emergency Management Act 2004 (SA), s 25(2)(n).
[147] Emergency Management Act 2006 (Tas), s 10(1).
[148] Emergency Management Act 2006 (Tas), s 40(2). The reason for declaring a state of emergency is to activate the responsibilities under emergency management plans created under the Act: ss 42, 44.

(a) ...an emergency is occurring or has occurred in Tasmania and, due to the occurrence of that emergency, there are reasonable grounds for the exercise of those powers for the purpose of –
  (i) protecting persons from distress, injury or death; or
  (ii) protecting property or the environment from damage or destruction; or
(b) is satisfied on credible information that an emergency that may impact on Tasmania is occurring elsewhere in Australia.

The difficulty in allowing an Emergency Commissioner to invoke emergency powers is compounded because the Tasmanian Act employs an overly broad definition of 'emergency'. The Act defines an emergency as an event, or significant threat of an event, that 'endangers, destroys or threatens to endanger or destroy human life, property or the environment, or causes or threatens to cause injury or distress to persons', and which requires a 'significant response' from the emergency services.[149] The qualifier of 'significant response' is welcomed, and the power is limited in the sense that it must be renewed after seven days with the consent of the Minister[150] and the State Controller must report his or her intention to activate the powers to the Minister either before doing so or as soon as is practicable afterwards.[151] But it is questionable as to whether this procedural safeguard is enough, because the definition of an emergency is so broad. It would be difficult, for example, to argue with a determination by a State Controller that the use of emergency powers is necessary to protect people from the injury or distress that may be caused by an emergency. This power is designed to be permissive and broad.

It should be noted that Tasmania's framework requires the Premier to make a formal declaration in order to engage 'special emergency powers'. That declaration may only be made when the Premier is satisfied on reasonable grounds that the special powers are necessary and that the 'ordinary' emergency powers provided for in Schedule 1 of the Emergency Management Act 2006 (Tas) are insufficient to manage the emergency.[152] Importantly, the ordinary 'emergency powers' described in Schedule 1, although broad, do not include the power to 'direct that the resources of the State and any council or other person be made available

[149] Emergency Management Act 2006 (Tas), s 3 (definition of 'emergency').
[150] Emergency Management Act 2006 (Tas), ss 40(4),(6)(b).
[151] Emergency Management Act 2006 (Tas), s 40(5)(a),(b).
[152] Emergency Management Act 2006 (Tas), s 42.

for emergency management'; this coordinative power is a special emergency power in Schedule 2 that may be only exercised once a declaration has been made by the Premier. The point is that even Tasmania's permissive framework categorically distinguishes special coordinative powers, that must be activated through some formal declaration, from general emergency powers.

6.4 Special Powers of Specific Application

In addition to the general special powers described in Section 6.3.2.2, the States, Territories and the Commonwealth have also enacted laws that provide special powers with respect to emergencies of a particular type. The particular emergencies that are the subject of concern are often in themselves a reflection of the global conversation around emergencies. International agreements tend to identify priorities and strategies for dealing with particular types of emergency with the potential to threaten the global public order, such as environmental catastrophes and pandemics, which nation-states must then give effect to within their own territorial borders and within the constraints of their own constitutional frameworks. This explains why special powers frameworks are designed, increasingly, to give effect to inter-governmental agreements distributing responsibility between the Commonwealth and the States for dealing with particular emergencies.

6.4.1 Environmental Emergencies

It is worth noting briefly that some States have enacted laws that confer a variety of special powers which are specifically designed to deal with an environmental emergency.[153] The general civil emergency frameworks

---

[153] Environmental Protection Act 1994 (Qld), ch 9 pt 4; Environment Protection Act 1993 (SA), pt 10 div 2; Environment Protection Act 1970 (Vic), s 30A; Environmental Protection Act 1986 (WA), s 75; Environmental Protection Act 1997 (ACT), pt 11 div 11.3. Other jurisdictions also provide similar powers or impose similar requirements by operation of law, but are not couched in the language of urgency or emergency: see, e.g., Environmental Management and Pollution Control Act 1994 (Tas), ss 74E and 74F (relating to the investigation and remediation of contaminated sites); Environmental Protection Act 1986 (WA), pt 5 div 4 (relating to various notices and directions that may be issued under the Act). New South Wales appears to deal with environmental emergencies, however defined, through grants; see, e.g., the NSW Environmental Trust's Emergency Pollution Clean Up Program administered pursuant to s 16 of the Environmental Trust Act 1998 (NSW).

are explicitly designed to respond to environmental emergencies, and so the continued relevance of these laws may be doubted.

However, these frameworks tend to be more narrowly tailored towards addressing an environmental emergency; some, by virtue of a narrowed definition directed at remedying environmental damage.[154] Some of these 'environmental special powers' reflect the general special powers provided for in civil emergency frameworks, in that they authorise warrantless entry into premises, as well as search and seizure.[155] Other powers are tailored to the particular circumstances of environmental emergency, in that they relate to the identification, disposal or storage of pollutants or waste or the remediation of polluted sites.[156]

6.4.2 Chemical, Biological, Radiological and Nuclear Emergencies

It is also important to briefly describe the Commonwealth and the States' shared framework for addressing emergencies involving so-called CBRN (chemical, biological, radiological and nuclear) hazards. Notwithstanding the potentially devastating effects of such emergencies, and the national implications, the inter-governmental agreements that address this question tend to adhere to traditional constitutional boundaries by providing that States and Territories are principally responsible for coordinating the response.[157]

---

[154] See, e.g., Environmental Protection Act 1994 (Qld), s 466B(b)(iii) (defining an emergency to include action to 'rehabilitate or restore the environment because of the harm'); Environment Protection Act 1997 (ACT), s 105(b) (activating emergency powers where an authorised officer is satisfied it is necessary to take 'immediate action to prevent, minimise or remedy' serious environmental harm).

[155] Environmental Protection Act 1994 (Qld), s 467; Environment Protection Act 1997 (ACT), ss 106–09.

[156] Environment Protection Act 1993 (SA), ss 93(3) (allowing an authorised officer to issue an emergency environmental protection order under s 93(2)(c), requiring a person to take or abstain from action, or take steps to combat pollution, if he or she is 'of the opinion that urgent action is required for the protection of the environment'), 99(3) (conferring the equivalent power to order an emergency clean up where satisfied that urgent action is required), 103J(5) (conferring the equivalent power to order an emergency site remediation where satisfied that urgent action is required); Environment Protection Act 1970 (Vic), s 30A (allowing for the emergency disposal or storage of waste); Environment Protection Act 1997 (ACT), pt 12 (providing for analysts to accompany officers who are exercising emergency powers to assist in determining whether there is or is likely to be environmental harm).

[157] See, e.g., National Counter-Terrorism Committee, *National Counter-Terrorism Plan* (2012), paras [126]–[131].

6.4 SPECIAL POWERS OF SPECIFIC APPLICATION

Some States have integrated the management of such hazards into their general emergency management legislation, which confers some dedicated special powers.[158] Others simply indicate that such hazards are within the definition of 'emergency' in respect of which the general special powers described in the previous section may be used.[159]

Section 73 of the National Health Security Act 2007 (Cth) provides health inspectors with some emergency powers, which they may use to search premises that they believe do not comply with the requirements of the Act, the regulations or the relevant standards for 'security-sensitive biological agents' or SSBA.[160] An inspector may enter a premises and conduct a search (but not seizure) without a warrant, may require a person to comply with the relevant rules and standards that apply to the SSBA if the inspector believes he or she has not complied, and may 'take such steps, or arrange for such steps to be taken, in relation to the thing as the inspector considers appropriate'.[161] An inspector may only exercise these powers in order 'to avoid an imminent risk of death, serious illness, serious injury, or to protect the environment',[162] and must notify the relevant State or Territory emergency response agency.[163]

Separate special powers are provided for nuclear and radiological hazards. These powers are generally similar to the SSBA powers in that they relate to search and seizure in the face of serious hazards. These powers are conferred at the federal level by the Australian Radiation Protection and Nuclear Safety Act 1998 (Cth)[164] and the Nuclear Non-Proliferation (Safeguards) Act 1987 (Cth).[165] At the level of policy, the CEO of the Commonwealth Australian Radiation Protection and Nuclear Safety Agency is responsible for promoting uniform law on radiation and

---

[158] See State Emergency and Rescue Management Act 1989 (NSW), s 60L; Public Safety Preservation Act 1986 (Qld), pt 3; Emergency Management Act 2006 (Tas), Sch. 1 s 1(1)(d), (e), (f)(i)–(iii), (h), (p), (4)(d); Emergency Management Act 2005 (WA), s 70.

[159] Emergency Management Act 1986 (Vic), s 3, Emergency Management Act 2013 (Vic), s 3 (defining 'emergency' as including contamination); Emergency Management Act 2004 (SA), s 3 (defining 'emergency' as including 'emissions of poisons, radiation or other hazardous agents').

[160] The responsible Minister must create a list of SSBA, which are 'biological agents that the Minister considers to be of security concern to Australia'. National Health Security Act 2007 (Cth), s 31(1).

[161] National Health Security Act 2007 (Cth), s 73(2)(a)–(e).

[162] National Health Security Act 2007 (Cth), s 73(1)(b), (3).

[163] National Health Security Act 2007 (Cth), s 73(4).

[164] Australian Radiation Protection and Nuclear Safety Act 1998 (Cth), s 63.

[165] Nuclear Non-Proliferation (Safeguards) Act 1987 (Cth), s 63.

nuclear safety across all Australian jurisdictions,[166] including uniform emergency responses.[167] The States and Territories have also legislated to provide a dedicated suite of special powers for nuclear and radiological hazards.[168]

Notwithstanding the presumption that a CBRN emergency is for the States and Territories to resolve, clearly, a nuclear attack on Australian soil would severely test this proposition and Australia's constitutional resilience more generally. But, as has been pointed out, the *National Health Security Agreement*, while not explicitly addressing such an event, provides a framework that would guide the allocation of emergency responsibilities in response to a nuclear attack.[169] It follows that there are public health dimensions to this problem, which are dealt with in the next Section.

6.4.3 Public Health and Biosecurity Emergencies

One of the major shifts in the allocation of special powers is in respect to emergencies that affect public health. In Australia, 'public health law is generally, and historically, seen as the States' responsibility'.[170] This has generally held true in times of emergency. Over time, however, the focus of public health has shifted towards 'biosecurity', a strategy for dealing with biological threats to human and animal life, as well as the environment.

In Australia, biosecurity has largely been conceived as a national responsibility, one that involves the exercise of broad regulatory powers

---

[166] Australian Radiation Protection and Nuclear Safety Act 1998 (Cth), s 15.
[167] See ARPANSA, *Recommendations for Intervention in Emergency Situations Involving Radiation Exposure* (2004).
[168] Radiation Control Act 1990 (NSW), s 19; Radiation Safety Act 1999 (Qld), s 148; Radiation Protection and Control Act 1982 (SA), s 42; Radiation Act 2005 (Vic), pt 8; Radiation Protection Act 2005 (Tas), s 64; Radiation Safety Act 1975 (WA), s 55; Radiation Protection Act 2006 (ACT), pt 3 div 3.7; Radiation Protection Act 2004 (NT), s 62. Some of these powers are explicitly designed to contain the CBRN hazard through decontamination: see, e.g., Radiation Control Act 1990 (NSW), s 19(1)(b); Radiation Act 2005 (Vic), s 96(1)(c), (d), (f); Radiation Protection Act 2006 (ACT), s 47(2)(c)–(e).
[169] Belinda Bennett, Terry Carney, Richard Bailey, 'Emergency Powers & Pandemics: Federalism and the Management of Public Health Emergencies in Australia' (2012) 31 (1) U Tas L Rev 37, 54–55. See also *National Health Security Agreement* (2008) paras [21]–[22].
[170] Christopher Reynolds, 'Public Health and the Australian Constitution' (1995) 19(3) Aus J Public Health 243, 243.

6.4 SPECIAL POWERS OF SPECIFIC APPLICATION

over material crossing over and within Australia's territorial borders. This reflects that, increasingly, public health matters have become an issue of international concern that are accordingly the responsibility of national governments.

The World Trade Organization *Agreement on the Application of Sanitary and Phytosanitary Measures* and the World Health Organization *International Health Regulations* are amongst the international agreements that address biosecurity issues. The third edition of the *International Health Regulations,* to which Australia is a signatory, has the purpose 'to prevent, protect against, control and provide a public health response to the international spread of disease in ways that are commensurate with and restricted to public health risks'.[171] To that end, it enjoins the States Parties to 'strengthen and maintain ... the capacity to respond promptly and effectively to public health risks and public health emergencies of international concern'.[172] The Regulations provide that an effective response includes the creation of a national public health response, including the creation of a national public health emergency response plan and control measures capable of preventing the spread of a disease.[173]

This is particularly relevant because, in Australia, the Commonwealth gains the authority to legislate with respect to the implementation of international treaties and agreements under the external affairs power provided for in section 51(xxix) of the Constitution. Accordingly, international agreements addressing public health have been suggested to form a foundation for the centralisation of public health powers in the Commonwealth.[174]

The Commonwealth's power to make laws with respect to quarantine in section 51(ix) of the Constitution also permits it to address some issues of public health. The scope of this power is, however, untested. Some High Court judgments have suggested that the power is not constrained by the restraints the Constitution otherwise imposes on executive detention by the Commonwealth or the protections it provides for political communication.[175] During the 2009 swine flu pandemic, in which

---

[171] International Health Regulations (2005), Art. 2.
[172] International Health Regulations (2005), Art. 13.1.
[173] International Health Regulations (2005), Annex 1, para [6].
[174] See, e.g., Brian Opeskin, 'The Architecture of Public Health Law Reform: Harmonisation of Law in a Federal System' (1998) 22(2) MULR 337, 342–43.
[175] *Kruger* v. *Commonwealth* (1997) 190 CLR 1, 111 (Gaudron J); *Al-Kateb* v. *Godwin* (2004) 219 CLR 562, 649 (Hayne J). See also Anthony Grey, 'The Australian Quarantine

154 people died and 4,440 were infected, it was invoked as a basis for the isolation of persons confirmed to be infected.[176] It has been observed, as a general matter, that the quarantine power could not itself authorise the exercise of unfettered emergency powers that went beyond the specific issue of quarantine.[177]

The Commonwealth's responsibilities in this field are accurately captured by the reasoning that also underpins the implied nationhood power as discussed in Chapter 3: that there exist uniquely national problems that are beyond the capacities of the States, because they extend beyond the boundaries of a State or involve logistical problems that the States are not well adapted to solve.

However, an attempt to extend emergency powers into intra-State emergencies, without State permission, would undermine the rationale for Australia's federalist system and the existence of the States as a separate level of government, by interfering with problems that State governments should be capable of solving. Moreover, emergency public health powers could not enable a Commonwealth Minister to direct State agencies in the exercise of their functions absent agreement, because it would affect the State's capacity to exercise its executive powers and thus breach the *Melbourne Corporation* doctrine.[178]

This is recognised by the inter-governmental agreement that underpins the National Health Security Act 2007 (Cth) - the law that gives effect to the *International Health Regulations* by establishing a framework for coordination and the sharing of information in response to public health emergencies. The *National Security Health Agreement* 'recognises that the States and Territories have responsibility for responding to significant public health events within their jurisdictions',[179] even as it identifies 'Public Health Events of National Significance', such as smallpox, SARS, viral haemorrhagic fevers such as

---

and Biosecurity Legislation: Constitutionality and Critique' (2015) 22 J Law Med 788, 794-800; Cristina Pelkas, 'State Interference with Liberty: The Scope and Accountability of Australian Powers to Detain During a Pandemic' (2010) 12 Flinders L J 41, 44-45.

[176] Quarantine Amendment Proclamation 2009 (Cth); Keith Eastwood, David N Durrheim, Michelle Butler, and Alison Jones, 'Responses to Pandemic (H1N1) 2009, Australia' (2010) 6 Emerging Infectious Diseases 1211, 1211.

[177] Grey (n 175) 803-04.

[178] *Melbourne v. Commonwealth* (1947) 74 CLR 31; *Austin v. Commonwealth* (2003) 215 CLR 185, 249; *Clarke v. Commissioner of Taxation* (2009) 240 CLR 272, 305-07 (Gummow, Heydon, Kiefel and Bell JJ).

[179] *National Health Security Agreement* (2008) para. [21]. See also the *National Health Emergency Response Arrangements* (2011) 10.

the Ebola virus, and other diseases that, inter alia, 'may have a serious public health impact', cause injury, disease or death to a degree that 'may require a significant national response', or pose a risk of spread across the borders of the Australian States or Australia's international borders.[180]

6.4.3.1 Public Health Emergencies

Public health powers are still generally held by the States, and State and Territory Acts provide for the declaration of public health emergencies and allow for a broad range of special powers to be exercised once a declaration is made.[181] As Christopher Reynolds has pointed out, these public health emergency powers should be 'read together with the more general [S]tate and [T]erritory emergency management acts ... to the extent that they are also relevant to public health emergencies'.[182] There is some variation between these Acts but, generally, they tend to confer broad powers that may be activated once the responsible Minister (or, in the case of Tasmania and South Australia, the relevant public official) considers it necessary to do so in order to address the emergency.

Public health emergency powers have been invoked by some jurisdictions in the context of the SARS and H1N1 influenza epidemics. At least some of this legislation is also explicitly designed to assert the enacting State's role in addressing a major public health emergency such as an epidemic or pandemic. For example, the Statutes Amendment (Public Health Incidents and Emergencies) Act 2009 (SA), which introduced public health emergency powers into the South Australian Public Health Act's predecessor, was justified in the Second Reading Speech as follows:

> It is critical that the State has adequate powers to address an outbreak of disease, such as an influenza pandemic, in the State and not be reliant on actions/directions from the Commonwealth. The two sets of powers and levels of government need to be able to work together in a co-ordinated manner.[183]

---

[180] Ibid 4 (definition of 'Public Health Event of National Significance to be Reported to the NFP').
[181] Public Health Act 2010 (NSW), s 8; Public Health Act 2005 (Qld), ch 8; South Australian Public Health Act 2011 (SA), pt 11; Public Health Act 1997 (Tas), pt 2 div 2; Public Health and Wellbeing Act 2008 (Vic), pt 10 div 3; Public Health Act 2016 (WA), pt 12; Public Health Act 1997 (ACT), pt 7; Notifiable Diseases Act 1981 (NT).
[182] Christopher Reynolds, *Public Health and Environment Law* (Federation Press 2011) 313.
[183] SA Parl Debs, LA, 12 May 2009, 2603.

The Acts provide for varying definitions of what is an 'emergency' for the purposes of activating public health special powers, but these formulations tend to be permissive. In Tasmania, under the Public Health Act 1997 (Tas), the Director of Public Health may declare that a 'public health emergency exists if satisfied that the situation requires it'.[184] In the ACT, the responsible Minister may declare a public health emergency 'if satisfied that it is justified in the circumstances'.[185] South Australia is slightly more specific; the Chief Executive may declare a public health emergency where it 'appears ... that an emergency has occurred, is occurring or is about to occur'.[186] That declaration may be informed by guidelines made pursuant to guidelines contained in the Public Health Emergency Management Plan made under the Emergency Management Act 2004 (SA).[187] New South Wales raises the threshold slightly by requiring that there be a 'risk to public health',[188] which Victoria raises further by requiring there be a 'serious risk'.[189] Queensland's legislation provides that the declaration must be 'necessary' to 'prevent or minimise serious adverse effects on human health'.[190] Western Australia's legislation is the most restrictive, stating that the Minister 'cannot' issue a declaration unless satisfied that 'a public health emergency has occurred, is occurring or is imminent'; and that 'extraordinary measures are required to prevent or minimise loss of life or prejudice to the safety, or harm to the health, of persons'.[191]

Surprisingly, given the permissiveness of the legislation, the special powers to address public health emergencies closely resemble in their substance the special powers conferred by the emergency management Acts described in Section 6.3.2. Some public health emergency powers are

---

[184] Public Health Act 1997 (Tas), s 14(1).
[185] Public Health Act 1997 (ACT), s 119(1).
[186] South Australian Public Health Act 2011 (SA), s 87(1).
[187] South Australian Public Health Act 2011 (SA), s 88. Different procedural requirements apply with respect to declarations made under each Act. In New South Wales, Queensland, Victoria and Western Australia, the Minister must consult with public officials, such as the Emergency Commissioners appointed under their emergency management legislation or the State's chief health officers. South Australia's Chief Executive of the administering Department must consult with the State Co-ordinator and the Chief Public Health Officer and seek the approval of the responsible Minister before declaring a public health emergency.
[188] Public Health Act 2010 (NSW), s 8(1).
[189] Public Health and Wellbeing Act 2008 (Vic), s 198(1).
[190] Public Health Act 2005 (Qld), s 319(3).
[191] Public Health Act 2016 (WA), s 167(2)(b),(c).

6.4 SPECIAL POWERS OF SPECIFIC APPLICATION

more extensive: for example, section 8(2) of the Public Health Act 2010 (NSW) goes beyond the enumerated special powers granted by the State Emergency and Rescue Management Act 1989 (NSW) by conferring a general power upon the Minister to 'take any such action' and 'give such directions' as he or she considers necessary to deal with a public safety risk. However, this makes sense given that the special powers provided for in this Act may only be used once a state of emergency is declared under the State Emergency and Rescue Management Act.[192]

No such procedural safeguard attends the Public Health Act 1997 (Tas), which allows the Director, who, it may be recalled, is also responsible for making a declaration of public health emergency upon satisfaction that it is required, to 'take any action or give any directions to', inter alia, 'manage a threat to public health or a likely threat to public health' or quarantine, evacuate or exclude persons from 'any area'.[193] The most recent enactment in this area, the Public Health Act 2016 (WA), is far more specific in its nature, conferring enumerated but purposive powers specifically directed at responding to a public health emergency, including the power to seize drugs and vaccines to use during a public health emergency.[194] The rationale for this is to confer powers that 'reflect the unique nature of health emergencies, which can typically be managed without the necessity to involve other agencies'.[195]

Of note are the special powers to quarantine and order persons to go under medical observation, examination and treatment.[196] Absent a formal declaration of emergency, public officers may still quarantine and treat people who are believed to have 'controlled notifiable conditions'.[197] However, special quarantine and treatment powers are freed

---

[192] Public Health Act 2010 (NSW), s 8(1). That section also provides that the Minister administering the Public Health Act must consult with the Minister administering the State Emergency and Rescue Management Act and decide 'on reasonable grounds that the emergency is, or is likely to be, a risk to public health'.
[193] Public Health Act 1997 (Tas), s 16.
[194] Public Health Act 2016 (WA), s 183.
[195] WA Parl Debs, LA, 26 November 2014, 8836.
[196] Public Health Act 2010 (NSW), s 8(3); Public Health Act 2005 (Qld), ch 8 pt 7; South Australian Public Health Act 2011 (SA), s 90(3); Public Health and Wellbeing Act 2008 (Vic), s 200(1)(a)–(d); Public Health Act 1997 (Tas), s 16(2)(a); Public Health Act 2016 (WA), ss 184, 185.
[197] E.g., listed conditions that are monitored by Australian governments and reported to the Commonwealth by operation of the *National Health Security Agreement* (2008) and the National Health Security Act 2007 (Cth), in fulfilment of Australia's international obligations in this regard.

from many of the procedural constraints imposed on the general quarantine powers. In some statutes, there are still special requirements to ensure these special powers are only used when necessary or, if they are used, with regard to certain overarching principles. Many Acts require that all powers therein be exercised with regard to principles such as prevention, transparency and proportionality.[198]

The South Australian Public Health Act 2011 (SA) distinguishes between quarantine powers in Part 10, which provides quarantine powers exercisable to detain people believed to have controlled notifiable conditions, and Part 11, which confers emergency powers. Using Part 11 frees the Chief Health Officer from a number of requirements, including having to first consider whether it would be more effective to issue a direction under section 75 of the Act instructing the person to, inter alia, isolate themselves or seek treatment.[199] However, section 90(3) provides that an authorised officer may only exercise a special power provided for in Part 11 to isolate a person if there is no reasonable cause to do so using the notified conditions quarantine scheme in Part 10 of the Act or the Mental Health Act 2009 (SA), or where there are 'significant public health advantages' to using the emergency quarantine powers.

6.4.3.2 Biosecurity Emergencies

A variation of the public health emergency is the 'biosecurity emergency'. 'Biosecurity', generally speaking, refers to 'the management of risks to the economy, the environment, and the broader community, of pests and diseases entering, emerging, establishing or spreading'.[200] Although biosecurity is closely linked to public health, it represents a different strategy: it is an integrated approach that amalgamates a series of different threats to human and animal life and health, as well to the environment, and which seeks to identify regulatory frameworks and powers that are sufficient to meet those threats. Those threats are potentially human-made, involving a biological attack, or natural, involving diseases such as Severe Acute Respiratory Syndrome (SARS), Ebola, or the Zika virus.

---

[198] Public Health Act 2010 (NSW), s 3(1); Public Health Act 2005 (Qld), s 7; South Australian Public Health Act 2011 (SA), pt 2; Public Health and Wellbeing Act 2008 (Vic), s 9, 10; Public Health Act 2016 (WA), s 3; Public Health Act 1997 (ACT), s 4.
[199] South Australian Public Health Act 2011 (SA), s 77(1)(b).
[200] Wendy Craik, David Palmer and Richard Sheldrake, IGAB Independent Review Panel, *Is Australia's National Biosecurity System and the Underpinning Intergovernmental Agreement on Biosecurity Fit for the Future?* (2016) 8.

6.4 SPECIAL POWERS OF SPECIFIC APPLICATION

In Australia, the Biosecurity Acts passed by the Commonwealth, New South Wales and Queensland[201] were designed to give effect to the idea that biosecurity is a 'shared responsibility between governments, industries and individuals'.[202] The Biosecurity Act 2015 (Cth), which replaced the Quarantine Act, reflects commitments made in the *Intergovernmental Agreement on Biosecurity*, reached by the Council of Australian Governments (with the exception of Tasmania) in 2012.

A key achievement under this agreement was the *National Environmental Biosecurity Response Agreement* of 2012, which sets out a coordinated framework for responding to biosecurity emergencies. This agreement, and the biosecurity legislation resulting from it, also reflects the recommendations made by a panel of experts headed by Roger Beale AO, in the so-called 'Beale Review' of 2008. The Beale Review made a number of recommendations relating to the harmonisation of Australia's biosecurity frameworks under the heading of the 'One Biosecurity' principle. To this end, the report also represented a shift in thinking about the Commonwealth's constitutional capacity and responsibility to deal with emergencies. The review asserted:

> The Commonwealth has constitutional powers to assume a much broader biosecurity reach. To manage the increasing biosecurity risks, the Commonwealth needs to take an assertive national leadership role underpinned by a strong partnership with the [S]tates and [T]erritories, businesses and the community. Modern and more comprehensive legislation is necessary.[203]

The rationale for this assertion was that there had been disagreement between the Commonwealth and the States as to the Commonwealth's responsibility for dealing with pests and disease once they were within the territorial borders of Australia, which created the risk that Australia could not comply with its international obligations.[204] On the other hand, some of the States, in particular Queensland, had suggested the need for model laws and the need for the Commonwealth to have greater

---

[201] Biosecurity Act 2015 (Cth); Biosecurity Act 2014 (Qld); Biosecurity Act 2015 (NSW). Other Acts focus more on agricultural biosecurity: see Plant Biosecurity Act 2010 (Vic); Biosecurity and Agriculture Management Act 2007 (WA). The Western Australian Act provides for some limited special powers to control pests: see Biosecurity and Agriculture Management Act 2007 (WA), pt 2 div 7.
[202] See, e.g., NSW Parl Debs, LC, 12 August 2015, 2381.
[203] Roger Beale AO, Dr Jeff Fairbrother AM, Andrew Inglis AM, and David Trebeck, *One Biosecurity: A Working Partnership* (Commonwealth of Australia 2008) x.
[204] Ibid 12–13.

emergency powers so as to provide a single framework for dealing with biosecurity emergencies.[205]

It follows that biosecurity emergencies are different from the emergencies dealt with under the framework of general special powers discussed in Section 6.3, or the public health emergencies discussed in Section 6.4.3.1. The *Intergovernmental Agreement on Biosecurity*, for example, provides that

> States and territories support the use of the Commonwealth's national emergency management powers in circumstances where the Parties agree that application of the emergency powers is necessary for a consistent national approach to control, reduce, or remove a threat associated with a biosecurity emergency.[206]

Indeed, the Biosecurity Act represents in some respects an attempt to shift the constitutional boundaries between the Commonwealth and States with respect to civil emergencies. It largely preserves the concurrent operation of State and Territory law,[207] but contains an entire Division dedicated to an invocation of the enumerated heads of power that authorise the Act and justify and limit its application, as well as a severability clause in the case of a successful constitutional challenge,[208] and makes certain action conditional upon consultation with the Health Ministers of the States and Territories.[209] Overall, the way constitutional authority is framed in the Act is designed to 'ensure that [it] is given the widest possible operation consistent with Commonwealth constitutional legislative power'.[210]

Even in the absence of an emergency declared under the Act's relevant provisions, the Biosecurity Act confers a range of broad powers upon the Commonwealth Ministers of Health and Agriculture and the administrative decision-makers who work under their supervision. The Act distinguishes between powers that are applicable to people (who are under the responsibility of the Health Minister) as opposed to plants

---

[205] Ibid 22–23.
[206] Council of Australian Governments, *Intergovernmental Agreement on Biosecurity* (2012), para [7.14] ('Emergency biosecurity powers').
[207] Biosecurity Act 2015 (Cth), s 8; cf s 172 (with regard to the exclusion of any State and Territory law that 'purports to prohibit or restrict the bringing or importation of particular goods into Australian territory').
[208] Biosecurity Act 2015 (Cth), ch 1 pt 3 div 2.
[209] See, e.g., a determination regarding a 'preventative biosecurity measure' made under the Biosecurity Act 2015 (Cth), ch 2 pt 2 div 5.
[210] Explanatory Memorandum to the Biosecurity Bill 2014, 92.

6.4 SPECIAL POWERS OF SPECIFIC APPLICATION 211

and animals (who are under the responsibility of the Agriculture Minister). These powers include those that one might expect the federal government to exercise, such as the Health Minister's power to impose entry and exit requirements on persons or operators of transport in the interests of preventing the entry or spread into Australian territory[211] of a 'listed human disease'.[212]

The Biosecurity Act also confers special powers that would necessarily involve some overlap with State special powers in public health. The germane example is the power to quarantine and treat people within the territorial borders of Australia. For example, under the Act, the Director of Human Biosecurity (the Commonwealth Chief Medical Officer)[213] may list a disease if he or she considers it may be communicable and cause significant harm to human health.[214] This decision must be made in consultation with the chief health officer for each State and Territory as well as with the Director of Biosecurity[215] (the Agriculture Secretary).[216] As the Act itself indicates, the main instrument for dealing with listed human diseases is the 'human biosecurity control order'.[217] A human biosecurity control order imposes 'biosecurity measures' that may include restricting the person to their place of residence; wearing certain protective clothing; being decontaminated; providing body samples; or receiving vaccinations or medication.[218] Individuals may consent to these measures or, if they do not, a direction compelling them to do so may be given by the Director.[219]

The application of control orders and biosecurity measures must be exercised with consideration to a range of principles, including that it be effective in addressing the risk; is appropriate and adapted to that risk; that the circumstances are 'sufficiently serious'; that its exercise is no more 'restrictive or intrusive than is required in the circumstances'; and

---

[211] Defined in s 12 of the Biosecurity Act 2015 (Cth) as '(a) Australia, Christmas Island, Cocos (Keeling) Islands and any external Territory to which that provision extends; and (b) the airspace over an area covered by paragraph (a); and (c) the coastal sea of Australia, of Christmas Island, of Cocos (Keeling) Islands and of any other external Territory to which that provision extends'.
[212] Biosecurity Act 2015 (Cth), ch 2 pt 2 div 2.
[213] Biosecurity Act 2015 (Cth), s 540.
[214] Biosecurity Act 2015 (Cth), s 42(1)(a) and (b).
[215] Biosecurity Act 2015 (Cth), s 42(2)(a) and (b).
[216] Biosecurity Act 2015 (Cth), s 544.
[217] Biosecurity Act 2015 (Cth), s 3.
[218] See generally Biosecurity Act 2015 (Cth), ch 2 pt 3 div 3 subdiv. B.
[219] Biosecurity Act 2015 (Cth), ss 71, 72.

only applies for as long as is necessary.[220] The powers are also to be exercised in order to manage the risk of a contagion or to prevent a listed human disease from 'entering, or emerging, establishing itself or spreading in, Australian territory or a part of Australian territory'.[221] Importantly, when biosecurity measures relating to medical examination and vaccination are to be imposed the Act requires that the person be given seven days to seek judicial review under the Administrative Decisions (Judicial Review) Act 1977 (Cth);[222] this does not extend to other measures, such as isolation.[223]

A closely related power is conferred upon the Director of Human Biosecurity to declare an area within a State or Territory a human health response zone if satisfied that 'it is necessary to do so for the purposes of preventing, or reducing the risk of, a listed human disease emerging, establishing itself or spreading in Australian territory or a part of Australian territory'.[224] The Director may specify requirements for people who are entering or leaving this zone, or prohibit them from entering, for up to three months.[225] The requirements must be appropriate and adapted to preventing the disease from spreading or reducing the risk that it will do so.[226]

Given the far-reaching nature of the Act into traditional fields of State competence, even absent an emergency, it is likely that the ultimate source of constitutional authority for such provisions lies in the Commonwealth's quarantine power.[227] The Commonwealth's ambitious reading of this power's scope is clear in that it does not solely restrain itself (as some other federal Acts do) to biosecurity events touching upon clear fields of Commonwealth authority, for example, inter-State trade and commerce or corporations.[228]

The constitutionality of the Act is pushed even further by the special powers provided for in Chapter 8 of the Act. That Chapter permits the Governor-General to declare a 'biosecurity emergency' (concerning threats to animal or plant life, or the environment) or a 'human

---

[220] Biosecurity Act 2015 (Cth), ss 32(2), 34(2).
[221] Biosecurity Act 2015 (Cth), s 34(1)(a),(b), 84.
[222] Biosecurity Act 2015 (Cth), s 74(1),(2).
[223] Biosecurity Act 2015 (Cth), s 74(3),(4).
[224] Biosecurity Act 2015 (Cth), s 113(1).
[225] Biosecurity Act 2015 (Cth), s 113(3).
[226] Biosecurity Act 2015 (Cth), s 113(4).
[227] See also Grey (n 175) 803.
[228] Biosecurity Act 2015 (Cth), s 24(2).

6.4 SPECIAL POWERS OF SPECIFIC APPLICATION 213

biosecurity emergency' (concerning threats to human life.). A declaration of emergency under Chapter 8 grants immense power to the relevant Minister for the duration of the emergency as specified by the Governor-General. For example, once a human biosecurity emergency is declared in respect of a listed human disease, the Health Minister gains the broad authority to 'determine emergency requirements during the human biosecurity emergency period' under section 477 of the Act.

The Biosecurity Act's explanatory memorandum elaborates on the purported content of this power:

> This power allows the Minister to set a requirement that applies to a class of people, goods or conveyances, to manage the disease risk. For example, the Minister may determine requirements that apply to people, goods or conveyances entering or leaving a specified place; restrict or prevent the movement of people, goods or conveyances between specified places; or require a specified place to be evacuated.[229]

Moreover, under section 478 the Health Minister gains the authority to 'give any direction, to any person, that the Health Minister is satisfied is necessary'. The power is intended to enable the Minister to engage in the 'large scale direction of people during an emergency, rather than for the management of individuals'.[230] This is why sections 477 and 478 prohibit the use of emergency powers to impose the aforementioned 'biosecurity measures' that would ordinarily be the subject of a human biosecurity order; the procedures and consideration of principles that precede the application of biosecurity measures must still be used.[231] The biosecurity emergency powers provided in the Act are similarly far reaching.[232]

Moreover, there are some important statutory limits to these far-reaching powers, which indicate the constitutional and logistical boundaries that could apply during a human biosecurity emergency. The most immediate limitation is the specified purposes for which the Health Minister or Agriculture Minister can exercise their emergency powers. The Health Minister, for example, must exercise those powers in order to prevent or control the listed human disease from entering Australian territory or from emerging or spreading within Australian territory; prevent or control the disease from spreading to another country; or in giving effect to a recommendation made by the World Health

---
[229] Explanatory Memorandum to the Biosecurity Bill 2014, 294.
[230] Ibid 295.
[231] Biosecurity Act 2015 (Cth), ss 477(6), 478(6).
[232] Biosecurity Act 2015 (Cth), ch 8 pt 1.

Organization under Part III of the International Health Regulations.[233] Another important limitation lies in the requirement that the emergency be a 'severe and immediate threat' and be occurring on a 'nationally significant scale', language that clearly resembles the federalism-inspired boundaries on the Commonwealth's emergency powers drawn in *Pape* as discussed in Chapter 3.[234]

The Commonwealth's consciousness of the nature and limits of its powers to deal with biosecurity emergencies is reflected in the explanatory memorandum to the Biosecurity Act, which uses a 'severe and widespread outbreak of foot-and-mouth disease that affects multiple Australian [S]tates' as an example of the kind of emergency that would justify the use of biosecurity emergency powers under Chapter 8.[235] It is worth noting that the distinguishing features of this example are that it is severe, widespread, and extends beyond the territorial boundaries of a single State, clarifying the emergency's uniquely national character and tying it closer to some of the Commonwealth's enumerated powers, such as the power to make laws with respect to inter-State trade and commerce in section 51(i) of the Constitution.

6.5 Ad-hoc Special Powers

Sometimes, Parliaments will confer special powers in response to a particular situation of emergency. These special powers frameworks are 'ad-hoc' because they tend to be tailored to the situation. State governments have passed legislation to, inter alia, address blockades,[236] union strikes,[237] ensure fuel rationing and price control,[238] control the price of beer,[239] and to protect important events and meetings.[240]

This Chapter will conclude by focusing on two recent examples of the Commonwealth's ad-hoc emergency interventions. The Commonwealth

---

[233] Biosecurity Act 2015 (Cth), s 477(1)(a)(i) and (ii), (b) and (c); s 478(1)(a)(i) and (ii), (b) and (c).
[234] Biosecurity Act 2015 (Cth), s 475(1)(a).
[235] Explanatory Memorandum to the Biosecurity Bill 2014, 44.
[236] Road Obstructions (Special Provisions) Act 1979 (NSW).
[237] Essential Foodstuffs and Commodities Act 1979 (WA).
[238] Motor Fuel Rationing (Temporary Provisions) Act 1977 (SA), Motor Fuel (Temporary Restriction) Act 1980 (SA); Fuel Prices Regulation Act 1981 (Vic).
[239] Beer Prices Regulation (Temporary Provisions) Act 1983 (Vic).
[240] See, e.g., Commonwealth Games Act 1982 (Qld); APEC Meeting (Police Powers) Act 2007 (NSW); Commonwealth Heads of Government Meeting (Special Powers) Act 2011 (WA).

6.5 AD-HOC SPECIAL POWERS

typically passes emergency ad-hoc legislation that has a funding element,[241] financial support being one of the Commonwealth's core responsibilities in this area. However, the Commonwealth's powers to intervene will depend on the nature of the emergency and, as the following example shows, where it occurs.

6.5.1 Northern Territory Intervention

The Commonwealth's controversial Northern Territory National Emergency Response, sometimes described as the 'Intervention', can be understood as involving ad-hoc special powers. The Intervention was an initiative of the Howard Liberal Government in reaction to a report published by the Northern Territory's *Board of Inquiry into the Protection of Aboriginal Children from Sexual Abuse*, 'Little Children are Sacred'.[242] The Government was galvanised by a number of findings in the report, in particular that the neglect of Aboriginal children and their abuse by men of both Aboriginal and non-Aboriginal backgrounds in the Northern Territory needed to be designated as an issue of 'urgent national significance'.[243] The report had recommended, inter alia, that police conduct consultations with Aboriginal communities with a view to supporting the communities in 'maintaining peace, law and order'.[244]

Instead, the Howard Government decided to 'declare an emergency situation and use the territories power available under the Constitution to make laws for the Northern Territory'.[245] This reflects that, under section 122 of the Constitution, the Commonwealth has a plenary power to make laws with respect to the Territories.[246] The Minister for Families, Community Services and Indigenous Affairs at the time, Mal Brough, described the Intervention as being into a 'failed society where basic standards of law and order and behaviour have broken down and where

---

[241] See, e.g., the Tax Laws Amendment (Temporary Flood and Cyclone Reconstruction Levy) Act 2011 (Cth) and the Income Tax Rates Amendment (Temporary Flood and Cyclone Reconstruction Levy) Act 2011 (Cth), passed by the Gillard Labor Government to temporarily raise income tax in the 2011–2012 financial year as a way of funding support for Queensland's recovery from Cyclone Yasi.
[242] Northern Territory Board of Inquiry into the Protection of Aboriginal Children from Sexual Abuse, *Ampe Akelyernemane Meke Mekarle: Little Children are Sacred* (2007).
[243] Ibid 82 (Recommendation 1).
[244] Ibid 115 (Recommendation 29).
[245] Cth Parl Debs, HR, 7 August 2007, 10.
[246] *Spratt v. Hermes* (1965) 114 CLR 226.

women and children are unsafe'.[247] The Commonwealth Parliament passed a suite of legislation including the Northern Territory National Emergency Response Act 2007 (Cth), and, to assist in the measures implemented by those laws, suspended parts of a number of laws including the Racial Discrimination Act 1975 (Cth), the Aboriginal Land Rights (Northern Territory) Act 1976 and the Northern Territory (Self-Government) Act 1978 (Cth).

It is impossible to go into the detail of the Intervention in this Chapter. The compulsory acquisition of a great deal of Aboriginal-owned property was one of the more controversial measures.[248] However, a number of public order measures were included in the Northern Territory National Emergency Response Act 2007 (Cth). It created 'prescribed areas', in which the sale of liquor was restricted and additional search and seizure powers were granted to officers to enforce these laws.[249] The Minister could declare that division 4 of Part VII of the Police Administration Act 1978 (NT), which provides for the warrantless arrest, detention, and search of persons reasonably believed to be intoxicated in a public place, applied within these prescribed areas.[250] Other powers were granted to police, for example, to search for and seize pornography.[251] Other measures involved the exercise of executive power: for example, the government increased police numbers in Aboriginal communities in the Northern Territory, and deployed the defence forces into the Northern Territory to perform logistical and support functions.[252]

6.5.2 The Global Financial Crisis

An ad-hoc Commonwealth response to an emergency of a very different kind concerned the Global Financial Crisis of 2008–2009. It was the

---

[247] Cth Parl Debs, HR, 7 August 2007, 10.
[248] For a more detailed account of the legal issues with the intervention, see Greg McIntyre SC, 'An Imbalance of Constitutional Power and Human Rights: The 2007 Federal Intervention in the Northern Territory' (2007) 14 James Cook U L 81.
[249] Northern Territory National Emergency Response Act 2007 (Cth), pt 10 div 2.
[250] Northern Territory National Emergency Response Act 2007 (Cth), s 18.
[251] Classification (Publications, Films and Computer Games) Act 1995 (Cth), pt 10.
[252] Greg McIntyre SC, 'An Imbalance of Constitutional Power and Human Rights: The 2007 Federal Intervention in the Northern Territory' (2007) 14 James Cook U L 81, 98. McIntyre argued that any attempt by the Commonwealth to assert these powers within a State as opposed to a territory 'would have impacted so significantly upon the legislative and executive power of the States as to disturb the federal balance of power which exists in the Constitution' (ibid 96).

Rudd Government's response to the Financial Crisis that produced the *Pape* litigation; the irony being that an ad hoc response to a novel emergency situation produced what are arguably general rules about national executive power and national emergency power. The Rudd Government's *Economic Security Strategy* and its *Nation Building and Jobs Plan* called for a $42 billion economic stimulus package in response to the emergency.[253] The package involved six pieces of legislation. The Appropriation (Nation Building and Jobs) Act (No. 1) 2009 (Cth) and Appropriation (Nation Building and Jobs) Act (No. 2) 2009 (Cth) funded the infrastructure projects proposed under the plan. The Household Stimulus Package Act (No. 2) 2009 (Cth) provided for a payment to be made to farmers, single-income families, families with school-aged children, those undertaking education, and others on low incomes. The Commonwealth Inscribed Stock Amendment Act 2009 (Cth) authorised the Treasurer to issue additional Commonwealth stock and securities, increasing the debt limit.

The Tax Bonus for Working Australians Act (No. 2) 2009 (Cth), challenged in *Pape,* authorised once-off payments of $250, $600 and $900 graded by income brackets up to $100,000. That Act was repealed by the Tax Bonus for Working Australians (Consequential Amendments) Act (No. 2) 2009 (Cth). In *Pape,* it was argued that the Tax Bonus for Working Australians Act (No. 2) was beyond the legislative power of the Commonwealth. As is recounted in Chapter 3, the Court rejected that argument by finding that the law was supported by section 51(xxxix) as a law incidental to the executive power of the Commonwealth.[254]

---

[253] Prime Minister Kevin Rudd, Deputy Prime Minister and Treasurer Wayne Swan, '$42 Billion Nation Building and Jobs Plan', Press Release, 3 February 2009.
[254] *Pape* (2009) 238 CLR 1, 64 [136].

7

Military Aid to the Civil Power

Use of the military other than for external defence, is a critical and controversial issue in the political life of a country and the civil liberties of its citizens.

R. M. Hope, *Protective Security Review*, (Parliamentary Paper No 397/1979), 142

7.1 Introduction

The topic of peacetime call-out of the Australian Defence Force (ADF) in the domestic arena was one which attracted scant attention for a long time. The rise of global terrorism has brought this topic to the forefront.[1] Terrorist attacks resulting in tragic loss of lives and widespread destruction of property in the major cities of a number of countries have cast the spotlight on the constitutional and legal parameters circumscribing the deployment of military troops to assist the civil power to maintain order and safety in the face of such attacks. Although the subjugation of the military forces to civilian authority is an entrenched part of the constitutional culture of Australia and many other vibrant democracies, it is important that the rules and criteria governing the call-out of the military forces are clearly set out to ensure the functioning of the rule of law.

---

[1] See generally: Elizabeth Ward, 'Call Out the Troops: An Examination of the Legal Basis for Australian Defence Force Involvement in "Non-Defence" Matters' *Research Paper 8 1997-98* (update of a Background Paper issued 5 September 1991); Peta Stephenson, 'Fertile Ground for Federalism? Internal Security, the States and Section 119 of the *Constitution*' (2015) 43 FLR 289; Cameron Moore, 'The ADF and Internal Security: Some Old Issues With New Relevance' (2005) 28(2) UNSWLR 523; Justice Margaret White, 'The Executive and the Military' (Paper presented at the 8th Annual Public Law Weekend, Constitutional Law Weekend, Canberra, 7-9 November 2003) <http://law.anu.edu.au/cipl/2003conference.asp>; Michael Head, 'The Military Call-Out Legislation: Some Legal and Constitutional Questions' (2001) 29 FLR 271.

7.2 Inquest into the Deaths Arising from the Lindt Café Siege

On 15 November 2014, a person by the name of Man Monis, described as a 'religious activist,' held eighteen persons hostage in Lindt Café in Sydney. The manager, who was one of the hostages, was directed by Monis to telephone the authorities and to say that the hostages had been taken by 'an Islamic State operative armed with a gun and explosives' and that he 'had stationed collaborators with bombs in other locations throughout the city'. Twelve hostages managed to escape during the siege. However, upon the execution of the manager by Monis the NSW Police immediately stormed the café and in the firefight Monis and one of the hostages were killed.[2] The New South Wales Coroner conducted an inquest into the deaths arising from the Lindt Café Siege.

In his report, the Coroner canvassed, among the issues, the extent to which the Australian Defence Force (ADF) was or could have been involved in the response to, and management of the siege.[3] The inquest in considering whether the ADF could have been called out within the terms of Part IIIAAA of the Defence Act 1903 (Cth), noted that Monis was a single armed offender and that 'responding to that threat was at all times within the capacity of the NSW Police Force. The inquest stated: 'The position might have been different if, for example, accomplices of Monis were engaged in other violent acts, or the capacity of the [Tactical Operations Unit] officers was exhausted by their attendance at other incidents.' It was of the view that the preconditions for a call-out set out in Part IIIAAA of the Defence Act 1903 (Cth) were not met 'because the NSWPF considered it had the capacity to respond effectively to Monis' actions and did not advise the NSW government otherwise.' The inquest concluded: 'The challenge global terrorism poses for state police forces calls into question the adequacy of existing arrangements for the transfer of responsibility for terrorist incidents to the ADF.'

The inquest viewed a foreshadowed comprehensive review of the ADF's role in domestic counterterrorism operations as an opportunity to review the call-out threshold. The review would include a review of

---

[2] 'Findings and Recommendations,' *Inquest into the Deaths Arising from the Lindt Café Siege* (2017) (hereinafter referred to as the 'Report') 3, [1] and [5].

[3] 'While the ADF has never been called out to respond to a terrorist incident, a number of steps have been taken to prepare for such an eventuality. In particular, the army has established two Tactical Assault Groups – TAG East and TAG West – based in Sydney and Perth, respectively. These groups are designed to be able to deploy rapidly to conduct domestic counterterrorist operations.' Report 384, para [19].

'the legislative and policy framework for call-out'. The inquest report recommended that 'the ADF Review confer with state and territory governments about the criteria governing applications for the ADF to be called out pursuant to the Defence Act 1903 (Cth) with a view to determining: whether further guidance is required on the criteria to be used by States and Territories in determining whether to apply for Commonwealth assistance; and if so, what criteria ought to be stipulated.'

The last occasion when the topic of military aid to the civil power was subjected to exegesis was in 1978 in the wake of a bomb blast at the Sydney Hilton Hotel.

7.3 The 1978 Sydney Hilton Bombing

On 13 February 1978, a bomb blast occurred at the Sydney Hilton Hotel. The blast occurred hours before the official opening of the Commonwealth Heads of Government Regional Meeting (CHOGRM).[4] Two men were killed and nine others injured.[5] The CHOGRM programme included a trip to Bowral. Acting on a report by the head of the Protective Security Co-ordination Centre[6] the Prime Minister (Malcolm Fraser) decided to call out the army to provide the conference with full security.[7] This domestic use of the Australian Defence Force[8] (hereafter the 'ADF') was authorised by an Executive Council minute of 13 February 1978.[9] In the minute, the Governor-General said he was satisfied that because of terrorist activities and related violence in New South Wales, it was necessary to call out the Defence Force. The minute stated that the call out was necessary (a) for the purpose of safeguarding the national and international interests of the Commonwealth of

---

[4] CHOGRM was attended by heads of government from a number of countries. See *Protective Security Review* (AGPS 1979), Appendix 3.
[5] One of the injured victims, a police constable, subsequently died in hospital.
[6] For information on the origin and functions of the Protective Services Co-Ordination Centre, see *Protective Security Review*, Appendix 14.
[7] For an account of the incident, see *The National Times*, 20–25 February 1978 and the editorial comment in *The Age*, 21 February 1978.
[8] According to David Letts and Rob McLaughlin, the term 'Australian Defence Force' 'only achieved legislative authority in 2016' as a result of changes to the composition of the ADF effected by the Defence Legislation Amendment (First Principles) Act 2015 (Cth). The changes came into force from 1 July 2016. See David Letts and Rob McLaughlin, 'Call-Out Powers for the Australian Defence Force in an Age of Terrorism: Some Legal Implications' (2016) 85 AIAL Forum 63.
[9] Commonwealth of Australia, *Gazette*, 14 February 1978, No. 530.

Australia; (b) for giving effect to the obligations of the Commonwealth of Australia in relation to the protection of internationally protected persons; (c) for the purposes related to those matters.

This call-out of the ADF, apparently the first instance of deployment in Australia's peacetime history, was highly controversial, and was particularly criticised as an overreaction. Professor Blackshield said:

> In terms of our popular social traditions, the idea is very firmly entrenched that the use of armed forces within the realm in peacetime is "not cricket". It is this longstanding social tradition that really underlies the disquiet surrounding the events at Bowral. But as soon as one asks whether this social tradition is reflected in any legal tradition that might be invoked as a constitutional restraint on the use of armed forces, one is plunged into an esoteric maze of uncertainties.[10]

In the wake of the Hilton bombing, R. M. Hope, a judge of the New South Wales Court of Appeal, was appointed by the Commonwealth Government to conduct a review of domestic security. His terms of reference included: 'The relationship between the Defence Force and civilian authorities in the matter of civilian security'; and, 'Security and protective arrangements in force in all Commonwealth departments and authorities, and the capacity of departments and authorities to provide support to the general protective security effort in various situations'.[11]

On 15 May 1979, Hope presented his *Protective Security Review* report to the Prime Minister. The report dealt comprehensively with a whole range of matters pertaining to counter-terrorism measures. One chapter, Chapter 10, set out recommendations by Hope regarding the Defence Force and civilian security. Appendix 9 of the report set out an opinion by Sir Victor Windeyer on issues concerning the position of members of the Defence Force when called out to aid the civil power. Sir Victor Windeyer was asked by the Commonwealth Attorney-General specifically to advise on the following questions:

---

[10] Anthony Blackshield, 'The Siege of Bowral – The Legal Issues' (1978) 4 Pacific Defence Reporter (March), 6. See also: NS Reaburn, 'The Legal Implications in Counter-Terrorist Operations' (1978) 4 Pacific Defence Reporter (April), 34–36; CM Doogan, 'Defence Powers Under the Constitution: Use of Troops in Aid of State Police Powers: Suppression of Terrorist Activities' (1982) 5(2) Journal of the Royal United Services Institute of Australia (October), 55.

[11] Cth Parl Debs, HR, 23 February 1978, 154–55. See also 'Legal and Constitutional Problems of Protective Security Arrangements in Australia' (1978) 52 ALJ 296, 297.

(1) What under the existing law are the powers and obligations of a member of the Defence Force when called out to aid the civil power?
(2) Whether changes in the existing law dealing with those powers and obligations are called for; if so, what these changes should be?[12]

This chapter will focus on the circumstances that govern the call-out[13] of the ADF, the legal umbrella under which they operate, the legal position of ADF members, and what safeguards should be available to prevent the misuse of the ADF.

At the outset, it is important to note that the concern is not with the utilisation of the ADF to counter the effects of natural disasters, to maintain services during strikes, for coastal surveillance, search and rescue, to provide bands and displays, or to render harmless explosive ordnance (for example, old bombs and hand grenades).

The real concern is with the relationship between the ADF and civilian authorities in matters of 'civilian security'. Hope construed that to mean 'aid to the Commonwealth and State governments and their civil authorities in meeting civil emergencies, especially terrorist attacks and other politically motivated violence, but also riots and the like'.[14] When the ADF are called out in such circumstances they are deployed to use force if necessary to support the civil power against a domestic threat.

7.4 Military Assistance Pursuant to Application by a State

The primary duty of preserving public order in a State rests with the government of the State. When emergencies arise that threaten the peace and tranquillity in a State, the State may have to resort to all the resources it can command to prevent such a breach. 'If [a police constable] sees an

---

[12] See 'Letter of 24 May 1978 from the Attorney-General to Sir Victor Windeyer': *Protective Security Review* (n 4) 277.

[13] For an explanation of the expressions, 'called out', 'call forth', see *Protective Security Review* (n 4), Appendix 9, 282–83.

[14] Since Federation, the services of the Defence Force have been employed on a few occasions. A notable controversial instance was when the army was sent to work the open-cut mines to break the coal strike of 1941: see Leslie Finlay Crisp, *Ben Chifley* (Angus & Robertson 1977) 360–67; Phillip Deery (ed), *Labour in Conflict: The 1949 Coal Strike* (Hale & Ironmonger 1978). In such a context the army was performing the role of coal-miners. Such a utilisation of the military forces is not unknown in other jurisdictions. In 1975, in Glasgow, troops were used to clear heaps of rotting refuse which had accumulated as a result of a ten-week unofficial strike by the dustcart drivers: *The Times*, 20 March 1975. The army was called out when Brisbane was severely affected by a cyclone in 1974 and when Darwin was devastated by a cyclone in 1974.

7.4 MILITARY ASSISTANCE TO STATE APPLICATION

affray, he must quell it and may arrest the offenders without warrant. It is his duty to disperse and put an end to an unlawful assembly. If there is a riot, it is his duty to suppress it, using such force as is necessary.'[15] Certain emergencies may, however, be beyond the capacity of the police to contain. The limited personnel of the police force may not be sufficient to enable them to control emergencies of an extreme magnitude. Furthermore, the police may lack highly sophisticated military hardware to cope with extremely dangerous emergencies, and it may be necessary to resort to the military forces. Such scenario is now becoming commonplace in a number of countries in Europe in the face of the ongoing 'war on terror'. The image of soldiers with heavy weaponry patrolling the streets in many European cities following a terrorist incident is now a familiar sight.

7.4.1 Sections 51(vi), 61, 68 and 114

The Commonwealth Parliament is empowered by the defence power in section 51(vi) to legislate with respect not only to 'the naval and military defence of the Commonwealth' but also with respect to 'the control of the forces to execute and maintain the laws of the Commonwealth'. Section 61 of the Commonwealth Constitution states that the executive power of the Commonwealth 'is vested in the Queen and is exercisable by the Governor-General as the queen's representative, and extends to the execution and maintenance of this Constitution and of the laws of the Commonwealth'. The Commonwealth Constitution, in section 68, expressly vests the 'command in chief of the naval and military forces' in the Governor-General as the Queen's representative.

Under section 114 of the Constitution, a State shall not, without the consent of the Commonwealth Parliament, raise or maintain any naval or military force. The language is mandatory, but the prohibition can be lifted if consent of the Commonwealth Parliament is obtained to set up a paramilitary force. On this score, Hope said:

> There is strong reason in our type of society to avoid the establishment of paramilitary forces. There may be constitutional difficulties in the way of any State setting up such a body. But quite apart from these difficulties,

---

[15] *Report of Inquiry on 'The Red Lion Square Disorders of 15 June 1974'*, (Cmnd 5919, 1975) para [116].

such a force would have a strength equivalent to that of a similar military body, but would have no military role, and would be without the traditional restraint of the Defence Force and without the system of legal and administrative controls which has been built up in respect of the Defence force over a long time. Moreover a paramilitary force could do nothing which a police force or the Defence Force, appropriately trained and equipped, could not do.[16]

The States do not have their own military forces and rely on their police force to maintain public order and protect safety. The 'war on terror' has made it starkly clear that a handful of militants armed with heavy weaponry can cause the loss of many civilian lives and destruction of property, and that the police may be unable to confront them. Hence, the States would have to rely on the ADF under the control of the Commonwealth. Seeking Commonwealth military assistance is provided for by the Commonwealth Constitution.

7.4.2   Section 119: Liability of the Commonwealth to Protect the States

Section 119 provides: 'The Commonwealth shall protect every State against invasion and, on the application of the Executive Government of the State, against domestic violence.'[17] The section is based mainly on article IV, section 4 of the US Constitution (the 'guaranty' clause). The US provision reads as follows:

> The United States shall guarantee to every State in this Union a Republican Form of Government, and shall protect each of them against Invasion; and on Application of the Legislature, or the Executive (when the Legislature cannot be convened) against domestic violence.

---

[16] *Protective Security Review* (n 4) 157. Hope's views correspond to those articulated by Sir Robert Mark, a former Commissioner of the Metropolitan Police in the United Kingdom: 'The Army High Command, the Home Office and the civil police have always been opposed to a third force and believe that the purposes it could achieve are better fulfilled by the police and the army about whose respective roles and accountability there is no ambiguity and who both enjoy public confidence.' New Scotland Yard, Press Release, 11 March 1976, 10.

[17] An attempt to substitute 'attack' for 'invasion' in the Melbourne Session of the Constitutional Convention was defeated. The mover of the motion, Mr Gordon, claimed that it would make it clear that a naval attack was included: see *Convention Debates*, Melbourne, 691–92. For an account of the drafting history of s 119, see Peta Stephenson, 'Fertile Ground for Federalism? Internal Security, the States and Section 119 of the Constitution' (2015) 43 FLR 289, 293–95.

The statutory embodiment of this provision states:

> Whenever there is an insurrection in any State against its government, the President may, upon the request of its legislature or of its governor if the legislature cannot be convened ... use such of the armed forces, as he considers necessary to suppress the insurrection.

The scope of these provisions has not been subject to judicial exegesis. Instead, past presidents 'have developed certain practices which have considerable force as precedents'.[18] A comparison of the Australian and the American constitutional provisions points to some important differences. First, article IV, section 4 contains an additional limb of guaranteeing a 'Republican Form of Government' to the States. Secondly, when there is resort to federal aid, the application must be in the first instance be made by the State legislature. It is only when the State legislature cannot be convened that the application is made by the executive. The absence of such a requirement enables the Australian States to have a speedier recourse to Commonwealth intervention.

Although section 119 uses the word 'shall', it does not follow that the Commonwealth is obliged to furnish military aid on any application by a State.[19] In 1912, an application was made by the Queensland government along the following lines:[20]

> In consequence of general strike riot and bloodshed are imminent in Brisbane. Police are not able to preserve order. Firearms have been used to prevent arrests of a man guilty of riotous conduct. Executive Government of State requests that you direct steps to be taken immediately to protect the State against domestic violence in terms of s 119 of *Commonwealth of Australia Constitution Act*.

The Governor-General, acting on the advice of the federal Government, replied:

> That whilst the Commonwealth Government is quite prepared to fulfil its obligations to the States if ever the occasion should arise, they do not admit the right of any State to call for their assistance under

---

[18] Note on 'Riot Control and the Use of Federal Troops' (1968) 81 Harv L Rev 638, reprinted in M Cherif Bassiouni (ed), *The Law of Dissent and Riots* (Charles C Thomas 1971) 365, 366.

[19] Section 119 refers to 'domestic violence' in contrast to the words 'domestic disturbances'.

[20] *Parliamentary Papers*, 1912, No 16. See also: Commonwealth of Australia, *Report of the Royal Commission on the Constitution* (1929); Brian Beddie and Sue Moss, *Some Aspects of Aid to the Civil Power in Australia*, (Occasional Monograph No 2, Department of Government, Faculty of Military Studies, University of New South Wales, 1982).

circumstances which are proper to be dealt with by the Police Forces of the States. The condition of affairs existing in Queensland does not in the opinion of my Ministers warrant the request of the Executive Government of Queensland contained in Your Excellency's message being complied with.

Hope identified two sets of circumstances requiring military intervention: '(a) when the police forces are unable to contain violence or to ensure the prevention of violence; and (b) when what is required to be done is not properly within the police role but is properly within the role of the Defence Force'.

Professor Blackshield has expressed the view that a *threat* of domestic violence would be sufficient for military aid to be invoked. He said:

> One argument is that when s 119 speaks of "domestic violence" it must refer to a continuing uncontrollable situation ... But ... it is easy enough to imagine other situations in which a real and continuing threat of "domestic violence" would justify the use of the section. The key word is "protect"; and obviously one can protect against threatened as well as actual aggression.[21]

7.4.3 The Defence Act 1903 (Cth)

The Defence Act 1903 (Cth) puts on a statutory footing the mechanics for the deployment of the ADF in aid of the civilian authorities. The Act was amended in 2000 in anticipation of the Sydney Olympics, and, in 2006, was 'updated' to address 'a range of shortfalls and problems identified in the 2000 scheme'[22] in anticipation of the Melbourne Commonwealth Games.[23]

Under section 51B of the Defence Act 1903 (Cth) as amended, the Governor-General may, by written order, call out the Defence Force and direct the Chief of the Defence Force to utilise the Defence Force to protect the State against the domestic violence 'if a State Government applies to the Commonwealth Government to protect the State against domestic violence that is occurring or is likely to occur in the State'.[24] The authorising Ministers must be satisfied that: '(a) the State is not, or is

---

[21] Blackshield (n 10) 6.
[22] See Letts and McLaughlin (n 8) 72.
[23] For a detailed analysis of the 2006 amendment, see Letts and McLaughlin (n 8) 72–77.
[24] If domestic violence occurs in any territory under the authority of the Commonwealth, s 51C contains provisions in pari materia to those of s 51B.

unlikely to be, able to protect itself against the domestic violence; and (b) the Defence Force should be called out and the Chief of the Defence Force should be directed to utilise the Defence Force to protect the State against the domestic violence; and (c) one or more of Divisions 2, 2A, 3 and 3B, and Division 4, should apply in relation to the order.' It is expressly spelt out in section 51B (2) that the Reserve Forces shall not be called out or utilised in connexion with an industrial dispute.

On 28 June 2018, the Defence Amendment (Call Out of the Australian Defence Force) Bill 2018 was introduced to the Commonwealth Parliament. The Bill seeks to make extensive amendments to Part IIIAAA of the Defence Act 1903 (Cth) to enhance the ADF's ability to protect the States, Territories and Commonwealth interests against domestic violence, including terrorism. A significant change proposed by the Bill is to make it easier for the States and Territories to request ADF support by lowering the threshold requirement for a call out. Instead of the current threshold requirement that the States and Territories are not, or are unlikely to be, able to protect themselves against the domestic violence, the authorising Ministers must consider the nature of the domestic violence and whether the utilisation of the ADF would be likely to enhance the ability of a State or Territory to protect the State or Territory against the domestic violence (proposed new section 35 of the Defence Act).

7.5 Commonwealth Intervention without State Application

An important issue concerns the ability of the Commonwealth to intervene on territory within a State. Section 119 of the *Constitution*, according to its text, would exclude unilateral action by the Commonwealth for the protection of the States against domestic violence. This does not mean that there are no circumstances under which the Commonwealth can employ military aid on its own initiative for its own protection.[25] In *R v. Sharkey*,[26] Dixon J, quoting from the *Constitution of the Australian Commonwealth* authored by Quick and Garran, said:

> The maintenance of order in a State is primarily the concern of the State, for which the police powers of the State are ordinarily adequate. But even

---

[25] See Cameron Moore, '"To Execute and Maintain the Laws of the Commonwealth" the ADF and Internal Security: Some Old Issues with New Relevance' (2005) 28(2) UNSWLR 523.
[26] (1949) 79 CLR 121.

if the State is unable to cope with domestic violence, the Federal Government has no right to intervene, for the protection of the State or its citizens, unless called upon by the State Executive. If, however, domestic violence within a State is of such a character as to interfere with the operations of the Federal government, or with the rights and privileges of federal citizenship, the Federal Government may clearly, without a summons from the State, interfere to restore order. Thus if a riot in a State interfered with the carriage of the federal mails, or with interstate commerce, or with the right of an elector to record his vote at federal elections, the Federal Government could use all the force at its disposal, not to protect the State, but to protect itself. Were it otherwise, the Federal Government would be dependent on the Governments of the States for the effective exercise of its powers.[27]

In the case of the Bowral affair, it was clearly not an operation under section 119 of the Constitution. There was no formal application by the government of New South Wales. The Prime Minister (Malcolm Fraser) consulted the Premier of New South Wales (Neville Wran). The Prime Minister made this clear in his statement to the Commonwealth Parliament:

The mechanism for the legal approach to the call-out was discussed with the Premier in two terms: In terms of a strict request from the State, and therefore in terms of aid to the civil power: or, secondly, in terms of the use of the Commonwealth's own authority and responsibility to protect people against possible acts of terrorism. For various reasons ... the second course was chosen, but the Premier had made it perfectly plain to me that if it was thought best to pursue it through the first mechanism, the Premier would certainly act in full co-operation.[28]

Professor Blackshield cogently explained why section 119 was inappropriate to provide the constitutional justification for the call-out of the ADF in the Bowral affair: 'The object of calling out the troops was not to protect the people of New South Wales against "domestic violence", but to protect 11 visiting heads of state against possible threats to their safety.'[29] The Executive Council minute of 13 February stated that the deployment of federal troops was necessitated by the Commonwealth's obligations in relation to 'the protection of internationally protected persons'. The Commonwealth's obligations arose from various statutes:

---

[27] Ibid 151.
[28] Cth Parl Debs, HR, 23 January 1978, 159.
[29] Blackshield (n 10) 7.

7.5 INTERVENTION WITHOUT STATE APPLICATION

the Public Order (Protection of Persons and Property) Act 1971 (Cth) and the Crimes (Internationally Protected Persons) Act 1976 (Cth).

The power to invoke military aid unilaterally can be based on the combined operation of sections 61 and 68. Section 68 vests the command of the naval and military forces of the Commonwealth in the Governor-General as the Queen's representative and that the executive power extends to the 'execution and maintenance of this Constitution and of the laws of the Commonwealth'. In the modern-day context of actions to counter terrorism, there could be reliance on justifying intervention by the invocation of an inherent executive power of self-protection. Hope said: 'One must accept the validity of relying on the inherent power for a source of power to counter terrorism directed against the Commonwealth government or hindering its legitimate activity, or attacking people in whom, or places or assets in which, the Commonwealth has a constitutional interest.'[30]

Under section 51A of the Defence Act 1903 (Cth), the Governor-General may, by written order, call out the Defence Force and direct the Chief of the Defence Force to utilise the Defence Force to protect 'Commonwealth interests' against the domestic violence if the authorising Ministers are satisfied, inter alia, that: '(a) domestic violence is occurring or is likely to occur in Australia; and (aa) the domestic violence would, or would be likely to, affect Commonwealth interests; and (b) if the domestic violence is occurring or is likely to occur in a State or self-governing Territory – the State or Territory is not, or is unlikely to be, able to protect Commonwealth interests against the domestic violence; and (c) the Defence Force should be called out and the Chief of the Defence Force should be directed to utilise the Defence Force to protect the Commonwealth interests against the domestic violence'. It has been pointed out that the expression 'Commonwealth interests' is not defined in the Defence Act itself or in other legislation.[31] The expression has been criticised for being 'unnecessarily vague' and that 'it could potentially be construed widely, such that any outbreak of domestic violence within a state could potentially pose a threat to Commonwealth interests' resulting in a dilution of 'the importance of s 119'.[32] Nevertheless, in

---

[30] *Protective Security Review* (n 4) 29–30.
[31] Peta Stephenson, 'Fertile Ground for Federalism? Internal Security, the States and Section 119 of the *Constitution*' (2015) 43 FLR 289, 303.
[32] Ibid.

practical reality it is not difficult to identify situations when Commonwealth interests are involved.

An expedited process is provided by the Defence Act 1903 (Cth) for the call-out of the ADF by the Prime Minister in the face of a 'sudden and extraordinary emergency' and where it is not practicable for an order to be made by the Governor-General.[33] The Act also prescribes for the other two authorising Ministers to make the call-out order if the Prime Minister is unable to be contacted for the purposes of considering whether to make, and making an order.[34] Furthermore, in the event that the Prime Minister and the remaining authorising Minister are unable to be contacted, an authorising Minister together with the Deputy Prime Minister, the Foreign Minister or the Treasurer may make the order for an expedited call-out.[35]

The Defence Amendment (Call Out of the Australian Defence Force) Bill 2018 also seeks to reduce the high threshold in relation to the protection of Commonwealth interests against domestic violence along the same lines as the change in relation to the protection of the States and Territories against domestic violence. Thus, the authorising Ministers are required to consider the nature of the domestic violence and whether the utilisation of the ADF would be likely to enhance the ability of those States and Territories to protect the Commonwealth interests against the domestic violence (as section 33).

The amendment Bill also seeks to provide for 'contingent call out' of the ADF to protect the States, Territories (as section 36) and Commonwealth interests (as section 34). Contingent call-out orders 'pre-authorise' the ADF to respond to threats or incidents of domestic violence, should specified circumstances arise.

7.6 The Soldier's Legal Position

Section 51T of the Defence Act 1903 (Cth) expressly states that a member of the Defence Force may use such force against persons and things as is reasonable and necessary in the circumstances. However, a member of the Defence Force must not, in using force against a person 'do anything

---

[33] Defence Act 1903 (Cth), s 51CA (1).
[34] Defence Act 1903 (Cth), s 51CA (2).
[35] Defence Act 1903 (Cth), s 51CA (2A). Under the 2018 proposed amendments, the Minister for Home Affairs (defined in the Bill as 'the Minister who administers the Australian Federal Police Act 1979') is added to the list of alternative Ministers.

that is likely to cause the death of, or grievous bodily harm to, the person unless the member believes on reasonable grounds that doing that thing is necessary to protect the life of, or to prevent serious injury to, another person (including the member); or subject the person to greater indignity than is reasonable and necessary in the circumstances.[36]

7.6.1 *Defence of Superior Orders in Certain Circumstances*

Section 51WB of the Defence Act 1903 (Cth) states that the fact that a criminal act was done, or purported to be done, by a member of the Defence Force under an order of a superior 'does not relieve the member of criminal responsibility'. However, the section allows for a defence of superior orders provided the following circumstances are satisfied: '(a) the criminal act was done by the member under an order of a superior; and (b) the member was under a legal obligation to obey the order; and (c) the order was not manifestly unlawful; and (d) the member had no reason to believe that circumstances had changed in a material respect since the order was given; and (e) the member had no reason to believe that the order was based on a mistake as to a material fact; and (f) the action taken was reasonable and necessary to give effect to the order.'[37]

---

[36] Under the 2018 amendment Bill, the contents of the current section 51T will be located in a new section 51N. It is interesting to note the contents of the proposed section 51N (3) states that a member of the ADF must not do anything that is likely to cause death of, or grievous bodily harm to, the person unless '(b) if a person against whom the force is to be used is attempting to escape being detained by fleeing – the person has, if practicable, been called on to surrender and the member believes on reasonable grounds that the person cannot be apprehended in any other manner'.

[37] Under the 2018 amendment Bill, the contents of the current section 51WB will be located in section 51Z.

8

The Judiciary and Emergency Powers

> *In* The Commonwealth *v.* Colonial Combing, Spinning and Weaving Co. Ltd. *[1922] HCA 62; (1922) 31 CLR 421, at p 442, Isaacs J. said that the well-known dictum in* The Zamora *(1916) 2 AC 77, at p 107, that 'those who are responsible for the national security must be the sole judges of what the national security requires' is 'unquestionable law'. The statement would nowadays be regarded as too absolute. It does not mean that when the executive seeks a special privilege or immunity on grounds of national security the courts will defer without question to the judgment of the executive as to what the national security requires.*
>
> Gibbs CJ, *A v. Hayden* (1984) 156 CLR 532, 548

8.1 Introduction

Previous chapters of this book have examined emergency powers in Australian law, both under the Australian Constitution, and pursuant to legislation. This chapter will focus on the extent to which there is, or may be, accountability with regard to the exercise of such powers as a result of the administrative law mechanism of judicial review. Specifically, the chapter will examine possible hindrances to the subjection of the exercise of emergency powers to judicial review. The chapter will be divided into two parts: In the first part, an examination will be made of the way in which judges, in exercising restraint, may hinder the bringing of successful review applications with regard to exercises of emergency power; in the second part, consideration will be given to express attempts by the legislature to limit the availability of judicial review, and consideration will be given to the possible impact of those attempts on the review of emergency powers.

8.2 The Exercise of Judicial Restraint

In this part, consideration will be given to three ways in which the exercise of judicial restraint may limit the extent to which successful applications for judicial review may be brought with regard to the exercise of emergency powers. First, the notion of non-justiciability will be analysed, and the impact that this may have upon the review of emergency powers considered. Secondly, an examination will be made of the effect that judicial deference in respect of the existence of jurisdictional facts may have upon the review of emergency powers. Finally, consideration will be given to the courts' preparedness to find that emergency powers legislation implies the existence of the hearing rule, in circumstances where the decision being impugned had to be made with urgency.

8.2.1 Non-Justiciability

In the context of judicial review, a decision will be justiciable if it is appropriate for it to be resolved through the review process.[1] If a court forms the view that a decision is not justiciable (and, therefore, is 'non-justiciable'), the court will determine not to review the decision, because to do so would be inapt.[2] Until relatively recently, the subject-matter of a decision was the crucial determinant of whether the decision was non-justiciable,[3] with all decisions pertaining to particular subject-matters being non-justiciable. For example, decisions regarding 'defence of the realm'[4] and 'national security'[5] were said not to be amenable to judicial review because of their subject-matter. Under this approach, no decision made pursuant to the exercise of emergency powers, and pertaining to (for instance) the defence of the realm or national security, would be amenable to judicial review.

---

[1] Timothy Endicott, *Administrative Law* (3rd edn, OUP 2015) 635.
[2] Peter Cane, Leighton McDonald and Kristen Rundle, *Principles of Administrative Law, Legal Regulation of Governance* (3rd edn, OUP 2018) 65.
[3] *Council of Civil Service Unions v. Minister for the Civil Service* [1985] AC 374, 418 (Lord Roskill).
[4] Ibid.
[5] *Re Minister of Arts, Heritage and the Environment v. Peko Wallsend* (1987) 15 FCR 274, 277 (Bowen CJ).

8.2.1.1 The Current Approach

However, this 'blanket' approach, whereby any decision pertaining to a particular subject-matter is regarded as non-justiciable, has been subject to severe academic criticism, principally on the basis that it is too undiscriminating.[6] Its application will, amongst other things, preclude the subjection of a decision to judicial review, even if the particular application for judicial review in question does not give rise to any issue of non-justiciability.[7] Although it would be going too far to say that the courts today act totally conformably with Daly's declaration that 'formal, a priori classification which would entirely exclude certain categories of decision from review must be rejected',[8] it is true that in recent years courts have tended to move away from an approach whereby judicial review would not be countenanced at all with regard to particular subject-matters.[9]

Rather, in determining whether a decision is non-justiciable, courts nowadays tend to have regard to whether the particular issues before the court[10] – and, more specifically, the actual propositions advanced by the applicant[11] – give rise to issues of non-justiciability. Elliott and Varuhas have gone so far as to say that this approach, which focuses on whether particular grounds of review give rise to issues of non-justiciability in the circumstances of the case at hand, is now the prevailing approach.[12]

Non-justiciability should not be understood as a simple notion, as it is underpinned by at least three concerns.[13] It is only if we properly understand the concerns underlying the notion of non-justiciability that we can determine whether a specific application for judicial review on a

---

[6] Cane, McDonald and Rundle (n 2) 65; Chris Finn, 'The Justiciability of Administrative Decisions: a Redundant Concept?' (2002) 30(2) FLR 239, 253. See also TRS Allan, *Constitutional Justice* (OUP 2001) 177; Paul Daly, 'Justiciability and the "Political Question" Doctrine' [2010] Public Law 160, 172.

[7] Mark Elliott and JNE Varuhas, *Administrative Law, Text and Materials* (5th edn, OUP 2017) 124.

[8] Daly (n 6) 160, 172.

[9] Cane, McDonald and Rundle (n 2) 65. See also Paul Daly (n 6) 160, 168; A Sapienza, 'Justiciability of Non-Statutory Executive Action: A Message for Immigration Policy Makers' (2015) 79 AIAL Forum 70, 79; *Aye v. Minister for Immigration and Citizenship* [2010] FCAFC 69, [103] (Lander J).

[10] Elliott and Varuhas (n 7) 124.

[11] Sapienza (n 9) 70, 79.

[12] Elliott and Varuhas (n 7) 124.

[13] Peter Cane, *Administrative Law* (5th edn, OUP 2011) 273.

8.2 THE EXERCISE OF JUDICIAL RESTRAINT 235

particular ground, or grounds, will conflict with one or more of these concerns, and so give rise to an issue of non-justiciability.

The three concerns are: the courts' inability to adjudicate 'polycentric' disputes; judicial (lack of) expertise with regard to particular substantive matters; and the courts' (lack of) political responsibility.[14] According to Fuller, a problem that is polycentric will normally affect a substantial number of people[15] who may be interconnected.[16] Accordingly, any intervention in the problem will have multifarious and complicated outcomes.[17] Courts, it is claimed, are poorly suited to adjudicating (including by way of judicial review) matters that are polycentric. In adjudicating cases before them, courts typically hear arguments from only two opposing parties, and do not have any inquisitorial or investigative role.[18] Consequently, a court hearing an application for judicial review will (normally at least) be rather limited, in terms of the material on which it can base its decision.[19] As a result of the lack of involvement of other affected parties, the court will not be adequately informed,[20] and will not be able to ascertain the full ramifications of any determination it might make.[21] By contrast, in making decisions, members of the executive will often be able to refer to information from disparate sources, reflecting multiple viewpoints.[22]

---

[14] See, for instance, Cane (n 13) 273–78; BV Harris, 'Judicial Review, Justiciability and the Prerogative of Mercy' (2003) 62 CLJ 631, 638–42.

[15] Lon Fuller, 'The Forms and Limits of Adjudication' (1978) 92 Harv L Rev 353, 397, referred to in John Allison, 'The Procedural Reasons for Judicial Restraint' [1994] PLR 452, 453.

[16] Ibid.

[17] Fuller (n 15) 353, 394, referred to in Allison (n 15) 452, 453.

[18] Cane (n 13) 275.

[19] Cane, McDonald and Rundle (n 2) 70.

[20] Allison (n 15) 452, 454.

[21] Ibid. A famous instance of polycentricity appearing to underpin a judge's determination that a decision is non-justiciable, in an Australian context, was contained in the judgment of Bowen CJ in *Minister for Arts, Heritage and the Environment* v. *Peko Wallsend* (1987) 15 FCR 274. The judge observed that the decision, was 'beyond review by the Court' because, amongst other things, 'the decision involved complex policy questions relating to the environment, the rights of Aborigines, mining and the impact on Australia's economic position of allowing or not allowing mining, as well as matters affecting private interests ...'

[22] Harris (n 14) 631, 643. But cf Craig's observation that nor should we idealise the quality of administrative decision-making. He says that a great deal of learning concerning administrative decision-making indicates that the issues considered by an administrative decision-maker in dealing with a particular matter will often be limited: Paul Craig, *Administrative Law*, (7th edn, Sweet and Maxwell 2012) 25.

The relevant expertise, for the purposes of non-justiciability, is that which pertains to the substantive subject-matter of application in question.[23] The argument is that, 'in some cases, at least', the judge's lack of expertise in the relevant area will render it inappropriate for them to hear the application for review.[24] It may be that the 'lack of expertise' justification for non-justiciability interacts, in at least some cases, with the 'polycentricity' justification, in the sense that the greater the number of parties that may be impacted upon by a decision, and the greater the number of a decision's 'interacting points of influence', the more a decision-maker would be assisted by expertise in the relevant area in making the decision (and the greater the extent to which their decision-making ability would be hampered by a lack of expertise).

Finally, it has been suggested that because courts are not representative or responsible to the populace, their involvement in the judicial review of certain matters of 'high policy' should be limited.[25] The idea is that the 'graver a matter of State and the more widespread its possible effects ... the more respect will be given ... to the democracy to decide its outcome.'[26] Consequently, the making of such a decision is the remit of the executive branch generally, and perhaps, specifically, the Cabinet.[27]

8.2.1.2 The Exercise of Emergency Powers – Non-Justiciable?

It is plain that some exercises of emergency powers would conflict with one or more of these three matters, and so be non-justiciable. Hence, assuming that the relevant emergency (or potential emergency) were of any magnitude, the exercise of emergency powers to deal with (or prevent) the emergency would not only affect a large number of people directly, but would also have considerable follow-on effects. Furthermore, it is entirely possible that some of the people affected would have disparate, or even conflicting, interests, with the result that they would be affected in quite dissimilar ways by the exercise of the emergency powers. It is thus likely that some exercises of emergency powers, at least, would be polycentric.[28]

---

[23] Peter Cane (n 13) 277. See, for example, *Aye v. Minister for Immigration and Citizenship* (2010) 187 FCR 449, 471 (Lander J).
[24] Peter Cane (n 13) 277–78.
[25] Ibid 274.
[26] *Marchiori v. Environment Agency* [2002] Eur LR 225, 245 (Laws LJ).
[27] MC Harris, 'The Courts and Cabinet: "Unfastening the Buckle"?' [1989] PL 251, 279.
[28] Consider, for instance, a decision taken under ss 198–200 of the Public Health and Wellbeing Act 2008 (Vic) (considered in Chapter 6) to quarantine a city block in the

8.2 THE EXERCISE OF JUDICIAL RESTRAINT

It is also the case that the exercise of emergency powers will often require such expertise with regard to particular substantive matters, and that judges will lack this expertise. Hence, the very determination of whether there is an emergency to begin with (and if so, its severity) may require considerable expertise. This is particularly a concern if that determination requires any degree of scientific proficiency, as may well be the case, for example, with regard to emergencies that may be caused by the spreading of contagious diseases. Then, subsequent determinations as to how best to deal with the emergency (including how best to allocate resources to deal with the emergency)[29] and then, finally, the decision that there is no longer an emergency may also require considerable expertise on the part of the decision-maker, with that expertise not being possessed by the courts.

Finally, the exercise of emergency powers may, in some instances, take the form of decisions in the way of policy. This is particularly so with respect to decisions made pursuant to section 61, with the executive being vested, under that section, with a 'nationhood' power.[30]

8.2.1.3 The Impact of Non-Justiciability

However, even if certain instances of the exercise of emergency powers are non-justiciable, the examination of the normative underpinnings of non-justiciability just undertaken strongly suggests that the impact of that categorisation upon an application for judicial review will be limited. The reason for this (and the manner in which review will be limited) is made apparent by way of the following argument, which will be outlined here, and then developed. As will be argued, the exercise by a judge of her supervisory jurisdiction will only conflict with the normative

---

event of a suspected outbreak of influenza or even Ebola. Such a decision (which may prevent people from both entering and exiting the quarantined area) would potentially safeguard the health of people within (and outside) the area, while perhaps, at the same time, adversely affecting the financial interests of businesses in the quarantined area, as well of those of people who worked for the businesses, and of entities that supplied the businesses with products. The interests of people who lived within the quarantined area would also potentially be affected – not least by virtue of their being unable to leave the immediate area in which they lived for the duration of the quarantine or, conversely, being unable to enter that area and, therefore, their homes (if they were outside the area when quarantine was declared).

[29] But cf Keith Syrett, 'Courts, Expertise and Resource Allocation: Is There a Judicial "Legitimacy" Problem' (2014) 7 Public Health Ethics, 112.

[30] See, generally, Anne Twomey, 'Pushing the Boundaries of Executive Power: *Pape*, the Prerogative and Nationhood Powers' (2010) 34 MULR 313, 327–42.

underpinnings of non-justiciability (and so be non-justiciable) if, in exercising her supervisory jurisdiction, she makes an assessment of the merits of the decision in question.[31] However (as will also be elaborated upon), the only ground of judicial review that requires judges to make such an assessment is the Wednesbury unreasonableness ground.[32] Accordingly, even if a decision is determined to be 'non-justiciable', the only impact that that determination will have on judicial review will be that it will render unreasonableness ground unavailable.

Let us begin by considering the first stage of the argument outlined – that the court's subjecting a decision to judicial review will only conflict with the normative underpinnings of non-justiciability if the court, in engaging judicial review, makes an assessment of the merits of the question under review. An objection to a court subjecting a decision to judicial review, on the basis that the decision is polycentric, centres around the merits of the decision in question. Because of the court's bipolar and adversarial adjudicative methodology, the court will be unable to appreciate the impact that the decision will have upon the many different (and differently) affected and potentially affected people and entities;[33] in other words, the court will be unable to properly assess the decision's merits. By contrast, there is no reason to think that the fact that a decision is polycentric will impede a judge from examining the process by which a decision is made, so as to determine whether that process was

---

[31] The idea that non-justiciability guards against courts assessing the merits of the decision in question is not novel. For instance, in *Council of Civil Service Unions* v. *Minister for the Civil Service* [1985] AC 374, Lord Roskill, in suggesting that certain species of prerogative power should not be subject to review, said that 'the courts are not the place wherein to determine whether a treaty should be concluded or the armed forces disposed in a particular matter or Parliament dissolved on one date rather than another' (ibid 418).

[32] It is recognised that a decision-maker's being satisfied as to the existence of a particular state of affairs, where the decision-maker's satisfaction is necessary if she is to exercise particular powers under statute, can be impugned on the basis that her being so satisfied is 'irrational'. However, such a determination does not require an assessment of the merits of the decision in question. Rather, the decision-maker's satisfaction as to the existence of a particular state of affairs will be irrational if 'only one conclusion is open on the evidence, and the decision maker does not come to that conclusion, or if the decision to which the decision maker came was simply not open on the evidence or if there is no logical connection between the evidence and the inference or conclusions drawn': *Minister for Immigration and Citizenship* v. *SZMDS* (2010) 240 CLR 611, 649–50 (Crennan and Bell JJ).

[33] Cane, McDonald and Rundle (n 2) 70.

8.2 THE EXERCISE OF JUDICIAL RESTRAINT

deficient; in making that assessment, the judge will simply not need to have regard to the polycentric nature of the decision at all.[34]

Similarly, it is certainly clear that a court's lack of expertise with regard to particular complex areas may make it difficult for the court to assess the pros and cons[35] of a decision that pertains to those areas (especially if the decision is polycentric). But, once again, it is difficult to see how the complex nature of the subject-matter would impede the court's assessment of whether the decision was made by way of the proper process. As Finn observes, if the court were to limit itself to assessing the way in which the decision was made, and did not assess the substantive decision itself, it would not need to engage with the complexities pertaining to the decision's outcome.[36]

Finally, it may well be the case that if a decision potentially affects a large number of people in gravely important ways, then, as a matter of principle, that substantive decision, on its merits, should be made by those who, unlike judges, have at least some degree of democratic accountability. However, it is not at all apparent that those normative concerns extend to examinations of the process by which the decision was made.

Moving on to the second stage of the argument, the only ground of review in Australian law that requires a court engaging in judicial review to assess the merits of the decision under review is the Wednesbury unreasonableness ground. As originally articulated, in *Wednesbury* itself, the ground would be made out if the decision-maker made a decision that was 'so unreasonable that no reasonable [decision-maker] could ever have come to it'.[37] It is thus axiomatic that where the Wednesbury unreasonableness ground is being applied, the court must assess the merits of the decision in question. It is recognised that, pursuant to the approach adopted by a plurality of the High Court in the *Minister for Immigration and Citizenship* v. *Li*,[38] it is no longer the case that the standard of unreasonableness that must be met for a decision to be impugned is a universal one that is applied in all cases where the ground is relied upon.[39] Rather, 'the legal standard of reasonableness must be the

---

[34] Finn (n 6) 239, 243–44.
[35] *Marchiori v. Environment Agency* [2002] Eur LR 225, 228 (Laws J).
[36] Finn (n 6) 239, 244.
[37] *Associated Provincial Picture Houses Ltd* v. *Wednesbury Corporation* [1948] 1 KB 223, 233–34 (Lord Greene MR).
[38] (2013) 249 CLR 364.
[39] Leighton McDonald 'Rethinking Unreasonableness Review' (2014) 25 PLR 117, 128, 129.

standard indicated by the true construction of the [relevant] statute.'[40] Nonetheless – and even though 'the legal standard of reasonableness should not be considered as limited to what is in effect an irrational, if not bizarre, decision'[41] – it remains that review on the unreasonableness ground involves the court engaging in an assessment of the merits of the decision review of which is sought.[42]

It is recognised that there are certain grounds of review, the making out of which will effectively disable the administrative decision-maker from making a particular substantive decision or decisions when the matter is sent back to her, subsequent to a successful review application. This is certainly the case, for instance, with the 'jurisdictional fact' ground of review. Broadly, a jurisdictional fact is a factual reference in a statute that the statute makes clear must exist, in the circumstances of the case, in order for the administrative decision-maker legally to exercise a particular power (and so to make a particular decision). Because the existence of the jurisdictional fact is a prerequisite for the exercise of a particular power, if the court, pursuant to an application for review of an exercise of that power, holds that the jurisdictional fact does not exist in the circumstances of the case, then the administrative decision-maker will be precluded from exercising the power (and so remaking the same decision) when the matter is sent back to her.

The position is the same with regard to the no-evidence ground of review under section 5(3)(b) of the AD(JR) Act. The ground will be made out if the person who made the decision being impugned 'based the decision on the existence of a particular fact, and that fact did not exist'. A fact will be a 'particular fact' for the purposes of section 5(3)(b) if it is a 'finding of fact without which the decision in question could not or would not have been reached'.[43] But if the particular substantive decision in question 'could not or would not' have been made 'but for' the existence of a particular fact, the finding by a judicial review court that that fact does 'not exist', would seem to preclude the administrative decision-maker from making the same decision again. Similarly, in respect of the improper purpose ground of review, where there are two

---

[40] *Minister for Immigration and Citizenship* v. *Li* (2013) 249 CLR 332, 364 (Hayne, Kiefel and Bell J).
[41] Ibid.
[42] McDonald (n 39) 117, 132. See also 119–22.
[43] *Minister for Immigration and Multicultural Affairs* v. *Rajamanikkam* (2002) 210 CLR 222, 240 (Gaudron and McHugh JJ).

or more operative purposes – at least one of which is proper – it is necessary, in order for the ground to be made out, that the decision would not have been made in the absence of the improper purpose (or purposes).[44] But if the decision at first instance would not have been made in the absence of the improper purpose (or purposes), it is difficult to see how the decision-maker to whom the matter had been remitted could re-make the same substantive decision in circumstances where she could not now rely on the improper purpose(s).

Because the successful establishment of any of these grounds will prevent an administrative decision-maker from making particular decisions, there is a sense in which review, on the basis of any one of them, can, like review on the basis of the Wednesbury unreasonableness ground, be described as 'substantive'.[45] However, despite this, and unlike the position with regard to Wednesbury unreasonableness, it does not follow that reliance by an applicant for review on any of these grounds will give rise to issues of non-justiciability.

This is because the making-out of the grounds does not engage any of the three issues underpinning justiciability. Hence, (and unlike the case with the Wednesbury unreasonableness ground) it is not necessary, in order for any of the jurisdictional fact, no evidence, or improper purpose grounds to be made out for the court to *assess* the merits of the decision under review. The quality of the substantive decision, for instance, or its likely impact, are simply not matters which the court need consider in determining whether any of the grounds is made out.

Nor is there any reason to think that it necessary, in order for any the three grounds under discussion to be established, for the court to possess particular expertise with regard to the substantive subject-matter of the decision. With respect to the three grounds, it will be necessary for the court, variously, to engage in statutory interpretation (to ascertain whether a factual reference in a statute is a 'jurisdictional fact', or to determine the purpose for which power under statute was conferred); to make findings of fact (did the jurisdictional fact exist in the circumstances of the case, or for what purpose or purposes did the decision-maker act, or on what 'evidence' did the decision-maker purport to rely in making the decision); to apply the facts of the case to the law so construed (did the decision-maker rely on a particular matter in coming

---

[44] *Thompson v. Randwick Municipal Council* (1950) 81 CLR 87, 106 (Williams, Webb and Kitto JJ).
[45] Elliott and Varuhas (n 7) 124, 262.

to her decision, or did she act for an improper purpose); and to answer questions of causation (but for the decision-maker's reliance on an improper purpose, or a certain fact, would she not have made, or have been unable to make, the substantive decision under review). But engaging in statutory interpretation, making findings of fact, applying the facts of a case to the law, and answering questions of causation are all activities engaged in routinely by judges, and are not dependent on the judge hearing a matter being an expert with regard to the subject-matter of the decision in question.[46]

Finally, the fact that a decision-maker will be precluded from making a particular substantive decision, pursuant to a judge's determination that one (or more) of the three grounds under consideration is made out, is only an *indirect* consequence of that determination. The judge has not ordered, in terms, that the decision in question must not be made. Rather, the fact that the decision in question cannot be made follows on from the judge's finding that the decision-maker has acted illegally by breaching one or more grounds of review. Accordingly, it is nothing to the point, in this connection, that the judge is not responsible to the electorate.

8.2.1.4 *Habib* and the Act of State Doctrine

The conception of non-justiciability discussed previously, resting on the three notions of polycentricity, lack of judicial expertise, and lack of judicial responsibility, is the conception of polycentricity that operates in the context of domestic judicial review. However, matters have been claimed to be non-justiciable in other contexts, and on other bases. One such basis is the 'act of state doctrine'. The act of state doctrine is a common law rule which, when given effect, 'prevents the [forum] court from examining the legality of certain acts performed in the exercise of sovereign authority within a foreign country or, occasionally, outside it'.[47] The Federal Court had reason to consider the act of state doctrine in *Habib* v. *Commonwealth of Australia*.[48] The court's observations, in that context, raise issues that invite discussion of the

---

[46] However, it may be the case that the decision-maker at first instance is expert with regard to the subject-matter of the decision in question. If this is so, then the court may accord a degree of weight, or deference, particularly to the decision-maker's finding that a jurisdictional fact existed in the circumstances of the case: see Section 8.2.2, under 'Deference'.

[47] *R* v. *Bow Street Metropolitan Stipendiary Magistrate; Ex parte Pinochet Ugarte (No 1)* [2000] 1 AC 61, 106 (Lord Nicholls).

[48] (2010) 183 FCR 62.

8.2 THE EXERCISE OF JUDICIAL RESTRAINT

operation of the notion of non-justiciability, in the context of the judicial review of emergency powers.

Habib, an Australian citizen, alleged that foreign officials had tortured him while he was detained in Pakistan, Egypt and Afghanistan, and at Guantanamo Bay, in contravention of, variously, section 6(1) of the Crimes (Torture) Act 1988 (Cth), section 7(2)(c) of the Geneva Conventions Act 1957 (Cth) and sections 268.26(1) and and 268.74(1) of the Criminal Code, being a Schedule to the Criminal Code Act 1995 (Cth). He also claimed that officers of the (Australian) Commonwealth – including officers of the Australian Federal Police, the Australian Security and Intelligence Organisation, and the Department of Foreign Affairs and Trade – had, in turn, aided, abetted or counselled those foreign officials in carrying out their unlawful conduct. If that were so, then, pursuant to section 11.2 of the *Criminal Code* – which states that 'a person who aids, abets, counsels or procures the commission of an offence by another person is taken to have committed that offence' – the officers of the Commonwealth would be deemed to have committed the various offences prohibited by the previously mentioned pieces of legislation. And if that were so, then the officers of the Commonwealth would have acted 'beyond the scope of the legal authority' under which they were purporting to act, namely that provided by section 61 of the Australian Constitution, and various pieces of legislation. That, in turn, would render them vulnerable to claims in the torts of misfeasance in public office and the intentional but indirect infliction of harm.

The Commonwealth sought to have the claims dismissed. Pursuant to section 11.2 of the *Criminal Code*, there can only be liability for aiding, abetting or counselling if 'the primary offence is first shown to have been committed'.[49] Accordingly, in order to be successful in his claims in tort against the Commonwealth officers, Habib would have to show, on the balance of probabilities, that the foreign officials in Pakistan, Egypt, Afghanistan and Guantanamo Bay had contravened the provisions of the Australian legislation. But this, said the Commonwealth, would contravene the act of state doctrine, since it would require 'a determination of the unlawfulness of acts of agents of foreign states within the territories of foreign states'.[50] Accordingly, said the Commonwealth, the claims should be dismissed.

---

[49] Ibid 71 (Perram J).
[50] Ibid 66 (Black CJ).

The court rejected this argument. Jagot J, with whom Black CJ agreed, observed that 'the foundation of the principal tort on which Mr Habib relies ... is conduct by Commonwealth officials in excess of [the] power'[51] they purported to exercise under section 61 of the Constitution, and legislation. Jagot J then observed that the court's jurisdiction to ascertain whether section 61 of the Constitution, or the legislative provisions in question, had been contravened (and, if so, to grant a remedy) was conferred under Chapter III of the Australian Constitution.[52] The act of state doctrine 'being a rule of the common law but no more, could not exclude the High Court's ... jurisdiction'[53] under Chapter III.

But that is effectively what would happen if the Court were prevented, pursuant to the act of state doctrine, from determining, pursuant to an application under section 75(iii) or 75(v) of the Constitution, whether the foreign officials contravened the various pieces of Australian legislation referred to previously. If the court were so prevented, then it would also be prevented, in turn, from ascertaining whether Officers of the Commonwealth had acted illegally by aiding, abetting or counselling the foreign officials in those contraventions. And if it were prevented from ascertaining that matter, then it would be prevented, in turn from determining whether Officers of the Commonwealth, purportedly acting pursuant to section 61 of the Constitution, or statute, had exceeded their power.

A question that arises is whether the sort of analysis relied on by the court in *Habib*, to exclude the operation of the act of state doctrine, might have the result, in the context of judicial review, of precluding reliance by the court on the notion of 'domestic' non-justiciability. It is suggested that the better view is that it would not, at least where the basis of the claim of non-justiciability was polycentricity or lack of judicial expertise (but not where the basis of the claim was that the decision in question was one involving matters of 'high policy'). There is a relevant difference between, on the one hand, the act of state doctrine, and, on the other, the notion of (domestic) non-justiciability in circumstances where the claim of non-justiciability is based on polycentricity or lack of judicial expertise. As will be shown, that difference renders the analysis relied on by the court in *Habib* to displace the act of state doctrine inapplicable in the context of non-justiciability.

---

[51] Ibid 99 (Jagot J).
[52] Ibid 100 (Jagot J).
[53] Ibid.

8.2 THE EXERCISE OF JUDICIAL RESTRAINT

Pursuant to the act of state doctrine, the court declines to do something – making an assessment as to the legality of the act of a foreign government – that it is *capable* of doing. But the position is different when the court declares a matter to be non-justiciable, at least on the basis of non-justiciability or lack of expertise. When that occurs, then the court is simply recognising that, in the circumstances of the case, it is incapable of properly applying the Wednesbury unreasonableness ground. There is no sense in which, pursuant to the notion of non-justiciability as just described, the court is declining to do something that it would (and could) otherwise do. Accordingly, in giving effect to the notion of non-justiciability, the court is not declining to exercise its jurisdiction under Chapter III of the Constitution. Rather, it is recognising that it is unable to ascertain whether a particular constraint on the exercise of power – that imposed by the Wednesbury unreasonableness ground – has been contravened.

It is recognised that the position is different where a matter is determined to be non-justiciable on the basis of the question at hand being one of 'high-policy'. In that case, it may be that the court could determine whether the decision was Wednesbury unreasonable, but declines to do because, as a result of its lack of a democratic mandate, making such a finding would be inappropriate. It may well be, then, that the reasoning in *Habib* does apply to preclude the operation of 'domestic' justiciability on this basis. If that were so, then a claim that an exercise of emergency powers were non-justiciable on the basis that the decision was one involving matters of 'high policy' would necessarily fail. And if that were the case, then review of the relevant decision would not even be precluded on the basis of the Wednesbury unreasonableness ground.

8.2.1.5 'Grounds of Review' and Section 61

It has been suggested above that non-justiciability, properly understood, applies only in respect of the Wednesbury unreasonableness ground of review. A related issue pertains to which so-called grounds of review are available with respect to executive power exercised under section 61 in the first place[54].

Relevantly for present purposes, section 75(v) of the Constitution – pursuant to which applications for review of decisions made under

---

[54] It is plain that all of the standard grounds of review apply to applications made under s 75(v) of the Constitution, and the Administrative Decisions (Judicial Review) Act 1977 (Cth).

section 61 are brought – will give the court jurisdiction to ascertain whether constraints on the exercise of executive power under section 61 have been breached, and, if they have been breached, to grant an appropriate remedy. However, section 75 does not, itself, impose those constraints.[55]

Rather, as Crawford suggests, the limits of the power deriving from section 61 of the Constitution 'are determined ... by interpreting s 61 ...'.[56] It is plain that there are some constraints on the exercise of the executive power under section 61 which are akin to certain of the grounds of judicial review, traditionally understood, which interpreting section 61 will reveal. For instance, it is apparent from the terms of section 61 that the section 61 executive power may only be exercised by the Governor-General (which, pursuant to convention, means the Governor-General acting on the advice of the Prime Minister and Cabinet).[57] Accordingly, it would seem that if the power under section 61 were purported to be exercised by someone other than the Governor-General acting on the advice of the Prime Minister or Cabinet, or by the Governor-General at the behest of someone other than the Prime Minister and Cabinet, then relief would be available under section 75(v).

Constraints upon the exercise of the executive power conferred under section 61, which are, in substance, similar to the grounds of judicial review, may also be inferred from the purpose of the power, and the context in which the power operates, namely power for the national government of a sovereign, independent and federal nation.[58] For instance, it is clear from *Williams v. Commonwealth*[59] that (as one would expect) certain types of activity will fall outside the scope of section 61,[60] and in that case concerns with federalism played a significant role in the

---

[55] See Lisa Burton Crawford, 'Who Decides the Validity of Executive Action? No-Invalidity Clauses and the Separation of Powers' (2017) 24 AJ Admin L 81, 88.

[56] Lisa Burton Crawford, *The Rule of Law and the Australian Constitution* (Federation Press 2017) 132.

[57] Sarah Joseph and Melissa Castan, *Federal Constitutional Law, A Contemporary View* (Lawbook Co 2014) 153.

[58] See, for example, *Pape v. Federal Commissioner of Taxation* (2009) 238 CLR 1, 83 (Gummow, Crennan and Bell JJ).

[59] (2014) 252 CLR 416.

[60] Although, see Hannah's argument that the scope of the Executive's 'nationhood power' under s 61 'is a non-justiciable question to be resolved by the political process': Andrew Hannah, 'Nationhood Power and Judicial Review: A Bridge Too Far?' (2015) 39 UWA L Rev 327.

court's conclusion that the activity in question fell outside the scope of section 61. Moreover, and given the mentioned purpose, it is probably the case that if power were exercised for some essentially 'private' purpose, or even, perhaps, if some essentially 'private' consideration were taken into account in the exercise of the power, that it might be rendered invalid, and relief available.

It is much less clear whether it is possible to infer from the text of section 61, or its purpose, whether other constraints may apply to the exercise of power under section 61, that are akin to the grounds of judicial review (like, for instance, the hearing rule or the rule against bias, or, indeed, Wednesbury unreasonableness). It is possible that modern English cases, providing for the judicial review of prerogative power, may help inform our understanding of the constraints that operate on the exercise of executive power under section 61,[61] (not unlike the way the general law might inform our reading of a statute dealing with similar subject matter, not as a *source of law* but as a source of understanding of context, meanings and purposes). Indeed, as French J has explained, 'the executive power may derive some of its content by reference to the royal prerogative'.[62] At the same time, however, it remains that caution is needed in relying on these cases, because they involve common law grounds of review being applied to a common law power, whereas section 61 is a constitutional conferral of power that, as suggested previously, has to be understood to bring its own grounds with it.[63] Accordingly, there is at least some possibility that the Wednesbury unreasonableness ground may not operate with regard to power (including emergency power) exercised pursuant to section 61 to begin with, whether or not a particular exercise of power may be described as 'non-justiciable'.

8.2.2 Deference

In addition to non-justiciability, another possible basis on which the judicial review of emergency powers could be hindered, pursuant to the exercise of judicial restraint, is by way of the notion of deference. In

---

[61] See, for instance, *Council of Civil Service Unions* v. *Minister for the Civil Service* [1985] AC 374.
[62] *Ruddock* v. *Vadarlis* (2001) 110 FCR 491, 549.
[63] *Re Ditfort; Ex parte Deputy Commissioner of Taxation (NSW)* (1988) 19 FCR 347, 369 (Gummow J); *Ruddock* v. *Vadarlis* (2001) 110 FCR 491, 540 (French J).

Corporation of the City of Enfield v. *Development Assessment Commission* (*'Enfield'*),[64] in the context of a discussion of the notion of 'jurisdictional fact', the High Court made it plain that, unlike the position in the US under *Chevron*,[65] in Australia, courts will not defer to executive interpretations of the law.[66] In explaining its position, the majority (Gleeson CJ, Gummow, Kirby and Hayne JJ) emphasised the observation of Brennan J in *Attorney-General (NSW)* v. *Quin*[67] (who, in turn, had been referring to the judgment of Marshall CJ in *Marbury* v. *Madison*[68]) that 'an essential characteristic of the judicature is that it declares and enforces the law which determines the limits of the power conferred by statute upon administrative decision-makers'.[69] Accordingly, the courts' deferring to the executive with respect to the meaning of legislative provisions would constitute an "abdication of judicial responsibility to interpret the law"[70] and a ceding of "interpretative authority"' to the executive branch.[71]

However, while (as we have just seen) the court in *Enfield* made it clear that courts should not defer to the executive's interpretation of the law, it also stated that, in certain circumstances, a reviewing court would have the choice (but would not be required) to place weight on the primary decision-maker's determination as to whether a jurisdictional fact – necessary if a certain power were to be exercised – was present in the circumstances of a particular case[72]. This would be the case if, amongst other things, the administrative decision-maker's particular expertise and knowledge made him or her especially well equipped to make that determination,[73] and the evidence before the court were 'in all significant respects ... substantially the same' as that before the administrative decision-maker.[74]

---

[64] (2000) 199 CLR 135.
[65] *Chevron USA Inc.* v. *Natural Resources Defence Council Inc.* 467 US 837 (1984).
[66] *Enfield* (2000) 199 CLR 135, 151–53.
[67] (1990) 170 CLR 1, 35–36.
[68] (1803) 1 Cranch 137, 177 (5 US 87, 111).
[69] *Enfield* (2000) 199 CLR 135, 153.
[70] Ibid 152, citing Stephen Breyer, 'Judicial Review of Questions of Law and Policy' (1986) 38 Admin L Rev 363, 381.
[71] *Enfield* (2000) 199 CLR 135, 152, citing Keith Werhan, 'Delegalising Administrative Law' [1996] U Ill L Rev 423, 457.
[72] *Enfield* (2000) 199 CLR 135, 155.
[73] Ibid relying on *R* v. *Alley; Ex parte NSW Plumbers & Gasfitters Employees' Union* (1981) 153 CLR 376 390.
[74] Ibid 155. See also Gaudron J, 158–59.

8.2 THE EXERCISE OF JUDICIAL RESTRAINT 249

Given this, it is possible that a court hearing an application for review of a decision made under Australian emergency powers legislation, where the making of the decision was dependent on the existence of a jurisdictional fact, might defer to the executive decision-maker's finding as to the existence of that fact. Under the Public Health and Wellbeing Act 2008 (Vic), for instance, particular emergency powers can be exercised only if a 'state of emergency' has been declared.[75] A 'state of emergency' may only be declared, in turn, if there is 'a serious risk to public health'.[76] The determination of whether such a risk exists, however, is not a simple matter. The Minister must seek the advice of the state's Chief Health Officer, and must have regard to each of: the number of people likely to be affected; the location, immediacy and seriousness of the threat to the health of people; the nature, scale and effects of the harm, illness or injury that may develop; and the availability and effectiveness of any precaution, safeguard, treatment or other measure to eliminate or reduce the risk to the health of human beings.[77] These are all matters, in respect of the ascertainment of which, relevant expertise would be of significant assistance.

There are very few cases in Australia where review has been sought of emergency powers exercised pursuant to statute, so it is difficult to predict what level of deference (if any) Australian courts would accord to the administrative decision-maker's determinations. However, it is certainly the case that in the US and England there is a long history of judges according deference to executive decisions made pursuant to emergency powers legislation, especially during times of crisis or emergency.[78]

A v. Secretary of State for the Home Department,[79] ('*Belmarsh*'), decided just over a decade ago, is seen, in an English context, as being strongly at odds with this tradition – certainly, at the very least a '[ray] of light'[80] in what had hitherto been the 'darkness' of excessive judicial deference to the executive in emergency powers cases, but also, perhaps, representative of a less deferential approach adopted by the House of

---

[75] Public Health and Wellbeing Act 2008 (Vic), s 199.
[76] Public Health and Wellbeing Act 2008 (Vic), s 198.
[77] Public Health and Wellbeing Act 2008 (Vic), s 3.
[78] See, for instance, John Ipp, 'The Supreme Court and the House of Lords in the War on Terror: *Inter Arma Silent Leges*?' (2010) 19 Mich St J Int'l L 1.
[79] [2005] 2 AC 68.
[80] David Dyzenhaus, *The Constitution of Law: Legality in a Time of Emergency* (CUP 2006) 166.

Lords in emergency powers cases, commencing in the period after 9/11.[81] For that reason alone, it would be worth examining *Belmarsh* here. However, there is also good reason to think that the judges, in deciding the case, did not actually depart from the courts' tradition of according deference to the executive in emergency powers cases nearly to the extent that some commentators have suggested.[82]

The appellants in *Belmarsh*, who were not British nationals, had been detained, without charge, under section 23 of the Anti-terrorism, Crime and Security Act 2001, on the basis that, in accordance with section 21 of the Act, the Secretary of State reasonably believed that their presence in the United Kingdom was a risk to national security, and reasonably suspected that they were terrorists (and had issued a certificate to that effect). The statutory regime just described (and which did not apply to British nationals) was almost certainly inconsistent with article 5 of the European Convention of Human Rights (the right to liberty and security), and as a result, the 2001 Act was vulnerable to having a declaration of incompatibility made in respect of it under section 4 of the Human Rights Act 1998. In order to avoid this possibility, the Home Secretary sought to derogate from the Article 5 right and, accordingly, purported to make a Derogation Order under article 15 of the Convention. Article 15, relevantly, provides that in 'time of war or other public emergency threatening the life of the nation' a contracting party 'may take measures derogating from its obligations under [the] Convention to the extent strictly required by the exigencies of the situation . . .'.

The appellants contended, in turn, that the Derogation Order was not valid. In accordance with the terms of Article 15, there were two main issues before the Court: whether there was a 'public emergency threatening the life of the nation' and whether the measures taken under the 2001 Act were 'strictly required by the exigencies of the situation'.

Certainly the court gave short shrift to – and so did not treat at all with deference – the government's claim, in relation to the second matter, that the regime in question was 'strictly required'. The view of most of the judges was, essentially, that since British nationals, who posed the same threat as foreign nationals, were not subject to the regime in question, but were dealt with by other means, the regime could not be regarded as

---

[81] Ipp (n 78) 1, 31–33, 56.
[82] This point is recognised by Ipp – see ibid 56.

8.2 THE EXERCISE OF JUDICIAL RESTRAINT 251

'strictly required' in the requisite sense.[83] Baroness Hale's blunt observation that 'if it is not necessary to lock up the nationals it cannot be necessary to lock up the foreigners',[84] is representative of, and conveys, the court's approach on this point. The judges' arguments as to why the regime was not 'strictly required by the exigencies of the situation' were made in the context of observations about the risk of the government, in cases involving national security, adopting measures which 'are not objectively justified',[85] and about the draconian nature of indefinite detention.[86]

However, the judges' approach to the first issue – whether there was 'a public emergency threatening the life of the nation' – was much more deferential. The judgments are replete with references to the 'expertise' of the executive branch in determining whether there was a 'public emergency',[87] with several of the judges also referring to judicial lack of expertise in that respect.[88]

Furthermore, most of the seven judges in the majority seemed to accept, conformably with the government's view, (and contrary to the view of Hoffmann LJ, who was in the minority on this point)[89] that a 'public emergency threatening the life of the nation' could be constituted by something considerably less than an existential danger to England as a socio-political entity.[90] While some of those judges sought support for this approach in cases decided by the European Court, not all did, and, in any case, as Tierney has pointed out,[91] such judgments are not strictly binding on English courts in making determinations about English legislation. That, combined with the relative paucity of analysis in the judgments concerning what is necessary for there to be 'public emergency threatening the life of the nation'[92] (as opposed to whether there was such an emergency on the facts of this case) has significant implications for the notion of deference in English law. It suggests that, unlike

---

[83] *Belmarsh* [2005] 2 AC 68, 129 (Lord Nicholls), 142 (Lord Hope), 149 (Lord Scott), 160 (Lord Rodger), 173 (Baroness Hale). But cf 167 (Lord Walker).
[84] Ibid 173.
[85] Ibid 155 (Lord Rodger).
[86] Ibid 148–49 (Lord Scott).
[87] Ibid 136–37 (Lord Hope), 152 (Lord Rodger), 162 (Lord Walker), 226 (Baroness Hale).
[88] Ibid 137 (Lord Hope), 152 (Lord Rodger).
[89] Ibid 132.
[90] Ibid 101–02 (Lord Bingham), 137–38 (Lord Hope), 148 (Lord Scott), 226 (Baroness Hale)
[91] Stephen Tierney, 'Determining the State of Exception: What Role for Parliament and the Court?' [2005] MLR 668, 670. See also in this regard Dyzenhaus (n 80) 179.
[92] See, especially, the judgment of Baroness Hale – in *Belmarsh* [2005] 2 AC 68 129, 172.

the position in Australia pursuant to *Enfield*, English judges – at least in cases involving the exercise of certain emergency powers – may defer to the executive's determination of the meaning of legislative requirements (and not just factual matters pertaining to whether those requirements are met).

8.2.3 Procedural Fairness and Urgency

A third way in which judicial restraint may impact upon the possibility of a successful judicial review claim being brought against the exercise of emergency powers pertains to the hearing rule. Where, due to the matters with which a decision is concerned, the decision must be made urgently (as will often be the case with regard to decisions made pursuant to emergency powers) the court may find the hearing rule impliedly excluded by the empowering legislation. This approach is not one that has only been recently adopted in emergency powers cases; it has been applied since the nineteenth century. Hence, in *R v. Davey*,[93] decided in 1899, Channell J held that an order, under the Public Health Act 1875, to 'remove an infectious person, likely to spread abroad the infection, to an infectious hospital' would need to be dealt with 'promptly' and so could be made *ex parte*.[94]

Twenty years prior to that, in *White v. Redfern*,[95] the court had held that a magistrate could make an order, again under the Public Health Act, that contaminated meat be destroyed without providing a hearing to the owner of the meat.[96] Nor was the statutory officer who seized the meat required to give notice to owner that the seizure was to occur.[97] For Field J it was very significant, in reaching those findings, that contaminated meat was a 'great evil'[98] which required 'prompt'[99] and 'immediate'[100] measures 'for its repression'[101]. The judge observed that while the 'legislature cannot generally be considered to have intended that a man's property be destroyed without giving him an opportunity of being heard,

---

[93] [1899] 2 QB 301.
[94] Ibid 306.
[95] [1879] 5 QBD 15.
[96] Ibid 18 (Field J).
[97] Ibid 18 (Field J), 19 (Manisty J).
[98] Ibid 17 (Field J).
[99] Ibid.
[100] Ibid 18.
[101] Ibid 17.

here the paramount object would appear to be the speedy destruction of a[n] ... unwholesome thing'.[102]

This approach, which may limit the operation of the hearing rule in cases involving the exercise of emergency powers, has recently received support from the High Court of Australia. *CPCF* v. *Minister for Immigration and Border Protection*[103] involved a claim brought by a Sri Lankan asylum seeker in respect of his detention, at sea, on a Commonwealth vessel. The relevant legislation, pursuant to which the detention had occurred, was the Maritime Powers Act 2013 (Cth). The court found that the common law hearing rule did not apply, by way of implication, to section 72(4) of the Act, the section which permitted the asylum seeker, by virtue of having been on a detained vessel, himself to be detained. Of the various judges, Gageler J, in reaching that conclusion, observed that 'maritime powers are powers which maritime officers must be able to exercise flexibly and quickly in the maritime environment, particularly in circumstances of urgency.'[104] Accordingly, 'it would be incongruous for the common law to imply a duty on a maritime officer to afford procedural fairness as a condition of the exercise of a maritime power.'[105]

8.3 Legislative Attempts to Prevent or Limit Review

This chapter so far has considered approaches by the courts that, if adopted, may have the consequence of limiting the availability of judicial review of emergency powers. Consideration will now be given to approaches that may be adopted by the legislature, that may have the consequence of removing or, at least, limiting, the availability of the judicial review of emergency powers. An examination will first be made of privative clauses then of 'no-invalidity' clauses.

8.3.1 Privative Clauses

The principal way, historically, in which the legislature would seek to limit the operation of judicial review was by way of 'privative' or 'ouster' clauses. A privative clause is a clause in legislation that purports to

---

[102] Ibid 18.
[103] (2015) 255 CLR 514.
[104] Ibid 622–23 (Gageler J).
[105] Ibid 623.

remove the court's jurisdiction to grant review of the decisions made under that piece of legislation (or, at least, under certain of its provisions). For many years, the 'classical'[106] statement of the operation of privative clauses at the Commonwealth level was contained in the judgment of Dixon J in *R v. Hickman; ex p Fox*.[107] Interestingly, this case plausibly involved the exercise of emergency powers, especially given its context.

The case was decided at the beginning of the Second World War, and involved the *National Security (Coal Mining Industry Employment) Regulations*. The regulations established Local Reference Boards, and held that the Local Reference Boards would have the power to settle disputes as to any matter 'likely to affect the amicable relations of employers and employees in the coal mining industry'[108]. Regulation 17 provided, relevantly, that the decision of a Local Reference Board 'shall not be challenged, appealed against, quashed or called into question, or be subject to prohibition, mandamus, or injunction in any court on any account whatsoever'.

It might be thought that regulation 17 would be in direct conflict with section 75(v) of the Australian Constitution (pursuant to which the High Court 'shall have original jurisdiction' in all matters in which 'a writ of Mandamus or prohibition or an injunction is sought against an officer of the Commonwealth') and should, therefore, have been be struck down. That was not, however, the approach adopted by the court. Rather the court – perhaps alert to the need, during wartime, for decisions of the Local Reference Boards to be protected from challenge – adopted a non-literal interpretation of the ouster clause, which permitted the ouster clause to have some effect, and yet still be consistent with section 75(v) of the Constitution.[109]

The judge said that in interpreting the ouster clause contained in regulation 17, it was necessary to reconcile two, conflicting,

---

[106] *Coal Miners' Industrial Union of Workers (WA) v. Amalgamated Collieries of Western Australia Ltd* (1960) 104 CLR 437, 455 (Menzies J), cited in *Deputy Commissioner of Taxation (Cth) v. Richard Walter Pty Ltd* (1995) 183 CLR 168, 210 (Deane and Gaudron JJ).

[107] (1945) 70 CLR 598.

[108] Regulation 14(1)(a).

[109] For an examination of English decisions, the outcomes of which were influenced by the hearing of the relevant matters during wartime, see JWF Allison, 'The Spirits of the Constitution' in Nicholas Bamforth and Peter Leyland, *Accountability in the Contemporary Constitution* (OUP 2013) 27, esp 48–55.

manifestations of Parliamentary intent.[110] On the one hand, there was the intention of Parliament, manifested in the language of the statute, that the decision-maker's power be limited. So, for instance, here the Local Reference Boards would, according to the terms of regulation 17, have the power to settle disputes as to any matter 'likely to affect the amicable relations of employers and employees in the *coal mining industry*' – not the steel industry, for example, or the wood chip industry.[111] One the other hand, there was the intention of Parliament, manifested in the ouster clause, that the decision-maker's power be effectively unlimited (because it cannot be subject to judicial review).[112]

According to the judge, when regulation 17 was interpreted in light of the limits in the legislation, it was apparent that the regulation did not seek to oust the jurisdiction of the court, including the jurisdiction of the court under section 75(v).[113] Rather, pursuant to this process of reconciliation, the jurisdiction of the Local Reference Boards was effectively expanded, so that some actions, which would otherwise have been made outside of jurisdiction, would now be within jurisdiction. Pursuant to this expansion, a decision of a Local Reference Board would be within jurisdiction if it was a bona fide attempt to exercise its power; related to the subject matter of the legislation; and was reasonably capable of reference to the power given to the tribunal.[114] (These conditions will henceforth be referred to as the *Hickman* provisos). Because, pursuant to this interpretation, the ouster clause would not purport to remove the court's jurisdiction under section 75(v) to grant a remedy when a Board had acted outside of jurisdiction – but instead rendered it less likely that a Board would act outside of jurisdiction in the first place – the ouster clause would not, in form at least,[115] conflict with section 75(v).

For many years, the approach just described, and relied on in *Hickman*, was thought to be the standard way in which privative clauses

---

[110] (1945) 70 CLR 598, 616–17.
[111] Ibid. Emphasis added in quote.
[112] Ibid.
[113] Ibid 614–15.
[114] Ibid 617. Subsequently, Dixon J added one more condition: in order to be valid, the decision could not be in breach of a specific statutory limitation on the body's power which, it was reasonable to suppose, the legislature had intended to be supreme (*R v. Commonwealth Rent Controller; Ex parte National Mututal Life Assurance Association of Australasia Ltd* (1947) 75 CLR 361).
[115] See Colin Campbell, 'An Examination of the Migration Legislation Amendment Bill (No 4) 1997 Purporting to Limit Judicial Review' [1998] AJ Admin L 135, 145–46.

(at least under Commonwealth legislation) should be interpreted.[116] If that approach were still relied on, then privative clauses in emergency powers legislation could at least have some effect. However, in *Plaintiff S157*[117], decided more than five decades after *Hickman*, the High Court, while still purporting to apply *Hickman*,[118] adopted a different approach.

Pursuant to the approach relied on in *Plaintiff S157*, the *Hickman* provisos do not describe the expanded jurisdiction of the administrative body in question but, rather, seem to serve as a kind of precondition – unless the decision in question complies with the provisos, the privative clause will not come into play in the first place.[119] The process of reconciliation, relied on by Dixon J in *Hickman*, still plays a role in the modified approach to the interpretation of ouster clauses in *Plaintiff S157*, and, as in *Hickman*, the process of reconciliation (so the court says) will reveal the protection purported to be provided by the ouster clause. Unlike in *Hickman*, though, the judges in *Plaintiff S157* give no indication as to what protection will purport to be provided in any particular case. That must be ascertained on a case-by-case basis by the court interpreting a particular privative clause.

Most significant, though, was the approach adopted by the court in *Plaintiff S157*, so as to permit the privative clause (whatever kind of protection it purported to afford the decision under consideration) to not conflict with section 75(v) of the Constitution. Pursuant to the relevant legislation,[120] the privative clause would afford protection (whatever that protection was) only to a 'privative clause decision'.[121] In reliance on reasoning that was essentially the same as that employed by the House of Lords in *Anisminic v. Foreign Compensation Commission*,[122] the court stated that a decision would not be a 'privative clause decision' for the purposes of the Act (and so would not be afforded protection by the privative clause), if it was attended by a jurisdictional error.[123] Because

---

[116] See Mark Aronson, Matthew Groves and Greg Weeks, *Judicial Review of Administrative Action and Government Liability* (6th edn, Lawbook Co 2017) 1066.
[117] (2003) 211 CLR 476.
[118] Ibid 502 (Gaudron, McHugh, Gummow, Kirby and Hayne JJ).
[119] Ibid.
[120] Migration Act 1958 (Cth).
[121] Migration Act 1958 (Cth), s 474.
[122] [1969] 2 AC 147, 169–71 (Lord Reid), 181–82 (Lord Morris), 199–201 (Lord Pearce), 207–10 (Lord Wilberforce), 205 (Lord Pearson). Curiously, and despite this, the High Court makes no mention of *Anisminic* in this case.
[123] *Plaintiff S157* (2003) 211 CLR 476, 506.

8.3 ATTEMPTS TO PREVENT OR LIMIT REVIEW

the privative clause would provide protection only against decisions attended by non-jurisdictional errors of law, it would not conflict with the High Court's jurisdiction, under section 75(v) to grant prerogative writs (since prerogative writs can be awarded only in respect of jurisdictional errors), and so would not be struck down.[124] At the same time, though, a decision which is attended only by a non-jurisdictional error is made 'within power' and so cannot be set aside on the basis of that error, at least pursuant to one or more the prerogative writs.[125] Accordingly, the approach to privative clauses in Commonwealth legislation adopted by the Court in *Plaintiff S157* preserved the Constitutional validity of the privative clause, but effectively eviscerated it.[126] It follows that it is very unlikely that privative clauses in Commonwealth legislation could have the effect of precluding judicial review of decisions made under that legislation, including legislation pertaining to emergency powers.

It is also the case that privative clauses cannot operate, under state legislation, to prevent state Supreme Courts from granting remedies in respect of decisions attended by jurisdictional errors of law. In *Kirk v. Industrial Court of New South Wales*,[127] the High Court held, inter alia, that the supervisory role of State Supreme Courts to grant 'prohibition, certiorari and mandamus ... was, and is, a defining characteristic of those courts'.[128] Accordingly, privative clauses, including in emergency powers legislation, that purported to prevent a State

---

[124] Ibid 508.

[125] Ibid. Note that s 75(v) also provides for the granting of an injunction, and that, typically, the award of injunctions is not limited to jurisdictional errors of law, and so may not be so limited in the context of s 75(v): see *Plaintiff S157* (2003) 211 CLR 476, 508. See also Aronson, Groves and Weeks (n 116) 12. However, note Cane, McDonald and Rundle's suggestion that such injunctive relief may only be available prospectively, and so may not be available in respect of decisions that have already been made: Cane, McDonald and Rundle (n 2) 109, 110. In this regard see also Benjamin O'Donnell, 'Jurisdictional error, invalidity and the role of injunction in s 75(v) of the Australian Constitution' (2007) 28 Aus Bar Rev 291, 298. But cf Charles Noonan, 'Section 75(v), No-Invalidity Clauses and the Rule of Law' (2013) 36 (2) UNSWLJ 437, 467.

[126] Cane, McDonald and Rundle make some interesting suggestions as to why the High Court may have adopted this approach, as opposed to simply holding that the privative clause conflicted with s 75(v) of the Constitution (with the result that it would be struck down): Cane, McDonald and Rundle (n 2) 255.

[127] (2010) 239 CLR 531.

[128] Ibid 581. See Oscar Roos, 'Accepted Doctrine at the Time of Federation *and Kirk v. Industrial Court of New South Wales*' (2013) 35 Syd L Rev 781 for a strong criticism of this conclusion in *Kirk*.

Supreme Court from granting such a remedy in respect of a jurisdictional error would be ineffective.[129]

8.3.2 No Invalidity Clauses

An alternate means by which Parliament can seek to limit the availability of judicial review with regard to decisions made under particular pieces of legislation – and which seems to have been more favourably received by the High Court – is by way of what are known as 'no-invalidity' clauses. A no-invalidity clause is a provision in legislation which states that certain – or, indeed, all – legal errors made under a particular Act are not jurisdictional in nature.

In *Commissioner of Taxation* v. *Futuris Corporation Ltd*,[130] the High Court of Australia interpreted a no-invalidity clause in the Income Tax Assessment Act 1936 (Cth). Section 175, the relevant provision, states that 'The validity of an assessment shall not be affected by reason that any of the provisions of this Act have not been complied with'. The Court interpreted the clause literally, stating – in words which closely mirror those of the section – that 'the validity of an assessment is not affected by failure to comply with any provision of the Act ...'.[131] The consequence was that where 's 175 applies, errors in the process of assessment do not go to jurisdiction and so do not attract the remedy of a Constitutional writ under s 75(v) of the *Constitution*...'.[132] Accordingly, as Noonan observes, a no-invalidity clause operates, effectively, to expand the jurisdiction of the administrative decision-maker, so that decisions that, in the absence of the no-invalidity clause, would have been attended by jurisdictional errors (and, so, therefore, made outside of jurisdiction) will now be made within jurisdiction.[133] In this sense, a no-invalidity clause operates in a fashion similar to the way in which privative clauses were thought to operate pursuant to *Hickman*.

---

[129] Hence it is unsurprising that recently drafted privative clauses pertaining to State legislation do not purport to protect decisions against judicial review with respect to jurisdictional errors of law. For instance, sub–s. 173(2) of the compilation table of the Public Health Act 2016 (WA) states that the privative clause contained in sub–s. (1) does not 'limit judicial review for jurisdictional error.' See also Biosecurity Act 2014 (Qld), s 498(1).

[130] (2008) 237 CLR 146.

[131] Ibid 153 (Gummow, Hayne, Heydon and Crennan JJ).

[132] Ibid.

[133] Noonan (n 125) 437, 459.

It might be thought, then, based on *Futuris*, that a no-invalidity clause in emergency powers legislation would significantly reduce the impact of judicial review.[134] However, it is not entirely clear that this is the case. As McDonald points out, in interpreting the no-invalidity clause, the Court regarded the availability of comprehensive appeal provisions in the Income Tax Assessment Act 1936 (Cth) as significant.[135] Accordingly, it is possible if that if an Act did not contain such provisions, the no-invalidity clause would be read more narrowly than was the clause in *Futuris*.[136] The argument has also been made that a widely drafted no-invalidity clause might be in breach of the implied doctrine of separation of powers in the Australian Constitution.[137] This is because, pursuant to the separation of powers, Parliament is unable to 'confer on a non-judicial body the power to determine conclusively the limits of its own jurisdiction'.[138] In order that the no-invalidity clause not be in breach, it would be necessary that the court not treat the clause as conclusively determining the validity of the administrative action in question.[139] Rather, it would be necessary that the court interpret the Act under which the decision was made, including the no-invalidity clause.[140] Pursuant to this approach, the no-invalidity clause may, after all, apply to some jurisdictional errors of law, with the result that a decision attended by those errors would not be invalid.[141] Finally, as noted previously, injunctions available under section 75(v) may not be restricted in their operation to jurisdictional errors of law (i.e. unlike the prerogative writs, they may be available in respect of non-jurisdictional errors of law), but may, nonetheless, be limited in their operation in other ways.[142]

---

[134] Note, though, McDonald's observation that the no-invalidity clause may not purport to operate, inter alia, with regard to restrictions that are implied by a statute: Leighton McDonald, 'The Entrenched Minimum Provision of Judicial Review and the Rule of Law' (2010) 21 PLR 14, 21.
[135] McDonald (n 134) 14, 21–22. See also Cane, McDonald and Rundle (n 2) 246.
[136] Cane, McDonald and Rundle (n 2) 247.
[137] Crawford (n 55) 81, 94–95. See also Noonan (n 125) 437, 465–66. But cf Will Bateman, 'The Constitution and the Substantive Principles of Judicial Review: The Full Scope of the Entrenched Minimum Provision of Judicial Review' [2011] FLR 463, 497–99.
[138] R v. Murray; Ex parte Proctor (1949) 77 CLR 387, 399–400 (Dixon J).
[139] Crawford (n 55) 81, 95.
[140] Ibid.
[141] Ibid 95–98.
[142] See note 125.

8.4 Conclusion

This chapter has examined some possible hindrances to subjecting the exercise of emergency powers – either pursuant to statute, or under section 75(v) of the Australian Constitution – to judicial review. The claim has been made that the 'judicial record in enforcing the rule of law' in emergency situations is 'at worst, dismal, and at best ambiguous'.[143] Despite this claim, the difficulties that may arise – specifically under Australian law – in seeking judicial review of decisions made pursuant to emergency powers should not be overstated. Hence, for instance, while the exercise of certain emergency powers may be non-justiciable, the notion of non-justiciability, properly understood, applies only to preclude the Wednesbury unreasonableness ground of review – and even then, only when the basis of the claim of non-justiciability is the polycentric nature of the decision in question, or the court's lack of expertise with regard to the subject-matter of the decision.

Furthermore, Australian courts, at least, will not accord deference to executive interpretations of the law. And, courts in Australia will not give effect to privative clauses, at least to the extent that they purport to exclude review for jurisdictional errors of law.

At the same, time, however, it is not all one way. Hence, Australia courts may, in certain circumstances, including those involving the exercise of emergency powers, accord deference to the executive's findings of fact. This may be especially significant in limiting the successful bringing of a review application especially when the facts in question are jurisdictional facts. Also, in cases involving emergency powers exercised under statute, and especially where those powers must be exercised as a matter of urgency, courts will routinely find that the administrative decision-maker in question is under no obligation to act in accordance with the hearing rule. Finally, there is at least some possibility that no-invalidity clauses might be interpreted by the courts so as to operate with regard to jurisdictional errors of law.

---

[143] Dyzenhaus (n 80) 17.

9

Conclusion

'The strength of our rule of law and human rights norms can only be measured by whether they can resist the temptations to surrender to fear in times of crisis'

– Louise Arbour, 'In Our Name and On Our Behalf' [2006] EHRLR (Issue 4) 371, 384

'It is of the essence of a free society that a balance is struck between the security that is desirable to protect society as a whole and the safeguards that are necessary to ensure individual liberty.'

– Brennan J in *Alister v. The Queen* (1984) 154 CLR 404, 456

The main thrust of this book has been to locate and evaluate the various sources of powers – both legislative and executive – available to the authorities to cope with emergency situations in Australia. While the Australian Constitution and all the State constitutions do not contain an elaborate framework of constitutionalised emergency powers, the conclusion that has been drawn in this book is that such omission has not rendered the Commonwealth or the States impotent in the face of crises. The invocation of exceptional powers by a vibrant democracy like Australia poses a dilemma, which is encapsulated in the following observation: 'Emergencies present enormous difficulties for democracies ... While democracy aims to diffuse power, emergencies concentrate it.'[1] The book also explores the constraints that are available to ensure that the invocation of those powers is consistent with the rule of law

At the national level, the defence power in section 51(vi) of the Constitution, through enlightened interpretation by the High Court of Australia, provides the Commonwealth with ample powers to deal with the most critical category of emergencies – namely, war. Although the

---

[1] Craig Forcese and Aaron Freeman, *The Laws of Government: The Legal Foundations of Canadian Democracy* (Irwin Law 2005) 576.

High Court is prepared to give the Commonwealth plenty of latitude by viewing the defence power as a power that ebbs and flows, the High Court is prepared to place a staying hand on the Commonwealth government when the Court forms the view that there has been an overreach in the invocation of the defence power, as exemplified by the *Communist Party Case*. However, in the face of global terrorism, a 'war' without an end in sight, the High Court has re-visited the jurisprudence on the defence power and, in *Thomas* v. *Mowbray*, has now given the power a greater latitude in its scope of operation.

In its history, the executive arm of government in Australia has always had at its disposal an armoury of legal weapons to combat riotous situations. Apart from the existence of a legislative power to deal with wartime emergencies and the on-going countering of global terrorism, the Commonwealth executive possesses powers equivalent to 'prerogative powers' by virtue of section 61 of the Australian Constitution. A number of recent decisions of the High Court have engaged in a re-evaluation of the scope of the executive power in section 61 of the Constitution. The Court's exegesis on the executive power raises doubt over the availability of a prerogative power to compulsorily requisition property without just compensation in times of crisis.

The Australian States are mainly responsible for the general maintenance of law and order in their own territory. The existence of criminal offences within their legal frameworks relating to unlawful assembly, riot and many other public disorder offences equips the authorities with ample powers to cope with civil disorders. An accommodation between many of these powers and the political freedoms jurisprudence of the High Court needs to be effected to ensure the validity of the statutory frameworks embodying these offences. Both federal and State legislatures have enacted legislation to arm the authorities with ample legal weapons to counter the threat of terrorism. The various State governments have also enacted a number of emergency statutes that provide the authorities with 'stand-by' special powers to be activated in the face of an emergency situation, particularly to natural disasters.

In extreme cases calling for the deployment of the Australian Defence Force to assist the civil power, the norms and protocols regulating their use are provided by the specific provision in section 119 of the Australian Constitution. The statutory framework giving effect to this constitutional provision now provides clear rules to govern the use of the military in aid of the civil power.

The role of the courts during an emergency raises difficult questions. In a democratic polity, such as Australia, the courts should not abdicate their role of protecting the rule of law. The performance of such a role requires courts to adopt a 'statesman-like' approach when scrutinising the validity of legal and executive measures and the objectives pursued by these measures. President Barak of the Supreme Court of Israel once said:

> This is the destiny of a democracy – it does not see all means as acceptable, and the ways of its enemies are not always open before it. A democracy must sometimes fight with one hand tied behind its back. Even so, a democracy has the upper hand. The rule of law and the liberty of an individual constitute important components in its understanding of security. At the end of the day, they strengthen its spirit and this strength allows it to overcome its difficulties.[2]

The experience of Australia relating to its role in the two World Wars, the *Communist Party Case*, and the lack of allegations of abuse of power on the part of the authorities pertaining to the control of natural disasters indicate an awareness of the fundamental importance of the rule of law. Michael McHugh[3] reminds us of the words uttered by Prime Minister Menzies upon the outbreak of World War II:

> Whatever may be the extent of the power that may be taken to govern, to direct and to control by regulation, there must be as little interference with individual rights as is consistent with concerted national effort ... [T]he greatest tragedy that could overcome a country would be for it to fight a successful war in defence of liberty and to lose its own liberty in the process.[4]

---

[2] A Barak, 'A Judge on Judging: The Role of a Supreme Court in a Democracy' (2002) 116 Harv L R 148. See also *A v. Secretary of State for the Home Department (No 2)* [2006] 2 AC 221, 299 (Lord Carswell).

[3] The Honourable Michael McHugh AC, 'Constitutional Implications of Terrorism Legislation' (2007) 8 TJR 189, 213.

[4] *Hansard*, Commonwealth of Australia, 7 September 1939, p 164. Also cited in A Lynch and G Williams, *What Price Security? Taking Stock of Australia's Anti-Terror Laws* (UNSW Press 2006) 12.

INDEX

A v Secretary of State for the Home Department, 249–50
Aboriginal Australians, 107
Aboriginal communities, 215
Aboriginal Land Rights (Northern Territory) Act (1976), 216
abortion clinic protests, 116–17
Act of Settlement (1701), 56
ad-hoc special powers, 214–15
Adelaide Company of Jehovah's Witnesses Inc v Commonwealth, 50–1
Administrative Decisions (Judicial Review) Act (1977), 212
Agreement on Australia's National Counter-Terrorism Arrangements (2002), 137
Agreement on the Application of Sanitary and Phytosanitary Measures (WTO), 203
Al Qa'ida, 151
alcohol sale regulations, 38
Alice Springs (Management of Public Places) By-Laws (2009), 100
alien doctors, 38
'all-hazards' approach, 181
alternative base of authority, 14
American Revolutionaries, 62–3, 82
ancillary special powers, 180
Andrews v Howell, 50
Anisminic v Foreign Compensation Commission, 256
anti-assembly powers, 103–17
anti-association measures, 117–21
anti-bikie laws, 88
anti-consorting laws, 120–1
anti-protest laws, 110–17

anti-terrorism legislation, 136–7
Appropriation (Nation Building and Jobs) Act (No. 1) (2009), 217
Appropriation (Nation Building and Jobs) Act (No. 2) (2009), 217
arbitrary executive detention, 80, 166
ASIO detention, 156–8
asylum seekers, 77–8
Attorney-General (NSW) v Quin, 248
Attorney-General (NT) v Emmerson, 159
Attorney-General (SA) v Corporation of the City of Adelaide, 102
Attorney-General (Vic) v Commonwealth, 40
Australia
    capacities of legal person, 69–71
    civil emergencies and special powers, 179–99
    constitutional system, 15
    emergency powers, 65–80
    nature and source of executive power, 56–62
    powers arising under statute, 66–9
    public order framework, 83–9
    sedition cases, 129–31
    war on terror, 1
Australian Capital Territory, 96
Australian Commonwealth Shipping Board, 40
Australian Communist Party, 67, 129–30
Australian Communist Party v Commonwealth
    defence power, 24, 40
    executive emergency powers, 66
    national survival, 18

overview of, 26–33
proportionality principle, 48–9
sedition offences, 128
summary, 262–3
Australian Constitution, 6–7, 15, 26, 64, 83, 172–5, 180, 254, 259
Australian Defence Force (ADF), 133, 218–20, 222
Australian Federal Police (AFP), 151–3, 243
Australian Law Reform Commission (ALRC), 134
Australian Radiation Protection and Nuclear Safety Act (1998), 201
Australian Security Intelligence Organisation Act (1979), 156, 243
authorisation of emergency powers, 123
authorised public assembly, 107–8
automation of special powers, 182

balance of probabilities, 146
Bali nightclub bombing, 2
Beale, Roger (Beale Review, 2008), 209
Belmarsh. *See A v Secretary of State for the Home Department*
Bhagat Singh & Ors v The King Emperor, 3
Bill of Rights (1688/89), 56
biological emergencies, 200–2
Biosecurity Act (2015), 209–11, 213–14
biosecurity emergencies, 202–5, 208–14
Board of Inquiry into the Protection of Aboriginal Children from Sexual Abuse, 215
body politic, 45–6
Brown v Tasmania, 111, 113–15
Burmah Oil Co Ltd v Lord Advocate, 79–80
Burns v Ransley, 129–31
business protests, 112–16

CBRN hazards, 200–2
'chameleon' doctrine, 149
chemical emergencies, 200–2
Christmas advertising regulations, 38
Chu Kheng Lim v Minister for Immigration, Local Government and Ethnic Affairs, 76, 165–6, 168

Civil Contingencies Act (2004), 177–80, 191
civil emergencies and special powers. *See also* military aid to civil power
ad-hoc special powers, 214–15
Australia, 172–5, 179–99
biosecurity, 202–5
chemical, biological, radiological, nuclear emergencies, 200–2
comparisons and differences, 190–9
defined, 170
environmental emergencies, 199–200
of general application, 175–99
global financial crisis, 216–17
introduction to, 170–2
Northern Territory National Emergency Response, 215–16
public health emergencies, 205–8
special public disorder, 121–2
of specific application, 199
United Kingdom, 176–9
Victoria's emergency framework, 183–99
civil regulation, 39
Clunies-Ross v The Commonwealth, 80
coal mining industry, 255
Coleman v Power, 87, 92
Commissioner of Police, 98
Commissioner of Taxation v Futuris Corporation Ltd, 258
common experience, 25
common law offence, 90–1
Commonwealth Australian Radiation Protection and Nuclear Safety Agency, 201
Commonwealth Heads of Government Regional Meeting (CHOGRM), 220
Commonwealth Inscribed Stock Amendment Act (2009), 217
Commonwealth of Australia Constitution Act, 225. *See also* Australian Constitution
Commonwealth Parliament powers, 67
Commonwealth Treasury, 72
Commonwealth v Australian Commonwealth Shipping Board, 40

INDEX

Communist Party, 66
Communist Party case. See Australian Communist Party v Commonwealth
Communist Party Dissolution Act (1950), 26, 28–9, 35–6, 47, 128
Community Protection Act (1994), 159
compartmentalisation, 147–8
compulsory acquisitions of property, 68
Condon v Pompano, 118
constitutional democracies, 83
constitutional dictatorship, 176
constitutional facts, 29
constitutional government, 3
constitutional law, 172
constitutional protection for political assembly, 85–9
constitutional theory, 33
constitutional validity, 74
constitutionalised framework of emergency powers, 7
Control of Weapons Act (1990), 124
control orders, 88, 117, 138, 141–2, 145–52, 211–12
Conway v Rimmer, 16
coordinative powers, 178
Corporation of the City of Enfield v Development Assessment Commission ('*Enfield*'), 248
counter-terrorism framework, 136, 140
Counter-Terrorism Legislation Amendment (Foreign Fighters) Act (2014), 135
CPCF v Minister for Immigration and Border Protection, 253
Crime and Misconduct Commission (CMC), 105–6
Crimes (Criminal Organisations Control) Act (2012), 120
Crimes (Internationally Protected Persons) Act (1976), 229
Crimes (Serious Crime Prevention Orders) Act (2016), 120
Crimes Act (1900), 115
Crimes Act (1914), 132–3, 153
Criminal Code Act (1995), 132, 134–5, 243

Criminal Code Amendment (Prevention of Lawful Activity) Bill (2015), 111
Criminal Investigation Act (2006), 124–5
criminal offense legislation, 76
Criminal Organisation Act (2009), 118
Cronulla Riots, 84–5, 101, 122
Cunliffe v Commonwealth, 131
Cyclone Debbie, 173

declaration of emergency, 212–13
declaration of war, 77
Defence (General) Regulations (1939), 144
Defence Act (1903), 138–9, 219, 226–7, 229–30
Defence Legislation Amendments (Aid to Civilian Authorities) Act (2000), 15
Defence of the Realm Act (1914), 177
defence power
  central conception of, 146
  Communist Party Case, 24, 26–33
  Farey v Burvett, 17, 19–23
  fluidity of, 145
  introduction to, 17–18
  limits of, 49–52
  Marcus Clark & Co Ltd v Commonwealth, 33–6
  peacetime phase, 40–1
  post-war phase, 38–40
  pre-*Thomas* phase, 18–20
  proportionality principle and, 48–9
  Stenhouse v Coleman, 23–6
  summary of, 52–3
  Thomas v Mowbray, 41–8
  variable scope of, 36–41
  war preparation phase, 41
  wartime phase of, 37–8
Defence Preparations (Capital Issues) Regulations, 34–5
Defence Preparations Act (1951), 34
deference in judiciary emergency powers, 247–52
democratic institutions, 54
democratic polity, 15

INDEX

Department of Foreign Affairs and Trade, 243
desired end of legislation, 25–6
Digest of the Criminal Law (Stephen), 128–9
direct choice, 68
Disaster Management Act (2003), 190, 195–6
Dixon, J., 5
domestic non-justiciability, 244
domestic violence, 224, 228–9

Ebola virus, 205, 208
economic dislocation/instability, 34
economic globalization, 84
emergency, defined, 3–7
Emergency Coordinators, 178
emergency fiscal policy, 74
Emergency Management Act (1983), 184
Emergency Management Act (1986), 186, 189
Emergency Management Act (2004), 196–7, 206
Emergency Management Act (2005), 194
Emergency Management Act (2006), 197–8
Emergency Management Act (2013), 184–9
emergency powers. *See* civil emergencies and special powers
in Australia, 65–80
capacities of legal person, 69–71
civil emergency, 121–2, 170–1, 173–5, 179–99
emergency, defined, 3–7
emergency frequencies, 13–15
executive power and, 62–5
general themes, 1–3
international norms, 11–13
over-reaction dangers, 8–11
overview, 15–16
powers arising under statute, 66–9
requisition during war, 78–80
special emergency powers, 121–7
summary of, 80–1
unfettered emergency powers, 204

Emergency Powers (Defence) Act (1939), 144
Emergency Powers Act (1920), 176–7, 180, 183
enemy resistance, collapse of, 39
enumerated powers, 65, 84
environmental emergencies, 199–200
environmental movement, 110
espionage activities, 27
Essential Services Act (1948), 183
Essential Services Act (1958), 183–4, 186
'essentials of life' for community, 183
European Convention on Human Rights, 12, 250
Ex parte Boilermakers' Society of Australia ('*Boilermakers*'), 148, 175
executive power
appropriate to national government, 71–8
Australia, 56–62
emergencies and, 62–5
inherent authority, 57–61, 66, 77
introduction to, 54–5
nature and source of, 55
transfers of, 20
United Kingdom, 55–6
executive preventative detention, 154
extraterritorial effect, 60

Farey v Burvett, 17, 19–23, 49–50
federal legislation in wartime, 22–3
federal trade unions, 28
federalism, 146, 246
Fraser v County Court of Victoria, 93
freedom of association, 142
freedom of expression, 84, 142
freedom of movement, 142
French revolution, 82
Fuel Emergency Act 1977, 184
fundamental freedoms, 169
fundamental liberties, 8

G20 (Safety and Security) Act (2013), 110–11
Geneva Conventions Act (1957), 243
Gibbs, Harry, 131–2

global financial crisis (2008-2009), 75, 216–17
global terrorism, 262
Government Gazette, 184
Gratwick v Johnson, 51
Grollo v Palmer, 150, 160–1, 169

habeas corpus, 82
Habib v Commonwealth of Australia, 242–5
Hamilton, Alexander, 52
'Henry VIII' powers, 178
Heydon, J., 4–5
High Court and control orders, 145–52
High Court of Australia, 61, 145–52
H1N1 influenza epidemic, 205
Holland v Jones, 30
Household Stimulus Package Act (No. 2) (2009), 217
Huddart Parker and Co Pty Ltd v Moorehead, 148
Human Rights Act (1998), 250
human rights law, 12
human rights restrictions, 14
humanitarian military intervention, 12

Illawarra District County Council v Wickham, 40
immigration, 84
immunities, 60, 171
In re Debs, 84
inadequate measures against emergency threat, 5
Inclosed Lands, Crimes and Law Enforcement Legislation Amendment (Interference) Act (2016), 113, 115
Inclosed Lands Protection Act (1901), 115
Income Tax Assessment Act (1936), 258–9
industrialisation, 14
inherent authority, 57–61, 66, 77
institutional integrity, 165–9
inter-State travel prohibitions, 51
Intergovernmental Agreement on Biosecurity (2012), 209–10

intergovernmental agreements, 137, 174, 180, 200, 204
intergovernmental immunities, 171
International Covenant on Civil and Political Rights (ICCPR), 12–13, 141
International Health Regulations (WHO), 203–4
international norms, 11–13
interpretative authority, 248
involuntary detention, 154
'Islamic gangs', 101

Japanese-Americans internment, 10–11
Jehovah Witnesses, 52
Joint Committee on the Draft Civil Contingencies Bill, 178–9
judicial notice, 26
judicially authorised warrants, 152–8
judiciary and emergency powers
  deference, 247–52
  defined, 148–9
  introduction to, 232
  judicial restraint, 233–53
  legislative attempts to prevent limit review, 253–9
  no validity clauses, 258–9
  non-justiciability, 233–47
  privative clauses, 253–8
  procedural fairness and urgency, 252–3
  public order framework, 88
  separation of, 147–8
  summary, 260
jurisdictional fact, 241

Kable v Director of Public Prosecutions (NSW), 88–9, 140, 158–65
Kamm v State of New South Wales, 167
Kirk v Industrial Court of New South Wales, 161–2, 257
Korematsu, Fred, 9–10
Kuczborski v Queensland, 118

'lack of expertise' justification for non-justiciability, 236
Lange v Australian Broadcasting Corporation, 86

INDEX

Law Enforcement (Powers and Responsibilities) Act (2002), 108, 115, 122, 124–6
law of defamation, 68
Le Front de Liberation du Quebec (FLQ), 8–9
legality principle, 63, 85–6
legislation in wartime, 22–3
legislative control executive power, 63–4
legislature of enumerated powers, 73
Levy v Victoria, 87
liberal democracy, 2, 62, 142
Lindt Café Siege, 219–20
Little v Commonwealth, 143–5
Liversidge v. Anderson, 144–5
Lloyd v Wallach, 37, 142, 145
Local Government Act (1989), 99
Local Government Act (2008), 100

Madzimbamuto v Lardner-Burke, 78
Malayan (Malaysian) Constitution, 5
manufacturing monopoly, 32
Marbury v Madison, 248
Marcus Clark & Co Ltd v Commonwealth, 33–6
Maritime Powers Act (2013), 253
McCloy v New South Wales, 86
McCulloch v Maryland, 22
Melbourne Corporation doctrine, 171, 204
Melbourne Corporation v Barry, 85, 94
Melbourne Corporation v The Commonwealth, 175
Mental Health Act (2009), 208
military aid to civil power
  defence of superior orders, 231
  introduction to, 218
  legislation, 223–4
  liability concerns, 224–6
  Lindt Café Siege, 219–20
  soldier's legal position, 230–1
  with State application, 222–7
  Sydney Hilton Bombing, 220–2
  without State application, 227–30
military control of naturalised persons, 37
military defence, 30, 147

Minister for Immigration and Citizenship v Li, 239
mobilised citizenry, 62
Model Arrangements for Leadership During Emergencies of National Consequence 2010, 173
Monis, Man, 219–20
Monis v The Queen, 87
move-on powers, 103–10
multiculturalism, 84
Municipal Council of Sydney, 40

nation states, 42, 46
National Environmental Biosecurity Response Agreement (2012), 209
national government executive power, 71–8
National Health Security Act (2007), 201
National Health Security Agreement (2007), 202, 204
National Security (Apple and Pear Acquisition) Regulations, 50
National Security (Coal Mining Industry Employment) Regulations, 254
National Security (General) Regulations, 143
National Security (Subversive Associations) Regulations, 51
National Security Act (1939–1940), 51, 143
National Strategy for Disaster Resilience (2011), 173
naturalised persons, 37
naval defence, 30, 147
New Zealand Law Reform Commission, 5–6
no-evidence ground of review, 240
no validity clauses, 258–9
non-emergency public disorder powers, 83
non-governmental religious organisation, 69
non-judicial function, 149
non-justiciability of emergency powers
  current approach, 234–6
  exercise of, 236–7

non-justiciability of emergency powers (cont.)
  Habib v Commonwealth of Australia, 242–5
  impact of, 237–42
  overview, 233–47
  Wednesbury unreasonableness ground, 239, 241, 245–7
non-statutory emergency powers, 71
non-violent protests, 125
North Australian Aboriginal Justice Agency Ltd v Northern Territory, 165, 167–8
Northern Territory (Self-Government) Act (1978), 216
Northern Territory National Emergency Response Act (2007), 215–16
NSW Commissioner of Police v Folkes, 100
nuclear emergencies, 200–2
Nuclear Non-Proliferation (Safeguards) Act (1987), 201

objective test in preventative detention, 143
obstruction offenses, 89–94
October Crisis, 9
offensive communications, 87
ouster clauses. *See* privative clauses
over-reaction dangers, 8–11

Pankhurst v Kiernan, 37
Pape v Federal Commissioner of Taxation, 4, 72–5, 175, 217
Parliamentary control, 13
Parliamentary Reform, 128
Party for Freedom, 100–2
'*pax est tranquilla libertas,*' 82
Peaceful Assembly Act (1992), 95, 110
peaceful protest, 113
peacetime phase of defence power, 40–1
Pearl Harbor attack, 9
Penalties and Sentences Act (1992), 118–19
permission systems, 94
Permit Model, 97–9

persona designata doctrine, 149–51, 153, 155
Police Act (1892), 83
Police Administration Act (1978), 165, 216
Police Offences Act (1935), 98
police powers, 83
Police Powers and Responsibilities Act (2000), 105, 107
political assembly, constitutional protection, 85–9
political communication, 69, 83, 86–7, 100–3, 203, 208–14
'polycentric' disputes, 235, 238
Polyukhovich v The Commonwealth, 17
post-*Thomas* phase of defence power, 18
post-war phase of defence power, 38–40
powers arising under statute, 66–9
pre-*Thomas* phase of defence power, 18–20
prerogative powers, 55, 58–9, 61, 71–80
presumption in favour of validity, 25
presumption of innocence, 142
preventative (preventive) detention, 138, 141–5, 152–8, 165–9
price controls, 38
primary aspect of defense power, 40
Privacy Act (1988), 133
privileges, as powers, 60
proclamation of emergency, 183
proclamation power, 32
property rights, as powers, 60
proportionality analysis, 48–9, 86
Protective Security Co-ordination Centre, 220
Protective Security Review, 221
protest and political communication, 100–3
Public Assemblies Act (1972), 96
public demonstrations, 98–9
public emergency, 251
Public Health Act (1875), 252
Public Health Act (1997), 206–7
Public Health Act (2010), 207
Public Health Act (2011), 208
Public Health Act (2016), 207

Public Health and Wellbeing Act (2008), 249
public health emergencies, 205–8
Public Health Emergency Management Plan, 206
public nuisance offences, 92
public order, 11
Public Order (Protection of Persons and Property) Act (1971), 93–4, 228–9
Public Order (Temporary Measures) Act (1970), 9
public order framework, 83–9
Public Order in Streets Act (1984), 97
public order maintenance
  abortion clinic protests, 116–17
  anti-assembly powers, 103–17
  anti-association measures, 117–21
  anti-consorting laws, 120–1
  anti-protest laws, 110–17
  business protests, 112–16
  constitutional protection for political assembly, 85–9
  Delegated Control Models, 94, 99–100
  framework of, 83–9
  introduction to, 82–3
  move-on powers, 103–10
  Notification model, 95–7
  permission systems, 94
  permit models, 97–9
  protest and political communication, 100–3
  regulation of political assembly, 89–100
  sedition offences, 127–35
  special emergency powers, 121–7
  subsequent reforms, 131–5
  unlawful assembly and obstruction offenses, 89–94
public safety and war on terror
  definition of judicial power, 148–9
  institutional integrity and preventative detention, 165–9
  introduction to, 136–41
  judicially authorised warrants, 152–8
  Kable principle, 158–65
  persona designata doctrine, 149–51, 153, 155

preventative (preventive) detention, 138, 141–2
preventative (preventive) detention, in wartime, 142–5
preventative (preventive) detention, overview, 138, 141–2
separation of judicial power, 147–8
summary of, 169
Totani v The State of South Australia, 163–4
Public Safety Preservation Act (1958), 183
Public Safety Preservation Act (1986), 122, 124–5, 190–1, 195–6
punitive detention powers, 165
purposive legislative power, 25

R v Burns, 128
R v Commonwealth Court of Conciliation and Arbitration; Ex parte Victoria, 18–50
R v Davey, 252
R v Foster, 38
R v Hickman; ex p Fox, 254
R v Kirby, 148, 175
R v Sharkey, 129, 227–8
R v University of Sydney, 50
Racial Discrimination Act (1975), 193
radiological emergencies, 200–2
reasonable suspicion, 104
regal dignity, 55
regulation-making power, 175
regulation of political assembly, 89–100
Reid Commission, 5, 172
religious diversity, 14
residue of power, 72
result-oriented test, 86
Review of the Criminal Organisation Act 2009 (Wilson), 118
right to liberty, 142
right to privacy, 142
rights-violating intention, 63
riot, defined, 90, 121–2
Roosevelt, Franklin, 9–10
rout, defined, 90
royal prerogative, 55
Ruddock v Vadarlis, 77
Rule of Law, 2–3, 26, 62

sabotage activities, 27
'*salus populi suprema lex esto*' ('Let the welfare of the people be the supreme law'), 11, 169
Schmitt, Carl, 62–3
Second World War, 5
security-sensitive biological agents (SSBA), 201
sedition offences, 127–35
September 11, 2001 terrorist attacks, 1–2, 62
serious civil disturbances, 6
Serious Crimes Act (2007), 119
Severe Acute Respiratory Syndrome (SARS) epidemic, 204–5, 208
'significant response' qualifier, 198
smallpox, 204
socio-political entity, 251
source of law, 247
South African constitution, 63
South Australian Public Health Act (2011), 205
sovereign authority, 242
sovereignty of nation-states, 11
special emergency powers, 121–7. *See also* civil emergencies and special powers
State courts and *Kable* principle, 158–63
State Disasters Act 1983, 185
State Emergency and Rescue Management Act (1989), 193, 206–10
Statutes Amendment (Public Health Incidents and Emergencies) Act (2009), 205
statutorily conferred power, 71
statutory authorisation, 78
statutory powers, 138
Stenhouse v Coleman, 23–6
Stephen Kalong Ningkan v Government of Malaysia, 3
strip searches, 125
subjective test in preventative detention, 143
'substantive' dimension of executive power, 75–6

Summary Offences Act (1953), 92–3
Summary Offences Act (1966), 107–8
Summary Offences Act (1966), 93
Summary Offences Act (1988), 95, 108
Summary Offences Amendment (Move-on Laws) Act (2015), 108
sumptuary laws, 22
supervisory jurisdiction, 237
Supreme Court of Israel, 263
Sydney Hilton Bombing, 220–2

Taskforce on Organised Crime Legislation, 119
Tax Bonus for Working Australians (Consequential Amendments) Act (No. 2) (2009), 217
Tax Bonus for Working Australians Act (No. 2) (2009), 217
tax refund, 73
telecommunications interception warrants, 169
temporary character of emergency threat, 5
terrorism offence/offenders, 135, 140–1
terrorist acts, 42, 44–5, 48–9, 157, 220
terrorist organisations, 53
Thomas v Mowbray
  control orders, 169
  defence power, 41–8, 53, 138–9, 145–6, 168
  overview of, 15, 151–2
  preventative detention, 168
  summary of, 262
tiers-of-scrutiny approach, 86
Totani v The State of South Australia, 163–4
Trade Practices Act (1974), 133–4
traditional jurisprudence, 53
'triple lock' of 'seriousness, necessity, and geographical proportionality', 179

UN Human Rights Committee, 13
UN Special Rapporteurs, 111
unconstitutional supersession of democratic institutions, 5
unfettered emergency powers, 204

United Kingdom
  civil emergencies and special powers, 176–9
  emergency executive powers, 73
  nature and source of executive power, 55–6
  prerogative powers, 79
United Nations Security Council, 12
unlawful assembly, 89–94
Unlawful Associations Act (1916), 37
urbanisation, 14
urgency of emergency threat, 5

Vagrancy Act (1966), 121
validity of a law, 32
validity of federal legislation in wartime, 22–3
Vicious Lawless Association Disestablishment Act (2013), 118
Victorian Chamber of Manufactures v Commonwealth, 50
Victorian Parliament's Scrutiny of Acts and Regulations Committee, 94
Victoria's emergency framework, 183–90
violent disorder, 91
viral haemorrhagic fevers, 204
vital industries, 27

War Measures Act (1914), 8–9
war on terror, 1–2, 4, 223. *See also* public safety and war on terror
War Precautions (Prices Adjustment) Regulations (1916), 21
War Precautions Act (1914), 21, 142
War Precautions Regulations (1915), 142
war preparation phase of defence power, 41
war prerogative powers, 80
wartime emergencies, 6, 19, 52–3
wartime phase of defence power, 37–8
Wednesbury unreasonableness ground, 239, 241, 245–7
White v Redfern, 252
widespread public disorder, 6
Williams v the Commonwealth, 69, 75, 246
Wilson, Alan, 118
Wilson v Minister for Aboriginal and Torres Strait Islander Affairs, 150–1
Windeyer, Victor, 221
Winterton, George, 26
Workplaces (Protection from Protesters) Act (2014), 111–12
World Health Organisation (WHO), 203
World Trade Organisation (WTO), 203
World War I, 37
World War II, 37, 39, 263. *See* Second World War
Wotton v Queensland, 102
Wotton v State of Queensland (No. 5), 126, 174–92

Zika virus, 208